Mr. Truman's War

University Press
of Kansas

MR. TRUMAN'S WAR

The Final Victories of World War II and the Birth of the Postwar World

J. ROBERT MOSKIN

MODERN WAR STUDIES

Theodore A. Wilson
General Editor

Raymond A. Callahan
J. Garry Clifford
Jacob W. Kipp
Jay Luvaas
Allan R. Millett
Carol Reardon
Dennis Showalter
David R. Stone
Series Editors

© 1996, 2002 by J. Robert Moskin

First published in the United States in 1996 by Random House, Inc., New York, and simultaneously in Canada by Random House of Canada Limited, Toronto.

Title-page photo: President Harry S Truman and British Prime Minister Winston Churchill inspect the Scots Guards at the prime minister's residence during the Potsdam Conference on July 18, 1945. Harry S Truman Library, Independence, Missouri.

Published by the University Press of Kansas (Lawrence, Kansas 66049), which was organized by the Kansas Board of Regents and is operated and funded by Emporia State University, Fort Hays State University, Kansas State University, Pittsburg State University, the University of Kansas, and Wichita State University

Library of Congress Cataloging-in-Publication Data is available.

ISBN 0-7006-1184-3 (pbk. : alk. paper)

Printed in the United States of America

10 9 8 7 6 5 4 3 2 1

The paper used in this publication meets the minimum requirements of the American National Standard for Permanence of Paper for Printed Library Materials Z39.48-1984.

For Lynn

Behold, I tell you a mystery: We shall not all sleep; but we shall all be changed in a moment, in the twinkling of an eye, at the last trumpet.

     —*Handel's* Messiah

Contents

History Is Our Memory
Preface to the Paperback Edition

Some years ago, I lay—unexpectedly—in a hospital intensive care unit and spent my better hours thinking about my life. I came to see that the end of World War II was the defining moment of my life—of our lives. Out of this epiphany came *Mr. Truman's War.*

Those of us who lived through World War II have always understood that this age began with the end of that war. Everything since then has been a continuum: the Korean War, the cold war, the end of political colonialism, the war in Vietnam, and the terrorists' attacks. Those of us too young to remember World War II, who know it only as a moment in history, also had lives changed "in the twinkling of an eye."

This book is the story of the five months in 1945 during which we fought and finished the most terrible war in mankind's history and gave birth to the world in which all of us still live. The story is told through an extraordinary "ordinary man," who was blessed with the ability to see the world clearly and make decisions. Some of the fateful decisions that Harry Truman made then are still being assailed and debated.

Today, the common wisdom is that Franklin D. Roosevelt, at his death, had the war won and the postwar world well in hand. His successor had only to mop up. As I researched this book, I saw that this was not so. FDR, a great President, had concentrated on winning a global war. He had taken the nation and the world a great distance toward victory and peace.

The day after Roosevelt died, Harry Truman signed his first official document as President, a proclamation to The People of the United States formally announcing President Roosevelt's death. It declared, with echoes of the story of Moses: "The leader of his people in a great war, he lived to see the assurance of the victory but not to share in it. He lived to see the first foundations of the free and peaceful world to which his life was dedicated, but not to enter on that world himself." Truman knew his Bible and knew he was Joshua to FDR's Moses.

History is our memory. We hope to learn from it. Joyce Appleby, the past president of the American Historical Association, has said that history is the quintessential Western discourse because, when done right, it gives witness to "the magnificence of the human effort to understand."

When Richard Nixon was asked how he thought history would treat him, he is said to have replied: "The judgment of history depends on who writes it." I don't want to believe that. I want to believe that historians try to approach objectivity—try to approach the truth.

A respected historian has suggested to me that there are three kinds of historians. Academic historians for the most part dig into the archives and add pieces to the jigsaw puzzle of historical knowledge. Official historians create a formal record of what has happened. And narrative historians seek primarily to synthesize and communicate the story of the past to a larger audience. (I count myself in this third group, whose priority is to communicate what happened in a coherent and comprehensible way.)

While researching this book, I encountered a fourth kind of historian—the "revisionists," who want to rewrite history. Today, they concern themselves especially with rewriting the history of the Holocaust, the origins of Western civilization, and the atomic bombing of Japan.

Obviously, there is nothing inherently wrong in updating history. There is always room for new information and reappraisal. Charles Beard revised our thinking about the self-interest of our Founding Fathers. Frederick Jackson Turner revised our understanding of the Western frontier. And we have great traditions of dissent. But to deny what happened or to contort the facts is unacceptable—and in the long run unpersuasive.

Something very dubious is happening when a British historian writes that the Auschwitz gas chambers were built by Poland after the war for tourism. Or when an American entitles his book on the Holocaust "The Hoax of the Twentieth Century."

Barton Bernstein of Stanford insists that the invasion of Japan would have cost no more than 46,000 American lives and that President Truman dropped the atomic bombs to intimidate the Russians. Ronald Takaki, a Berkeley historian, asserts that Truman ordered the atomic bombs dropped because he hated the Japanese. Psychologist Robert Jay Lifton insists that Truman was irrational and dropped the bombs because as a boy he had not been good at sports and he still feared being called a "sissy." John Dower of MIT is quoted as saying, "That we used the bomb simply to win the war and save American lives is a myth." Gar Alperovitz is persuaded that the atomic bombing has been a "fifty-year deception."

Why is such "revisionism" surfacing now?

First, I think we live in an age when man is questioning whether what he was taught to believe is true—about himself, about science, about faith. And secondly, we cannot overlook the differences of generations. I doubt my generation includes many revisionists on the questions of Hiroshima or the Holocaust. It is not surprising to find the later generations stunned by the terribleness of the atomic bombing of Japanese cities.

War is insanity. And no one on earth thinks the atomic bombs were compassionate weapons. But some historians who came to judgment in the 1960s misdirect their guilt and their disgust against the use of an horrific weapon instead of against the horror of war itself. In a war in which sixty million people were killed, and in which the United States fire-bombed its enemies' cities mercilessly, it is difficult to argue that a responsible President should not use a new weapon that could in a single stroke stop the killing.

Harry Truman made another wartime decision that is attacked by some latter-day revisionist historians. That was the demand for "unconditional surrender"—a requirement affirmed by Roosevelt at Casablanca and confirmed by Truman to a Joint Session of Congress and at Potsdam. During the war, the American people would have accepted nothing less.

Since then, revisionists have contended that the requirement for "unconditional surrender" made the Germans and Japanese fight harder and to the last man. There is no persuasive evidence of this cause and effect. The evidence is that Roosevelt's and Truman's demand assured our enemies, our own people, and our allies that our leaders were not going to bargain with Hitler or the Japanese militarists.

While this drama was being played out, I was a young Army sergeant in the Philippines. On the night Japan surrendered, thousands of Americans and Filipinos fired their weapons and lit up the sky above Manila to celebrate the end of the war. It was a thrilling, unforgettable moment. There would be no invasion of Japan. We were going home.

The atomic bombings did save large numbers of American lives. This is not a myth. And those horrendous bombs cost fewer Japanese lives than an American invasion would have done.

When the killings stopped in August 1945, a Thirty-One-Year-War ended and the world was a different place. I have come to see World War I and II as two parts of a single war, a convulsion that shook the world loose from its bearings. Europe no longer dominated the rest of the world; classic Western colonialism had been virtually exterminated. Within Europe, power shifted away from the center; England, France, and Germany gave way to the two new superpowers on the periphery. And the United States, which only twenty-six years earlier had refused to join the League of Nations, was now irreversibly a world power.

The war's effects reached far beyond politics. The lives of American women and of African-Americans were revolutionized by the war. Advances in science and medicine altered life forever. They have also, it must be said, created a worldwide population explosion that is now our greatest problem.

Japanese recipient of the Nobel Prize for Literature Kenzaburo Oe visited the city of Hiroshima on August 6 some years ago and wrote: "As a child I did not believe the old saying that one's whole life can be decided by the events of a few days." Now we all have learned that our lives can be changed in a moment.

After V-J Day, Truman warned that, although we had won World War II, "we're facing another fight, and we must win the victory in that. That is a fight for a peaceful world, a fight so we won't have to do this again, so we won't have to maim the flower of our young men, and bury them."

Half a century later, this victory is not yet won. Whatever surprising forms the battle has assumed in our time, we have wished more than once that our leaders would act with the integrity, the judgment, and the decisiveness of Harry Truman. As this story of five months in Truman's life shows, the character of leadership is often decisive.

Mr. Truman's War changed all our lives. The change it spawned that troubles me most is the skepticism and cynicism with which we have been left. Historian Joyce Appleby says: "We live in an age without consensus." We have still to figure out the role, in this troubled world, of our power, our wealth, and our democratic principles of freedom. And we do not always agree on how to decipher the memory of our past. But we keep trying.

—*J. Robert Moskin*
January 2002

Source notes for quotations and references in the Preface to the Paperback Edition:

Barton Bernstein, *Foreign Affairs,* February 1995, p. 151.

Ronald Takaki, *Newsweek,* July 24, 1995, p. 30, review of Takaki, Ronald, *Hiroshima: Why America Dropped the Atomic Bomb* (Little, Brown, 1995).

Robert Jay Lifton, *New York Review of Books,* September 21, 1995, p. 29.

John Dower, *Civilization,* January–February 1997, p. 37.

Gar Alperovitz, *The Decision to Use the Atomic Bomb* (Alfred A. Knopf, 1995), p. 640.

Kenzaburo Oe, *Hiroshima Notes* (Grove Press, 1996), p. 7.

Introduction

This is the story of five surprise-filled months during the spring and summer of 1945, when the world changed forever. The Nazi Thousand-Year Reich was destroyed, Japan bombed into defeat, the United Nations born, the atomic age launched, colonialism began to die, and the seeds of the Cold War were planted. In these five months our era began—with new political orders, radical war-fed science, a nuclear menace, and fresh aspirations for human freedom.

This is the story of a mighty changeover from war to peace and the men who led it. Many stories have been told of World War II, and others of the postwar era and the Cold War. But this book targets the exciting and painful transition—and the complex, even tragic decisions that made up the birth pangs of our age. To understand the times we live in, to perceive where we stand in the constantly running stream of history, we must know this climactic moment.

In the traditional wisdom, the Civil War is always cited as the defining event in American history. The Civil War opened the industrial age and terminated slavery. But the world wars—and especially, World War II—jump-started the postmodern, postindustrial age we live in. World War II was the great defining event in American history, transforming our society and our world.

Throughout history, humankind has repeatedly experienced periods, some brief and others extended, of enormous and fundamental change. They have been given names like the Birth of Christianity, the Renaissance, the Age of Exploration, the Industrial Revolution. But none has been more revolutionary than this "twinkling of an eye" at the end of history's most devastating conflict.

These five months climaxed the global cataclysm that spanned the three decades from 1914 to 1945. The world's five billion people found themselves interdependent, insecure about the future, and confused about why they are here on earth. Then, four postwar decades of superpower confrontation were followed by self-centered tribalism, nuclear-based fear, and arrogant fundamentalism. The world's population exploded out of control. The result is our time of both violence and hope.

Arthur M. Schlesinger, Jr., called this "a turbulent age for America and the world." World historian Theodore Von Laue wrote, "Humanity has now entered an utterly unprecedented new era."

The leaders of the triumphant moment in which this new age was born were giants.

Winston Churchill rallied all free people to halt the rampaging dictatorships against enormous odds and even despair—yet he was the most pragmatic of leaders, with his gaze fixed on the future well before others were prepared to face it.

Josef Stalin, stubborn and ruthless, led a people who suffered more than twenty million deaths and fought across vast landscapes to throw back the German invaders.

Charles de Gaulle made himself into a figure of grand opera and lifted his nation off its knees after years of submission and collaboration to regain faith in its grandeur.

Above all, there was Harry S Truman, who came off a farm and a county political job to decide global issues that would change humankind's future. The man from Missouri at the center of this story had no experience with international problems, but he commanded the world's most powerful nation. Within hours after Franklin D. Roosevelt died on April 12, 1945, Harry Truman began to deal with Churchill, Stalin, and de Gaulle to win the war and shape the postwar world.

Truman was unlike the aristocratic, sophisticated FDR. A politician to the bone, he was both a romantic and a realist. He liked people and loved politics. He was plainspoken but thin-lipped. He did much more than just continue in the role of the dead FDR. He had to make a host of difficult decisions in his own, very different style.

Believing in the causes Roosevelt believed in, Truman picked up the fallen baton and had to solve the unfinished and unexpected problems of the greatest war in man's history, shape the fragile peace, and give form to a new and archetypical age.

Of all the responsibilities of leadership and all the achievements of Harry Truman's eight-year presidency—even fighting and winning what Dean Acheson called the "limited war for limited objectives" on the Korean peninsula—the decisions he made that conditioned the final victories of World War II and the birth of the postwar world were truly *Mr. Truman's war.*

Mr. Truman's War

Chapter 1

"Jesus Christ and General Jackson!"

Thursday, April 12, 1945

The Georgia April morning was sunny and warmed the bones. Outside, the quince were in bloom and the dogwood were beginning to drop their white and pink blossoms.

Most of the world was entangled in war. The vast armies of the Soviet Union paused impatiently on the banks of the Oder River, waiting for the signal to charge ahead fifty miles and conquer Berlin; west of the German capital, the American Ninth Army was forcing a crossing of the Elbe. On the Asian side of the globe, American soldiers and Marines advanced slowly, at a terrible price, against the dug-in Japanese defenders of the island of Okinawa, 350 miles south of Japan's home islands. And hundreds of B-29 Superfortresses fire-bombed Tokyo.

On this bright morning in the living room of the Little White House in Warm Springs, Georgia, a prematurely old man—his face gray and gaunt, deep pouches beneath his eyes, his hand palsied, but his mind still full of spark—sat in his favorite large leather armchair near the fireplace, reading official papers set out on a card table in front of him. The Russian-born artist Madame Elizabeth Shoumatoff was sketching him for a watercolor portrait commissioned by his loving friend of thirty years, Lucy Mercer Rutherfurd, for her youngest daughter.

Franklin Roosevelt had arrived at the Little White House on March 30, two weeks earlier, exhausted—to recuperate from the grueling, tense summit conference with Soviet Premier Josef V. Stalin and British Prime Minister Winston S. Churchill at Yalta in the Crimea. (Secretary of War Henry L. Stimson always believed that "President

Roosevelt hastened his death by traveling to the Crimea in order to meet with Stalin, who reported himself forbidden by his doctor to make a long voyage.")

Mrs. Rutherfurd, who had joined Roosevelt just three days before, sat on the couch facing the fireplace. Her brown hair had a wisp of gray, but she was tall and attractive. Roosevelt and she had been in love ever since 1914 when his wife, Eleanor, had hired her as a social secretary.

His cousin Laura "Polly" Delano was filling a vase with roses, and another cousin, Margaret "Daisy" Suckley, crocheted nearby. Across the room, the Filipino houseboy quietly started setting the dining table for lunch, and Roosevelt looked at his watch; it was one o'clock. He said he could give Madame Shoumatoff only fifteen minutes more. He hoisted himself by his arms from his large armchair into a straight-backed movable one on casters, stuck a cigarette into his holder, lit it, and went on reading papers.

The fifteen minutes were almost up when Roosevelt raised his left hand to his temple, then dropped it again and pressed the back of his neck. "I have a terrific headache," he said gently. He slumped forward.

Madame Shoumatoff screamed, and the women called for Dr. Howard Bruenn, the young U.S. Navy cardiologist who was taking care of Roosevelt and who was then at the swimming pool. Roosevelt's valet, Arthur Prettyman, and the houseboy, Irineo "Joe" Esperancilla, came over on the run and lifted Roosevelt's deadweight into the bedroom. His head lolled; he was breathing in great gasps.

By 1:30 Dr. Bruenn had dressed and was driven to the house. He tore away Roosevelt's clothing and injected papaverine and amyl nitrate. Madame Shoumatoff and Mrs. Rutherfurd were hurried out of the house. Grace Tully, his secretary, sat in the corner; her lips moved in silent prayer.

Finally, the breathing stopped. Dr. Bruenn injected the heart with Adrenalin. There was no response. He could do nothing more. At 3:35 he pronounced Roosevelt dead. Dr. Bruenn closed his eyes with his thumbs. Ms. Tully walked over and kissed the President lightly on the forehead.

An hour later, William D. Hassett, Roosevelt's correspondence secretary, summoned the reporters into the living room—at a moment coordinated with the White House in Washington—and said, "Gentlemen, it is my sad duty to inform you that the President of the United States is dead." Franklin Delano Roosevelt was only sixty-three.

* * *

Twenty minutes after President Roosevelt died—it was now five minutes before 5 P.M. Washington time—Vice President Harry S Truman, wearing a double-breasted gray suit and blue polka-dot tie, his blue eyes magnified by his thick steel-rimmed glasses, entered the hideaway office of House Speaker Sam Rayburn, poured himself a bourbon, and sat down on the arm of an overstuffed black leather chair. The little room on the ground floor of the Capitol was known to intimates as the "Board of Education"; the powerful "Mister Sam" invited congressional leaders there for some informal conversation and refreshment.

The vice president had had a busy day, starting when he dropped his daughter Margaret at George Washington University, where she was a student, and then answering mail in his Senate office until it was time to preside over the Senate. "It's my job to get 'em prayed for—and goodness knows they need it—and then get the business to going by staying in the chair," he wrote "Mamma and Mary," his ninety-two-year-old mother and his sister, Mary Jane, back on the family farm in Grandview, Missouri. This Thursday he had presided over an interminable, boring debate on a water treaty with Mexico; the Senate had not adjourned until almost 5 P.M. Then he had walked over to Sam Rayburn's hideaway to relax with his friends.

When Truman had settled into the leather chair, Lewis Deschler, the House parliamentarian, reminded Speaker Rayburn that Truman was supposed to return a call to Stephen T. Early, a senior presidential assistant, at the White House. Truman dialed National 1414 and heard Steve Early's strained voice: "Please come right over and come in through the main Pennsylvania Avenue entrance."

Early's urgency startled him. Truman turned pale; he said under his breath: "Jesus Christ and General Jackson!"

He instantly recognized that because Early had directed him not to come as usual through the East Executive Avenue entrance of the White House, which would keep him off the official caller list, the moment he feared had arrived.

Asking Rayburn not to mention the call, he half ran through the narrow basement passageway of the Capitol building through the old Crypt to his official black Mercury, which was waiting on the far Senate side of the building.

Truman unintentionally lost his Secret Service guard, and Tom Harty, his government chauffeur, drove him alone through the misty rain and the rush-hour traffic to the White House; he arrived at 5:25.

He went up slowly in the small paneled elevator to the second floor and entered the sitting room, where Mrs. Roosevelt was waiting for him with her son-in-law and daughter, Colonel John Boettiger and Mrs. Anna Roosevelt Boettiger, and Steve Early. Mrs. Roosevelt rose, came forward, put her arm around Truman's shoulder, and said, "Harry, the President is dead."

There was a long, paralyzing silence. Truman could not speak. Finally he asked, "Is there anything I can do for you?"

She replied, "Is there anything we can do for you? For you are the one in trouble now."

Truman fought back tears.

Now that the vice president was at the White House, Steve Early went to his office and telephoned the three wire services simultaneously. International News Service moved the news fastest. At 5:47 P.M. it sent its clients: "FLASH WASHN—FDR DEAD." The word circled the world in seconds.

Truman would write his mother and his sister, Mary, "I had hurried to the White House to see the President, and when I arrived, I found I was the President." Later he remembered his feelings at the moment: "Now the lightning had struck, and events beyond anyone's control had taken command. America had lost a great leader, and I was faced with a terrible responsibility."

Upstairs in the White House, Secretary of State Edward R. Stettinius, Jr. (whom Dean Acheson described as "snow-capped and episcopal"), knocked and entered the sitting room. He was weeping. Truman calmly took charge. He asked Stettinius, Early, and Secretary of the Senate Leslie Biffle to telephone all the members of the cabinet to meet in the Cabinet Room at 6:15, and he arranged for a government plane to fly Mrs. Roosevelt to Warm Springs. He walked over to the west end of the White House and called Mrs. Truman and Margaret. Margaret answered the telephone and teased her father about not coming home for dinner. "In a voice of steel," he told her to put her mother on the line. Then he sent a car for them. After that he telephoned Chief Justice Harlan Fiske Stone and asked him to come over as soon as possible and swear him in.

Truman went downstairs to the Cabinet Room, where cabinet members and congressional leaders had started gathering. When all the cabinet members who were in town were present, he asked for their attention and announced formally what they already knew— that Roosevelt was dead.

Truman stood at the end of the huge cabinet table and picked up a Gideon Bible that had been found in an office nearby. Chief Justice Stone recited the oath; Truman, standing rigidly erect, placed his left hand flat on the Bible, raised his right hand, slowly repeated the oath, kissed the Bible, and became the thirty-third President of the United States. He glanced at the clock on the mantel beneath Woodrow Wilson's portrait; it said 7:09. He looked at the faces crowding around him; many people were weeping and distraught. He thought: "None of us could believe F.D.R. was gone." Roosevelt had been dead less than two and a half hours.

The brief ceremony over, most of those present departed. The members of the cabinet stayed behind at President Truman's request and took their places around the great table.

Early entered the Cabinet Room and said that members of the press were asking whether the San Francisco conference to create the United Nations was still scheduled to meet on April 25. Truman said it certainly was. He remembered later, "I said that it was what Roosevelt had wanted, and it had to take place if we were going to keep the peace. And that's the first decision I made as President of the United States."

President Truman emphasized to the cabinet that he would continue Roosevelt's policies at home and abroad, and he asked them to stay at their posts. "They were all so broken up and upset that . . . none of them did much talking." He urged them to tell him if they thought he was wrong but made it clear that he would make the final decisions.

He asked Secretary of War Stimson and Secretary of the Navy James V. Forrestal to meet with him and the Joint Chiefs of Staff the next day. The cabinet meeting was short, and when the cabinet members silently filed out, Stimson stayed behind.

White-haired, greatly respected, and seventy-seven years old, Stimson had been a Wall Street lawyer and secretary of war under President William Howard Taft and secretary of state under President Herbert C. Hoover long before Roosevelt had appointed him in 1940. Now he told Truman that he had an urgent matter to discuss. He said that "the Pasco project"—so named for Pasco, Washington, on the Columbia River and the location of the Hanford Engineering Works—was developing an explosive of incredible power.

Truman was puzzled. He knew almost nothing of the building of the atomic bomb, which had been kept secret from members of Congress. And Stimson brought him no details. Truman had tried to investigate the Hanford Works when he was the chairman of the Senate Special Committee to Investigate the National Defense Program, but Stimson had stopped him then. Stimson had come to his Senate office and asked him to stop sending his men to the top secret plants in Tennessee and Washington State. On Stimson's word and in the face of his unyielding opposition, Truman had called off the investigations. He said later, "Stimson was a man you could trust—one hundred percent."

This rainy April afternoon, as daylight was dying, portrait photographer Yousef Karsh arranged his bulky equipment in the State Department office of Assistant Secretary of State Dean Acheson, a six-foot-three, elegant Yale alumnus who had a major diplomatic career ahead of him. Karsh readied his camera and a screen, lowered the blinds, and focused his lights on Acheson's chair. Barbara Evans, Acheson's secretary, opened the office door suddenly and said, "The President is dead."

Acheson walked to the window and raised a blind. The White House flag was already at half-mast. They continued their photographing.

Acheson had met Harry Truman only two days before; they had discussed the wish of Senator Pat McCarran of Nevada to attend the United Nations Conference in San Francisco. Acheson wrote his son soon after Truman became President that he was impressed with the man. "He is straight-forward, decisive, simple, entirely honest. He, of course, has the limitations upon his judgment and wisdom that the limitations of his experience produce, but I think he will learn fast and will inspire confidence."

Washington insiders' reactions to his ascension to the presidency varied.

Charles E. "Chip" Bohlen, who had served Roosevelt as interpreter and would do the same for his successor, was dubious:

> We in the State Department shared the concern of all Americans whether the "little man from Missouri" could rise to the occasion. I had not met Truman at the time he became President. He was an obscure Vice-President, who got to see Roosevelt much less than I did and who knew less than I did about United States foreign relations. . . . It took some months for Americans to discover the decisiveness of their new President.

Republican Senator Robert Taft of Ohio worried about Truman's lack of "education or background to analyze soundly the large problems which are before him." Eager young Democratic Congressman Lyndon B. Johnson from Texas did not think Truman could take command; he told his secretary, "There is going to be the damnedest scramble for power in this man's town for the next two weeks that anyone ever saw in their lives."

The older, more seasoned former Vice President John Nance Garner, also from Texas, wrote wisely, "Truman is honest and patriotic and has a head full of good horse sense. Besides, he has guts. All of this can be made into a good President."

As the bells of Washington's churches began tolling Roosevelt's death, Supreme Court Justice Felix Frankfurter and Lord Halifax, the British ambassador, were walking in Washington's Rock Creek Park, discussing how to make it possible for scientist Niels Bohr to see Roosevelt. The Danish theoretical physicist wanted to present his conviction that the United States should discuss with the Soviet Union the mutual dangers of a nuclear arms race in order to prevent such a race after the Russians learned of the existence of the atomic bomb.

When word of the President's death reached the desolate mesa of Los Alamos, New Mexico, Dr. J. Robert Oppenheimer, director of the Los Alamos Scientific Laboratory, came out onto the steps of the administration building and spoke simply and movingly to the people who had gathered there spontaneously.

In Berlin, Adolf Hitler waved a paper and shouted, "The war isn't lost. Read it! Roosevelt is dead."

In Moscow, the news arrived after midnight while U.S. Ambassador W. Averell Harriman was hosting a party at Spaso House. Soviet Foreign Minister Vyacheslav M. Molotov insisted on coming over in person and emotionally expressed his great sadness at the world's loss. He promised that the Soviet government would have confidence in Truman because he had been selected by Roosevelt. And he informed Ambassador Harriman that Stalin wanted to see him the next day. Harriman remembered, "When I saw Stalin he appeared deeply shaken and more disturbed than I had ever seen him. He held my hand for some time."

In London, Prime Minister Churchill received the news of Roosevelt's death early Friday morning, London time, April 13, in his study at 10 Downing Street. He felt as if he had been struck a physical blow. He went to the House of Commons, which met at 11 A.M., and in an unprecedented step immediately obtained the members' unanimous consent to adjourn.

Churchill wanted to fly over for Roosevelt's funeral, and Truman encouraged him, saying he hoped they could meet and talk. But Churchill was dissuaded and sent a message to Truman that he could not change his plans. Years later, Churchill said he regretted not taking up Truman's invitation. He was appalled that Roosevelt had not had Vice President Truman participate in decisions of foreign affairs; he himself kept Anthony Eden, his foreign secretary, informed so that he could take over at any moment. Churchill felt that, although Truman was "a resolute and fearless man, capable of taking the greatest decisions," in those first months, he would face great difficulties.

When President Truman assured the cabinet that he would continue FDR's policies, he did not yet realize how many problems remained to be resolved: Germany, Poland, Palestine, colonial empires, the future of the Japanese Emperor, the use and control of atomic energy, the feeding of a starving Europe, a postwar economic program.

The Soviet Union was already forcing Communist regimes on Romania and Czechoslovakia and nailing down control over Poland. Relations between Stalin and Roosevelt had deteriorated and become overladen with suspicion and mistrust. On April 3 Stalin had written to Roosevelt, accusing him of dealing with the Germans behind his back. Roosevelt had been infuriated.

As Churchill would write perceptively, "The destruction of Germany's military power had brought with it a fundamental change in the relations between Communist Russia and the Western democracies. They had lost their common enemy, which was almost their sole bond of union."

Not yet aware of the problems with Stalin, Truman first turned his attention to the U.N. conference in San Francisco. After the cabinet meeting, he, Stettinius, Early, and Presidential Secretary Jonathan Daniels went into the White House's Oval Room to draft a statement that would scotch any rumors that plans for the San Francisco meeting would be changed. Truman's priorities were to win the war and "to win an organized peace."

Then, Truman decided, "the best thing to do was to go home and get as much rest as possible and face the music."

It was almost 9:30 when he arrived at the Trumans' five-room apartment at 4701 Connecticut Avenue. His wife, daughter, and mother-in-law were next door at the neighbors', who gave the brand-new President a turkey-and-ham sandwich and a glass of milk. Then, from his own bedroom, he telephoned and reassured his mother and brother, Vivian, in Grandview. They had been listening to developments on the radio.

He wrote in his diary, "I was very much shocked," but he never said he was surprised. When he had been nominated to be vice president, he had realized that this was the possibility. Insiders all knew that Roosevelt was a dying man. That responsible aides like Admiral William D. Leahy and Secretary Stimson had not made an effort to draw in the new vice president and familiarize him with the crucial wartime issues seems, in retrospect, incredible. But no one had prepared Harry Truman to take over when this day suddenly arrived. He had good reason to be shocked.

He called an old friend, Edward D. McKim, his World War I sergeant, with whom he had planned to play poker that evening at the Statler Hotel, and told Eddie, "I guess the party's off. They've got me fenced in out here."

Chapter 2

The Man

The man who came to the presidency suddenly in the midst of worldwide war had been vice president for less than three months. He had not been kept informed about either the progress of the war or U.S. relations with other powers; he was a novice at diplomacy and international affairs.

But he was a careful, thorough, principled politician who liked people and knew what makes them tick, and he was well grounded in the nation's domestic affairs. What people knew best about him was that he had been a senatorial watchdog on war production and expenditures, an army captain in World War I, and a failed haberdasher. In fact, there was more.

Harry Truman was born on May 8 1884, in tiny Lamar, Missouri, 120 miles south of Kansas City. His family were Baptists and Democrats; they had been in Jackson County since 1846. His father, John Anderson Truman, was a mostly unschooled farmer who died in 1914. His mother, Martha Ellen Young Truman, came from a more prosperous family and was better educated. Harry and his younger brother, Vivian, and sister, Mary Jane, grew up on a 600-acre Jackson County farm owned by his mother's family, the Youngs. Harry's father and maternal grandfather grew wheat and corn and raised cattle, hogs, sheep, and mules. A dozen farmhands worked for them. A promoter building a railroad from Kansas City to Springfield, Missouri, set a station a mile south of the farm, on a crest of land he called Grandview, and that gave the Young-Truman farm a place name. Harry experienced the pleasures and performed the chores of a farm boy. Much later, he remembered, "Those were wonderful days and great adventures."

Like Franklin Roosevelt, Harry Truman was the son of a strong mother. When he was six, his mother moved the immediate family to South Crysler Street in Independence, Missouri, twenty miles from Grandview, so that the children could go to a better school.

Independence had been the jumping-off point for the Santa Fe and Oregon trails and was still an unreconstructed southern country town. Harry's father, a small, feisty man, operated a farm outside town and was passionate about politics. Because Harry's mother wanted to escape from the Baptist country churches, she sent her children to the more fashionable Presbyterian Sunday school. There he met Elizabeth Virginia "Bess" Wallace, the blond tomboy daughter of a prominent local family. They went to public school together from the fifth grade through high school. Harry said of Bess, "I only had one sweetheart from the time I was six."

In 1892, the year Grover Cleveland was elected President, Harry entered school and started wearing glasses, which eliminated him from most rough-and-tumble games and turned him to reading and the piano. He always felt he was a bit of a sissy.

By the time he was fourteen, he said later with proud exaggeration, he had read all the books in the Independence Public Library. He was fascinated with history and said it taught him "that a leader is a man who has the ability to get other people to do what they don't want to do, and like it." He took another lesson from his reading of history: "I saw that it takes men to make history, or there would be no history. History does not make the man."

Harry's first job was cleaning Jim Clinton's drugstore on the corner of the square, starting at 6:30 in the morning before he went to school. At the end of his first week he received three silver dollars. He knew his father could not afford to send him to college—he had lost everything he had saved speculating on grain futures—so Harry studied hard, hoping to be admitted to one of the service academies at West Point or Annapolis. But when he graduated from high school in 1901, his poor eyesight prevented him from winning an academy appointment. In his graduating high school class were Bess Wallace, who would become his wife, and Charlie Ross, the quiet, gentle class valedictorian, who would become his White House press secretary. Harry liked to say that Independence, Missouri, was to him what Hannibal, Missouri, was to Mark Twain.

After high school, Harry found a job as timekeeper for a contractor who was double-tracking the Atchison, Topeka and Santa Fe Railroad; he worked ten hours a day for fifteen cents an hour, living in hobo camps along the Missouri River. His second full-time job was in the mail room of the *Kansas City Star* at seven dollars a week, and after that he worked in a couple of Kansas City banks.

In 1905 he joined Battery B of a new National Guard unit of horse-drawn light artillery in Kansas City. He enjoyed living in the big city.

In 1904 the family had moved back to the farm near Grandview, and two years later Harry joined them, staying on the farm until the United States entered World War I. He milked cows by hand and plowed with a four-horse team, sowing corn, wheat, and oats. Running the farm was hard work and became harder after his father died. Harry increased the farm's wheat production from thirteen to nineteen bushels per acre, oats from eight to fifty. He joined the Masonic Order and in 1917 organized a lodge in Grandview. And he still found time to read; Mark Twain was his "patron saint in literature," he told Bess. "I managed to save dimes to buy all he has written."

This was a young man with only a high school education who worked hard, who felt strong ties to the land and history and family, and who had a sense of humor and made friends easily. His letters to Bess often contained wry anecdotes about farming life. He loved Mozart and Chopin, as well as dancing and playing cards, even if that bothered some of his more straitlaced friends. He was proud when he sowed seventy acres of oats in five days ("That is moving some") but he did not express arrogance or any overweening ambition.

The young farmer grew up in an isolated and outspokenly prejudiced time. The Civil War was still a bitter memory; his mother was not sorry that Abraham Lincoln had been shot; Negroes were inferior and Jews despised. Even though Harry and his post–World War I business partner Edward Jacobson were close for many years, the Trumans never had Eddie and his wife, who were Jewish, to their home. Young Harry who would become a civil rights leader and help create the state of Israel had a long distance to go.

In 1911, before taking a trip to South Dakota, Harry wrote Bess:

> I bet there'll be more bohunks and "Rooshans" up there than white men. I think it is a disgrace to the country for those fellows to be in it. If they had only stopped

immigration about twenty or thirty years ago, the good Americans could all have had plenty of land and we'd have been an agricultural country forever. You know as long as a country is one of that kind, people are more independent and make better citizens. When it is made up of factories and large cities it soon becomes depressed and makes classes among people. Every farmer thinks he's as good as the President or perhaps a little bit better.

Even when he was first in the White House, he wrote in his private diary: "The Jews claim God Almighty picked 'em out for special privilege. Well I'm sure He had better judgment. Fact is I never thought God picked any favorites. It is my studied opinion that any race, creed or color can be God's favorites if they act the part—and very few of 'em do that."

None of this is to suggest that Harry Truman was bigoted. In his youthful political battles in Missouri, he fought the Ku Klux Klan openly. And his daughter attested: "I had never heard an anti-Semitic word uttered in our house." Campaigning for the Senate in 1940, he boldly told an all-white farm audience in Sedalia, "I believe in the brotherhood of man, not merely the brotherhood of white men but the brotherhood of all men before the law." That was not popular in rural Missouri, although it probably won him some of the state's 250,000 black voters. And when he was the vice presidential candidate in 1944, his enemies claimed he was one-fourth Jewish and his middle initial stood for "Solomon" (his grandfather's given name). Truman replied: "I'm not Jewish, but if I were I would not be ashamed of it." He was a man who could grow.

As the years passed on the farm, he dreamed of better things. In the fall of 1913 Bess agreed to be engaged to him, and he wrote her half insecurely, half prophetically:

How does it feel being engaged to a clodhopper who has ambitions to be Governor of Montana and Chief Executive of U.S. He'll do well to be a retired farmer. . . . But I intend to keep peggin' away and I suppose I'll arrive at something. You'll never be sorry if you take me for better or for worse because I'll always try to make it better."

When the United States entered World War I, Harry, now beyond draft age, rejoined the National Guard. The artillery batteries in Kansas City and Independence were expanded into a regiment, and the batteries of the regiment elected their own officers. Harry was elected first lieutenant of the newly organized Battery F—his first elective office. In August the regiment became the 129th Field Artillery of the 35th Division of the U.S. Army.

The colonel appointed Harry regimental canteen officer, and he asked Eddie Jacobson, whom he had met in Battery F, to help him. They collected $2,200 from the men and set up a store, a barber shop, and a tailor shop. In six months they paid back the $2,200, plus $15,000 in dividends, while other canteens in the division were failing.

Lieutenant Truman shipped overseas to France as battalion adjutant of the 2nd Battalion and subsequently was given command of Battery D, which consisted of four guns and 194 Irish Catholics from Kansas City. With him, Truman carried a photograph of a young woman; on its back she had written: "Dear Harry, May this photograph bring you safely home again from France—Bess."

He landed at Brest on April 13, 1918 (precisely twenty-seven years before his first full day in the White House). And he first saw action on the night of September 6 in the Vosges Mountains west of the Rhine River. The Germans replied to American artillery fire, panicked the men, and killed six horses. Later, as the artillerymen moved forward in the Meuse-Argonne offensive, a French 155mm battery fired over their heads, and ever after Harry Truman had trouble hearing.

His men fired on three German batteries, destroying one and putting the other two out of action. He was threatened with a court-martial for firing out of his division's sector, but he believed he had saved the lives of men in the 28th Division, on their left. In October he received word that he had been promoted to captain five months earlier. In the final days of the war, his men were firing in support of the 81st Division in front of Verdun. At eleven o'clock on the morning of November 11, the armistice began and Captain Truman wrote, "The silence that followed almost made one's head ache."

Given leave, he went to Paris, where he enjoyed the opera and found the Folies-Bergère "disgusting." He reached New York on Easter Sunday, April 20, 1919; was discharged on May 6; and went home to the farm. Less than eight weeks later, on June 28, Bess Wallace and he were married in the Trinity Episcopal Church in Independence. They moved into the home of Bess' mother. He was thirty-five.

Bess had made it clear she did not want to be a farmer's wife. Truman and Eddie Jacobson opened a menswear store at Twelfth and Baltimore streets in Kansas City near the Muehlebach Hotel. The store made money the first year.

One of their customers was James Pendergast, who had been an artillery officer with Truman in France. Jim's father, Michael J., was a Democratic leader in Jackson County for the political machine. Truman had been Democratic clerk in every election from 1906 on and before the war had been postmaster of Grandview. Local politics intrigued him.

In 1921 the Pendergast political organization offered Truman its support for the Democratic nomination for judge of the county court for the Eastern District of Jackson County. Each county in Missouri had a county court of three judges; two represented districts and the third was elected for the county at large. The court was not judicial but administrative; it levied taxes to support roads, homes for the aged, and schools for delinquent children.

The store was in trouble, and Truman accepted the Pendergast offer immediately. As one of five candidates, most of them backed by local political organizations, he had a rough battle for the nomination. He threw himself into the fight and traveled through all seven townships in the Eastern District in a hard-riding Dodge roadster. He had relatives all over the county, and his wife was related to even more voters. He won the primary with a small plurality. The county voted overwhelmingly Democratic, and he easily won the election.

Falling farm prices and the onset of a recession dropped the value of Truman & Jacobson's inventory by two thirds. They closed the store in 1922, hopelessly in debt. Truman blamed the economic policies of President Warren G. Harding and Secretary of the Treasury Andrew Mellon, who had forced down farm prices and raised interest rates. Over time, the two business partners settled with their creditors and paid all of them, except the banks, in full. They both tried hard to avoid bankruptcy. But after several years Jacobson could not meet the pressure of debts totaling $10,676 and filed for bankruptcy. The bank could not push Truman as hard because he was by then a public official; he eventually settled with it.

When Judge Truman ran again in 1924, he was defeated; another political faction had not received its share of the jobs he had handed out. That was to be the only election defeat Truman ever experienced. He was now forty, out of a job, and in debt.

The Trumans' daughter, Mary Margaret, was born on February 17, 1924. He found a job with the Automobile Club of Kansas City and was active in the Reserve Officers Association and the Masons. In 1926 Mike Pendergast wanted him to run for county collector and took him to meet his brother Thomas J. Pendergast, the boss of the Kansas City Democratic political machine. But "Boss Tom" had promised the job to someone else and persuaded Truman to run for presiding judge of the county court. He was elected by 16,000 votes and served for eight years. He built roads and public buildings and worked to put the county onto a sound financial footing without a tinge of scandal. He raised money against tentative tax levies, but he got an interest rate of 2.5 percent from banks in Chicago and St. Louis while the local bankers had been charging 6 percent. As presiding judge, he was the executive officer of the largest and richest county in Missouri. (St. Louis was a city without county government.) He was responsible for spending $60 million in tax funds and bond issues, and he did it all with a spotless record.

When he first had contracts to let, Truman received a telephone call from Tom Pendergast, who said some friends were eager to see him about those contracts. Truman met with them and told them he would let the contracts to the lowest bidders, as he had promised the taxpayers he would. Pendergast said to the contractors, "I told you he's the contrariest man in the state of Missouri." He supported Truman, saying, "You carry out the agreement you made with the people of Jackson County."

He was reelected in 1930 by a majority of 58,000 votes. He said later, "I came out of the county courts after ten years service a damn sight worse off than when I went into it. No man can get rich in politics unless he's a crook."

Biographer Robert H. Ferrell describes Truman well at this time:

> It was the era of George F. Babbitt, and Truman was a good deal like Babbitt. He was full of his American Legion activities and his Masonic initiations; he took friends and acquaintances to the Kansas City Club, dressed with care, and sported the flashy neckties of the time. He looked like a thousand other middle-aged denizens of downtown Kansas City, maybe several thousands of them."

In 1934 Truman wanted to run for Congress, but the Pendergasts convinced him to campaign, instead, for the U.S. Senate. Biographer

Ferrell figures Truman was "Boss Tom's" fifteenth choice; some of Truman's friends even believed the Pendergasts would not mind if he lost. But he seized the opportunity. He had built political support throughout the state, and he campaigned hard to beat two congressmen for the nomination and then defeat the conservative Republican incumbent by more than a quarter of a million votes. His strength was in the country counties, and the machine gave him 90 percent of the vote in Kansas City. This was the turning point of Harry Truman's political life, lifting him from Jackson County to the national stage.

When he left for Washington, he went to say good-bye to Tom Pendergast in Kansas City. "Boss Tom's" advice was: "Work hard, keep your mouth shut, and answer your mail."

Truman was fifty when, on January 3, 1935, he took his seat in the U.S. Senate. He arrived in a Washington dominated by Franklin Roosevelt and his New Deal Democrats. Across the Atlantic, Adolf Hitler had already exercised dictatorial power for two years. Alan Bullock, Hitler's respected biographer, wrote, "The street gangs had seized control of the resources of a great modern state, the gutter had come to power."

Truman confessed to Bess that he saw his new responsibilities as an enormous challenge. He was a financial failure, he wrote her, because he would not be "a pirate." But, he added, "I am hoping to make a reputation as a Senator, though if I live long enough that'll make the money successes look like cheese. But you'll have to put up with a lot if I do it because I won't sell influence and I'm perfectly willing to be cussed if I'm right."

He was pleased to be appointed to the Senate Appropriations Committee and the Interstate Commerce Committee and disappointed not to receive a seat on the Military Affairs Committee. A thoroughgoing New Dealer, he supported Franklin Roosevelt's program, voted for legislation against the poll tax and lynchings, and was an early supporter of national defense and military preparedness. He backed the Wagner Labor Relations Act and the Social Security Act. He even sided with Roosevelt's attempt to pack the Supreme Court, but he voted to override Roosevelt's veto of a bill to advance the payment date of the soldiers' bonus.

By the time Truman's first term in the Senate was over, Hitler had gobbled up Austria and Czechoslovakia and had begun World War II in Europe by invading Poland on September 1, 1939. In the spring of 1940, eighty-nine German divisions overran Holland, Belgium, Denmark, and Norway and invaded France, and on June 14 the Nazis goose-stepped into Paris. Only Britain, where Winston Churchill had replaced Neville Chamberlain as prime minister, still stood to do battle with Hitler, and the Führer then prepared to invade England. In the Battle of Britain, the Royal Air Force stood off the Luftwaffe and prevented a German amphibious assault across the English Channel.

When Truman sought a second Senate term, the opposition was formidable; both the governor and the state's attorney general wanted his seat. Missouri's big-city newspapers opposed him because of his New Deal stands. Tom Pendergast was now in prison in Leavenworth for income tax evasion, and the Missouri Democratic organization had fallen into disrepute. Truman formed his own political organization and created a strategy of going primarily after the farm vote and organized labor. He won the nomination narrowly and then took the election.

One person who helped Truman financially was Bernard M. Baruch, the South Carolina–born financier and advisor to President Roosevelt, whom Senator James F. Byrnes of South Carolina convinced to contribute $4,000 to Truman's money-tight campaign.

As Truman started his second term in 1941, the nation was frantically preparing for war. The government spent huge sums to build a two-ocean navy and arm and train a million men a year for five years. During the first few months of 1941, defense expenditures exceeded $25 billion. Truman, by now a member of the Military Affairs Committee and the military subcommittee of the Appropriations Committee, became concerned about how that money was being spent. He traveled to war camps and defense plants and identified himself only if asked. He saw that contracts were often let through favoritism and defense industries were concentrated in the big cities, making it difficult for small businessmen to participate in the war effort. And the contracts were usually drawn on a "cost-plus" basis, allowing a contractor to increase prices and then add a profit on top of them—the higher the price, the larger the profit.

On February 10, 1941, he submitted a resolution for a special committee to investigate the national defense effort. The Senate authorized a Special Committee to Investigate the National Defense Program with seven members, including two Republicans, and a budget of $15,000. Hugh Fulton, an assistant to Attorney General Robert H. Jackson, became its chief counsel. The committee examined the link between the military bureaucracy and big business and immediately uncovered vast waste and lack of planning in military camp construction. It tackled the labor-management dispute that was preventing coal from being mined; the threat of public exposure pushed the coal operators to a settlement. The committee showed that the cost-plus-fixed-fee contracts for government work allowed contractors to run up profits. Then it plunged into an investigation of the shortages of such vital war materials as aluminum, copper, lead, and zinc. In response to the committee's work, Roosevelt created the War Production Board, with Donald M. Nelson as its head.

On June 22, 1941, Hitler reversed course and attacked the Soviet Union. With 150 divisions, totaling three million men and 2,700 aircraft, he invaded the Soviet Union from the Arctic Circle to the Black Sea. The Nazis seemed invincible.

The Germans powered ahead for six months and were within sight of Moscow when, on December 6, a hundred fresh Soviet divisions counterattacked in forty-degree-below-zero weather and threw back the Nazi invaders.

The very next day, the Japanese attacked Pearl Harbor. Hitler trumpeted that he would make war on the decadent, "half Judaized, half negrified" Americans. He did not yet see that the aroused alliance of the British Commonwealth, the Soviet Union, and now the United States would obliterate all his dreams.

After the United States entered the war, the work of the Truman Committee, as it was now widely known, took on new urgency. The committee exposed bureaucratic waste and red tape, duplication of effort, and conflicts between military and civilian agencies in the rapid and enormous buildup for war. It discovered that German U-boats had destroyed twelve million tons of Allied shipping during 1942—said to be one million tons more than all the American shipyards were then producing. The Navy publicly denied the figures, but Secretary of the Navy Frank Knox admitted them to the committee in executive session. The United States increased ship production and concentrated on trying to wipe out German submarine domination of the shipping lanes to Europe. The committee also revealed the production of defective airplanes and engines and other defense procurement imperfections and illegalities. Truman chaired the committee until, in August 1944, he was nominated for the vice presidency of the United States.

By then the tide of the war had turned. American Marines had landed on Guadalcanal (August 7, 1942); Soviet forces had crushed the Germans at Stalingrad (January 30, 1943) and at Kursk (July 17, 1943); the Western Allies had entered Rome (June 4, 1944) and landed at Normandy (June 6, 1944). The massive Soviet-German battle front, on which three million German soldiers faced five million Russians, was constantly shifting westward. The great German and Japanese offensives were finished.

Truman received the nomination for vice president after a political struggle between the popular and very liberal incumbent Henry Wallace and the southern conservative and former Catholic James Byrnes, a former U.S. senator, justice of the Supreme Court, and "Assistant President." FDR, in his usual political style, kept everyone guessing about whom he would support. Truman actually went to the Democratic National Convention in Chicago prepared to nominate Byrnes. (Much later, Truman said he thought Byrnes had asked Truman to nominate him to prevent Truman from accepting the nomination himself.) When FDR finally told Democratic Party leaders to "clear it with Sidney," labor leader Sidney Hillman vetoed Byrnes. Roosevelt then secretly tapped Truman, who had the backing of the leaders of organized labor, including Hillman, and support in the southern elements of the party. Edward J. Flynn, the powerful Democratic boss of The Bronx, also spoke up for Truman over Byrnes.

In essence, the party bosses regarded Byrnes as too conservative and Wallace, the most popular choice, as too liberal, so they settled on Truman. Truman was seen as a conservative, a politician who would "go along." National Democratic Chairman Robert E. Hannegan, a Missourian and a Truman partisan, told Truman at the convention in Chicago that Roosevelt wanted him to run and showed him a handwritten note that simply said: "Bob, it's Truman. F.D.R."

On the first ballot, Wallace received 429 votes to Truman's 319. When "Boss" Flynn switched 74 New York votes to Truman on the second ballot, he won the nomination overwhelmingly. Byrnes, who had believed to the end that he was FDR's choice, was furious.

After the convention, Truman had lunch with FDR on the South Lawn of the White House (which Truman called "the back yard"). In their shirtsleeves, they sat in white lawn chairs under a large tree reputedly planted by Andrew Jackson, Truman's hero, and endured a prolonged session of photographing. Then the ill, polio-limited Roosevelt told the junior senator from Missouri that he would have to do the campaigning for both of them, or, as Truman wrote Bess, "a lot of hooey about what I could do to help the campaign." Truman said he would fly around the country, but Roosevelt said, "Don't fly. Ride the trains. Can't both of us afford to take chances."

Truman was appalled by FDR's worn appearance and his shaky

hands. He could not pour cream into his coffee and had difficulty talking. Truman thought Roosevelt, who was only two years older than he was, looked like an old man. The seriousness of his condition was too apparent to be a secret. Truman added later, "I knew he was a sick man. And what he said about both of us not being able to take chances, why, what more did you need?"

Truman toured in a railroad car, making some fifty-four speeches; Roosevelt, despite his weakened condition, did a bit of campaigning just before the election in order to convince the electorate that he was strong enough to continue in the job for a fourth term. During the campaign, Thomas E. Dewey, the Republican candidate and governor of New York, who would run against Truman four years later, said that with the help of Sidney Hillman the Communists were taking over the New Deal and the U.S. government. This was only the beginning of the vicious attacks to come.

The election was close; but when it was over, Truman said he had always thought that Dewey never had a chance. Even though many disliked Roosevelt running for a fourth term as President, the country did not want to change leaders in the middle of a war.

Harry Truman and some of his Battery D friends spent election night together waiting for the returns in a suite in Kansas City's Muehlebach Hotel. He played the piano while they drank and listened to the radio. It was a long night; Dewey finally conceded at 3:45 A.M. Then Truman threw out his friends except for one old pal, Harry Easley, and tried to relax. Easley remembered, "He told me that the last time that he saw Mr. Roosevelt he had the pallor of death on his face and he knew that he would be President before the term was out."

When Truman was elected vice president, the war was still being fiercely fought around the globe; but by now the Soviet forces were fighting on German soil and in the suburbs of Budapest; Paris was back in Allied hands; and the Americans had seized Aachen, the first German city to fall. In the Pacific, the Americans had retaken Guam and conquered Saipan, Tinian, Tarawa, Peleliu, and Leyte in the Philippines.

Franklin Roosevelt's time was running out; and like it or not, however they voted, the American people were going to have to change presidents in midwar. In reality, they had chosen between Thomas Dewey and Harry Truman.

As 1945 opened, Churchill asked Stalin to quick-start his next giant offensive in order to ease German pressure in the Battle of the Bulge in Belgium. Stalin cooperated by opening his campaign on January 12 with 180 divisions; Hitler could mount only 75 divisions to meet them. The Soviet army captured the shattered remains of Warsaw on January 17 and two days later took Cracow. Soviet Marshals Georgi K. Zhukov and Ivan Stepanovich Konev massed their forces along the eastern bank of the Oder River.

On January 20, a snowy, sleeting Saturday in Washington, President Roosevelt, to save his strength, was inaugurated on the jam-packed south portico of the White House. It was the third wartime inauguration in the nation's history; the first had been Madison's and the second Lincoln's. Retiring Vice President Wallace administered the oath to Harry Truman; then Roosevelt stood up painfully in his braces, his hands shaking, his face worn, and Chief Justice Stone swore him in for his fourth term. Afterwards, Vice President Truman dutifully telephoned his mother in Grandview. She said firmly, "Now you behave yourself."

Exactly a week later, Soviet infantrymen stumbled upon the gigantic Nazi death camp at Auschwitz in Poland. They found its horrible mechanisms for mass extermination and seven thousand starving survivors.

Two days after the Inauguration in Washington, Roosevelt left for the summit conference at Yalta. He met with Churchill and Stalin at the resort town in the Crimea on February 4. In February the Americans in the Pacific assaulted Iwo Jima and liberated Manila.

At Yalta, the Big Three coordinated the Western Allied war effort with the Soviet offensive, which was meeting increasing German resistance, and looked ahead at some of the problems of postwar Europe. They discussed dividing Germany among the victors. They agreed on zones of occupation, with a French zone to be carved out of the American and British zones. Stalin was unbending about keeping his versions of a pro-Soviet Polish government and Poland's borders.

Roosevelt returned from Yalta exhausted and listless; he was in Washington only thirty more days before his death. Truman served as vice president for eighty-two days.

The man who now became President was a self-made Midwesterner who enjoyed poker (he called it "a study in probabilities") and a shot of bourbon. He never smoked; he used barracks language when among men. At five feet ten, his bearing was erect, his grip firm. Originally left-handed, he had been taught to use his right hand. Not especially sophisticated, he was an optimist and friendly; he liked a good story and playing the piano. He had enormous energy, rarely seemed to tire, and was decisive in giving his associates directions. He was the first President since Ulysses S. Grant who had worked in his adult life as a dirt farmer.

Chapter 3

"Plowing a Field with a Mule"

Harry Truman began his first full day as President on Friday the 13th by rising at 6:30 in his Connecticut Avenue apartment. After he had breakfast while chatting with Hugh Fulton, who had been his chief investigator on the Truman Committee, the Secret Service led the two men out the back way. As the President entered the White House car, he spotted Ernest B. "Tony" Vaccaro, the Associated Press Capitol Hill correspondent, standing in the driveway behind the apartment house, and called, "Come on in, Tony. Let's get started." They drove to the White House together. In the car, Truman said a silent prayer that he could live up to the task he now faced.

The White House executive office, then known as the Oval Room, was still filled with ship models, ship prints, and other Roosevelt mementos. Truman asked that the desktop be cleared so he could work but that nothing else be touched for the present. Roosevelt's personal staff were preoccupied with the funeral.

Fleet Admiral William Leahy, chief of staff to the Commander-in-Chief, lay before Truman a stack of papers, reports, and correspondence. Each presented a problem.

Eddie McKim dropped by, and Truman apologized for canceling their poker game the night before. Then Secretary of State Stettinius was Truman's first official caller. They discussed plans for the United Nations Conference, and Truman asked to be given regular reports from the Department of State on the principal problems with other nations. He had to catch up. He would study State Department reports every night before going to bed.

At 11 A.M. he met with the secretary of war, the secretary of the navy, and the Joint Chiefs of Staff and listened to a briefing on the overall military situation. The World War I artillery captain was suddenly the Commander-in-Chief of armed forces totaling sixteen million people.

In reply to Truman's question, the military leaders predicted that Germany would not be defeated for six more months, and Japan for a year and a half. The war, which had already killed 196,999 Americans (total American casualties were 899,390), was still going to be long and hard.

When the others had left, Truman asked the crusty, outspoken Admiral Leahy to stay at his post as personal chief of staff to the President. Although Leahy felt that Truman would be too malleable to make a good President, he agreed.

Then, in a surprise move, Truman had himself driven over to the Capitol for a private lunch with selected leaders of Congress, thirteen senators, and four representatives. By traveling to the Capitol, he purposely set out to strengthen the ties between the executive and legislative branches and ease the frictions that had built up during the Roosevelt years. At lunch he admitted to them that he felt overwhelmed. Truman arranged to address a Joint Session of the Senate and House on Monday, after Roosevelt's funeral. He said he wanted to let the country know that he intended to continue the policies of the dead President and that he would seek continued bipartisan support for the conduct of the war.

Lunch over, Truman waded through a line of reporters and page boys waiting to greet him. He shook hands with each one and said to the reporters, "Boys, if you ever pray, pray for me now." He said he felt that the moon and the stars and the planets had all fallen on him.

Back at the White House, Truman signed his first official document as President—a proclamation to The People of the United States formally announcing President Roosevelt's death. It said in part, with clear echoes of the biblical story of Moses:

> The leader of his people in a great war, he lived to see the assurance of the victory but not to share in it. He lived to see the first foundations of the free and peaceful world to which his life was dedicated, but not to enter on that world himself.

All around the globe, national leaders wondered how the inexperienced new President would meet the sudden, crucial challenges before him. Messages poured in. Churchill said he hoped to "renew with you the intimate comradeship in the great cause we all served that I enjoyed through these terrible years with him." Stalin, starting out on a most positive note, called Roosevelt "a great world statesman and herald of world organization and security after the war."

At 2:30 James Byrnes, who had flown up from his home in Spartanburg, South Carolina, came in to see Truman. He was five years Truman's senior and had been Roosevelt's "assistant president" until the beginning of April. But his unhappiness with Roosevelt had been festering ever since the 1944 election. Byrnes had been insulted and embarrassed when he was passed over in favor of Truman, who now sat in the White House where Byrnes knew he might have sat.

Byrnes had gone to Yalta with Roosevelt, and Truman was anxious to learn from him what had taken place there. Truman had heard that Byrnes had kept shorthand notes of the secret meetings he had attended at Yalta. He asked Byrnes to have his notes typed up. Truman thought that Byrnes had sat in on all the meetings of Churchill, Stalin, and Roosevelt, but this was not the case. Roosevelt had enabled Byrnes to attend only some of the meetings and record only carefully selected portions of what was discussed.

These limits on access had increased Byrnes' displeasure with Roosevelt. As soon as the Western Allies' armies had crossed the Rhine that spring, Byrnes had resigned as "Assistant President."

Truman was eager to assuage Byrnes' disappointment at not being the President. He informed Byrnes that after the San Francisco U.N. conference, he wanted to appoint him secretary of state. He said later, "I thought that my calling on him at this time might help balance things up."

And Truman had another, more presidential reason for proposing this change. The line of succession to the presidency at that time went directly from the vice president to the secretary of state, and Stettinius, the forty-five-year-old former chairman of the board of the United States Steel Corporation, had never held elective office. Truman thought a person who had held elective office would make a stronger successor, and Byrnes had served in both the House and the Senate. "At this time I regarded Byrnes as the man best qualified."

At their Friday afternoon meeting, Byrnes also told Truman that the government had been developing "an explosive great enough to destroy the whole world." But, in fact, Byrnes was not well informed about the atomic project; Truman would have to wait until Secretary of War Stimson came back to brief him.

At 3 P.M. Truman met with Roy Roberts, the managing editor of the *Kansas City Star,* which had fought the Pendergast political organization. Roberts, in Washington for the Gridiron Dinner that had been scheduled for the next night, had had a long-standing lunch date with Truman. When the press asked Roberts what he thought of the new chief executive, he said, "I have confidence in him and think he will do a fine, common-sense job. And I think that the people of this country will rally to him."

Half an hour after Roberts left, Truman faced his first major international problem; he had to deal with Premier Stalin. He was visited by Secretary Stettinius and Charles Bohlen, the State Department expert on the Soviet Union. They wanted him to declare his opposition to the Soviet Union's domination of Poland. Truman heard, for the first time, that Stalin was not living up to the Yalta agreements.

Stalin planned to use Poland as a buffer against the West. With the Soviet army occupying Poland, Stalin insisted on establishing a Polish government friendly to the Soviet Union. And he wanted to move Poland's borders westward by taking some Polish land adjacent to the Soviet Union and giving German territory to Poland in exchange. The Western powers objected vigorously. The concept of buffer states was an old-fashioned idea that made many informed Americans uncomfortable. Poland was to become one of Truman's most nettlesome problems.

Churchill had recently proposed to Roosevelt that they issue a joint public statement informing the world of the Soviet moves to control Poland. Roosevelt, the day before his death, had replied, "We must be firm." Now, late on the afternoon of the thirteenth, following the advice of his holdover counselors, Truman sent Churchill a message saying that he agreed with sending a joint note from Churchill and himself to Stalin but that he felt it should not be made public at this time.

His first instinct was to try to get along with Stalin, even while those around him were urging him to be tough. Soon he would start to feel suspicious of those who could see no good whatsoever in the Soviet Union. He wrote in his diary on June 7, "I'm not afraid of Russia. They've always been our friends and I can't see any reason why they shouldn't always be."

He wanted to live at peace in a world with intense ideological differences. He believed that "the dictatorship of the proletariat is no different from the Czar or Hitler. There is no socialism in Russia. It's a hotbed of special privilege."

And he came to see that Stalin had already solidified his hold on the Eastern European countries he had freed from the Nazis, particularly Poland, and was starting the East-West confrontation that would soon split Europe down its middle. But Truman was determined to live at peace with the Soviet Union and its leader.

Truman immediately faced a second problem with Stalin. The Soviet premier refused to send Foreign Minister Molotov to the U.N. conference in San Francisco; Stalin thought it enough to send Molotov's deputy, Andrei Y. Vishinsky. In Washington, this was taken as a signal of the Soviet Union's lack of interest in the United Nations.

When Averell Harriman met with Stalin in Moscow this same day, the ambassador took advantage of Roosevelt's death and urged Stalin to send Molotov to meet the new President and attend the conference. Stalin agreed to order Molotov to attend the San Francisco conference if Truman would make the request. On his way, Molotov would stop and visit with the President. Truman promptly sent the request.

On Saturday, April 14, the new President was up by five o'clock, even earlier than usual. Franklin Roosevelt's body was to arrive at Washington's Union Station from Warm Springs. Before breakfast, Truman worked on his address to Congress and thought through the instructions he would give the U.S. delegation to San Francisco. The delegation members faced some prickly issues, such as the presidency of the conference, trusteeships, and how many votes the Soviet Union was to have. Stalin was pressing to have two Soviet republics represented: White Russia and the Ukraine.

As soon as Truman reached the White House, he appointed his close friend John W. Snyder, vice president of the First National Bank of St. Louis, to the vacant post of federal loan administrator. He telephoned Secretary of Commerce Jesse H. Jones, the former loan administrator, and informed him that "the President" had appointed Snyder.

"Did he make that appointment before he died?" Jones asked.

"No," Truman replied. "He just made it now."

After a quick meeting with Secretary of the Treasury Henry Morgenthau, Jr., Truman drove to Union Station with Henry Wallace and James Byrnes, the two men who might have been President in his place. He chose these companions as a public statement of conciliation and confidence.

The train bearing Roosevelt's body arrived at ten. Truman, accompanied by Wallace and Byrnes, went aboard to pay his respects to Mrs. Roosevelt. Then the funeral procession formed—and snaked through the hot, muggy streets of Washington, the flag-draped casket and its caisson drawn by six white horses. Up Constitution Avenue to the White House, the streets were crowded with silent, grief-stricken mourners, many of them weeping openly.

In the East Room, flowers were banked up against the walls, and the casket, adorned with lilies and roses, lay in state. Five members of the armed forces stood guard. An American flag stood on one side and the blue presidential banner on the other. Truman spoke again with Mrs. Roosevelt and went back to the executive offices.

Harry Hopkins, who had been Roosevelt's personal representative and confidant, had left his sickbed in the Mayo Clinic at Rochester, Minnesota, to attend the funeral and had just arrived at the White House. Truman knew him well and was eager to see him.

When Hopkins came in, they had lunch sent in on trays and talked for two hours. Hopkins was pale and thin; Truman thought he looked "like a ghost." The President soaked up everything Hopkins could tell him about relations with the Soviet Union and about Stalin, Churchill, and the various conferences that had been held during the long war.

Hopkins explained candidly, "Stalin is a forthright, rough, tough Russian. He is a Russian partisan through and through, thinking always first of Russia. But he can be talked to frankly." Hopkins had always been successful in talking with Stalin, and Truman regarded his advice as important. Truman said later of Hopkins, ". . . he knew exactly how to do it. He talked tough to them all the time. I don't know how he did it, but he got it done."

Ed Flynn, the Democratic boss of The Bronx in New York City, was the next caller; but when he began to discuss the political consequences of Roosevelt's death, Truman stopped him, saying it was too soon.

At 2:15 Leahy and Byrnes brought Truman two messages just in from Churchill. The first dealt with the approaching meeting of the Anglo-American and Soviet armies in the middle of Europe and suggested that Truman, Stalin, and Churchill all broadcast an announcement of the event when it occurred. Truman agreed easily.

Churchill's second cable discussed the American proposal for a final all-out air attack on Germany to smash the war industries that still survived. Churchill opposed the U.S. Joint Chiefs of Staff's scheme to send against the German war plants pilotless old bombers loaded with explosives and guided by remote control. He feared that the Germans would retaliate against London. But he added that if the U.S. military leaders thought it essential, he would accept the ploy. After consulting with the Chiefs of Staff, Truman promised Churchill he would veto the suggestion.

Then another cable arrived from Churchill, this one dealing with the Polish problem. Anthony Eden, the British foreign minister, was on his way to San Francisco and wished to stop off and see the President about the proposed joint message to Stalin on Poland.

The rain of messages from Churchill was not haphazard. Harry Hopkins had suggested to Lord Halifax, the British ambassador to Washington, this concerted program so that the wartime leaders could get to know each other across vast distances and under great daily stress.

At the same time, Lord Halifax informed Churchill about the new President: "It may be of interest that Truman's hobby is history of military strategy, of which he is reported to have read widely. He certainly betrayed surprising knowledge of Hannibal's campaigns one night here. He venerates Marshall." Truman would later call George C. Marshall "the military man I liked best" and "one of the most remarkable men who ever lived."

While Truman struggled to familiarize himself with all the complex European issues, he also had to consider a British request for his agreement to urgent military cooperation in Asia. Japan had recently seized Indochina, and Admiral Lord Louis Mountbatten, commander of the Southeast Asia Command (SEAC), was preparing clandestine guerrilla operations before his regular forces advanced. American units under Mountbatten's command were already active in such operations in Burma, and a French resistance force was also in the field in Indochina.

Mountbatten had conferred with Lieutenant General Albert C. Wedemeyer, the American military advisor to Generalissimo Chiang Kai-shek; and they now proposed that Mountbatten keep Wedemeyer informed of his moves and undertake no operation until the generalissimo approved. Truman cabled Churchill his endorsement of this arrangement.

Just before 4 P.M., Mrs. Truman and Margaret joined the President, and together they went to the East Room for the brief service conducted by the Right Reverend Angus Dun, bishop of the Episcopal Diocese of Washington. Outside, the sultry day had broken into fiercely wind-whipped rain. The room was jammed with silent dignitaries and foreign diplomats; both Mrs. Woodrow Wilson and Thomas E. Dewey were there, as were British Foreign Secretary Eden and Soviet Ambassador Andrei Gromyko. But nobody stood up when the new President entered the room. Truman did not even notice.

Mrs. Roosevelt had asked that there be no eulogies. Everyone sang Franklin Roosevelt's two favorite hymns, "Eternal Father, Strong to Save" and "Faith of Our Fathers." Bishop Dun included in the service the well-remembered statement from Roosevelt's first inaugural address in 1933: "The only thing we have to fear is fear itself."

After the service, the Trumans returned to their Connecticut Avenue apartment. At 9:30 P.M., as the Marine Band played the national anthem, President Roosevelt's body, accompanied by Mrs. Roosevelt and the family, was carried to Union Station—through streets packed six deep with mourners—and placed aboard the funeral train for the trip to the Roosevelt family home at Hyde Park, New York. The President, Mrs. Truman, and Margaret boarded the train an hour later. Cabinet members, Supreme Court justices, military leaders, government officials, friends of the Roosevelts, and members of the press filled the seventeen-car special train.

The party arrived at Hyde Park at 9:30 on a beautiful cool spring Sunday morning. Cannon sounded twenty-one times as the coffin was moved from the train to a caisson drawn by six brown horses. A seventh horse stood there hooded, stirrups reversed, sword and boots turned upside down—the symbols of honor for the fallen warrior.

To muffled drums the procession walked silently up the gravel road in the sunshine to the hemlock-hedged rose garden behind the house in which Roosevelt had been born. The Corps of West Point cadets in gray uniforms stood at motionless attention. Eight servicemen lowered the coffin into the grave. The cadets fired three volleys. A bugler sounded Taps. Harry Truman stood there, hat in hand, his head bowed, as Franklin Delano Roosevelt was buried in the Roosevelt garden.

Monday, April 16, was the day Soviet Marshal Georgi Zhukov crossed the Oder River and opened his final drive on Berlin. That morning, Truman polished his speech to Congress, and at 10 A.M. he met with Foreign Minister Eden and Lord Halifax. Eden judged Truman to be "honest and friendly. . . . I believe we shall have in him a loyal collaborator, and I am much heartened by this first conversation."

They reviewed Churchill's version of the joint communication on the Polish question and came to agreement. The message restated firmly the Anglo-American understanding that Poles from the government-in-exile in London would participate in the formation of a new Polish government. Truman sent off a copy to Ambassador Harriman in Moscow with instructions to hand it to Marshal Stalin.

Then, led by a single motorcycle policeman and followed by a Secret Service car, Truman was driven to the Capitol. The District police had had eighteen motorcycle officers ready to escort him, but he set his style for presidential travel by turning down all the escorts but one. The day was bright and invigorating, and he noticed the tulips blooming in the White House garden.

He was taken to the Speaker's office, where he had dropped by for a chat only four days before. At one o'clock, he was ceremoniously led to the House floor and down the main aisle to the rostrum. There, before a battery of microphones, nervous and overcome by the moment, he began: "Mr. Speaker." Quickly, Speaker Sam Rayburn leaned over and, in a whisper that could be heard over the radio, said, "Just a minute, Harry, I want to present you."

Truman readily admitted that he was a neophyte and had large shoes to fill. Reading slowly from a black notebook, he said, "In His infinite wisdom, Almighty God has seen fit to take from us a great man who loved, and was beloved by, all humanity. No man could possibly fill the tremendous void left by the passing of that noble soul." He promised to carry on.

Truman assured Congress and the assembled dignitaries, as well as the vast public listening over the radio, that he would carry out the war and peace policies of President Roosevelt. He asserted, "America will never become a party to any plan for partial victory. . . . Our demand has been, and it remains—Unconditional Surrender!" His voice rose as he said those last two words. He was interrupted by applause fifteen times in his seventeen minutes, and when he promised to insist on unconditional surrender, everyone in the chamber rose. He closed with the words of King Solomon: "Give therefore Thy servant an understanding heart to judge Thy people, that I may discern between good and bad: for who is able to judge this Thy so great a people?"

That evening, Truman and his family moved from their Connecticut Avenue apartment into Blair House, across Pennsylvania Avenue from the White House. They would live there until Mrs. Roosevelt could move out of the White House. Truman was pleased that he could now walk to and from his office, not realizing the security precautions that required. When he walked home at five o'clock, he was surprised to see that until he reached the entrance of Blair House, the traffic lights at Pennsylvania Avenue's intersection with Executive West turned red in all directions.

Inundated with new and perturbing problems, he buckled down to studying a pile of reports. One that troubled him most was about the shortages of the world's foodstuffs, as well as cotton, wool, and coal. He became aware that these essentials were scarce in many liberated areas and that chaos was flaring up in some countries. The report urged him to emphasize a "tightening of the belt" at home in order to reduce domestic consumption.

Truman soon started putting some structure into his new life. He revived his daily habit of taking a walk every morning at 6:30, moving out at the 120 steps per minute he had learned in the army. He covered two miles in little more than the half hour he allotted for this part of his routine. He felt it gave him a buoyant start to the day.

He husbanded his strength, took a half-hour nap after lunch, and then worked until 6 or 6:30, followed by taking a swim or a stroll around the grounds. His days were devoted mostly to seeing people and his evenings to the endless paperwork and frequent social events.

He certainly displayed more energy than most of the men around him, with his long schedule, physical workouts, and the amount of reading he devoured. He worked at his job.

Tuesday morning he met with the members of the U.S. delegation to San Francisco. He gave them his vision of their mission: they were to help set up an international organization that would prevent another world war. He wanted the U.N. Charter to be a document that would pass the U.S. Senate and not arouse opposition like that which had defeated President Wilson after World War I.

Then he signed an extension of Lend-Lease for another year. Hardly a month earlier, as vice president, he had cast the deciding vote in the Senate to continue Lend-Lease.

At 10:30 A.M. he held his first press and radio conference. Standing at his desk, he told the 348 reporters bluntly, "If you want to ask me anything, I will try to answer; and if I don't know, I will tell you." The press conference allowed for fifteen minutes of questions. He decided to reduce the number of press conferences to one a week and to continue FDR's policy of no direct quotation of his replies to questions. After the session, the reporters applauded his performance. He returned to the host of problems waiting for him.

Years later, looking back at those first days and the flood of visitors, Truman wrote: "I like people. I like to see them and hear what they have to say. But seeing people takes time and effort. It is more than a ceremonial duty, and although it is a heavy burden on the President, he cannot share it with anyone, for in the White House he is the only directly elected representative of all the people."

He was very conscious in those first days that he was replacing a great President. He wanted to make his own mark and achieve the things he wanted to accomplish.

Much later, he said it another way: "Plowing a field with a mule is the most satisfying thing a man can do. And at the end of the day, looking over what you've done, you can feel a real sense of accomplishment, and that's a very rare thing." The field ahead of him that April was long and uncharted. He had barely begun. The challenges were tremendous. He wondered if he could meet them— if he could do the job.

Chapter 4

"The So Recently Arrogant Enemies of Mankind"

As the presidency changed hands in Washington, both the Soviet and Anglo-American armies were fighting inside Germany, and some people thought that no problems remained for Harry Truman to solve in order to finish the European war. General Dwight D. Eisenhower's grandson, David, went so far as to write years later that General Eisenhower "was acting in the void left by Roosevelt's illness and death." In truth, there was no void.

Truman came to the White House less than a month before the war in Europe ended. Victory now appeared inevitable, but the battling and killing continued and the unresolved issues which would impact the new world being born, were numerous, complex, and intensely debated. He was bombarded by problems, all of which were new to him and about which his advisors' opinions differed passionately. These problems demanded decisions made swiftly and under great pressure. The war would not stop while he caught up.

He had Roosevelt's experience and wisdom as reference points, but he had to risk acting on his own judgment. In the beginning, he kept Roosevelt's military and political advisors in place to guide him, and he had to pick and choose among their conflicting ideas. Fortunately, he was direct and decisive; he understood politicians and their manipulations; and, being a "common man" himself, he sensed people's fears and hopes.

He soon learned that in wartime the generals and admirals possessed extraordinary power and authority. He had never, either as an artillery captain in Europe or as an investigative senator in Washington, developed any great respect for the regular military establishment. Now, as President, he discovered that in meetings with his Chiefs of Staff the question of military subordination to civilian government was never fully addressed. He found the Chiefs of Staff and generals such as Eisenhower, Douglas MacArthur, Joseph W. Stilwell, and Wedemeyer, as well as Admiral Harold R. Stark playing frontline foreign policy roles with considerable independence. He repeatedly relied on the judgment of Eisenhower, the supreme commander of the Western Allies in Europe, for solutions to the difficult and controversial military-related issues there. And he used Generals Marshall and Lucius D. Clay and other men in uniform to manage major foreign policy problems.

By that spring of 1945, the fighting had swept back and forth across all of Europe, from the Atlantic to the Urals, for nearly six years. Now, after the destruction of millions of lives on both sides, Adolf Hitler and the Nazis, rather than attacking and invading, were defending the bombed-out cities of what was to have been their glorious Thousand-Year Reich.

Three great army groups were advancing against Germany from the west. General Omar N. Bradley's U.S. 12th Army Group—comprising four field armies, nearly a million men—was charging eastward across the middle of Germany. American GIs of three fast-moving divisions of General William Simpson's U.S. Ninth Army (part of Bradley's command) were hurling themselves against the Elbe River, the last barrier preventing the Americans from closing on Berlin from the west. On Bradley's left, to the north, General Sir Bernard Law Montgomery's British 21st Army Group advanced toward Lübeck, and on his right, to the south, General Jacob L. Devers' U.S. 6th Army Group moved southeast toward Austria and Czechoslovakia.

Over on the eastern side of Germany, the Soviet forces massed more than two million men against the German defenses along the Oder River.

All that winter, the Germans had held the Americans at the Rhine River in western Germany. Then, on March 7, the Germans failed to blow up a railroad bridge at Remagen, and the U.S. 9th Armored Division was unexpectedly able to cross the river. For the first time since Napoleon, an enemy of Germany had crossed the Rhine. After that, the Americans fought rapidly eastward. In the next five weeks, Allied spearheads—American, British, and French—were established deep inside Germany.

On the eastern front, Soviet forces overwhelmed the German Sixth Panzer Army and entered Vienna in force in the first week of April. The Viennese did not resist, but the German Army fought in the streets, even in the central Ringstrasse itself. The battle destroyed the heart of this city which had been in so many ways the capital of central Europe.

Directly east of Berlin, stiff German opposition halted the Soviet advance along the Oder River and the spring mud immobilized the Soviet tanks. The Soviet leaders were also not adverse to pausing and letting the Western Allies, who had landed at Normandy only ten months before, absorb their share of the human cost of wearing down the enemy. But when the Western and Soviet armies, now less than fifty miles from their respective sides of Berlin, would meet in the heart of Germany, the Reich would be sliced in half and the final campaign of the European war would begin.

Who would capture Berlin? Both the Soviet and Anglo-American forces appeared to be rushing toward the Nazi capital. One of the more romantic American contingency plans called for the paratroopers of the 82nd Airborne Division and other units to jump and seize Berlin. It was to be "the final battle."

But appearances were not fact. Before Truman ever took office, General Marshall, the U.S. Army chief of staff, and Eisenhower had decided that they wanted the Russians to fight for Berlin. This decision was strengthened when the bridge at Remagen was captured, shifting the Americans' prime opportunity to the south. In the north, Montgomery, who could have led the advance on Berlin, did not cross the Rhine until March 23. In any case, the Americans were not eager for Montgomery and the British to be the conquerors of Berlin.

Berlin symbolized Nazi Germany. Once Berlin was conquered, the Germans might still thrash about, but their second attempt in a lifetime to master Europe would have failed. Despite the importance of Berlin as the hub of Nazi power, Eisenhower hoped his civilian superiors would not require him to advance on the capital and confront the vastly larger Soviet force. He viewed Berlin, deep inside the agreed-upon Soviet zone of occupation, as strategically unimportant and militarily difficult to capture. In addition, western Germany was in chaos and his armies there were busy with a lifesaving mission to bring food and medical care to the freed slave laborers and displaced persons, as well as to tens of millions of Germans.

Churchill and the British Chiefs of Staff repeatedly insisted to

Roosevelt and Eisenhower that Montgomery's 21st Army Group must advance across northwest Germany and seize the German capital. Churchill wanted to show the Soviet Union that it had not won the war by itself. And he wanted all the bargaining chips he could collect for negotiating with the Russians. He felt Berlin would be a very large chip. Churchill cared who took Berlin; Eisenhower cared only that it be taken.

Eisenhower saw his job as achieving military victory, not as political maneuvering. He told General Marshall that his three military objectives were (1) to split German forces with a thrust through the middle of Germany, (2) to anchor German forces in the Lübeck area in the north and prevent them from retreating onto the Danish peninsula and into Norway, and (3) "to disrupt any German efforts to establish a fortress in the southern mountains." It was a paradox that this most political of generals seemed not to comprehend that his decisions, based supposedly only on military considerations, were inevitably political decisions too and would have long-lasting consequences.

He did write Marshall, "I am the first to admit that a war is waged in pursuit of political aims, and if the Combined Chiefs of Staff should decide that the Allied effort to take Berlin outweighs purely military considerations in the theater, I would cheerfully readjust my plans and my thinking so as to carry out such an operation." Military objectives must come first unless he was overruled at a higher political level. No one overruled him.

Ambassador Harriman in Moscow would write later, "Some think that General Eisenhower should have taken Berlin, but if he had done that, our Third Army wouldn't have been in Austria, and Austria, which is a free and independent country, probably would have been occupied largely by the Red Army and might have been turned into a satellite."

Behind these strong and contrasting views were differing ideas about how to handle the Soviet Union and its tough-minded premier. Even the British government and Foreign Office were at odds over this fundamental question. How the Allies' power, now overwhelming, was used in these final weeks would help shape postwar Europe.

Marshall and the Joint Chiefs of Staff desired to establish "an agreed-upon line of demarcation" between the Western and Soviet forces to prevent any clashes. Marshall proposed that Eisenhower arrange with the Soviet leaders that this line follow clear geographical markers, the Elbe and Danube rivers. Implicit here was that Eisenhower would halt at the Elbe and not attack Berlin.

Eisenhower swiftly put into action his plan to cut through the center of Germany; he brought back Simpson's U.S. Ninth Army, which had been lent to Montgomery in the North during the Battle of the Bulge, to Bradley's command in the center. This infuriated the British because Eisenhower's action virtually eliminated the possibility that Montgomery could take Berlin and concentrated American strength on bisecting Germany through its center. That was Eisenhower's intention. And when the British Chiefs of Staff attacked the supreme commander, Marshall backed him without question. Marshall told the British that the commander in the field was the best judge of how to destroy the German armies and finish the war.

The huge Soviet force on the Oder stood ready to attack Berlin. But the German winter offensive in Belgium and the battle for the Ruhr pocket had left only the lead elements of the Western forces in position to advance from the Elbe to Berlin.

On March 28 Eisenhower sent Stalin "an unprecedented 'personal' message" to coordinate the movements of their armies, which were about to meet. The message explained that Eisenhower was sending the U.S. Ninth Army southeast toward Leipzig and Dresden, not north to Berlin. That implicitly ruled out an Anglo-American advance on Berlin. The message, with its primary objective of dividing Germany in half, pleased Stalin but angered Churchill and the British government. Berlin's fall, the prime minister cabled Roosevelt, "will be the supreme signal of defeat to the German people." Eisenhower had stirred up a controversy that would not be extinguished for years.

Stalin, replying to Eisenhower on April 1, agreed that Berlin had lost its strategic importance. But at the same time he was planning a 750,000-man offensive aimed directly at Berlin. He ordered the short, stocky, extremely popular Marshal Georgi Zhukov and his rival commander, the tall, gruff, former political commissar Marshal Ivan Konev, to race each other for the German capital.

Two days later, Eisenhower told General Marshall that "Berlin itself is no longer a particularly important objective."

With Roosevelt's agreement, Marshall replied that the battle for Germany should be finished on the judgment of the field commander. Like Eisenhower, Marshall believed that "the single objective should be quick and complete victory." And even though Churchill regarded Berlin as a matter of state to be decided by heads of government, Roosevelt would not interfere with Eisenhower's operational plan.

On Wednesday afternoon, April 11, a reconnaissance group from the U.S. 2nd Armored Division dashed into the thirteenth-century cathedral city of Magdeburg on the west bank of the Elbe, directly west of Berlin. If the Americans could cross the river, they expected to charge on to Berlin.

Firing machine guns, the American GIs terrified the afternoon shopping crowds; German civilians and soldiers scattered in all directions. The American scout cars sped over and sprayed the city's airport. The Germans counterattacked with heavy fire; the recon unit lost one scout car and pulled back.

The 2nd Armored Division was approaching the river in five great tank-led columns, and as more American units reached the Elbe, both south and north of Magdeburg, the Germans started blowing the bridges.

At 11 p.m. the 67th Armored Regiment's advanced elements were almost on the bridge at Schönebeck, three miles south of Magdeburg, when the Germans' massed fire drove them away. At dawn the Germans dynamited that bridge.

At noon on the twelfth, a platoon of 5th Armored Division tanks cruised into Tangermünde, forty miles north of Magdeburg, site of another bridge. The GIs found the main square deserted, but suddenly antitank guns fired on them from all sides. Two tanks were hit. The Americans and Germans fought house to house. German engineers destroyed the bridge with a terrific explosion. The Americans had still not made it across.

The American commanders, realizing that they would not be able to seize a bridge as they had done at Remagen, decided to cross the Elbe with an amphibious assault and then construct a pontoon bridge.

That night—Harry Truman was now President—two battalions of 2nd Armored Division infantry ferried across the Elbe in amphibious vehicles (DUKWs) at the small town of Westerhüsen, south of Magdeburg. By dawn three battalions of armored infantry were across; they dug in on the east bank and began connecting the floating units of a pontoon bridge. But accurate German artillery fire destroyed the pontoons. The three American battalions on the eastern shore were isolated.

On the afternoon of the thirteenth, still another crossing place was found farther south, and DUKWs towed a heavy cable across the river. The cable was to be used to pull across pontoons loaded with vehicles and guns—a laborious process.

The Germans battled for every river crossing. Wrote one commentator, "Had the division been able to secure either a bridge or a bridgehead across the Elbe, the 2nd might have roared right on to Berlin without ever waiting for orders."

At last, on that evening of the thirteenth, just south of the site of the cable, the Americans got a break. Men of the 83rd Division came to the river unopposed at the town of Barby, fifteen miles south of Magdeburg. The bridge had already been blown, but a battalion, without specific orders, rushed across in boats and was able to hold. Here was formed the first solid bridgehead across the Elbe. The engineers erected a treadway bridge and a sign honoring the new President: TRUMAN BRIDGE.

The American troops expected to keep advancing and take the German capital, and the crossing of the Elbe forced Eisenhower to reexamine the situation. He asked Bradley's judgment on what it would cost to push on from the Elbe to Berlin. Figuring that even if the Germans had little strength left between the Elbe and the capital, they would defend Berlin to the death, Bradley estimated one hundred thousand Allied casualties. He called that "a pretty stiff price to pay for a prestige objective." (It would ultimately cost the Russians three times that many lives to take Berlin.)

Eisenhower saw no reason to pay such a price. And he had at least three more reasons not to go on and capture Berlin. His troops had advanced a considerable distance in a very short time, and he was concerned with his supply lines' ability to keep pace. The Soviet Union had two million troops facing the city, while the Americans had only their spearhead in position to attack Berlin. And finally, because the Americans were already fighting in a section of Germany that had been designated as part of the Soviet Union's postwar occupation zone, he felt it did not made sense to fight into the German capital and then have to back out again.

On Sunday, April 15, Eisenhower gave the order to halt at the Elbe. He would leave the conquest of Berlin to the Soviet army. His field commanders were appalled, but the U.S. Joint Chiefs of Staff supported him. Bradley summoned Simpson to Wiesbaden and told the angry Ninth Army commander he was not to take Berlin. He was to stop at the Elbe. This was to be the high tide of the Western Allies' battle across Europe.

That same day, Harry Truman, who had been in office for less than three days, was watching Franklin Roosevelt's burial at Hyde Park. Although Truman had had no part in the decision on Berlin, he later supported it: "It was always a basic condition of all our military planning that we would not expose our troops to any greater danger than was necessary. Our plans for the advance eastward always had this in mind. The military commanders, General Eisenhower and his staff, decided on how far they could advance without exposing our troops to unnecessary casualties." He would not over-rule his commanders in the field. The very next day, Monday, the Soviet forces opened their giant offensive against Berlin.

At 11:30 on Thursday, April 19, Truman reviewed with General Marshall the draft of a message he planned to release as soon as the Western and Soviet armies met. It began, "The Anglo American armies under the command of General Eisenhower have met the Soviet forces where they intended to meet—in the heart of Nazi Germany. The enemy has been cut in two. This is not the hour of final victory in Europe, but the hour draws near." The moment, he wrote, signals "to ourselves and to the world that the collaboration of our nations in the cause of peace and freedom is an effective collaboration." Truman cabled the draft to Churchill, who promptly accepted it verbatim.

As Truman assumed the responsibilities of office, he became much more involved in another military problem with political implications. When should American and British troops withdraw from areas of Germany that were scheduled to be in the postwar Soviet zone of occupation? This question caused a serious conflict between Truman and Churchill.

Truman's attention was first directed to the zones of occupation by a telegram from Churchill on April 18. The prime minister's eye was always fixed on the postwar consequences of military moves.

Now he made the point that Germany was divided into "tactical zones," areas that the armies had conquered, and "occupational zones" to which the victors were to retire after V-E Day "with dignity." The zones of occupation had been drafted by the European Advisory Commission and approved at Yalta. Churchill asserted, "I am quite prepared to adhere to the occupational zones, but I do not wish our Allied troops or your American troops to be hustled back at any point by some crude assertion of a local Russian general."

The prime minister wanted the triumphant Western armies to advance as far as possible to the east and to hold onto whatever they conquered. He protested that the Americans should not fall back 150 miles in the center of Europe when there were still serious issues to settle with the Soviet Union. He regarded controlling the timing of the withdrawals as another of the few bargaining chips he and Truman still had with Stalin.

Since the Americans had done most of the advancing in the West and Truman supervised the movement of American forces, he was in a position to take the lead in deciding how and when the armies would rearrange themselves. Truman discussed Churchill's telegram with his advisors, mostly military, and replied to Churchill that they recommended that American and British troops pull back as soon as the military situation made it possible. He intended to honor the Yalta agreements.

The generals might advise him, but only the new President himself could stand up to the great British leader's ardent advocacy. When Truman had been President for barely a week, he was ready to do this. And because he was willing to defy Churchill, he set the policy.

Churchill did not give up on this point he judged so important. Over and over, he hammered home his fear of the effect of American withdrawals and transfers of troops to the Pacific while the fate of Eastern Europe was, in his view, still unresolved.

On April 12 Eisenhower, Bradley, and Lieutenant General George S. Patton came together at Hersfeld, Germany, where Patton was using a Wehrmacht cantonment for a command post, and held a series of meetings to plan further strategy, including a swing by Patton's U.S. Third Army into Austria. They discussed rumors that the top Nazis—the German High Command, the SS, and elements of the army—planned to prolong the war with a last-ditch stand in a huge "national redoubt" in the mountains of Bavaria, Austria, and northern Italy, all centered on Hitler's mountaintop retreat at Berchtesgaden. Final Allied strategy had to take this possibility into account—a long, drawn-out resistance would cost many more lives—even though in time the redoubt proved to be fantasy.

Between meetings, the three generals, with their entourage, descended two thousand feet into a salt mine near the city of Gotha, Germany, to inspect a hoard of $250 million worth of twenty-five-pound gold bars and two thousand crates of art that the Nazis had stolen from all over Europe. The Germans had painstakingly hidden the gold behind a brick wall and a steel door; an American soldier using a half stick of TNT had simply blown a hole in the brick wall.

Then the generals experienced the Holocaust for the first time. They walked through a newly captured Nazi concentration camp for political prisoners a few miles to the south in the little village of Ohrdruf. Although American soldiers of the U.S. 6th Armored Division had entered the Buchenwald concentration camp the day before and found corpses piled like dead fish and 21,000 emaciated survivors, Ohrdruf was the first Nazi camp these generals had seen. They were overwhelmed by the evidence of Nazi atrocities. Patton was moved to tears and became violently ill. Eisenhower walked through the death houses ashen-faced, teeth clenched.

The generals inspected the facilities for torturing and executing prisoners, the crowded barracks, and the "hospitals" where wasted prisoners waited for death. Outside were stacked lice-covered corpses, each with a bullet through its head. In the fields lay 3,200 more corpses. The stench of death was overpowering.

Eisenhower immediately asked Washington and London to send legislators and reporters to witness the Nazi brutality. Patton ordered that the citizens of Gotha be marched through the camp, at bayonet point if necessary, and made into work parties to bury the dead. All American soldiers in the area were ordered to visit the camp. Eisenhower turned to one GI sentry and asked, "Still have trouble hating them?" He wrote home that he had never thought "that such cruelty, bestiality and savagery could really exist in this world! It was horrible."

The mayor of Gotha and his wife were forced to tour the camp; then they went home and hanged themselves. Eisenhower mused: "Maybe there is hope after all."

The Nazis arrogantly believed they should decide who had the right to live. They had caused millions of men, women, and children, whom they regarded as subhuman, to be rounded up, starved, tortured, and worked to death—and then had fed them into the gas chambers and the flames of the crematoria—six million of them simply because they were Jewish. In the twelve years from 1933 to 1945, two out of every three European Jews had been exterminated. The Germans had murdered millions of human beings for no reason other than that they were different from some mythic Hitlerian "super" race.

Alan Bullock made the essential point about the Nazis' rise to power: "The Nazi campaign could not have succeeded as it did by the ingenuity of its methods alone, if it had not at the same time corresponded and appealed to the mood of a considerable proportion of the German people." That their sadistic efforts, first in Germany and eventually throughout Europe, should have been carried out by a people whose heritage includes the greatness and humanity of a Goethe and a Beethoven speaks to the mystery of the dichotomy between human caring and bestiality.

By the spring of 1945, the Nazis were no longer able to condemn human beings to slave-labor and extermination camps. All that remained of the Holocaust was desperation, stealth, and murder on the part of the Germans and discovery and the saving of survivors on the part of the advancing Allies.

At the end of the day, the generals flew back to Patton's Third Army Headquarters at Marburg and went to bed just before midnight. Eisenhower and Bradley shared a small house, and Patton slept in his trailer. Patton's watch had stopped, so he turned on the radio to get the time signal from the British Broadcasting Corporation. That is how he heard that President Roosevelt had died. He woke Bradley, and the two went to Eisenhower's room.

The three men, in their bathrobes, talked for a long time about what Roosevelt's death meant to the war. They had trouble accepting Truman as President, although Bradley, a Missourian like Truman, had a favorable impression of him. They knew that Truman greatly respected General Marshall and felt that boded well for the war effort.

Eisenhower was deeply disturbed by the news and worried about the nation's future. He wrote later, "It seemed to us, from the international viewpoint, to be a most critical time to be forced to change national leaders. We went to bed depressed and sad."

The Russians opened their drive on Berlin from the line of the Oder River at 4 A.M. on Monday, April 16, with an earth-shaking barrage of 500,000 shells, rockets, and bombs. The Germans, long expecting the onslaught, had retreated to the Seelow Heights, out of harm's way, and bought a little time.

Marshals Zhukov and Konev commanded two vast forces of assault troops, who crossed the Oder in small boats, on rafts and logs, and by swimming; guns and supplies were floated across. Combat engineers, shoulder deep in ice-cold water, bolted together prefabricated wooden bridges.

Zhukov and Konev led twenty-two divisions to establish bridgeheads west of the Oder and Neisse rivers and south and north of Berlin. Three thousand tanks churned westward. The Germans destroyed many of them with point-blank fire and mowed down infantry with small arms. They momentarily stopped Zhukov's force, but then both marshals headed for Berlin. Stalin urged them on, expecting the Germans to invite in the Western Allies in order to avoid surrendering to the Russians.

Hitler, in his bunker, had all the autobahn bridges leading to Berlin blown up and issued an Order of the Day: "He who gives the order to retreat is to be shot on the spot."

On the day the Russians opened their offensive, the British Chiefs of Staff made one last stab at persuading the Combined Chiefs of Staff to direct Eisenhower to take Berlin. But it was meaningless; the Russians had acted. The next afternoon, with a major Soviet-German battle building on the Oder, American forces collecting at the Elbe, and a new President in the White House, Eisenhower flew to London to confer with Churchill personally.

That morning, Churchill addressed Parliament and expressed the sorrow of the House of Commons at the death of President Roosevelt. He praised FDR's generous heart and his anger at aggression and oppression. And the prime minister said, "He has left a successor who comes forward with firm steps and sure convictions to carry on the task to its appointed end."

Then he met with Eisenhower at 10 Downing Street. Chief among the military-political issues before them were the north-to-south demarcation line between the Western Allies and the Soviet army and the undetermined fate of both Denmark and Czechoslovakia. They talked about Berlin and Eisenhower's decision to halt at the Elbe; about Vienna, which Soviet forces had already entered, and Prague, toward which both the Americans and the Russians were advancing. They discussed the French occupation zone that was to be carved out of the American zone, and how to assure de Gaulle that he would have a zone of his own. In the end, Churchill and Eisenhower agreed that Montgomery should take Lübeck and free Denmark while Patton pushed south of Stuttgart and into Czechoslovakia and Konev seized Prague.

Churchill still sought to delay the Americans' withdrawals to their own occupation zone to make sure the Russians lived up to agreements such as Western access to Berlin and Vienna and participation in an Austrian Allied Control Commission. However, the withdrawal question applied to American forces and Churchill had to give way. This was to be Eisenhower's last meeting with Churchill and the British Chiefs of Staff during the war in Europe.

On April 22 columnist Drew Pearson published in *The Washington Post* that on April 13, Truman's first full day in the White House, U.S. patrols had reached Potsdam, "which is to Berlin what the Bronx is to New York City." Pearson wrote that they had then pulled back fifty miles to the Elbe to keep "a previous agreement," which, he said, Roosevelt had made with Stalin at Yalta to let the Russians occupy Berlin. This conspiracy scenario was total fiction, and Harry Hopkins denied that any secret deal had been made. But that did not quiet the controversy. The ugly little incident came to be viewed in retrospect as foreshadowing the Cold War. The seedlings of distrust were being planted.

This growing distrust between the Soviet Union and the Western democracies was also the cause of one of the most loathsome decisions of the war. Britain and the United States, fearing that the Russians would mistreat British and American prisoners they liberated from the Germans, agreed to return home, even against their will, large numbers of Soviet and Eastern European civilian war refugees and soldiers who had been prisoners of the Germans.

Although Truman stood up to Churchill on withdrawing American troops from the Soviet zone of occupation, he played a less stalwart role when it came time to carry out this forced repatriation of Soviet and Eastern European nationals.

The Churchill cabinet had agreed to the forced repatriation of Soviet nationals in August 1944, well before Truman assumed the presidency. The British wanted to give the Russians no excuse to refuse to repatriate British prisoners of war they liberated. By the time of Yalta, the British had returned 17,500 Soviet citizens, willing or not. British Foreign Secretary Eden helped convince Admiral Leahy, Roosevelt's chief of staff, that "it is not advisable for the United States Government to proceed otherwise." And Eisenhower pushed for the early and swift repatriation of millions of displaced Soviet nationals his command had on its hands.

Just before the Yalta Conference, U.S. Embassy officials in Moscow, especially Ambassador Harriman and George Kennan, had agreed to send liberated Soviet prisoners back to the Soviet Union. Acting Secretary of State Joseph C. Grew cabled Stettinius at Yalta opposing forced repatriation and received this reply: "The consensus here [in Yalta] is that it would be unwise to include questions relative to the protection of the Geneva Convention." At Yalta the Big Three endorsed forced repatriation without a murmur.

Concern that the Russians would mistreat British and American prisoners they liberated from the Germans outweighed the knowledge, obvious ever since the Soviet purge trials of the 1930s, that the Soviet government treated savagely its own citizens who differed with the Communist Party's rule. And there could be no doubt about what would happen to turncoats like General Andrei Vlasov and other Soviet citizens who had fought for Germany against the Communists.

Truman accepted the rationale that this policy of repatriation would ensure the safety and well-being of American and British nationals who had been taken prisoner by the Germans and were now in Russian hands. Although it has been said that Truman quietly fortified Dean Acheson's opposition to indiscriminate repatriation, the President did not speak out about the principle of forced repatriation until the Korean War, when the issue of repatriation of prisoners of war prevented agreement on an armistice.

In 1952 Truman said:

> Communism is a system that has no regard for human dignity or human freedom, and no right-thinking government can give its consent to the forcible return to such a system of men or women who would rather remain free. . . . I would not agree to any trade of prisoners that might result in forcibly returning non-Communists to Communist control.

The shameful experience of 1945 contributed to the strength of his conviction seven years later.

Toward the end of the war in Europe, the Germans held an estimated 235,000 Anglo-American prisoners and were cautioned to treat them properly. (The Japanese held about 132,000 Anglo-American prisoners. Of the POWs held by the Germans, 4 percent died in captivity; of those held by the Japanese, 27 percent died.)

On April 23 leaflets signed by Truman, Churchill, and Stalin were dropped over territory still under German control. They warned:

> Any person guilty of maltreating or allowing any Allied prisoners of war, internees or deported citizens to be maltreated, whether in battle zone, on lines of communication, in a camp, hospital, prison or elsewhere, will be ruthlessly pursued and brought to punishment.

Such a threat was the right tactic to use with the Germans, but ensuring the safety of Westerners in Soviet hands required negotiations and reassurances. The American and British leaders may have meant well in agreeing to repatriate people against their will, but their decision turned out to be a massive moral disaster.

Unlike the British, the Americans at least refused to repatriate civilians who had left the Soviet Union before 1939 and those from areas added to the Soviet Union since then. And the Americans refused to repatriate Poles who had fought with the Western Allies against the Germans. The line of morality had to be drawn somewhere.

Once the Soviet and Western Allied armies linked up, trainloads of former prisoners and slave laborers were shipped back to the Soviet Union. More than five million Soviet nationals, who either had been captured by the Germans or had simply moved out of the war's path, were returned. Of those five million, three million had been prisoners of war of the Germans, and at least two million were civilians. Many of them were sent back against their will, against the Geneva Convention and against all moral principles.

The Soviet Union never announced what happened to the repatriates, but the best historical analyses judge that 2.5 million were sent to Soviet prisons or forced-labor camps in the Gulag; 1.1 million were drafted into the Soviet army; and 1.3 million were shipped into exile or allowed to go home. As Mark R. Elliott noted, "Stalin had the remainder, some 300,000 repatriates, executed for service in the enemy ranks or simply for being captured alive by the Germans." Additional large numbers of Soviet civilians and soldiers who had deserted to the Germans and been recaptured committed suicide.

The whole issue became a nightmare of fears and fantasies. Pressure from military leaders like Marshall, Eisenhower, and General John R. Deane of the American military mission in Moscow—who were worried that Russian ruthlessness would be applied against GIs stranded in Eastern Europe—swamped the milder objections of civilians like Secretary of War Stimson, Acting Secretary of State Grew, Attorney General Francis Biddle, and many lower-echelon officers of the Department of State and other American agencies, who raised questions about the Geneva Convention and the principle of political asylum.

On the one hand, General Deane feared *German reprisals* if the United States repatriated Russians in German uniforms, while General Marshall, Secretary of State Stettinius, and Charles E. Bohlen, who was later to be the U.S. ambassador to Moscow (and who admitted to misgivings about the agreement), saw a greater danger from *Soviet reprisals* if Soviet nationals were not returned.

The attitude of many Americans (and Russians)—including the director of the United Nations Relief and Rehabilitation Administration and the editors of *The New York Times*—was that Soviet nationals who did not want to go home must be either Soviet army deserters or civilian free-will collaborators with the Nazis. Therefore, they presumably should expect to be punished when they were returned to Soviet custody.

Ambassador Harriman said apologetically later on, "Our officers were thinking of the welfare of our own prisoners, some seventy-five thousand men, who without exception could not get home quickly enough. We had no idea that hundreds of thousands of the Soviet citizens would refuse because they had no reason to suspect they would be sent to their deaths or to [NKVD head Lavrenti] Beria's prison camps. That knowledge came later."

If Harriman "had no idea," certainly the officers and GIs ordered to enforce the repatriation policy did. Some American soldiers reported in sick to avoid sending desperate men, women, and children to death or imprisonment. William Sloane Coffin, Jr., tells this story:

> Despite the fact that there were three GIs to every returning Russian, I saw several men commit suicide. Two rammed their heads through windows sawing their necks on the broken glass until they cut their jugular veins. Another took his leather bootstraps, tied a loop to the top of his triple-decker bunk, put his head through the noose and did a backflip over the edge which broke his neck.

As the Soviet army started its final drive against Berlin, the Canadians took Arnhem in Holland; the British army, meeting ferocious resistance, fought for a week to win Bremen on the German coast. The U.S. First Army rolled into Leipzig on April 19, and Nuremberg, the scene of the Nazis' great self-glorifying rallies, was captured the following day, Hitler's fifty-sixth birthday. That morning, Hitler was greeted by Soviet artillery, only fifteen miles away, shelling Berlin for the first time.

By the Führer's birthday, the outcome of the battle for Berlin was, in truth, already plain. But the Germans continued to defend Berlin like a fortress, even though they could not muster enough troops to save the huge city. Its defense relied on teenage members of the Hitler Youth and Home Guardsmen in their sixties and seventies. Its outer defenses, half-finished makeshift fortifications, were twenty miles from the city center; inside were two, more solid, defensive rings. The middle one was based on the Berlin railway system, and the last-ditch inner ring was in the city's heart and depended on monumental government buildings linked together with concrete walls.

That Friday afternoon, the Führer ventured out of his reinforced concrete bunker, fifty feet underground, to the booming of Zhukov's guns and the birthday cheers of the Hitler Youth teenagers and the old men who were defending the city. Hitler was bent and trembling.

(Among the medals handed out to honor this birthday was a War Merit Cross, First Class, with Swords to Army Lieutenant Kurt Waldheim, who was then stationed in Zagreb and who much later would become the Secretary General of the United Nations.)

Back in the bunker, Hitler led a chaotic war conference. He broke down in a tearful rage, declaring the war lost and accusing his generals of treachery. He swore emotionally that he would stay in Berlin until the end and kill himself so that the Russians could not take him prisoner.

The next morning, the Western Allies' bombers made their last massive raid on Berlin, igniting fires across the city; it was the three hundred sixty-third air raid against the German capital. Zhukov's artillery now laid direct fire into the city, killing and maiming civilians in the street. His guns hit the Brandenburg Gate, the Reichstag, Unter den Linden, and the Kurfürstendamm. The bombardment was incessant and random. With electric power gone, refuse uncollected, and streetcars and subway halted, the city was already half dead.

Zhukov's soldiers began to outflank Berlin on the north, while Konev's tanks raced in from the south. Konev's tankers captured the German High Command Headquarters at Zossen intact and dashed at Berlin. They cracked its southern defenses and entered the city at dusk on Sunday, a full day ahead of Zhukov.

On the twenty-third Stalin resolved the intense rivalry between his commanders by dividing Berlin between them. Zhukov received the prize: the Reichstag; Konev's troops were to stop 150 yards to the west.

The city was now commandeered by civilian looters, Berliners trying to survive. Zhukov's and Konev's veteran assault troops began to take over the city, fighting their way through the streets and parks.

On April 25 the two Soviet spearheads met northwest of Potsdam and encircled Berlin. And on this same afternoon, patrols of the U.S.

69th Division met soldiers of Konev's 58th Guards Rifle Division of the Fifth Guards Army at the villages of Torgau and Leckwitz, twenty miles apart on the Elbe's western bank. At Torgau, at 4:40 P.M., an American second lieutenant and a Soviet private squirmed across a girder of a blown Elbe River bridge, shook hands, and pounded each other on the back.

Germany was cut in half and Berlin surrounded. Stalin ordered a salute of 24 salvos by 324 guns.

Anticipating that the Allies would slice Germany in two, Hitler had established two military commands, north and south. And on April 22, Field Marshal Hermann Göring, who had fled south and assumed that Hitler had abdicated when he decided to stay, and if necessary die, in Berlin, asked for confirmation that he would be Hitler's successor. Hitler immediately dismissed him and ordered his arrest.

In Washington, excited rumors prophesied that the Germans were about to surrender unconditionally. Truman checked with Eisenhower, called in the White House press corps, and announced that the rumors were false. He issued a statement he had worked out with Marshall: "The enemy has been cut in two. . . . [T]he last faint, desperate hope of Hitler and his gangster government has been extinguished."

Also on April 25, Harry Truman spoke directly with Winston Churchill for the first time. Truman did not know it in advance, but the subject of their transatlantic conversation was another indicator that German resistance was crumbling.

Truman was startled when he received a message through U.S. Ambassador John G. Winant in London that Churchill wanted urgently to speak with him. This was highly unusual; Truman wondered what had occurred to make Churchill change his mode of operation so dramatically.

After a morning filled with a procession of visitors and an hour-long conference with Secretary Stimson, Truman left the White House secretly, in a pelting rain, and drove over to the Pentagon so he and Churchill could talk over a secure telephone; at 3:10 P.M. (8:10 P.M. in London), they were straining to hear each other.

Thus, Truman learned that Reichsführer SS Heinrich Himmler, the German Gestapo chief, had approached the Swedes and proposed to surrender all the German forces on the western front.

This was not the first effort by German leaders to avoid falling into Soviet hands, but Churchill sounded intrigued with the offer; he told Truman, "We thought it looked very good."

Truman was instantly skeptical, despite Churchill's obvious interest. The President asked: "Has he anything to surrender?" Truman was not swayed by the excitement of the moment and the sudden prospect that the German opposition might evaporate. He had been in the presidency less than two weeks, but he would stick to the principle all three allies had agreed to, even if it meant disagreeing with the British prime minister. He told Churchill: "I think he should be forced to surrender to all three governments, Russia, you and the United States. I don't think we ought to even consider a piecemeal surrender."

Churchill backed off immediately but, in one final attempt to win Truman's agreement, said that perhaps this was a local surrender that Eisenhower was authorized to accept. He knew, of course, that he was stretching the agreement among the Big Three. Very clearly, they had agreed not to let the Germans facing the Americans and British surrender while the rest of the German forces continued to fight the Soviet army. Nothing would enrage Stalin more.

Truman quietly listened to the story of what had happened. Himmler had met with Count Folke Bernadotte of the Swedish Red Cross four times during the previous week. The final meeting was at night in Lübeck, and an air raid had forced them down into the basement. The electricity failed, and even in the wavering candlelight Bernadotte thought Himmler looked exhausted and nervous, despite his stubborn efforts to appear calm and confident. After midnight they returned upstairs and continued their discussion, still by candlelight.

Himmler painted for Bernadotte a picture of a Germany hanging on the ropes. Hitler had decided to stay in Berlin and die there; he was desperately ill with a brain hemorrhage, Himmler said, and would be dead in a few days, if he were not already. Therefore, Himmler wanted the Swedish government to arrange for him to meet with Eisenhower so he could surrender the whole western front while he continued fighting the Soviet forces in the East.

Bernadotte thought this proposal would not be acceptable to the Allies, and he would not even forward the request to the Swedish government unless Norway and Denmark, still occupied by German troops, were included in the capitulation. Himmler agreed, but he stipulated that the Russians must not be informed of his overture.

Bernadotte carried Himmler's request to the Swedish minister for foreign affairs, who called in Sir Victor Mallet, the British minister to Sweden, and Herschel Johnson, his American equal. They both felt that Himmler was trying to make trouble between the West and the Soviet Union. The Swedish foreign minister urged them to report to their governments and to notify the Russians if they wished.

On the transatlantic telephone, Truman and Churchill agreed that Himmler had to surrender unconditionally and to all the Allies at once. Churchill said he had sent Truman a telegram, which had not gotten through; after waiting two hours, he had also notified Stalin of Himmler's overture and reassured him that the war would continue on the western front "with the utmost vigor." Churchill read to Truman the telegram he had already sent to Stalin, and Truman asked him to read it a second time so he could send a similar message immediately. Their conversation concluded:

> Truman: I hope to see you someday soon.
>
> Churchill: I am planning to. I'll be sending you some telegrams about that quite soon. I entirely agree with all that you've done on the Polish situation. We are walking hand in hand together.
>
> Truman: Well, I want to continue just that.
>
> Churchill: In fact, I am following your lead, backing up whatever you do on the matter.
>
> Truman: Thank you. Good night.

Three days later, Himmler's scheming leaked to the delegates and the press at the San Francisco conference establishing the United Nations. News reports informed the world, including Hitler, of Himmler's disloyalty.

The frantic Himmler had even approached Charles de Gaulle and proposed an entente between France and a defeated Germany. Playing insidiously on de Gaulle's paranoid suspicions of his allies, Himmler had warned him that the Americans and British would make a satellite of France. Himmler claimed that the men coming into power in Germany after Hitler wanted de Gaulle to lead them so he could become "the greatest man of all time." De Gaulle replied that that evaluation contained "an element of truth," but he did not go along with Himmler's intrigue.

Himmler's plotting failed totally. A British patrol arrested him on May 22. He was in disguise trying to escape but admitted his identity. While he was being questioned, he bit open a phial of cyanide and died almost instantly.

Meanwhile, the war on the Italian front was progressing even faster than the British and American advance across Germany. Bologna fell on April 21; two days later, the 10th Mountain Division of the U.S. Fifth Army crossed the Po River, and the Germans collapsed. On April 25 Italian partisans led a general uprising and seized control of Milan and Venice. And two days later, partisans shot to death Benito Mussolini at the village of Dongo. His body was taken to Milan, where a mob wired it up by the feet from the roof of a gas station, like slaughtered beef.

Nearly a million Germans in Italy surrendered to Field Marshal Sir Harold Alexander and General Mark W. Clark on April 28, and hostilities south of the Alps ceased at noon on May 2. Truman used the Italian victory to issue a statement: "Let Japan as well as Germany understand the meaning of these events. Unless they are lost in fanaticism or determined upon suicide, they must recognize the meaning of the increasing, swifter-moving power now ready for the capitulation of destruction of the so recently arrogant enemies of mankind."

The day Mussolini was executed, Soviet infantry were fighting block by block through Berlin, tunneling from cellar to cellar. Eight Soviet armies were crushing Berlin; the streets were littered with rubble and the dead. The Soviet forces seized Tempelhof airport, blasted their way across the Teltow Canal, battled the Germans for Wannsee Island and pushed into Charlottenburg. Small units of Germans fought until they were exterminated.

Hitler wrote out his final testament in the early hours of April 29. He blamed the war on "International Jewry" and predicted: "Through the sacrifices of our soldiers and my own fellowship with them unto death, a seed has been sown in German history that will one day grow to usher in the glorious rebirth of the National Socialist movement in a truly united nation." His testament cast Göring and Himmler out of the party. He named Grossadmiral Karl Dönitz as President to succeed himself and Joseph Goebbels as Reichschancellor. And he married Eva Braun, his mistress.

That same April 29, U.S. Seventh Army troops reached the concentration camp at Dachau, just north of Munich, where the Third Reich had held as many as thirty thousand prisoners. Horrified and enraged by the piles of rotting corpses and the starving survivors, the Americans—and some of the inmates—killed more than five hundred German guards and garrison troops within the hour. Of the 2,539 Jewish prisoners who still survived when Dachau was freed, only 73 would be alive two months later.

A few days later, the 82nd Airborne Division liberated another concentration camp. As the division commander, Major General James M. Gavin, described it:

> One could smell the Wobelein Concentration Camp before seeing it. And seeing it was more than a human being could stand. Even after three years of war it brought tears to my eyes. Living skeletons were scattered about, the dead distinguishable from the living only by the blue-black color of their skin compared to the somewhat greenish skin, taut over the bony frames of the living. There were hundreds of dead about the grounds and in the tarpaper shacks. In the corner of the stockade area was an abandoned quarry into which the daily stack of cadavers were bulldozed. It was obvious they could not tell many of the dead from the living.

At 1 A.M. on Monday, April 30, Field Marshal Wilhelm Keitel told Hitler no relief forces could reach them. Soviet tanks were a half mile away. At 3:30 Hitler and Eva Braun killed themselves. Their bodies were laid in a shallow ditch in the Chancellery Garden, burned with gasoline, and the remains buried in a shell crater.

The Russians captured Himmler's Ministry of the Interior and stormed the Reichstag. A sergeant of the 756th Rifle Regiment had the honor of leading the final attack into the building that symbolized the Nazi Reich. At 10:50 that night, a "Red Victory Banner" was finally raised over the Reichstag. Inside, Germans and Russians still fought to the death.

The news of Hitler's death was solemnly broadcast over the German radio to heroic music of Wagner and Bruckner's Seventh Symphony.

At 5 A.M. on May 2, General Helmuth "Karl" Weidling officially surrendered Berlin. Small-unit fighting continued until finally, at 3 P.M. on May 3, the Soviet guns ceased firing. There was a great silence.

Alan Bullock wrote, "Europe may rise again, but the old Europe of the years between 1789, the year of the French Revolution, and 1939, the year of Hitler's War, has gone for ever."

Truman was surprised that Hitler's fanaticism had not forced him to fight to the very end. He had left Germany's military leaders to surrender the nation.

German commanders scrambled to find Western generals who would permit them to escape Soviet vengeance. The Berliners were left to the mercy of the Soviet army. The first-line veterans were well disciplined, but the troops following them wanted revenge and booty. They robbed German homes and raped the women.

The battle for Berlin had cost half a million casualties. A hundred thousand civilians died in the city. The Soviets lost 304,000 killed, wounded, and missing in the two weeks since advancing from the Oder on April 16. And they took 134,000 German prisoners of war.

The war for Europe was not quite over. A conflict, similar to that over who was to capture Berlin, arose over Prague, the beautiful Czech capital, which so far had been untouched by the war. More than 750,000 Soviet soldiers were advancing into Czechoslovakia from the east, and Patton's U.S. Third Army was closing in from the west.

Eisenhower planned to halt Patton's advance on the 1937 boundary of Czechoslovakia. Later, when the Soviet forces were still seventy miles from Prague and engaged in heavy fighting, they agreed that the Americans should advance to the line of Karlsbad–Pilsen–Budějovice inside Czechoslovakia. But Stalin intended to occupy the capital, Prague.

British Foreign Secretary Eden pressed for the Americans—not the Russians—to capture Prague, and on April 30 Churchill made the point directly to Truman: the Americans should carry out the liberation of Prague and western Czechoslovakia because what happened there would significantly affect postwar Europe.

The U.S. Department of State agreed and recommended to Truman and the Joint Chiefs of Staff that the Americans take the Czech capital. Asking Eisenhower for his opinion, Marshall said, "Personally and aside from all logistic, tactical or strategical implications I would be loath to hazard American lives for purely political purposes."

Eisenhower took exactly the same position in regard to Prague that he had on Berlin: "I shall not attempt any move I deem militarily unwise merely to gain a political prize unless I receive specific orders from the Combined Chiefs of Staff." The supreme commander believed his job was to destroy enemy forces, not to divide up the great capitals of central Europe.

Truman, under pressure from both Churchill and the State Department to persuade Eisenhower to advance into Czechoslovakia, turned to the U.S. Joint Chiefs of Staff for advice, but they supported Eisenhower. On May 1 Truman sent Churchill a message declaring that Eisenhower's attitude toward operations in Czechoslovakia "meets with my approval." Prague would be Russian.

Truman certainly knew that it would be better to have Berlin, Vienna, and Prague under Western control. But he was also pragmatic. He recognized that "these cities were under Russian control or about to fall under her control. The Russians were in a strong position, and they knew it." Still, after the war, second-guessers would ask why Eisenhower had not moved across an open front to occupy the Czech capital.

Actually, Eisenhower changed his mind briefly on May 4, when the citizens of Prague demonstrated in the streets, tore down German-language street signs, ripped up cobblestones, and erected barricades. Eisenhower notified General Aleksei I. Antonov, Chief of the Soviet General Staff, that the uprising convinced him to move the U.S. Third Army into Prague. Antonov objected strenuously, so Eisenhower dropped the idea. Stalin quickly ordered Marshal Konev and the Second Ukrainian Front, already fighting in eastern Czechoslovakia, to move on Prague.

Fighting with the Germans inside the city was General Andrei Vlasov, a Russian officer who had served in the defense of Moscow in 1942. He had been taken prisoner and become an officer for the Germans. In Prague, he was now trying to build an anti-Soviet "third force," including non-communist Czech partisans, who would hold out until the American army arrived.

Just after midnight on May 6, Radio Prague broadcast an appeal to the U.S. Army to send tanks to Prague. Three U.S. Army vehicles actually reached the suburbs of Prague, but they were not followed up. At 5 A.M. on May 8, the Czech National Council announced the surrender of the German forces in Prague. The next morning, after the Germans had already surrendered, Soviet tanks entered Prague alone. Patton's forces stayed in western Czechoslovakia. (Later that summer, in celebration of the end of the war, GIs of the U.S. 94th Division paraded with Soviet troops in Pilsen as a momentary symbol of good fellowship.)

Some Czech leaders who fell into Soviet hands were tortured, hanged, transported to slave-labor camps, or forced to commit suicide. General Vlasov and his men managed to surrender to the U.S. Third Army but were promptly turned over to the Russians, who executed Vlasov as a traitor.

At the same time as the fate of Czechoslovakia was being played out, Truman had to deal with the Soviet occupation of Vienna. On

April 30 Churchill anxiously pointed out to him that the Russians had set up a provisional government in Austria without consulting the British and Americans.

Truman protested to Stalin that he had learned about the provisional government from the press. In strongly worded messages, both Truman and Churchill complained to Stalin that ever since the Soviet Union had occupied Austria and Vienna, it had refused to admit missions from the Western Allies. The Western objections were futile.

Once the Russians occupied Warsaw, Vienna, Berlin, and Prague, their prime concern switched from the commitments and cooperation of Yalta to holding on to what they had conquered.

Chapter 5

First of All—Poland

Truman soon began to realize that Stalin was an adversary as well as an ally. He swore to a friend that he would not let the Soviet dictator beat him at a poker game. In the international game that Truman had just joined, the first hand to be played was Poland. Unfortunately, Stalin held most of the cards.

Still, Truman clung to the hope that the Russians and the Western Allies could come to an accommodation on Poland. That country, which had been re-created after World War I, had not only triggered World War II but was now threatening to split the Great Powers. When Truman was apprised of the tensions Roosevelt had endured over Poland—and when he experienced Soviet recalcitrance for himself—he had to summon up all his Missouri-mule stubbornness to deal with Stalin.

At the heart of this heated issue were two seemingly intractable problems: the location of Poland's borders and the makeup of its government. The United States and Britain wanted Poland's prewar borders restored and an independent, representative government based on the Polish government-in-exile in London. The Russians wanted to move the Polish-Russian frontier west as far as possible and to install a pro-Soviet regime based on the Communist-dominated "Committee of National Liberation" or the "Lublin-Warsaw Committee." The Soviet army was firmly on the ground, and Truman was faced with not just implementing Western policy but trying to change Soviet policy—a tough order.

At Yalta, Stalin, whose armies by then were occupying the country, would not compromise on Poland. The Big Three worked through many problems, including the Soviet Union's entrance into the war against Japan, a Great Power veto in the U.N. Security Council, and a French occupation zone in Germany—but not Poland.

Churchill and Roosevelt searched for some middle ground; they accepted a Russian-Polish border close to the so-called Curzon Line, which had been designed in 1919 by the Versailles Treaty and had placed parts of Poland in Russia. As compensation, the Poles would acquire German territory—but the Powers and the various Polish factions disagreed over how much.

Stalin insisted that the frontier between Poland and Germany be set along the Oder River and the Western Neisse River; Roosevelt and Churchill wanted it to run along the Eastern Neisse. The fate of some four million Poles and eight million Germans depended on whether the border would be drawn along the eastern or western branch of the Neisse. In actual fact, the Soviet-controlled "Provisional Government of Poland" had already advanced its control to the Western Neisse.

But the makeup of the Polish government provoked the most intense disagreement at Yalta. The three leaders agreed that the provisional government should be a mix of the Committee of National Liberation, based in Lublin and Warsaw, and the Western Allied–recognized government-in-exile, based in London. Despite Soviet reluctance, a commission was organized to include democratic leaders both from Poland and from abroad in a new Government of National Unity. But its membership was never spelled out, and subsequently, in Western eyes, the Russians failed to live up to the agreement.

At the same time, the Russians also rejected Anglo-American demands for tripartite supervision of elections in Bulgaria. Here, in Poland and Bulgaria, the Soviet Union was forcing a division of Europe that would lead to the North Atlantic Treaty Organization, the Warsaw Pact, and the Cold War.

As the end of the European war approached, a sense of distrust and unease surged up between the Soviet Union and the Western Allies. This tension surfaced whenever Western leaders lifted their heads from their battle maps and contemplated the difficulties of building a peace.

The new President's political instincts gravitated to working out compromises to problems and getting along with the Soviet Union. But he ran into strong sentiments among his inherited advisors and the British for solving these problems by demonstrations of strength and confrontation.

Churchill warned Truman, as he had repeatedly warned Roosevelt, that the Soviets were violating the agreements they had made at Yalta. The U.S. Department of State forecast postwar conflict with the Soviet Union. The Office of Strategic Services (OSS), the wartime American intelligence organization, had predicted on April 2 that after the war the United States would face a threat from the Soviet Union even greater than the danger that had been posed by the rise of Japan and Nazi Germany. The OSS reported, "In the easily foreseeable future Russia may well outrank even the United States in military potential."

U.S. Ambassador Averell Harriman, a respected public servant and son of the railroad tycoon E. H. Harriman, had held a consistent view of the Soviet Union since his first trip there in 1936. Now it was intensified by his firsthand experience in Moscow:

> I became convinced that the Bolshevik Revolution was in fact a reactionary revolution and that it was not "the wave of the future." It denied the basic beliefs that we value so deeply—the rights and dignity of the individual, the idea that government should express the will of the people. The Bolshevik conception was that the few knew what was good for the many and ruthlessly forced their will on the people. The individual was the servant of the state. Nothing has happened since to alter my conviction that the Bolshevik Revolution, for all its manifest achievements, has been on balance a tragic step backward in human development.

George F. Kennan—already an articulate Foreign Service officer and minister-counselor to Ambassador Harriman—was also apprehensive about the Soviet Union's role in the postwar world. He even went so far as to oppose the efforts in Washington to encourage the Soviet Union to participate in the creation of the United Nations. He would write later, "Just at the time of my return to Russia [in July 1944] I found our government, and the British, busily engaged in pressing the wary and unenthusiastic Russians to join in talks looking to the formation of a future international organization for peace and security. I considered this effort of persuasion to be unwise and regrettable."

Kennan perceived no need for a new world organization; he believed we should "occupy ourselves seriously and minutely with the sheer power relationships of the European peoples." Stalin, he said, was interested only in his own personal power. Of the discussions at Yalta and elsewhere over the formation of the United Nations, Kennan said he "rather hoped, I must confess, that they would fail."

Stalin's refusal in the summer of 1944 to send the Soviet army to the aid of the Polish underground fighters whom the Germans were slaughtering during the Warsaw Uprising had persuaded Kennan that the Western Allies should no longer support the Soviet war effort.

When Truman, as his first international political act, recommended to Churchill that they send Stalin a joint declaration on the makeup of Poland's government and the location of her borders, Churchill was impressed that, although the issues were familiar to the more experienced political leaders like Roosevelt and himself, Truman committed himself on them so promptly. Truman reasoned that if the Russians did not keep their word on the Polish issues, the Senate would reject U.S. participation in the United Nations, which he supported so strongly.

Stalin predictably denied he was breaking any of the Yalta agreements. He interpreted them as allowing him to shape a Poland submissive to the Soviet Union because he believed that the vital interest of the Soviet Union—its future life and death—was at stake. Invading armies had repeatedly attacked Russia through Poland, and Stalin was determined to prevent that in the future by having a Poland with a government responsive to Soviet concerns and frontiers far enough westward to give the Soviet Union space to defend itself.

Stalin countered that it was Churchill who was reneging on the Yalta agreements by insisting on strengthening the non-communists in the proposed Polish government. To turn the tables, he demanded that Greek communists be included in the pro-British government being installed in Greece. He attacked Churchill's policy as colonial, imperialist, and anti-Soviet. The truth was that, although ideologically light-years apart, the rulers of Europe intended to retain their power in the postwar world.

Stalin had addressed Roosevelt just as harshly, and when Truman was shown how Stalin had accused Roosevelt of deceit, he was furious. He began to see why his advisors urged that the United States take a tougher attitude toward Stalin and his maneuvering.

Truman first participated directly in this East-West struggle on April 22, when he had been in office only ten days. This was a face-to-face confrontation with Soviet Foreign Minister Molotov, whom Stalin had sent to meet with the President before attending the U.N. Conference in San Francisco.

Molotov flew from Moscow to Washington across Asiatic Russia and the Pacific; he landed and slept over at Great Falls, Montana. Ambassador Harriman, by taking the shorter route across the Atlantic, reached Washington ahead of him. Harriman was in a hurry: "I felt I had to see President Truman as soon as possible in order to give him as accurate a picture as possible of our relations with the Soviet Union. I wanted to be sure that he understood that Stalin was already failing to keep his Yalta commitment."

Harriman had cabled ahead that Molotov's deputy, Andrei Y. Vishinsky, told him that the Russians planned to conclude a Soviet-Polish treaty immediately. Harriman warned Vishinsky against signing such a treaty before the Soviet Union and the Western Allies agreed on a Polish government.

Harriman's information infuriated Truman. He had three reactions. He protested to Moscow against signing a Soviet-Polish treaty. He wished that the terms agreed to at Yalta had been clearer. And he decided to talk bluntly to Molotov—as Harriman put it later, "perhaps too bluntly."

As soon as Harriman reached Washington on Friday, April 20 (Hitler's birthday), he joined a policy meeting Truman had called at noon to discuss relations with the Soviet Union. Also present were Secretary Stettinius, Undersecretary of State Grew, and Soviet specialist Charles Bohlen. This was the first time Truman had met Harriman, and he welcomed a firsthand report from the perspective of Moscow.

The Russians, Harriman explained to the President, were pursuing two contradictory policies simultaneously: they were trying to cooperate with Britain and the United States while at the same time carving out their own sphere of dominance in Eastern Europe. Some men around Stalin, he reported, thought the United States was soft and the Soviet Union could do as it liked in Eastern Europe.

In Harriman's view, the Soviet Union did not want to break with the United States because it would need U.S. help with postwar reconstruction. Therefore, he advised, the United States could afford to stand firm. Truman assured Harriman that he would be firm on a give-and-take basis.

Europe, Harriman warned, faced a "barbarian invasion." Whenever the Russians conquered a country, they installed the Soviet system and their secret police crushed all freedom of speech. The democracies could still work with the Russians, Harriman thought, but the West should not expect Stalin's government to conduct international affairs in accordance with Western principles.

Truman interjected that he understood this and did not expect it to accept 100 percent of what the United States proposed. He ventured, rather naïvely, that he would be satisfied with 85 percent.

The United States had to decide whether it would accept Soviet domination of Poland, Harriman asserted. And Truman had to consider how he would react if Stalin rejected the Western proposals in the joint note and empowered the Lublin-Warsaw group.

Harriman asked how important the Polish problems were to the proposed world organization, and Truman replied that if the Polish issues were not resolved according to what had been agreed on at Yalta, the Senate would never accept American participation. He was speaking from his personal knowledge of what the senators thought. He said he would make this clear to Molotov.

What if the Russians dropped out of the world organization? Harriman asked. Without the Soviet Union, Truman said, there would not be a world organization.

This discussion persuaded Harriman that the President saw "eye to eye" with him. It also hardened the American leaders' attitude toward the Soviet Union. This was intensified the next day when the Soviet government, ignoring all warnings, made a twenty-year treaty of friendship with its puppet government in Warsaw. To do this on the eve of the Truman-Molotov meeting was seen in Washington as an affront to the new President.

At 8:30 on Sunday evening, April 22, Truman received Foreign Minister Molotov in Blair House. He had reached Washington only hours before. Truman began by assuring Molotov that he stood behind all the commitments and agreements that Roosevelt had made.

Molotov, one of the few surviving "old Bolsheviks," was tough, curt, and cold. The rapid military victories of the past few weeks, he began, had given political questions a new urgency. Truman agreed: that was why he had wanted this meeting.

Truman went directly to the most difficult question between them: Poland. Solutions were vital, he asserted, because a large number of Americans were personally interested in Poland. Rejecting the President's argument, Molotov retorted that Poland was even more important to the Soviet Union because it and Poland had a common border.

Molotov turned to his own agenda; he wanted Truman to confirm that the agreements Roosevelt had made at Yalta about East Asia still held—specifically, that the Soviet Union would receive territorial concessions in Asia if it entered the war against Japan within three months after the Germans surrendered.

Soviet participation in the Asian war was then important to U.S. planners. The American victories on Iwo Jima and Okinawa were still in the future, the atomic bomb was an unknown quantity, and the invasion of Japan was a bloody likelihood. The United States needed the Soviet armies to pin down Japanese forces on the Asian mainland.

Truman assured Molotov that he would abide by the Yalta agreements, and as Molotov left to meet with the British and American foreign ministers across the street at the Department of State, Truman said he looked forward to meeting with Stalin soon.

The meeting at State went badly. The representatives of both East and West were intransigent on Poland. Foreign Minister Eden, discouraged, reported to Churchill that he doubted that the Soviet Union would ever understand the Western Allies' concern about Soviet domination of Poland. And without all three Powers working together on the basis of Yalta, Eden saw no ground for the U.N. Conference in San Francisco. Churchill replied to Eden more optimistically: "My appreciation is that the new President is not to be bullied by the Soviets."

At two the next afternoon, April 23, Truman gathered his diplomatic and military advisors at the White House to review the Polish questions before he held his substantive meeting with Molotov. Secretary of State Stettinius reported that at the State Department Sunday evening and Monday morning Molotov's apparent good spirits had faded and it was evident that the Soviet Union intended to keep the Lublin-Warsaw Provisional Polish Government in power.

Truman went around the table asking for opinions. Secretary Stimson opposed a head-on confrontation with the Soviet Union. Perhaps, he suggested calmly, the Russians were being more realistic than the Americans about the importance of Eastern Europe to Soviet security. The secretary of war affirmed that the Russians had kept their word on military matters; why would they not do the same in regard to their border countries? He warned that the Russians obviously took the Polish matter seriously; was not Molotov insisting on a seat at San Francisco for the Lublin-Warsaw government? Stimson recommended that the President go slowly and avoid an open break.

Navy Secretary James Forrestal disagreed. The former president of Dillon, Read and Company emphasized that Poland was not an isolated case; the Soviet Union had shown repeatedly that it wanted to dominate adjacent countries. It had taken similar unilateral positions in regard to Bulgaria, Romania, Turkey, and Greece. Differing totally with Stimson, he advised having a showdown now rather than later.

Ambassador Harriman speculated that Soviet stubbornness was increasing because, after Stalin and Molotov had returned home from Yalta, they had sensed the weakness of the Lublin-Warsaw government. They feared including any democratic Polish leaders who might overwhelm the handpicked Soviet puppets. But in Harriman's view a break with the Russians could still be avoided.

When questioned by Truman, Admiral Leahy remembered that he had left Yalta feeling the Soviet Union would not permit a free government in Poland, and he said he did not expect them to act any differently now. He urged that, although a break with the Russians would be serious, the United States should continue to insist on a free and independent Poland.

General Marshall introduced another concern. Now that the military situation in Europe was secure, he looked for Soviet participation in the war against Japan. But he did not want the Soviet Union to come into that war after "we had done all the dirty work." Right now, he felt, it would be a serious matter to risk a break.

Truman was prepared to take that risk, and he wanted to make the U.S. government's position unmistakable. Most of his advisors were urging him to stand up to Molotov; the Soviet Union should not be allowed to continue to ignore its Yalta commitments. If one part of the agreements was breached, the President should consider the entire Yalta agreements no longer binding. He would tell Molotov that the United States expected the Soviet Union to carry out all the Yalta agreements, but he was not ready to deliver an ultimatum. So far, Truman said, our agreements with the Russians have been a "one-way street," and he would not continue that. He intended to move forward with the plans for San Francisco, and if the Russians backed out, they could "go to hell."

Stimson was worried. He confided to his diary that day that he thought Truman had been maneuvered into taking a tough position. These issues among the Great Powers should have been resolved before the public meeting in San Francisco was convened. He wrote, "I am very sorry for the President because he is new on his job and he has been brought into a situation which ought not to have been allowed to come in this way."

At 5:30 P.M., Truman met with Molotov—this time in the Oval Room of the White House. The President was primed for a showdown. He told Molotov he was sorry to learn that no progress had been made on the Polish problem at the State Department meeting; Molotov said he was too. Truman asserted that he thought the U.S. position on Poland was fair and the U.S. government could not be party to a Polish government that did not represent all Polish democratic elements and provide for free elections.

Truman reminded Molotov that Roosevelt had emphasized to Stalin that no United States policy could succeed without public and congressional support. The U.S. government would be able to help the Soviet Union financially after the war only if it had the public's backing, and this obviously first required the resolution of the Polish questions.

The United States would honor all its Yalta commitments, Truman insisted, but it was getting tired of waiting for the Soviet Union to carry out its agreements to let the Eastern European countries establish democratic regimes. The Polish government must include non-Lublin Poles; the United States would not recognize a Polish government that did not represent all democratic elements.

The President was taking no new positions, but he was demonstrating determination and strength—only eleven days after assuming the presidency. He wanted no misapprehension in the Kremlin that Roosevelt's death had left Washington weaker. He did not mind at all if his assertions created tension in the Oval Room.

Truman said he wanted the United States and the Soviet Union to be friends, but the Soviet Union had to carry out its part of the Yalta agreements. He asked Molotov to communicate to Stalin his concern over the failure of the Soviet government to live up to those agreements and handed him a message reiterating this, which he asked Molotov to send to Stalin immediately.

Obviously taken aback by Truman's undiplomatic bluntness, Molotov warned the President against two allies imposing their views on the third. He denied that the Soviet Union was violating Yalta, and he assured Truman that he was convinced that all their difficulties could be overcome.

Truman said sharply that all Stalin had to do was to keep his word. Truman wanted friendship, but not as a "one-way street."

Molotov said, "I have never been talked to like that in my life."

Truman replied, "Carry out your agreements and you won't get talked to like that."

That was how both Truman and Harriman, who was present,

remembered the exchange. Charles "Chip" Bohlen, who was acting as Truman's interpreter, made more measured notes in which he recorded that the President said simply, "That will be all, Mr. Molotov. I would appreciate it if you would transmit my views to Marshal Stalin." Molotov was dismissed—and left quickly.

However he answered, this was vintage Truman—direct, candid, "unadorned by the polite verbiage of diplomacy," as Admiral Leahy put it. As far as Truman was concerned, a man stood by his word. Years later, an interviewer in Independence, Missouri, asked him what he had been taught about a man keeping his word. He answered:

> Unless you were a man who stood by what he said, you were not well thought of around here and you never got very far, never got anywhere at all in this part of the country. . . . In those days, in the time I was growing up and when I was a young man, people thought more of an honest man than any one thing, and if a man wasn't honest, he wouldn't stay long in the neighborhood. They would run him out. And I have never changed my mind since.

Truman was pleased with his handling of Molotov, and Bohlen recalled his own pleasure in his memoirs: "How I enjoyed translating Truman's sentences! They were probably the first sharp words uttered during the war by an American President to a high Soviet official."

But Stimson felt the American attitude toward the Soviet Union was hardening under Truman. Now the dominant view was that Soviet foreign policy was expansionist.

On the night of April 24, Truman received a message from Stalin in response to his sent via Molotov. Stalin asserted that at Yalta it had been decided that the Provisional Polish Government should be the "kernel," the core, of the new government of national unity. Now, he said, the American position seemed to refute that agreement.

"It is also necessary to take into account the fact that Poland borders on the Soviet Union, which cannot be said of Great Britain and the United States," Stalin argued again. "The question of Poland has the same meaning for the security of the Soviet Union as the question of Belgium and Greece for the security of Great Britain." He reminded Truman that he had not been consulted when governments were established in Greece and Belgium; because of their importance to Britain's security, he had not claimed a right to interfere there. But he could not renounce the security of his country.

This emphatic message disturbed Truman. "It showed plainly," he wrote, "that Churchill and I were going to have persistent, calculated resistance from Stalin in our dealings with the Russians." He added, "Without any attempt to hide his role in diplomatic niceties, Stalin for the first time in addressing Churchill and me used the 'Big I Am.' "

Churchill was also pressuring Stalin to add to the Lublin-Warsaw group representatives from other Polish elements, including those in London. But he was talking conciliation. The West, he reminded Stalin on April 29, had made a concession by agreeing to place the Russian-Polish border on the Curzon Line, where Stalin wanted it. And, accepting Stalin's argument of Soviet self-interest, he asked him to meet the West partway and agree to "the sovereignty, independence, and freedom of Poland, provided it is a Poland friendly to Russia." He urgently tried to persuade Stalin that they should not divide Europe into two camps: "their quarrel would tear the world to pieces and . . . all of us leading men on either side who had anything to do with that would be shamed before history." War over Poland was unthinkable.

Truman appreciated Churchill's skill and applauded his message, but he doubted it would change Stalin's mind. And the next day, when the U.S. delegation in San Francisco reported that discussions there on Poland were stalemated, Truman "felt as if I had lived through several lifetimes."

One of the ongoing contretemps on which Churchill confronted Stalin in his long cable of April 29 was the case of "the fifteen Poles."

This referred to a repulsive affair. In March the Russians had invited the leaders of the Polish underground to discuss forming a united Polish government. They were given a written guarantee of personal safety. On March 27 and 28 they met with Soviet representatives in the suburbs of Warsaw. None of them returned from that meeting.

Six weeks later, on May 4, in San Francisco, Molotov admitted that the Poles were being held in the Soviet Union. Churchill, disturbed, urged Truman that "you and I should consult together very carefully on this matter."

The next day, Churchill received an unequivocal message from Stalin: unless Britain recognized the Lublin-Warsaw Committee as the foundation of a future government of national unity, no solution of the Polish question was possible.

Churchill now concluded, and advised Truman, that only a personal Big Three summit conference could make any progress on Poland. And he warned Eden in San Francisco that what threatened to become a permanent division of Europe, half dominated by the Soviet Union, must be resolved before U.S. forces withdrew from Europe, or it would not be resolved at all.

The Polish problems seemed to move a bit closer to solution when the Soviet Union on June 11 finally allowed the commission of Molotov, Harriman, and Clark Kerr, Britain's ambassador to Moscow, which had been created at Yalta, to issue invitations to democratic Polish leaders to consult about reorganizing the Polish Provisional Government. The meetings would take place in Moscow starting on June 15; the hope: to form a Polish Provisional Government of National Unity.

In his press conference on June 13, Truman announced that Potsdam, in the Soviet occupation zone of Germany, would be the site of a Big Three Conference. Stalin had recently agreed to a summit meeting. At the press conference Truman also took a conciliatory stance toward the Soviet Union on Poland—at least in public:

> Q.   Mr. President, has there been any change in American policy which has caused the Russians to change their position on the Polish issue?
> The President.   No. There has been no change in American policy. There has been a very pleasant yielding on the part of the Russians to some of the things in which we are interested, and I think if we keep our heads and be patient, we will arrive at a conclusion; because the Russians are just as anxious to get along with us as we are with them. And I think they have showed it very conclusively in these last conversations."

When reporters pressed him on how the London Polish Government-in-Exile would fit in with the hoped-for Government of National Unity, Truman reacted sharply:

> Don't get this thing tangled up now. What we are trying to do is to get the situation worked out that has been causing us a lot of embarrassment. And for God's sake, don't you go muddying it all up so as to make it worse! We have made arrangements so that all these factions can

get together, the present Polish Government, the people in Poland who are not in the Polish Government, and the people in London, to see if they can't sit down and work out a government that will be satisfactory to Poland. Now, that's what this conference is for. We have succeeded in getting that far. But don't upset the applecart. Say we have made some progress and that I believe that we can get results that will do what we want, which is a free Polish Government.

Truman told the reporters that the American and British governments were trying to help the Poles whom the Russians had arrested; he had sent Harry Hopkins to Moscow for that purpose, among others. But, he added, he wanted to avoid saying anything that would embarrass the Soviet government. Despite his caution, the Soviet Union suddenly announced that the arrested Polish leaders would be tried. Truman found the deliberate timing of the trial "provocative and discouraging."

The trial opened in Moscow on June 18, in the same great hall where the infamous purge trials had been held in the 1930s. The Poles were charged with plotting to form a Western European bloc that would fight the Soviet Union and even murdering Russian officers.

After three days, twelve of the Poles were sentenced to prison terms ranging from six months to ten years. The commander of the Polish Home Army was sentenced to ten years and the deputy prime minister of the Polish Government-in-Exile-in London to eight. Thus, Stalin liquidated much of the leadership of the Polish underground that had fought the Nazis.

Despite these ugly events, the commission of Molotov, Harriman, and Kerr met and agreed to broaden the Polish Provisional Government. But the majority would come from Stalin's Warsaw allies. Harriman and Kerr asserted that the Yalta agreements would be fulfilled only when the new government held truly free elections. Truman decided this was as much as could be achieved now. In the final analysis, Stalin and his army controlled the situation.

On Harriman's recommendation and with Churchill's reluctant concurrence, Truman announced on July 5 that the United States was establishing diplomatic relations with the new Polish Provisional Government of National Unity, which had promised to hold "free elections."

Even if everyone kept his word, this compromise was at best

half a loaf. Stalin had the kind of Polish government he wanted: sympathetic and subservient. Truman had spoken up for the Poland he believed in: independent and democratic. But he had learned that in a rough-and-tumble world the truth was that he who commanded the troops on the ground called the tune. Both sides realized that enough blood had been spilled over Poland; no one was prepared to go to war for Poland now.

The passionate argument over Poland was not over. But it would have to wait until the Big Three sat together in Potsdam. Then Truman and Stalin would debate postwar Poland face to face.

Chapter 6
"The Flags of Freedom"

On Saturday evening, April 28, Washington was swept by reports that the Germans had surrendered. Thousands of jubilant people piled into the streets to celebrate. Lafayette Park in front of the White House was jammed with happy Americans.

Harry Truman remembered that World War I had also had a premature ending, which Americans across the country had cheered only to be let down again. He had Admiral Leahy check with General Eisenhower's headquarters and then called a sudden press conference at 9:30 P.M. Newsmen rushed in, certain the war was over, but the President announced, "There is no foundation for the rumor." The disappointed crowds quickly disappeared.

Four days later, there was solid reason to celebrate. Marshal Zhukov accepted the unconditional surrender of Berlin; the fighting ended in Italy; and in the north the British and Americans reached Lübeck, made contact with Soviet forces, and cut off the Germans in Denmark and Norway. Wernher von Braun, who had developed the V-2 rocket for Hitler, was captured at Oberammergau and flown to the United States.

The next day, the British marched into Hamburg, and a German delegation led by Grossadmiral Hans Georg von Friedeburg, anxious not to surrender to the Russians, opened negotiations at Field Marshal Montgomery's headquarters on the nearby Lüneburger Heide. Field Marshal Wilhelm Keitel, chief of the German High Command, was eager to hand over to Montgomery two German armies facing the Russians; he was refused. But the following day, Montgomery did accept the surrender of all German forces opposite the British army in northwest Germany.

The Americans entered the Flossenburg concentration camp north of Nuremberg and liberated, among others, the former prime minister of France, Léon Blum; the former chancellor of Austria, Kurt von Schuschnigg; and Pastor Martin Niemöller, who had been a prisoner of Hitler for more than seven years.

On May 5, Admiral Friedeburg, representing Admiral Dönitz, Hitler's heir as president of the Third Reich, came to Eisenhower's Supreme Headquarters, Allied Expeditionary Forces, at Reims, France. Eisenhower asked the Soviet High Command to send a representative, and the Russians sent Major General Ivan Susloparov.

The next day, General Alfred Jodl, chief of the Operations Staff of the High Command of the German armed forces throughout the war, joined Admiral Friedeburg. Jodl was a shrewd professional officer who had come to believe in Hitler's "genius" and would eventually be hanged for murdering captured Soviet Communist Party members. He offered to surrender only the German forces facing west.

The two German officers seemed to be stalling to allow as many German soldiers as possible to be shifted from the Russian to the western front. Eisenhower sent word that unless the negotiators surrendered unconditionally he would cut off all discussions, seal the western front, and prevent German refugees from entering the Allied lines. They would end up in Russian hands.

The German representatives, left with no choice, telegraphed Admiral Dönitz requesting authority to surrender all German forces on all fronts, with the fighting to cease forty-eight hours after signing. Since that would still leave in German control the decision as to when the cease-fire would begin, Eisenhower refused to accept it. He insisted on unconditional surrender effective forty-eight hours from midnight. Dönitz empowered Jodl to sign.

At 2:30 A.M. on May 7, Generals Jodl, Bedell Smith, and Susloparov, together with other Allied officers, sat down around a doughnut-shaped table and eleven minutes later signed an unconditional surrender. General François Sevez signed for France as a witness. All military operations would cease at 11:01 P.M. on May 8. (The last major battle, in Prague, actually finished at 5:04 A.M. on May 7, when the German units in the city surrendered unconditionally to the Soviet forces.)

After the signing, General Jodl asked to speak to Eisenhower and was led upstairs where the supreme commander, unsmiling, stood behind his desk at attention. Eisenhower tersely asked Jodl if he understood all the provisions he had signed.

"Ja," he answered.

Eisenhower said, "You will, officially and personally, be held responsible if the terms of this surrender are violated, including its provisions for German commanders to appear in Berlin at the moment set by the Russian High Command to accomplish formal surrender to that government." The purpose of the second signing was to display Allied unity and to emphasize to the Germans that they were surrendering to all the victors, not just the Western Allies.

Eisenhower told Jodl that the Germans would now take orders from the Allies. Jodl nodded. Eisenhower dismissed him with a curt: "That is all!"

Jodl saluted, did a military about-face and marched out of the room.

Eisenhower's face broke into a huge smile. He sent the Combined Chiefs of Staff a message: "The mission of this Allied force was fulfilled at 0241, local time, May 7, 1945."

The Allied officers adjourned to Eisenhower's house. They opened bottles of champagne and sat around reminiscing. Years later, Eisenhower had forgotten his broad smile and remembered only his overwhelming tiredness; he wrote, "Exhaustion rather than exultation was my first reaction to victory in Europe."

The Americans, Russians, and British could not, each for their own reasons, agree even on the date of announcing the official German surrender. Churchill pressed for May 7; Truman for May 8 (which happened to be his sixty-first birthday); and Stalin, uncertain that the Germans on the Russian front would quit, for May 9. They finally decided to announce V-E Day on Tuesday, May 8, at 9 A.M. Washington time.

The German High Command appeared in the rubble of Berlin on May 9 and at the Soviet army headquarters signed the formal ratification of the surrender. British Air Chief Marshal Arthur Tedder represented Eisenhower and Marshal Zhukov, the Soviet Union. Field Marshal Keitel signed for Germany.

On V-E Day Harry Truman had been President two days less than four weeks. Early that morning he wrote his mother and his sister,

Mary, about the end of the European war and added, "Isn't that some birthday present?"

At 8:15 A.M. the cabinet gathered at the White House to hear the President announce the victory in Europe. Twenty minutes later, Truman, surrounded by dignitaries, met the press in the Executive Office. He began, "This is a solemn but a glorious hour. I only wish that Franklin D. Roosevelt had lived to witness this day. General Eisenhower informs me that the forces of Germany have surrendered to the United Nations. The flags of freedom fly all over Europe." But, he reminded the American people, "Our victory is but half won."

Then, he read a second statement warning the Japanese to expect the "utter destruction" of their war-making power. He told them that to continue the war would be in vain; he promised them only unconditional surrender. But, he added, "Unconditional surrender does not mean the extermination or enslavement of the Japanese people."

Following the press conference, at 9 A.M., Truman—surrounded by his wife and daughter, members of the cabinet and Congress, and top U.S. and British military leaders—broadcast to the nation over a battery of microphones. He told the American people that Germany had surrendered unconditionally and asked all Americans not to take time out to celebrate but to turn to winning the war in the Pacific and then to winning the peace. Until the last battle is won, he said, "Let no man abandon his post or slacken his efforts."

By midmorning of May 9 in Moscow, thousands of young Soviet citizens, singing and waving banners, marched in the huge square in front of the U.S. Embassy. Chargé d'affaires George Kennan sent an employee across the roof of the National Hotel next door and obtained a Soviet flag, which was hung on the embassy, next to the American flag. The crowd cheered. Kennan climbed up onto the pedestal of one of the great columns in front of the building and yelled in Russian: "Congratulations on this day of victory! All honor to the Soviet allies!" The crowd shouted back.

The fighting across Europe had lasted six years, ten months, and sixteen days. It had ranged over a vast area from Norway to North Africa and from Stalingrad to Normandy. The total number of troops engaged was estimated at nine million. The sixty-eight American combat divisions in Europe, including the Italian theater, were the most powerful force the United States had ever put in the field. The Germans lost four million people, while Soviet deaths reached some twenty-five million, only one third of them military. United States deaths in Europe totaled 135,576. The struggle was over.

Each nation on the winning side would trumpet its part in the victory, but, as one historian of the war wrote years later, "whatever the scale of measurement, the decisive role in defeating the 'Fascist bloc' was played by the Soviet Union." The long, man-killing, massive battling on the eastern front had Nazi Germany staggering, though not beaten, before the Western Allies ever stepped ashore in Normandy. Then two great forces crushed the Nazi Reich.

Eleven months after the landing on D-Day, the Allies' triumph left Europe in a shambles. Truman's euphoric V-E Day statement that "the flags of freedom fly all over Europe" would prove to be premature.

Chapter 7

Unconditional Surrender

Just four days after he replaced Franklin Roosevelt, and eager to reassure the nation and the world that he would continue FDR's policies, Harry Truman announced in his Address to the Joint Session of the United States Congress that he would carry out Roosevelt's demand for the "unconditional surrender" of the Allies' enemies.

The representatives and senators rose to their feet cheering. Their applause reflected the American people's mood. They wanted the war won and the enemy crushed; they had no wish to compromise.

A June 1 public opinion poll reported that, even if Japan offered to surrender on the sole condition that the United States would not send in an army of occupation, the Americans questioned, by an overwhelming nine-to-one margin, wanted to continue fighting and would not accept the peace offer. They demanded that Japan be defeated totally.

Harry Truman sensed and shared this popular attitude. As a consequence, his insistence on "unconditional surrender" prodded the leaders of both Nazi Germany and militaristic Japan to keep fighting to the finish, and it compelled military invasions of their countries. It certainly altered the postwar world.

Of course, that was its purpose.

"Unconditional surrender" was a tough-minded reaction to the memory of World War I, which had ended while German armies were still fighting in France and Belgium. The Allied armies never penetrated Germany in 1918, enabling many Germans to deny they had been beaten on the field of battle. German nationalists and Adolf Hitler claimed that Germany had been stabbed in the back by its politicians, and they renewed the world war that had been halted only twenty-one years before. In World War II, the Allies were determined to prevent the Germans—and the Japanese—from again dreaming up political excuses for their defeat. This time, defeat on the battlefield would be unquestionable and unconditional.

Unconditional surrender is a trade-off between submission and resistance. For the victor, it means complete conquest and control, even if he has to pay a higher price in lives and treasure. For the vanquished, it means putting oneself completely in the hands of the enemy. Most embattled nations will fight on to avoid it.

Of course, unconditional surrender can mean anything from disarming the enemy's armed forces to a fundamental reordering of his society and political system. To the Allies' political leaders in World War II, it established that the war had been won in combat, controlled the future governments and military resources of the defeated powers, and prevented the Germans and Japanese from splitting the Allies' international coalition. Roosevelt, Truman, Stalin, and Churchill all were determined to destroy their enemies' aggressive power and, this time, to maintain peace in the postwar world.

Early in World War II, when he was still a senator, Truman had concluded that victory would have to be total. Having fought in World War I and later seen how Hitler had converted that German defeat into a renewal of the hating and the killing, Truman wrote his wife on April 30, 1942, "If Britain were to run out on us, or if China should suddenly collapse, we'd have all that old isolation fever again and another war in twenty years. We must take this one to its conclusion and *dictate* peace terms from Berlin and Tokyo. Then we'll have Russia and China to settle with afterwards."

Roosevelt had first explored the concept of "unconditional surrender" with the Joint Chiefs of Staff on January 7, 1943, before he left to meet Churchill at Casablanca in French Morocco. There, at the press conference closing the Casablanca Conference, Roosevelt announced that their enemies would have to surrender unconditionally. (Accounts differ as to whether Churchill had agreed to this policy in advance.) Roosevelt continued:

> The elimination of German, Japanese and Italian war power means the unconditional surrender by Germany,

Italy, and Japan. That means a reasonable assurance of future world peace. It does not mean the destruction of the population of Germany, Italy, or Japan, but it does mean the destruction of the philosophies in those countries which are based on conquest and the subjugation of other people.

He digressed to tell the reporters the story of Major General Ulysses S. "Unconditional Surrender" Grant as he was called "in my, and the Prime Minister's, early days." The term "unconditional surrender" had become famous in American history as Grant's reply when the Confederate commander sent a note asking what terms Grant would give if he would surrender Fort Donelson on the Tennessee River. (The Confederate commander, by a coincidence of history, was Brigadier General Simon Bolivar Buckner, Grant's friend and the father of the American commander who was killed in the battle for Okinawa.)

Why was this policy announced at the Casablanca Conference in 1943, when the Allies were still such a long way from winning any kind of surrender? The immediate reason was that Roosevelt and Churchill had just agreed on military plans that would further delay the opening of the second front that Stalin was demanding in Western Europe. The "unconditional surrender" statement was designed to reassure Stalin that his allies would not negotiate an end to the war. It was supposed to replace with crystal-hard clarity the ambiguity of the usual phrases about Western war aims such as "complete victory" and "final victory."

Stalin was not consulted before the Casablanca announcement. But the Soviet government formally endorsed the idea at a meeting of Hull, Eden, and Molotov in Moscow in the fall of 1943. And the Chinese ambassador to Moscow was permitted to sign the document on behalf of his government. From then on, until victory was finally won more than two years later, the Allies consistently demanded "unconditional surrender."

As the end of the war approached, it became Harry Truman's responsibility to decide whether the Allies should adhere to the principle and pay the higher price. In the view of Truman and his advisors, no alternatives to Hitler survived in Nazi Germany, and, therefore, compromises with the German generals would be profitless. But Japan was known to have both hawks and doves, and there might be other options in Tokyo.

On the morning of May 8, when Truman announced the surrender of Nazi Germany, he included this mollifying message to the Japanese people:

> Our blows will not cease until the Japanese military and naval forces lay down their arms in *unconditional surrender*. Just what does the unconditional surrender of the armed forces mean for the Japanese people? It means the end of the war. It means the termination of the influence of the military leaders who brought Japan to the present brink of disaster. It means provision for the return of soldiers and sailors to their families, their farms, and their jobs. And it means not prolonging the present agony and suffering of the Japanese in the vain hope of victory. Unconditional surrender does not mean the extermination or enslavement of the Japanese people.

Years later, Truman came to have doubts about the idea of unconditional surrender. He eventually came to believe that negotiated or conditional settlements were preferable to unconditional surrenders.

And he was not the only one to develop belated second thoughts. In 1964 Eisenhower said that the policy had lengthened the war against Germany by sixty to ninety days and that General Marshall had also agreed that the policy had been "a mistake." Charles Bohlen came to believe it had been Roosevelt's "greatest single mistake" and had prolonged the war in Europe. Fleet Admiral Ernest J. King, wartime commander in chief of the United States Fleet, would also criticize the policy.

But theirs was late-in-the-day wisdom. Certainly, in 1945 no general or admiral was urging "conditional" surrender on either Roosevelt or Truman. And the Department of State's leaders were divided.

Hindsight, stimulated by the Cold War and the postwar courtship of Germany and Japan, softened the conviction that unconditional surrender had been necessary. Truman was firmly persuaded that unconditional surrender was sound policy. The Germans and Japanese had begun an ugly, aggressive worldwide war, and they would have to admit they had been defeated.

Chapter 8

France Shall Rise Again

Harry Truman discovered he needed to make peace with the nation's allies as urgently as with its enemies. On his first day in office, he asked Secretary of State Stettinius for a report on the status of the United States' major problems abroad. The report, which the President read that evening at home, began not with Germany and Japan but with Britain—most particularly the warning that Winston Churchill was determined to press the Soviet Union on the Yalta agreements "with what we consider unnecessary rigidity as to detail."

Second, the State Department report emphasized problems with France, now led by General Charles de Gaulle. It said the French people "are at present unduly preoccupied . . . with questions of national prestige." It listed unresolved issues regarding the French Army; French participation in the European Advisory Commission, the Allied Reparations Commission, and the occupation of Germany; and Indochina, where the French, the Department of State felt, "showed unreasonable suspicions of American aims and motives."

Next, the report itemized the Soviet government's "firm and uncompromising position on nearly every major question that has arisen in our relations," especially on Poland, the Yalta agreements on liberated areas, the exchange of liberated prisoners of war and civilians, and the San Francisco conference to create an international organization.

Even with his allies, Truman had his hands full.

* * *

Stalin aside, the most exasperating leader Truman faced was de Gaulle—the abrasive, obstinate symbol of France's idea of honor. The French general had come to power the previous August 25, when the Allies had liberated Paris, and he was now pushing to extend France's borders and postwar influence both in Europe and overseas. He was elbowing France to the victors' table and unremittingly insisting on respect for France. He believed he had been called on to lift France out of the depths of occupation, collaboration, and disgrace. It could be brought back to the ranks of the great powers only by rebuilding French pride.

Among those who doubted that it would be possible to restore France's "honor" was Secretary of War Stimson, who wrote in his memoirs (using the third person):

> He [Stimson] had shared the aspirations of his old friend [former Premier Édouard] Herriot, who sent him by a neutral diplomat in 1942 his verbal assurance that the old France would rise again. But when a man he had trusted as he had [former Premier Pierre] Laval became "a mere Quisling," when [former Premier Henri Philippe] Pétain, who had been a fine soldier, permitted in senility outrageous crimes against Frenchmen by Frenchmen, when French North Africa would join the Allies only on the word of a [Admiral Jean] Darlan, when fighting France would find no greater leader than a man with twisted pride and out-of-date political ideas—then Stimson could say only that this was not the France he had known.

With de Gaulle and the French—as well as with the Japanese in their reverence for the Emperor—national pride played a powerful role in shaping relationships between nations and in molding the postwar world. Insisting on the preservation of the Emperor as their national symbol would help the Japanese keep a shred of dignity in defeat and build postwar self-confidence and vigor, but devotion to national pride would carry de Gaulle to the brink.

Despite the value he placed on pride, the French general immediately jettisoned the leaders of the Resistance who had battled the Nazis from inside France. These relatively young men and women thought they constituted a new generation of moral leaders who would share power with the old leadership. De Gaulle quickly dissuaded them. One Resistance intellectual, Jean Bloch-Michel, an editor of the underground newspaper *Combat,* later wrote, "We had believed that the conduct of public affairs required more good faith than experience, more imagination than systemic thinking, and more common sense than ruse. We were childish." De Gaulle taught them reality.

Truman personally tangled with de Gaulle's stubbornness for the first time when the general, defying Eisenhower, bullheadedly refused to remove the French army from the newly conquered German city of Stuttgart.

This *cause célèbre* began in mid-April, when the French and American generals together authorized the French First Army to capture this major city and then move south and allow the American Seventh Army to occupy it.

French tanks entered Stuttgart on April 20, and the French 3rd Algerian Division captured the city. On April 27, as agreed, General Jacob L. Devers, commander of the Sixth Army Group, ordered Lieutenant General Alexander M. Patch's U.S. Seventh Army to take over and General Jean de Lattre de Tassigny's French First Army to move out and mop up the nearby Black Forest.

De Gaulle countermanded that order. He told de Lattre to keep his First Army in Stuttgart. He believed that by staying and occupying Stuttgart, France would gain leverage to have its own zone of occupation in Germany. De Lattre was in the impossible position of trying to accommodate military orders from Devers and contradictory political orders from de Gaulle. As de Gaulle put it, "The roses of glory grew thorns as well."

The situation turned even more unpleasant because of the French 3rd Algerian Division's three infantry regiments, one was Algerian, one Tunisian, and one made up of *maquisards,* European French from the Maquis Resistance. The Maquis of this third regiment hated the Germans, and their hatred enflamed the French obstinacy. When prisoners freed from concentration camps looted the battle-torn city and American military police tried to stop them, French soldiers supported the displaced people. Such direct confrontation between French and American allies was intolerable.

Despite de Lattre's clear responsibility to obey the orders of his army group commander, his loyalty was divided; he told General Devers the issue was beyond them and had to be solved by their governments.

Devers referred the dispute to Eisenhower, who ordered him to stand fast. When de Gaulle insisted that French national prestige was at stake, Eisenhower, always conciliatory, offered the French an arrangement by which they would symbolically occupy a part of Stuttgart. De Gaulle recognized Eisenhower's gesture as soothing but kept the French garrison in Stuttgart.

Eisenhower bristled. He warned the French commander that if his orders were not obeyed he would inform the Combined Chiefs of Staff that he could not use French forces in the future and they should not be equipped from Allied resources.

The conflict was brought to President Truman; he had to decide it himself. He agreed that Eisenhower must be obeyed and the French must leave Stuttgart. He notified de Gaulle directly on May 4 that he would rearrange the structure of command, and he reinforced Eisenhower's warning that the flow of American equipment to the French would be halted.

De Gaulle said sardonically that he found Truman's "message stamped with a certain acidity." He replied sharply to the American President that he expected the Allies to include the French in discussions about the occupation of German territory. Truman was not intimidated. He angrily told his staff, "I don't like the son of a bitch."

Truman actually ordered supplies to the French army stopped and forced de Gaulle's hand; at last, on June 25, having pushed his allies as far as he could, de Gaulle began moving the French army out of Stuttgart. Still, Truman tried to reassure de Gaulle that both the Americans and the British wanted to see France restored as a power and that a French occupation zone would be carved out of the American zone. De Gaulle would always say that the French withdrew from Stuttgart in exchange for a large section of the American zone of occupation. That, of course, was nonsense. But he had forced his allies to pay attention to France—and to him.

During the previous nine months, de Gaulle had repeatedly stirred up crises that Roosevelt had had to deal with. They had been intended to benefit de Gaulle and France; they had certainly done nothing to help defeat the Germans.

De Gaulle had traveled to Moscow in December to seek Stalin's support for France against her own allies. He found Stalin "possessed by the will to power." De Gaulle proposed a treaty between Moscow and Paris; Stalin refused, saying that he would have to discuss such an arrangement with the United States and Britain.

Stalin impressed on de Gaulle that Poland had always been the corridor through which Germany invaded Russia and that the corridor must be closed. From the heat of Stalin's remarks, de Gaulle recognized the importance of the Polish question to him.

At that moment, Churchill telegraphed Stalin, proposing a tripartite security pact among the Soviet Union, Britain, and France. De Gaulle chose to resent Churchill addressing himself exclusively to Stalin on a subject involving France, and he refused to accept a tripartite treaty. He continued to seek a pact between France and the Soviet Union alone.

Stalin took advantage of de Gaulle's peevishness and broached a deal. He would now agree to a narrow Franco-Soviet treaty against German aggression if France understood that the Soviet Union must have an anti-German Polish government, and that was not possible with the London government-in-exile, which he said was anti-Russian.

De Gaulle accepted. And during the following days the foreign ministers, Georges Bidault and Molotov, worked out such a plan.

De Gaulle was visited by members of the Soviet-controlled Lublin-Warsaw Committee, which proposed an agreement with the French government. But de Gaulle saw that the committee did not represent an independent Poland; what its members said sounded too much like the Soviet line.

At 4 A.M. on December 10, in Molotov's office, the two foreign ministers signed a twenty-year agreement that they would take common measures to oppose any new German threat. In the end, fortunately, de Gaulle would not go so far as to support a Soviet-sponsored government for Poland, and Stalin would not make a full-fledged treaty with de Gaulle alone. But they did combine their self-interests enough to make a mutual defense pact without Britain and the United States.

The next serious clash between de Gaulle and his allies erupted in January 1945 over Strasbourg, the capital of Alsace, an important source of coal and iron. Because the city had swung between French and German control in 1871 and 1918, de Gaulle asserted that it carried a heavy emotional meaning for the French. In November 1944 the French 2d Armored Division, led by General Philippe Leclerc, the conqueror of Paris, had entered Strasbourg and "restored the entire city to France."

When the Germans counterattacked in the Ardennes on December 16 and opened the Battle of the Bulge, the Allied command decided to pull out of Alsace as a defensive move. De Gaulle declared the evacuation of Alsace "was not acceptable" to France. He ordered General de Lattre, commander of the French First Army, to hold Strasbourg even if the Allies fell back. He wrote Eisenhower, "Whatever happens, the French will defend Strasbourg."

This refusal to move out of Strasbourg angered Eisenhower. On January 3 de Gaulle went to see the supreme commander at Versailles; Churchill joined them. In a long and antagonistic meeting, de Gaulle insisted his government would fall if he gave up this French territory to the Germans without a major fight; if necessary, he would fight on alone. "Alsace is sacred ground."

Eisenhower pointedly warned de Gaulle to consider just how the French First Army would fight if it were cut off from the Allied armies. De Gaulle counterthreatened that an outraged French people might forbid the Allies to use their railroads and communications. To prevent a rupture, Eisenhower finally agreed to cancel the Allied retreat from Strasbourg. De Gaulle had his way. Fortunately, the German advance soon spent itself, and American troops were not required to sacrifice their lives for a French political icon.

De Gaulle's next explosion against his Allies came when he was not invited to the Yalta Conference. He blamed Roosevelt and retaliated by questioning whether decisions made there would bind France.

A week before the Yalta summit opened, Harry Hopkins visited de Gaulle as Roosevelt's special emissary, hoping to ease some of the tension. But de Gaulle rebuffed him in the most candid language:

> The United States does not give us the impression that it regards its own destiny as linked with that of France, that it wishes France to be great and strong, that it is doing all it can to help her remain or become so once again. Perhaps, in fact, we are not worth the trouble. In that case, you are right. But perhaps we shall rise again. Then you will have been wrong. In either case, your behavior tends to alienate us.

De Gaulle even blamed the United States for the rise of Hitler. The United States had not entered World War I until France was exhausted from three years of battle—and, after that war, the United States had refused to allow France to have security guarantees and the reparations due her. "The result," he said, "was Hitler."

As to the future, de Gaulle said he did not understand how the

United States could conceive of organizing Europe's future in the absence of France.

Of course, the Allies had no intention of ignoring France; they needed a stable, prosperous France to balance the presence of Germany and the Soviet Union in Europe.

De Gaulle's paranoia burst out again when, after the Yalta Conference, Roosevelt cordially invited him to meet in Algiers on Roosevelt's way home from the Crimea. De Gaulle took offense and stipulated that FDR come to Paris instead. Roosevelt declined. Back home, on March 2, when Roosevelt addressed Congress, he referred to "prima donnas" who had thwarted a useful discussion.

Next, de Gaulle complained that the Americans wanted to leave the French troops sitting west of the Rhine and prevent them from participating in the occupation of Germany. Indeed, the British asserted, there was no military reason for the French to occupy the Rhineland and cross the river into the heart of Germany. But de Gaulle persisted. He later wrote, "Our troops, too, would have to cross the border. They would do so, if possible, within the interallied framework. If this was not possible, they would do so on our own account. In any case, they would seize a French zone of occupation on the right bank of the Rhine."

After the Americans captured the bridge at Remagen on March 7 and won a foothold on the Rhine's east bank, de Gaulle ordered de Lattre to cross the river in boats if necessary. The 2nd Moroccan Division finally crossed over in boats on March 30. Although they had the assistance of the American army, the French, in the view of one respected French military historian, bungled the crossing. Only three of their twenty assault boats survived the German fire and made it to the east bank. The French had to wait until dark to establish their bridgehead.

De Gaulle's threat to seize a zone of occupation in Germany by force was totally unnecessary. Churchill supported a French zone of occupation; he wanted France to be a counterweight to the Soviet Union after the war. And since the British zone was to be in the north, where Belgium and the Netherlands stood between France and Germany, it fell to the Americans to share their zone with the French. General Devers and General de Lattre agreed that French troops would occupy an area between the German border and the Rhine. From there the French army moved southeast, absorbing more of the American zone.

By this time, Truman was President and had to deal with de Gaulle's European unilateral power plays over Stuttgart and northern

Italy. He quickly grew fed up with the French general's machinations and hubris.

De Gaulle's final confrontation in Europe with his wartime Allies came at the end of April, when the French initiated, and fought in, an offensive in the Italian Alps. The purpose of this campaign was to seize for France enclaves then in Italy's possession.

De Gaulle established, under General Paul Doyen, an "Alpine Special Command" that would extend the French frontier to the strategic Alpine mountain peaks, acquire the French-speaking cantons of Tende and La Brigue, and claim the Val d'Aosta (Aosta Valley). He wanted a French occupation zone in Italy extending from Villefranche to the Val d'Aosta, which had a French-speaking population. Eventually, he planned to confirm his aggression with a referendum. He was, as always, trying to enlarge a Greater France.

French troops began seizing scarce food supplies, hauling down Italian flags, and posting notices ordering the people to accept French currency. French roadblocks even stopped the movement of U.S. troops.

On May 5 Field Marshal Alexander, the Allied commander in Italy, asked Eisenhower to remove the French troops because he feared they would cause clashes with the local population. When Eisenhower ordered the French to return to France, the local commander, denying Eisenhower's authority, replied that he needed instructions from his government. Meanwhile, the French continued to pour troops into the area.

By May 8 the situation had become another crisis between de Gaulle and the Allies. The Americans and British demanded that the French withdraw to their 1939 borders and that all boundary changes wait for the final peace treaties. With injured dignity, de Gaulle insisted he only sought amiable frontier adjustments. And he advised Eisenhower that with the end of the war against Germany the movement of French troops had become solely a French concern.

In Washington on May 18, when the guns in Europe were already silent, Truman received, at de Gaulle's request, French Foreign Minister Bidault, whom Truman respected for his courageous leadership in the wartime resistance movement. Truman was firm with his visitor, however; he did not like what was going on in Europe. Unless the French troops were ordered to obey the American general under whom they were serving, the United States could not supply them. Bidault thought the situation could be straightened out. It would not be that simple.

Bidault conveyed de Gaulle's desire to share in the invasion of Japan's home islands and requested that the United States transport French troops to Asia. Truman was determined not to let de Gaulle create the same problems there that the Allies were having with the French in Europe; if the French did join the Pacific war, he warned Bidault, they must obey the orders of the American commanding general. Truman wrote on his appointment sheet, "They would be under our command and they would have to agree to obey—they had not obeyed before and we did not like that sort of procedure and we might as well lay the cards on the table."

In the meantime, the conflict with de Gaulle in Italy grew more acrimonious. Major General Willis D. Crittenberger, commander of the U.S. IV Corps in northwestern Italy, tried to remove the French troops; General Doyen rashly threatened that he would go to "the extreme consequences" to carry out de Gaulle's orders.

In letters to Major General Crittenberger on May 30 and June 2, General Doyen asserted that the establishment of an Allied military authority in the area would "assume a clearly unfriendly character, even a hostile character, and could have grave consequences." The French, Doyen warned, would act "by all necessary means without exception." The Americans were shocked. The clear implication was that the French would fire on American soldiers.

When Admiral Leahy, the chief of staff to the Commander-in-Chief, came and told Truman of these incredible developments, the President snapped: "The French are using our guns, are they not?" Leahy confirmed that they were, and Truman acted instantly: "All right, we will at once stop shipping guns, ammunition and equipment to de Gaulle." He instructed General Marshall to draft a message in which the President personally notified de Gaulle that he had halted supplies and that he would hold to his order until the French army left the Val d'Aosta.

Truman was astounded, he informed de Gaulle, that General Doyen's statements "contain the almost unbelievable threat that French soldiers bearing American arms will combat American and Allied soldiers whose efforts and sacrifices have so recently and successfully contributed to the liberation of France itself."

Truman's message concluded unequivocally: "While this threat by the French Government is outstanding against American soldiers, I regret that I have no alternative but to issue instructions that no further issue of military equipment or munitions can be made to French troops. Rations will continue to be supplied. Truman."

De Gaulle later wrote disingenuously, "I did not take Truman's communication too seriously." Again distorting the facts to fit his personal vision, he blamed London for creating friction between Washington and Paris.

Churchill called General Doyen's pronouncements "astonishing." He said that if Truman made his statement to de Gaulle public, it would cause his overthrow. De Gaulle, Churchill declared, was a danger to European peace. Truman discussed the crisis with Secretary Stimson; they agreed that de Gaulle was a psychopath, but Stimson urged Truman to act prudently.

Truman's message achieved his purpose; de Gaulle backed down. On June 9 he ordered the withdrawal of the French troops from the Val d'Aosta, though he continued to sponsor an autonomy movement among the French-speaking Italians. The French forces pulled back to the 1939 border, and the disputed areas remained Italian. To the French people, de Gaulle announced baldly that he had withdrawn "for reasons of the highest rank on which depends the main interest of the country."

De Gaulle's maneuverings overseas had an even greater impact on the world's future than his European scheming did. At the same time as he was roiling the waters in Europe, he set out to recover France's colonies in Algeria and Indochina and its League of Nations Mandates in Lebanon and Syria. And it usually fell to Truman, in the last instance, to rein in the stiff-necked, nationalistic general.

Earlier in the war, de Gaulle had sided with the British against the Vichy French, and Free French and British troops had together fought Vichy troops in Lebanon and Syria. The victorious British had allowed French soldiers in the area to choose—man by man— whether they would join the Free French or the Vichy forces. Fifteen thousand joined the Free French and helped stop German General Erwin Rommel in the North African desert.

The Allies recognized Lebanon and Syria as independent countries and made them members of the United Nations. De Gaulle ignored this. In April 1945 he reinforced his small garrisons in Syria. The British objected. De Gaulle insisted that more men were needed to maintain order, which, he said, only the French could do. On May 5 Churchill reminded de Gaulle of Britain's continuing interest in the area and the need to make certain that communications and oil kept flowing to the Indian and Pacific theaters of war. He asked de Gaulle to stop sending in reinforcements and to release the local troops he commanded to the governments in Damascus and Beirut. De Gaulle assured him that once the French had worked out their strategic, economic, and cultural interests, they would terminate their mandate in the Middle East.

Starting on May 8, V-E Day, Arab troops attached to the British forces rose up and demonstrated against de Gaulle's attempts to reinstall French rule. The French were convinced that the British were behind the uprising.

Despite Churchill's admonition that de Gaulle not reinforce the French forces, on May 17 he landed more troops at Beirut. As Churchill later wrote, "An explosion followed." Anti-French strikes and demonstrations broke out. The French charged that the disturbances had been provoked.

Truman, thoroughly upset by the French efforts to revive colonialism in the Middle East, on May 27 approved a note asking de Gaulle to treat Syria and Lebanon as independent states. Churchill even won Truman's approval to intervene with a British armed force to end the fighting and restore order.

Starting in Damascus the next day, Lebanese and Syrian soldiers murdered their Free French officers and for two days fought French Senegalese troops. French artillery shelled the capital, and French troops occupied the Syrian parliament buildings.

Churchill called for a cease-fire in Damascus and clashed publicly with de Gaulle. By the end of the month, some two thousand people had been killed or injured. General Sir Bernard Paget, Commander-in-Chief Middle East, was instructed to restore order. British aircraft and armor appeared at Beirut.

In the face of this show of force, French General Paul E. Beynet ordered his troops to their barracks as the British demanded. But, with de Gaulle's backing, Beynet refused to take orders from the British. Infuriated, Truman told a White House staff meeting on May 31, "Those French ought to be taken out and castrated."

In the end, the British and French avoided firing on each other. But even de Gaulle's supporters thought he had gone too far. Efforts were made to repair the damage, and Churchill went out of his way to be conciliatory.

General Beynet regrouped his troops outside the major cities, which the British promptly occupied. They ordered all French citizens expelled. The French gave up their authority over the Syrian troops. The Syrian president sent Churchill a note of gratitude for the British intervention.

Churchill proposed a conference of France, Britain, and the United States on the Middle East. When Stalin wanted to be included, de Gaulle was delighted on June 2 to throw "a pebble in their diplomatic pond" and urged instead a five-power conference with the Soviet Union and China. Not wanting to encourage a Soviet presence in the Middle East, the United States and Britain rejected this idea.

"The end of the war was very bad for the French army," says one French military historian. The French eventually would choose to get out of Lebanon and Syria, which had been League of Nation Mandates, and try (unsuccessfully) to hold on to colonies in Indochina and Algeria, which had French populations.

The most dramatic and portentous example of the effort to restore French colonialism was de Gaulle's determination to regain possession of Indochina.

Although Indochina spent the war under Vichy's nominal rule, the Japanese were its real masters. Japan chose not to crush French sovereignty but to establish its own bases and troops in Indochina. The naval base at Cam Ranh Bay, for example, helped put Japan within reach of the Philippines, the Dutch East Indies, and Malaya. The French in Indochina were neutralized and isolated.

As early as 1943, Roosevelt had proposed that Indochina be placed under a postwar United Nations trusteeship. Churchill had resisted the idea, fearing that the end of the French empire would lead to the end of the British. The U.S. State Department had also disapproved; it wanted France present in East Asia as a counterforce to the Soviet Union. Later, Roosevelt had partially come around to the State Department view and had allowed American air forces in China to help the French in Indochina when they were able to fight the Japanese.

Once France itself was liberated, the French colonials in Indochina, including some fifty thousand scattered troops, tried to put aside their differences and rally under de Gaulle. French officers parachuted in to build an underground resistance movement on the style of the Maquis.

On March 9, 1945, the Japanese ordered the French military commanders in Saigon and Hanoi to surrender in order to forestall their making common cause with the Free French. When they refused, Japanese troops attacked the French garrisons and interned almost all French troops and civil servants. De Gaulle was not displeased. He wrote later with tough-minded cynicism, "French blood shed on the soil of Indochina would constitute an impressive claim."

The Japanese struck down the local government and disarmed and killed French soldiers. They imprisoned the French engineers responsible for the dikes on the Red River delta. This, combined with Allied air bombardments, flooded vast areas of rice fields that summer and brought famine the next fall. More than a half-million villagers died of starvation. At the same time, French underground activities against the Japanese were thwarted by Vietnamese hostility. De Gaulle began assembling for service in East Asia a French expeditionary force of troops training in Africa and Madagascar.

On June 22 the U.S. State Department, following a policy review, produced a paper that defied the Roosevelt-Truman position against colonialism in Indochina. The State Department opposed a U.N. trusteeship over Indochina and favored France's return there.

The paper predicted that at the end of the war conditions in northern Indochina would be unstable. "It is believed that the French will encounter serious difficulty in overcoming [local] opposition and in reestablishing French control." The State Department hedged its political bets, advocating French sovereignty while supporting Indochina's eventual independence. But the paper concluded clearly: "The United States recognizes French sovereignty over Indochina."

As part of reestablishing the French presence in East Asia, de Gaulle also wanted to participate, at least symbolically, in the invasion of Japan. A visible role in the Pacific war, he believed, would help qualify France as a world power and as a member of the U.N. Security Council.

Early in July the Pentagon let de Gaulle know that he could send two divisions to the war against Japan. Always pushing for France's advantage, he replied that if he did, he also wanted to send forces to Burma to fight in Indochina.

The Allies decided that the British would take the Japanese surrender and occupy southern Indochina below the 16th Parallel, while Nationalist China would do the same in the north. France, which by now had every expectation of regaining its colony, objected to allowing in the Chinese because they would be difficult to dislodge. De Gaulle had no trouble accepting the presence of the British, who were so openly procolonial.

With the end of the war against Japan, de Gaulle wanted the return of French authority everywhere in the world; then he would decide in which places France wished to remain. He chose a difficult strategy.

In order to return to Indochina, for example, he had to create a French military force, win British and Chinese agreement to let it enter Indochina, and then ship it there. He had no problem with Lord Mountbatten, supreme allied commander of Southeast Asia, who welcomed the return of French troops to Indochina.

Elements of the French 2nd Armored Division and the 9th Colonial Infantry Division were prepared to go. But shipping was not available, and the United States refused to supply any. Between September and December, *Richelieu* and other French warships carried troops out to Indochina. The British general commanding in Saigon helped the French disembark and maintain order.

Vietnamese nationalist and communist guerrillas, organized as the Vietnamese Independence League, or Vietminh, defied the return of French authority; they wanted independence. The League, with Ho Chi Minh as its political leader and Vo Nguyen Giap as its military leader, was supported by the American Office of Strategic Services during the war and afterward formed the Democratic Republic of Vietnam.

On August 15 de Gaulle unwisely appointed as the high commissioner of Indochina Rear Admiral Georges Thierry d'Argenlieu, who had been his arrogant, tactless high commissioner for the Pacific. A rigid defender of colonialism, the admiral set up a puppet government in south Vietnam, opposed his government's recognition of the Democratic Republic of Vietnam, and played a major role in stimulating the long and violent war between the French and the Vietnamese.

At Truman's invitation, de Gaulle arrived in Washington on August 22 and was greeted with enough pomp and ceremony to make him feel he was "a great ally, wounded but victorious, and above all, needed." Truman, meeting de Gaulle for the first time, greeted him under a green canopy at the south portico of the White House. After a military ceremony on the South Lawn, de Gaulle was introduced to Mrs. Truman and the cabinet. The two presidents spent a total of seven hours together over three days.

By now, after little more than four months in office, Harry Truman had moved beyond many of the positions he had inherited from Roosevelt. And he had gained enormously in self-confidence. These changes were very clear, even seen through the prism of de Gaulle's distorted view of the world. De Gaulle found Truman "extremely positive" but lacking Roosevelt's "vast idealism." Truman, according to de Gaulle, did not expect world harmony but foresaw the rivalry between the free world and the Soviet bloc as the world's most important political problem. His goal, as de Gaulle saw it, was to prevent more nations from going Communist.

De Gaulle viewed the United States as the only major power still intact, optimistic, and energetic. But he judged Truman simplistic, believing that Europe's perplexing problems could be solved with democracy and the leadership of the United States alone. Truman told him that he planned to withdraw American troops from Europe, except for occupation forces in Germany and Austria, because the Soviet Union, despite its rivalry with the West, would not risk war for a long time.

Truman wanted to help Germany recover and not again be torn between communism and fascism. But de Gaulle, haunted by the fact that Germany had invaded France three times in the past seventy-five years, wanted assurance that the German threat would not re-emerge. Germany could flourish, but France wanted guarantees. From his viewpoint, Britain and the United States had destroyed Europe's equilibrium by permitting the states of central Europe and the Balkans to become satellites of the Soviet Union. Now, only by demonstrating that the German threat no longer existed could these satellites develop their own national interests; if they sensed a German threat, they would seek shelter in the Russians' embrace.

De Gaulle told Truman that he expected the colonial peoples of Asia and Africa would achieve independence in the era now beginning; but if this occurred too fast, it would lead to xenophobia, poverty, and anarchy from which only the Soviet Union would benefit. The worst thing would be rivalry among the Western powers, and exactly this was already taking place in the Middle East. He objected to the support the United States was giving there to British intervention, as against the French. "Ultimately," he told the President, "the West will have to pay for this error and this injustice."

When Truman assured de Gaulle that the United States did not object to the return of the French army and authority to Indochina, he retorted sharply that France did not need permission or approval but that he welcomed Truman's intentions. He protested, furthermore, that the Allies there had been making arrangements without consulting France. France wanted neither British troops in southern Indochina nor Chinese troops in the north. He added that he knew that American agents were infiltrating Tonkin and were in touch with the native revolutionaries.

De Gaulle went home with a long-term loan of $650 million, which would help fill the gap when Truman terminated Lend-Lease on September 2.

He also went home with admiration for Truman's frankness. He wrote, "As Chief of State, Truman impressed me as equal to his task, his character firm, his mind oriented toward the practical side of affairs—in short, a man who doubtless promised no miracles but who could be counted on in a crisis."

In the end, Truman was responsible for the decision that made it possible for the French to return to Indochina in force and fight the indigenous movement seeking independence, a decision that would lead to thirty years of destruction and death for the local people.

Chapter 9

Like Running Jackson County

"As long as I have been in the White House, I can't help waking at 5 A.M. and hearing the old man at the foot of the stairs calling and telling me get out and milk the cows," Harry Truman once said. He never needed an alarm clock.

The Truman family moved over from Blair House on V-E Day and brought a small-town atmosphere to the White House. When they were alone, the President and Mrs. Truman would usually each have one bourbon old-fashioned and then dine together with their twenty-one-year-old daughter, Margaret. They seldom entertained privately. They enjoyed each other's company and would play Margaret's piano and chat. Mrs. Truman liked listening to the Washington Senators night baseball games on the radio and playing Ping-Pong with Margaret. The President often worked in the study after dinner. At bedtime, the President would wind the clocks and check the doors and windows. He slept in his own room in a four-poster bed.

He liked to walk and often swam the breaststroke in the White House pool with his glasses on. He worked out on a rowing machine and did twenty-five sit-ups each day.

A typical workday started with a visit to the so-called Map Room, which was actually the White House's secret intelligence center. There, he would be briefed on overnight military developments and disasters and pick up messages from Churchill, Stalin, and his own ambassadors abroad. Then, he would dictate, answering his mail for some forty-five minutes before discussing the coming day with his chief aides. And he would begin to see the endless stream of what he called his "customers"—"usually Senators, Congressmen, Cabinet members and Missourians."

Friday, April 27, exemplified how Truman had to concern himself with domestic issues even in wartime. He started by having breakfast with Judge Lewis Schwellenbach of Washington State. At 9:15 he met with Senator Owen Brewster of Maine; and then spent fifteen minutes each with Senator Robert M. La Follette of Wisconsin and House Speaker Sam Rayburn. At 10, he saw Treasury Secretary Henry Morgenthau, Jr., followed by Acting Secretary of State Joseph C. Grew and other State Department officials and assistant secretaries of war and navy. Next came Oliver Lyttleton, minister of production in the British war cabinet; then, at fifteen-minute intervals, Agriculture Secretary Claude R. Wickard, Commerce Secretary Henry Wallace, and Representative Paul Shafer of Michigan.

That morning, Truman held his first conference with labor leaders, receiving a party from the railroad brotherhoods. At noon he saw former Senator Samuel Jackson of Indiana and then former Senator George H. Williams of Missouri and his son, followed by Federal Security Administrator Paul V. McNutt. At 12:45 the President welcomed his first official black visitor, J. E. Mitchell, editor and publisher of the weekly *St. Louis Argus,* and finally General Marshall. The list suggested the range of his problems and responsibilities.

Truman sent the *Sacred Cow,* the Presidential plane, to bring his mother and sister from Grandview to Washington for Mother's Day on Sunday, May 13. It was his ninety-two-year-old mother's first visit to Washington and her first airplane ride. "Mama got a great kick out of the trip," he noted.

As an unreconstructed Rebel, she balked at sleeping in the bed Lincoln had slept in and threatened to lie on the floor. The President wanted to put her in the Rose Room, but she insisted on sleeping in a small adjoining room, and his sister slept in the Rose Room.

The next morning, Truman was back hard at work with a full schedule of callers. This Monday brought him chiefly foreign policy rather than domestic problems. He met for forty minutes with British Foreign Secretary Anthony Eden, who was en route to San Francisco, and Deputy Prime Minister Clement Attlee. He conferred with Chinese Foreign Minister T. V. Soong about Lend-Lease to China; Senator Millard E. Tydings, who was leaving to make an economic study of the Philippines; Senator George L. Radcliffe about postwar shipping; Democratic committeeman from Texas Myron Blaylock; and Donald

M. Nelson, who was departing after completing five years of government war-production work.

Once, when Bess was in Independence and he was at the White House, he wrote her, describing a common failing: "I didn't get to phone you last night. I lost the phone number you gave me by putting it where I could find it. Whenever I do that with an important paper or memo it is as effectually lost as if it had never existed."

He lovingly worried about the effect of their new life on the family, especially Margaret. He once confided to his diary, "The family left for Missouri last evening. Went to the train with them and rode to Silver Spring just as I did with my mother and sister a week or so ago. Daughter was in a very unsatisfactory humor. I hope—sincerely hope—that this situation (my being President) is not going to affect her adversely."

He went on to say, "I'm always so lonesome when the family leaves. I have no one to raise a fuss over my neckties and my haircuts, my shoes and my clothes generally. I usually put on a terrible tie not even Bob Hannegan or Ed McKim would wear, just to get a loud protest from Bess or Margie. When they are gone I have to put on the right ones and it's no fun."

The Trumans were not pretentious. Harry Truman said it another way: "The only things worth learning are the things you learn after you know it all."

The new President found his eyes troubling him from reading the endless papers he forced himself to study; cannily, he examined every memorandum as if it had a catch in it somewhere. He enjoyed his first night out on May 27 when he was invited to a dinner at the Burning Tree Club. And then he had to sit through some "very boresome speeches." On request, he played several numbers on the piano for which he was given a prize: a marked deck of cards and some loaded dice. "Will never use either, I hope."

After the official dinner, he was led upstairs, where some friends had organized a poker game. That was more to his liking. "To be fair" he announced that he had to quit at midnight. "For some reason I was lucky enough not to lose any money. Luck always seems to be with me in games of chance and in politics." He felt he had been so lucky since he had become President that he attributed it to God. "He guides me, I think."

He soon realized that some of "my boys" whom he had brought in to help him were letting their closeness to the President of the United States go to their heads. He commented, "It's hell when a man gets in close association with the President. Something happens to him." He kept an eye open for the rare person who was not seduced by the glamour.

Less than two months in office, he wrote Bess, "It won't be long until I can sit back and study the whole picture and tell 'em what is to be done in each department. When things come to that stage there'll be no more to this job than there was to running Jackson County and not any more worry."

Bess was one person who did not succumb to the allure of the White House and who—too often for her husband—was back in Missouri taking care of her mother or just escaping from Washington's pressures. On June 12 the ex-farmer from Grandview sat upstairs in the White House and wrote to his wife in Missouri:

> Dear Bess:
> Just two months ago today, I was a reasonably happy and contented Vice President. Maybe you can remember that far back too. But things have changed so much it hardly seems real.
> I sit here in this old house and work on foreign affairs, read reports, and work on speeches—all the while listening to the ghosts walk up and down the hallway and even right here in the study. The floors pop and the drapes move back and forth—I can just imagine old Andy and Teddy having an argument over Franklin. Or James Buchanan and Franklin Pierce deciding which was the more useless to the country. And when Millard Fillmore and Chester Arthur join in for place and show the din is almost unbearable. But I still get some work done. . . .
> Write me when you can—I hope every day.
> Lots of love,
> Harry

The country was beginning to get a reading of this quiet man on whom had suddenly been dumped the burden of governing. *Washington Post* columnist Ernest Lindley wrote that "the United States must be carrying a rabbit's foot in its pocket" because "so far, he has been better than pretty good. He has been first-rate." Lindley reported that even "a number of sagacious Republicans" agreed with that appraisal.

The early judgment on the President, Lindley wrote, was that

"Truman seems to run on well-oiled bearings. He runs fast, too, without detours. His ability to listen, to grasp the problem quickly, and to make up his mind, has been astonishing. . . . The fact is that, hour by hour, Truman transacts more business than Roosevelt ever did."

By the time Harry Truman came to the presidency, the citizens of the United States sensed they were approaching the eagerly wished-for end of this war. The crucial—and not always recognized—fact in their lives was that this was an overseas war; and, as a result, civilian Americans at home had escaped the horrors of trying to survive on a battlefield. Over the years, the dangers, the deaths and wounds, the disruption of life and careers, the separations of families had taken their toll on the American people—although nothing, surely, compared to the suffering of the peoples in Europe, Asia, and Africa, who were experiencing war at home.

Truman faced an array of postwar issues that in good part Roosevelt had ignored because he had concentrated most of his energies on winning the global war. Only during his last year or so had he begun to focus on the problems of the postwar world. For example, one of the issues FDR had paid attention to was the plight of the returning servicemen. He had proposed, among other things, the unprecedented and enormously significant GI Bill of Rights, under which the government would help pay for veterans' education and enable thousands who otherwise could never have afforded it to go to college.

In dedicating himself to fulfilling Roosevelt's objectives, at home and overseas, Truman had promised to carry out the "Second Bill of Rights," which FDR had put forth in his January 1944 State of the Union Address. This was FDR's most dramatic summation of the goals of the New Deal: every American, regardless of station, race, or creed was entitled to a useful job; to earn enough for food, clothing, and recreation, a decent home, adequate medical care; protection from the economic fears associated with old age, sickness, and unemployment; and finally a good education. This was the promise of the New Deal that Harry Truman found waiting to be fulfilled.

Americans grew restless as victory approached. The tensions of deaths and casualties, the rationing of food and gasoline, and the demands of war production had built up strains that created problems as soon as people felt that the dangers were receding. The plaintive songs of the moment said some of it: "I Left My Heart at the Stage Door Canteen"; "Don't Sit Under the Apple Tree."

CIO President Philip Murray and AFL President William Green came to the White House and asked Truman to raise the wages of all industrial workers by 20 percent, half to cover cost-of-living increases and half to allow for increases in productivity. They anticipated that this would absorb the losses in take-home pay when war plants reduced their workweek from forty-eight to forty hours.

The American people were winning the war in good part because they had been willing to mobilize all their resources, their entire economy, their manpower, their lives. They were willing to put up with price controls and rationing. Harry Truman believed the nation's wartime "price control and stabilization program has been one of the most remarkable achievements of this war."

Albert Speer, who had organized the Nazis' industrial war effort, said, "One of the most surprising aspects of this war is that Hitler wished to spare his own people the privations that Churchill and Roosevelt imposed without hesitation on theirs."

What Speer failed to consider was that in 1939 the United States still had ten million unemployed and two thirds of its steel plants had been idle. The Depression had left room for an enormous military and industrial expansion for war. The Germans were already building tanks and dive-bombers and attacking their neighbors when the prospect of war put American workers back on the job.

By the time Truman was seated in the White House, Americans were beginning to strain at the bonds of discipline and sacrifice that had made their war effort successful. And when the war in Europe was over, millions of American men and women had to be demobilized and provided housing and jobs to start their lives again.

America had changed forever. The nation now had commitments around the world. Rural Americans had flooded into the cities' war plants. Millions of women were now in the labor force. The automobile and the airplane were making people more mobile than they had ever been. And there were wrongs that cried out to be corrected. The descendants of American slaves were churning with discontent accentuated by their wartime experiences, and race relations were climbing to the forefront of domestic concerns. And the injustice done after Pearl Harbor to 120,000 people of Japanese birth or descent— many of them American citizens—by locking them in remote concentration camps because of their race had to be remedied.

This tragic racist action had been taken, with Roosevelt's approval, by responsible men. After the war, Secretary of War Stimson, who had ordered the incarcerations, admitted they had done a personal injustice to loyal American citizens; but he continued to defend them in his postwar memoirs, saying bizarrely that they had produced "a distinctly healthier atmosphere for both Japanese and Americans."

Then-Senator Truman had disapproved of the entire action against the Japanese Americans and years later acknowledged that the so-called evacuation sites had been concentration camps and that Roosevelt should never have allowed it. The action had special meaning to Truman, who was known to tell emotional stories about how in 1863, during the Civil War, Federal troops had removed his grandmother and his mother, along with many people in that part of Missouri, to a "post," or concentration camp, in Kansas City. Truman credited the experiences his family had endured during the Civil War and the prejudices and vindictiveness he had witnessed long afterward with shaping his mature views against loyalty oaths, for civil rights for blacks, and for the healing of postwar wounds as he sought to do in Europe.

That spring and summer of 1945, Truman repeatedly reminded the American people that they still had to win the war against Japan. But millions of Americans were tired of rationing and shortages, and hundreds of thousands of young servicemen wanted only to get home from Europe and pick up their lives.

Such tensions erupted into a tenacious dispute between American mineworkers and the coal mine operators. On May 1 John L. Lewis pulled his 72,000 United Mine Workers out of more than three hundred anthracite mines, despite a War Labor Board order that they continue to produce coal while their differences were being settled.

Truman accused Lewis of making a power play for postwar domination of labor: "I would not stand for that." He later said, "Here we were in the midst of one of the gravest conflicts in the history of civilization. Men were dying in battle. Our citizens were tightening their belts and making every sacrifice to help save the world from tyranny."

He did not quibble. He issued an Executive Order commanding Secretary of the Interior Harold L. Ickes to take possession of any mines in which production was interrupted or threatened. The miners were then working for the government.

But workers' willingness to go on strike in order to protest wartime restraints spread to many smaller companies, such as the Diamond

Alkali Company of Painesville, Ohio, producer of chemicals essential to the war effort, and the R. R. Donnelley & Sons Printing Company of Chicago, a major printer of national magazines and other publications.

Unions were not the only organizations eager to return to business as usual. Before the United States had gone to war in 1941, the automobile industry, for one, had been reluctant to respond to the government's call to convert to military production. The industry had just begun to make profits following the long Great Depression and insisted on expanding its output of passenger cars. Labor leader Walter Reuther was one of those who pressed the industry to change over to aircraft production more rapidly.

The federal government was forced to order reductions in the number of cars produced, erect new plants itself to build tanks and aircraft, and then turn over the plants to Chrysler and Ford to manage. The attack on Pearl Harbor had changed all that, and the last civilian automobile rolled off the assembly line on February 10, 1942. At war's end, the auto industry was naturally impatient to return to the profitable production of civilian products.

President Truman had to resolve many such problems that now surfaced. Because armament and shipping production had increased sufficiently, he was able to recommend on May 2 that Congress cut $7.4 billion out of the proposed budget for 1946. The next day, he vetoed a congressional resolution that would have given draft deferments to agricultural workers. He declared, "No group should be given special privileges."

He actively supported the bipartisan congressional ratification of the Bretton Woods international monetary agreements, which made billions of dollars available to guarantee long-term loans to war-devastated and underdeveloped countries and helped stabilize currencies.

Calling racial discrimination "un-American in nature," he intervened to break up a House Rules Committee logjam that was preventing the establishment of a permanent Fair Employment Practices Commission. Otherwise "the principle of fair employment practices will have been abandoned by the House of Representatives," and that, he felt, was "unthinkable."

He advocated raising the pay of members of the House of Representatives and the Senate from $10,000 a year to at least $15,000, once wage controls over private industry were lifted; Congress should not be a rich man's club, he declared. Speaking from his own experience as a senator, he told a press conference that he had had to put his wife on the payroll as his secretary in order to meet his bills. He said that neither he nor his wife had liked the arrangement and some of the press had tried to make a political issue out of it; but, he added with a smile, apparently the people had liked it.

Still, Truman took time to keep his political fences mended. He had already visited the Senate; and on May 1, he visited the House of Representatives, had lunch with the Speaker, Majority Leader, and Minority Leader, and then was introduced to those of the 435 members of the House whom he had not met. A fourteen-year-old red-headed page boy went through the presidential reception line twice; Truman spotted him, laughed, and shook hands a second time.

Just before V-E Day, Truman instructed Director of the Budget Harold Smith to initiate studies on how the nation should convert to a peacetime economy and deflate the size and complexity of its wartime government. The federal government was now a monster with 2.9 million paid civilian employees on a $7 billion payroll. The war had stopped the Great Depression, and it would take planning to ensure that the war's end would not revive depression conditions.

Truman intended to reshape the White House, reorganize the Labor Department, put public health services under a cabinet officer, and establish a Welfare Department. Even while leading the war to its climax, he was clearly giving domestic issues, with which he had long familiarity, a lot of attention.

As these domestic issues regained importance, some expected Truman to come down on the side of the conservative Democrats, but he reacted more like a New Dealer. He accepted the principles of government spending and making loans abroad to keep up employment at home. This became important when war production jobs were cut back drastically, throwing many people out of work or reducing their working hours.

The war had enormous impact on the relationship between "black" and "white" Americans—Americans with African roots and those with European. Here Truman played a bold and defining role. This Southerner, whose mother would not sleep in Lincoln's White House bed and who in private had used nasty words like "nigger" and "kike," grew into a surprisingly forceful leader bringing the races together in a divided and often bitterly antagonistic society. He believed, "If you just give people a chance to be decent, they will be."

At the time of Pearl Harbor, 51 percent of all jobs in America's defense industry had been closed to blacks. Under the growing wartime need for workers and pressure from the Roosevelt administration, the number of blacks in all manufacturing industry had increased from half a million in 1940 to one and a quarter million in 1944. But there was still plenty of prejudice around.

Black Americans responded to the need for their participation in the war effort. Hundreds of thousands moved from the rural South to war production jobs in the North and on the West Coast. Blacks who served in the armed forces were almost totally segregated, but black units served valiantly in combat. Despite many ugly racial incidents—Stimson was infuriated when he could not bring to justice southern policemen who had murdered a black army military policeman—black servicemen gained self-pride and won recognition from many white Americans.

Achieving this new fluidity in American society had its price. The new rules and the new juxtapositions of blacks and whites exploded during the war into race riots in Detroit, Mobile, Harlem, Beaumont. On the other hand, people's understanding of the nation's race problem also grew during the war, aided by the publication of such books as Gunnar Myrdal's *An American Dilemma*, Richard Wright's *Black Boy*, and Lillian Smith's *Strange Fruit*. All these were both the products of change and the creators of change.

Black servicemen began coming home to a country that was, of course, still segregated. Almost 90 percent of the 32,892 churches in the Southern Baptist Convention, one of the largest Protestant denominations in the nation, refused to admit blacks. But discrimination based on skin color was not only a southern problem; it was all America's greatest form of social immorality.

Harlem-born author James Baldwin said that prejudice "is a human characteristic but an American vice." And the Reverend Martin Luther King, Jr., said, "While the race question has economic and sociological and political factors, it is at bottom a moral issue—a question of the dignity of man. Segregation is morally wrong because it relegates persons to the status of things."

The war opened the eyes of black Americans. They saw what their lives could be like and were encouraged to fight for equal treatment.

American women revolutionized the role of women in the American labor force, and ultimately in society and the family. In 1940, 11 million women were employed in the United States, half of them in low-paid clerical, sales, and service jobs. The war brought many more women into the labor force; 49 percent of the women employed in war industries had not worked before the war.

For example, in 1940 only 30,445 women were employed in the automotive and aviation industry with its better-paying jobs ("the foremost mass-production industry in the United States")—that is, 10.5 percent of the workforce. By November 1943 the number of women had risen to 203,300, 26 percent of what was then the total force.

As a consequence of the massive influx of women throughout the labor force, the gap between men's and women's wages narrowed, especially after the National War Labor Board's landmark adoption of the equal-pay-for-equal-work principle.

On the twenty-fifth anniversary of the constitutional amendment granting suffrage to women, President Truman recognized women's contribution to the war effort. He walked a tightrope in his brief statement, saying that to praise women for "doing their share in winning the war would be an act of condescension." But he lauded them anyhow: "In the total war through which we have just passed the home front has been no mere phrase, but truly a battlefront where women bore a major part of the struggle. Women walked into the pages of today's history as good citizens and good soldiers."

Many men assumed that women would return to the kitchen after the war, but a survey discovered that 84 percent of the women employed in manufacturing during the war wanted to continue working.

Industry and unions alike faced the formidable problem of how to make room for both the returning servicemen and the women who had replaced them during the war and wanted to go on working. Both industry and unions applied pressure to restore male veterans to their wage-earning jobs, and women workers had to fight a variety of discriminatory practices in transfers, layoffs, recalls, and violations of their seniority rights. Women walked picket lines outside plant employment offices and union halls, usually in a losing cause. Most of them were dismissed as men were released from military service and plants cut back to peacetime production.

Another war-based tremor rumbled through American society with the emergence of the political extremism that would swiftly degenerate into the "politics of fear" of the McCarthy era. Here Truman was troubled but not much help.

Before the war was over, the growing ideological and political tensions with the Soviet Union spilled over at home. Some Americans, by perceiving and capitalizing on threats in the shadows, endangered the very freedoms of speech, press, and belief they feared for. Those alarmed enough by communism to be willing to smother freedom of speech did not have to wait for a senator from Wisconsin to lead them.

On June 6, 1945, with the ink of Germany's surrender barely dry, the Federal Bureau of Investigation arrested six persons after finding classified documents in the office of the small magazine *Amerasia*, which supported the Chinese Communists. Among those arrested was John Stewart Service, a Foreign Service expert on China who had served with Lieutenant General Joseph Stilwell, had studied the Chinese Communists firsthand, and had been forced out of China by U.S. Ambassador Patrick J. Hurley.

United States policy sought a reconciliation between the Chinese Nationalists and the Chinese Communists, but conservative Ambassador Hurley argued that the Communists should be supplied with arms to fight the Japanese only through Chiang Kai-shek—which would give the Nationalists a veto over the Communists. John Service and his professional Foreign Service colleagues disagreed and tried to persuade the State Department to win the Communists' friendship because they would be major players in China after the war.

Ambassador Hurley, enraged by what he regarded as personal disloyalty, broke up the group of State Department China experts who had opposed him. And he won support in Washington for his policy of obtaining Chiang's consent for any help sent to the Communists. John Service returned to Washington the very day Truman became President and subsequently briefed various editors on the China situation, including Philip J. Jaffe, the coeditor of *Amerasia,* which was already under FBI surveillance.

Navy Secretary Forrestal was told about the *Amerasia* case on May 28, because one of those against whom charges were being brought was a navy lieutenant. Anticipating that the press would give the affair an anti–Soviet Union cast while President Truman was busily negotiating with Stalin, Forrestal telephoned J. Edgar Hoover, director of the FBI, and urged caution in order not to embarrass the President. Then Forrestal called the White House to make sure the President was fully informed.

Acting Secretary of State Grew went to see Truman and protested that Forrestal was interfering with prosecution of the case. As a result,

Truman angrily ordered the Department of Justice to proceed with its investigation; he did not care who wanted it stopped or who would be hurt by it. Sensitive to any charges of undue influence on the investigation, Truman put his weight on the side of security.

Amerasia editor Jaffe and one other man were found guilty and fined. Service was arrested but never indicted, and the State Department returned him to duty.

The *Amerasia* case was one early-warning signal of a tidal wave of postwar hysteria. Other early signs that spring included the efforts of Congressman John Rankin of Mississippi, chairman of the House Veterans' Committee, to force medical news reporters like Albert Deutsch and Albert Q. Maisel to reveal their sources for articles criticizing patient care by the Veterans Administration. Such incidents foreshadowed an era of controversial and divisive events such as Truman's Federal Employees Loyalty and Security Program, the trial of Alger Hiss, and the fear-mongering of Senator Joseph R. McCarthy.

Truman made a serious mistake when Leo Crowley, the foreign economic administrator, and Acting Secretary of State Grew asked him to sign an order authorizing the Foreign Economic Administration and the State Department to cut back on Lend-Lease as soon as Germany surrendered. He was told that Roosevelt had approved but not signed the order. Under it, only Lend-Lease matériel needed for the war effort against Japan or for completing industrial plants would still be shipped. This made sense to Truman; he was fully aware that the diversion of wartime Lend-Lease funds to pay for reconstruction in Europe was a political hot potato in Washington. On May 11 he signed the order.

This unleashed an international storm. Interpreting the order simplistically, Crowley slapped an immediate embargo on all shipments to the Soviet Union and other European nations and even had ships turned around, returned to port, and unloaded.

Stalin indignantly told Harry Hopkins that the order to curtail Lend-Lease was an example of American enmity toward the Soviet Union and that if Truman meant to pressure the Soviet Union, he was making a fundamental mistake.

Seeing how the order was being interpreted and how Stalin was reacting, Truman rescinded it and ruled that the ships be sent out again. He did not want to risk having the Soviet Union fail to help finish off the war against Japan. Lend-Lease to the Soviet Union would be phased down gradually. Angry both at Crowley and Grew and at himself, Truman swore he would get rid of Roosevelt's hold-over aides and build his own team to whom he could delegate serious matters with confidence.

In contrast, self-styled anti–Soviet Union hard-liner George Kennan drafted a memorandum saying in part, "I know of no justification, either economic or political, for any further granting of Lend-Lease aid to Russia . . . without equivalent political advantage to our people."

Truman received a telegram from Churchill on May 28, emphasizing his concern that American assistance to Britain would be decreased. This sent Truman into discussions with congressional leaders, where he stressed the need for the Allies to continue every effort to win the war against Japan. He acknowledged that the Lend-Lease Act did not authorize postwar use of Lend-Lease aid. But this still left a major question: Since V-E Day did not mean the war was over, could Lend-Lease materials be used against Japan?

The wartime Lend-Lease program, which gave out the equivalent of $42 billion and equipped thousands of foreign soldiers, was one of the great weapons through which the United States served as "the arsenal of democracy." And Truman was convinced the program had saved many American lives. Expecting that the Soviet Union would join the war against Japan, the Lend-Lease budget submitted to Congress for the year following V-E Day included a contingency sum of $935 million for the Soviet Union.

Later, when Truman ordered the Foreign Economic Administration to discontinue all Lend-Lease operations, Attlee and Churchill objected, and Acheson called the decision "ill-considered." Of course, the economic repercussions of the war continued; and years later Truman agreed that this termination, too, had been a grave mistake.

The war built up pressures for basic changes in the way the American military establishment was to be organized to fight future wars. The twin competitive Pacific campaigns—one led by the U.S. Army through New Guinea and the Philippines and the other by the Navy and Marine Corps through Tarawa and Okinawa—especially pointed up the power and rivalries of the individual military services.

Truman believed strongly that the military should no longer be run by separate and independent civilian secretaries and an interservice military committee, the Joint Chiefs of Staff; as a result, the President became the vortex of controversy in the long, bitter postwar battle over military "unification."

When Senator Truman had been the nominee for vice president, he had published an article in *Collier's* magazine, expressing his disgust at how bureaucrats and interservice rivalry were damaging the war effort through "a dreary succession of wastes, duplications and ugly conflict." He urged that the Joint Chiefs of Staff be replaced with a centralized General Staff and that Congress put "every element of America's defense under one authoritative, responsible head." He said that the war would have ended much earlier if the army and navy had fought the enemy as they fought each other.

Inside the military, General Marshall and the army led the drive for a single secretary of defense and a single chief of staff. Airpower advocates in the Army Air Corps campaigned for a separate air force. The navy and Secretary Forrestal vehemently opposed unification; Forrestal saw the battle over future military organization as army versus navy and predicted that the army would prevail.

The future roles and missions of each of the services had to be thought through afresh. In addition, who would control the new technologies that had come out of the war, such as the long-range bomber and the atomic bomb, and how could an effective intelligence organization be organized?

On June 13 Truman told Forrestal that he wanted a single military command at the top, but he would still keep the War and Navy Departments as separate entities. When Forrestal suggested that the State Department also be involved in such a plan, Truman said "there wasn't much material in the State Department to work with." But he wanted to review the whole question of government organization to create a more effective machinery.

Forrestal immediately enlisted Ferdinand Eberstadt, a former business associate who had worked with the War Production Board, to make a study of postwar military organization. Eberstadt's 250-page report was completed by September 25 and became a principal basis for the first unification act adopted two years later.

That act was a compromise. It called for three separate military departments—army, navy, and air force—each headed by a civilian of cabinet rank; the continuation of the Joint Chiefs of Staff; and the creation of a number of new agencies, including a National Security Council and a Central Intelligence Agency.

Truman asked Congress to create a single overall Department of National Defense with subordinate army, navy, and air components. After nineteen months of friction and lobbying, he would sign into law the National Security Act of 1947 and nominate Forrestal, the man who had opposed unification, as the first Secretary of Defense. Thus the lessons of two world wars reshaped the American armed forces into a more effective arm for a world superpower.

Almost from the beginning, Truman wanted to change the Roosevelt cabinet he had inherited into a Truman cabinet. The cabinet members who were there when he arrived did not awe him a bit—except perhaps for Henry Stimson. The new President felt an urgent need to surround himself with cabinet members who had political experience, who could persuade the Congress and the public that his policies were correct, and who would be loyal to him.

He wrote on his appointment sheet:

> In my opinion the Cabinet members were simply a Board of Directors appointed by the President, to help him carry out policies of the Government; in many instances the Cabinet could be of tremendous help to the President by offering advice whether he liked it or not but when [the] President [gave] an order they should carry it out. I told them I expected to have a Cabinet I could depend on and take in my confidence and if this confidence was not well placed I would get a Cabinet in which I could place confidence.
>
> I told the Cabinet members a story about President Lincoln—when he was discussing the proclamation—every member of his Cabinet opposed to him making [the] proclamation—he put the question up to the whole Cabinet and they voted No—that is very well, the President voted Yes—that is the way I intend to run this.

He waited only six weeks before announcing the first changes, to take effect on June 30. Then four of the ten cabinet members would be his own appointees. All four of them came from west of the Mississippi River (as did also Secretary of Commerce Henry A. Wallace of Iowa). Judge Lewis B. Schwellenbach of Washington State replaced Frances Perkins as secretary of labor. Robert E. Hannegan of Missouri, chairman of the Democratic National Committee, succeeded Postmaster General Frank C. Walker. Congressman Clinton P. Anderson of New Mexico replaced Claude R. Wickard as secretary of agriculture. And Tom C. Clark of Texas replaced Francis Biddle as attorney general.

Biddle had had an extra strike against him. Despite the wishes of Senator Truman of Missouri, he had refused to replace Maurice M. Milligan as U.S. district attorney for the Western District of Missouri; Milligan had prosecuted political boss Tom Pendergast. Two weeks after Truman became President, he got rid of Milligan himself.

Truman was eager to drop Secretary of State Edward Stettinius but wisely waited until after the San Francisco conference establishing the United Nations. He had already promised the job to the sixty-six-year-old James F. Byrnes. Stettinius, the President noted, was handsome and amiable "but never an idea new or old."

Another reason Truman wanted to replace Stettinius was that under the law at the time the secretary of state became President if Truman should become incapacitated or die. There was, of course, no vice president. Stettinius had never held elective office, while Byrnes had served in both the House of Representatives and the Senate. This was important to Truman; he recommended to Congress that the line of succession be changed; instead of having the secretary of state next in line, the speaker of the House should become the President's (or the vice president's) successor, followed by the president pro tempore of the Senate. In the meantime, the secretary of state, Truman felt, had better be qualified for the presidency; he wrote much later with faint praise, "At this time I regarded Byrnes as the man best qualified."

As soon as the San Francisco conference was finished, Truman appointed Byrnes as secretary of state and nominated Stettinius to represent the United States at the United Nations. Truman was convinced of Byrnes' ability, although Samuel I. Rosenman, a Texas-born New York judge and speechwriter for Roosevelt, warned him that Byrnes was always thinking primarily of himself. Years later, Truman told an interviewer, "After I got to be President, I knew every time Jimmy and I talked that he thought it ought to be the other way around. He ought to be sitting where I was sitting."

Truman announced one more cabinet change on July 6, just before leaving for Potsdam: Fred M. Vinson, a Kentuckian who was the director of war mobilization, to replace Henry Morgenthau, Jr., as secretary of the Treasury. Morgenthau had come to Truman just the day before and asked to accompany him to Potsdam, presumably to further the Morgenthau Plan, which would make Germany a purely agricultural country. Truman did not like the Morgenthau Plan, and when he refused to take Morgenthau to Potsdam, the secretary resigned. He had been in the office for more than eleven years.

While Truman was in Potsdam, Morgenthau asked that his replacement's appointment be made effective as soon as possible. Truman sent Vinson's nomination to the Senate on July 16, and it was confirmed the following day.

Now Wallace, Ickes, Forrestal, and Stimson were the only members of the Roosevelt cabinet left.

Chapter 10

"The Architects of the Better World"

Harry Truman was certain that a peaceful postwar world would require that the United States, Britain, and the Soviet Union work together. After World War I, the United States—vast, continental, self-absorbed—had refused to join the common effort to form a "league" of nations. After World War II, could America's leaders persuade the people and their representatives to choose a different course?

A direct attack on the American Pacific Fleet had been required to provoke the United States into combat when the second worldwide war had already been raging for two years. By 1945 the lesson some Americans drew from the two bloody global wars was that they ought to stay out of the world's endless conflicts. American isolationism was not dead, and U.S. participation in a future organization of nations was not incvitable. If the farmer-president from Missouri had been indifferent, it might never have happened. But Truman was determined.

Both Roosevelt and Truman believed fervently in the need for an international organization to prevent a third world war. Truman had no illusions about the difficulty of creating such an organization; perfecting the constitutional foundation of the United States, he observed, had required many trials and changes, even a civil war. He had studied King Henry IV of France's "Grand Design," which in the sixteenth century had proposed a federation of European Protestant states to prevent them being swallowed up by the Catholic House of Hapsburg. He had read Woodrow Wilson on the League of Nations and knew precisely how a small group of "willful men," to use Wilson's epithet, had sideswiped American participation.

Roosevelt, of course, had already pursued his vision of a "United Nations" as the bulwark of peace. The Big Three foreign ministers, with China as an honorary member, lay down the blueprint for such an organization at Dumbarton Oaks in Washington, D.C., in September 1944. Their efforts were so widely admired that Thomas E. Dewey, Roosevelt's opponent in the presidential elections that fall, chose not to make them an issue.

Still, many influential Americans regarded the proposal of a "united nations" as foolish idealism. To them, the world had to remain divided into Bismarckian spheres of influence and alliances of nations; it could not be ordered by international parliaments and canons of world law. Powerful nations, they were convinced, would never surrender significant parts of their sovereignty; the world would continue to be fueled by self-interest.

An elegant exchange of letters between the diplomat-intellectual George Kennan and his fellow foreign service officer, the Soviet Union expert Charles E. "Chip" Bohlen, expressed these two basic and contrary views about postwar Europe. Kennan candidly expounded his position in a long, pessimistic letter from Moscow: the plans for the United Nations should be buried.

Bohlen replied just as frankly that some of Kennan's suggestions were naïve—"as practical suggestions they are utterly impossible" in a democracy. The Soviet Union, he asserted, "is here to stay, as one of the major factors in the world." Abandoning the United Nations would be a tremendous mistake, and accepting a Soviet sphere of influence in Europe "would compound the felony."

"As hopeless as the outlook seemed, the United States must try to get along with the Soviets," Bohlen wrote. And one important value of the United Nations would be to prevent the United States "from slipping back into isolationism."

Walter Lippmann, the respected conservative commentator and columnist, was also convinced that relying on international cooperation could not sustain the peace. He advocated self-interested Great Power collaboration. His book *U.S. Foreign Policy* preached the spheres-of-influence viewpoint. It became an instant best-seller, and a paperback edition was among the books the U.S. armed forces distributed to the troops during the war. Lippmann and those who agreed with him were ready to involve the United States in a new system of military alliances like those that had already dragged the world into two global bloodbaths.

Lippmann pursued his spheres-of-influence logic further with a book entitled *U.S. War Aims,* in which he proposed granting the Soviet Union an area of dominance in Eastern Europe. This new book, however, found little acceptance.

Senator Robert Taft of Ohio, himself a most conservative man, was among those who spoke out against Lippmann's position; he said "if world federalism was impractical, a postwar military alliance as advocated by Walter Lippmann and others was frightening." It would lead to American imperialism.

A pragmatic question posed by both those who advocated spheres of influence and those who favored international organization was: How would the Soviet Union meld with the free world, how could communism be contained? Even before Nazi Germany was defeated, some in the West saw Soviet containment as the key to postwar peace. Truman thought that Soviet participation was essential to a United Nations organization.

Both Roosevelt and Truman were committed to persuading the leaders of both U.S. political parties to support an international organization. Both presidents wanted to avoid repeating Woodrow Wilson's debacle. To this end, they made sure that Republicans as well as Democrats were included in the U.S. delegation to the San Francisco conference that would establish the organization. Truman instructed Secretary of State Stettinius to consult Senators Thomas Connally and Arthur II. Vandenberg, the ranking Democratic and Republican members of the Senate Foreign Relations Committee, about his every move. Stettinius was also to call Truman at the end of each session and at any hour and keep him informed. Truman was prepared to intervene if he were needed.

Truman talked to the United States delegates for the first time on his second day in the presidency, just before they left for San Francisco. He assured them that he was willing to transfer to the new organization enough power to prevent another major war.

The question of national sovereignty hung over all considerations of the emerging U.N. Charter. Truman hoped that in time the world could operate under a legislative system that echoed that of the United States, but he recognized it was not possible at this stage of national rivalries.

The delegates went to San Francisco with directives agreed on at Dumbarton Oaks the previous fall and modified to some degree with Truman's approval. They wanted to include in the purposes of the United Nations a statement on the respect for human rights and fundamental freedoms. The Dumbarton Oaks proposal had referred to this only in the chapter on economic and social cooperation. Truman preferred a world "bill of rights." And the U.S. delegation wanted to empower the General Assembly to discuss any question and to admit new members—and to provide for a conference of the U.N. members to review the Charter.

Truman instructed the U.S. delegation to cast the United States' vote to admit into membership the two Soviet republics of Russia and the Ukraine, as Roosevelt had promised at Yalta, in order to stimulate Soviet enthusiasm for the world organization. Stalin had originally proposed that the Soviets be given sixteen votes, one for each republic of the Soviet Union; Roosevelt had countered that then the United States should be given forty-eight votes, one for each state. Stalin had quickly abandoned his demand.

At 7:35 P.M. on April 25, Truman opened the conference by speaking from the White House over the major radio networks. He told the delegates of forty-seven nations gathered in San Francisco, "You members of the conference are to be the architects of the better world." He reminded them that they were not supposed to draft a peace treaty or settle such issues as territories, boundaries, and reparations. Their job was to set up "the essential organization to keep the peace. . . . We can no longer permit any nation, or group of nations, to attempt to settle their arguments with bombs and bayonets."

Secretary Stettinius' first progress report to the President from San Francisco emphasized two points: the need to provide for amending the Charter as conditions changed and the conviction that the United Nations Organization must be based on the unity of the major powers.

But not everyone was sanguine. At Stettinius' request, Ambassador Averell Harriman held three off-the-record press conferences in San Francisco and hammered away at his view of the Soviet Union and its intentions. He said:

> I told [the press] we would have real difficulties with the Soviet Union in the postwar period. This came as a great shock to many of them. At one meeting, I explained that our objectives and the Kremlin objectives were irreconcilable; they wanted to communize the world, and we wanted a free world. But I added that we would have to find ways to compose our differences if we were to live in peace

on this small planet. Two men were so shocked that they got up and left . . . some even suggested that I should be recalled as Ambassador.

The two journalists who walked out, Walter Lippmann and radio newscaster Raymond Gram Swing, were horrified by Harriman's insistence that U.S. and Soviet objectives were irreconcilable and believed the ambassador was exaggerating the differences between the two powers.

Two days after the conference opened, its steering committee faced the persistently difficult question of Poland. Truman did not want Poland to become a member of the United Nations until its government was reorganized in keeping with the Yalta agreements. Soviet Foreign Minister Molotov pressed to have Poland admitted immediately. The arguments raged back and forth until Paul-Henri Spaak, Belgium's foreign minister, in an emotional speech, pleaded that this controversy not stymie the conference. He offered a compromise: Poland would be represented as soon as the powers that had sponsored the conference recognized its government. Spaak's resolution passed 33–0.

But Molotov would not let the matter rest. On May 1 Mexico and Chile proposed the admission of pro-fascist Argentina to the conference in the cause of Western Hemisphere solidarity. Molotov used this debate to argue Poland's case again. Why admit Argentina, which had helped the enemy during the war, while Poland was kept out?

In San Francisco, Eden, Molotov, and Stettinius discussed among themselves what was to be done with "war criminals." Understandably, "war crimes" were one of the last multinational issues to be thought through. Roosevelt had repeatedly recommended a U.N. commission to investigate war crimes, but at his death the Allies had still not decided what should happen to the Axis' "war criminals." Now Truman appointed Associate Justice Robert H. Jackson of the United States Supreme Court to represent the United States and serve as chief counsel when European war criminals were prosecuted.

What was a war criminal? A leader who had lost a war? War criminals were always scarce on the winning side. The debate among the Allies—and inside Washington—over what was to be done with war criminals was intense. Churchill wanted the Nazi leaders shot without trial. He favored this so-called executive action because international law did not cover many of the Nazis' horrendous crimes.

Truman was resolved that they be tried and face justice under law; he felt Churchill's solution would both violate principles of justice and enable the Germans to convert the Nazi leaders into martyrs. Stalin also wanted them to be tried. In Britain, the war cabinet, learning that Truman and Stalin favored an international trial, agreed that the six top Nazis should be tried—and then shot.

The foreign ministers finally decided that the leading Nazis would be brought before a military tribunal consisting of representatives of the United States, the United Kingdom, the Soviet Union, and France, with perhaps three representatives from smaller U.N. members. Most other war criminals were returned to and tried in the countries where their crimes had been committed.

The victors had no legal basis for extending the concept of "war crimes" beyond those crimes directly related to the waging of war. Lawyers like Henry Stimson had trouble punishing Nazis for the torture, killing, and use as slave labor of millions of people—separate from waging war. Stimson especially opposed an international court trying "those responsible for excesses committed within Germany both before and during the war which have no relation to the conduct of the war . . . in precisely the same way that any foreign court would be without jurisdiction to try those who were guilty of, or condoned, lynching in our own country." (The parallel was not worthy of Stimson. The Nazis' crimes had been official; lynching was private murder.)

Two radically new categories of international crimes were finally agreed on: in addition to crimes related to the conduct of war, the international court would also deal with crimes against peace and crimes against humanity. The definition of war crimes was thus expanded to include waging aggressive war; that is, crimes against peace.

Stimson felt more comfortable with this, because for him "the central moral problem is war and not its methods." Aggression would be the crucial fact, not trying to judge whether a war had been fought by criminal means. And individuals as well as governments would be held responsible: "the man who makes or plans to make aggressive war is a criminal." For the first time, aggressive war was declared to be a crime punishable under law.

The principle, Stimson wrote, went back into the distant past to the first case of murder in which the tribe replaced the victim's family as the judge and punisher and in which killing was first treated as an offense against the community. War, like murder, Stimson said, is justifiable only in self-defense.

An International Military Tribunal was established and, meeting in Nuremberg, Germany, eventually found twenty-two Europeans guilty of war crimes under the new rules. (Nine leading Nazis were hanged; Göring took cyanide.) Although aggressive war was now recognized as a war crime, no one had yet figured out how to identify and bring to justice war criminals on the winning side.

Truman summoned Stettinius to the White House for a face-to-face discussion of the unresolved problems in creating the United Nations. A major sticking point was the proposed use of the veto by the major powers to preserve a large degree of their national sovereignty. At Yalta, the "sponsoring powers" of the United Nations had agreed that each of them would retain a veto in the Security Council. In San Francisco, this proposal came under severe attack from the smaller countries.

Truman knew that unless the Charter provided for a Great Power veto, the Senate would not ratify the United States' membership. Therefore, the American delegation insisted on having veto power over any amendments to the U.N. Charter but bent a little to allow settlements without unanimity if the Great Powers were not involved in the dispute.

Truman also instructed Stettinius to work for an international court of justice that would eventually have compulsory jurisdiction. And he accepted the reality that other nations would not agree to a prohibition against withdrawing from the United Nations Organization.

The main issue still dividing the major powers was whether a permanent member of the Security Council could use the veto to prevent discussion of a dispute. The Russians demanded that right; the other sponsoring powers and France opposed it. Truman felt such use of the veto would seriously hobble the Security Council.

Stettinius raised the question to Truman of whether Stalin actually understood the position his delegation was taking on discussions in the Security Council. Truman instructed Ambassador Harriman and Harry Hopkins, who were both in Moscow at the time, to go over it with Stalin in person. Hopkins reported back to Truman on June 6 that Stalin indeed had not understood the problem. A lengthy debate had taken place in which Molotov had participated, and Stalin finally overruled his foreign minister and accepted the American position. That impasse was over. No single state could stop the Security Council from hearing a dispute.

The final objection the Soviet delegations raised at the conference was against the proposal that any nation in the General Assembly could bring any issue to the attention of the Security Council. The vast majority of the smaller nations demanded that this provision be adopted; the Soviet delegations opposed it. Again the issue had to be resolved in Moscow. Truman asked Stettinius to take it up with Molotov, and if necessary the President was prepared to talk with Stalin directly. But Molotov agreed to a modification by which the General Assembly could discuss and refer to the Security Council any question involving international peace and security.

Truman was delighted when this last barrier was surmounted but kept things in perspective with humor. He wrote Bess, "Yesterday was a hectic day. Had both good news and bad. Stalin agreed to our interpretation of the veto at San Francisco and a reconsideration of the Polish question, but we lost the election in Montana and the Republicans are jubilant over it."

In another letter written on Saturday, June 16, he noted that the deed to the family house had arrived and that meant his mother and sister would have a rent-free home for the rest of their lives. He said the work of the presidency seemed to agree with him; he had gained twelve pounds since January. And he reported that General Alexander M. Patch, Jr., had come by and presented him with Hermann Göring's baton. He wrote:

> I always get those dirty Nazis mixed up but it makes no difference. Anyway it's the fat Marshal's insignia of office. It is about a foot and a half long, made of ivory inlaid with gold eagles and iron crosses with diamond studded ends and platinum rings around it for engraving. Must have cost several thousand dollars—maybe forty—to make. Can you imagine a fat pig like that strutting around with a forty thousand dollar bauble—the poor taxpayer's expense and making 'em like it? It goes to a military museum.

On Monday he hosted a dinner for 110 guests to honor Eisenhower and in the afternoon pinned on the general a second Oak Leaf Cluster to the Distinguished Service Medal. Afterwards, Truman wrote home,

"It was a gaudy affair if gold braid counts." But he added a more heartfelt comment to Bess:

> P.S. Eisenhower's party was a grand success. I pinned a medal on him in the afternoon. He is a nice fellow and a good man. He's done a whale of a job. They are running him for President, which is O.K. with me. I'd turn it over to him now if I could.

The next day, Truman flew to Olympia, Washington, to spend a few days relaxing as the guest of Governor Mon C. Wallgren, an old friend and a former colleague on the Truman Committee. It was the first nonstop cross-country flight by a President as well as his first chance since taking office to escape the Washington routine. At Olympia, he did some hiking and salmon fishing, dutifully worked at his papers, exchanged messages with Churchill and Stalin, and called and sought the support of senators whose votes he thought he needed for the U.N. Charter. His stay with the governor was extended until the U.N. conference was ready to wind up.

Monday, June 25, he flew to Portland and toured a veterans hospital; then he went on to San Francisco to address the closing day of the U.N. conference. He was driven to the Fairmont Hotel in a seventy-five-car parade under a rain of ticker tape and through cheering throngs.

The next afternoon at three, Truman accompanied the American delegation to the Veterans' War Memorial Building to witness the signing of the United Nations Charter. He stood at Secretary Stettinius' right shoulder while he signed for the United States and then shook the secretary's hand.

Following the ceremonies, they walked to the Opera House, where Truman addressed the representatives of the fifty nations attending the final session of the conference. He called the Charter "a solid structure upon which we can build a better world . . . you have won a victory against war itself." He said, "If we had had this Charter a few years ago—and above all, the will to use it—millions now dead would be alive." And then, in a burst of hopefulness, he stretched out his arms and exclaimed, "Oh, what a great day this can be in history."

Afterwards, he flew via Salt Lake City to Kansas City and was driven the fifteen miles to Independence, coming home to see family and friends for the first time since he became President. He was rested from his stay in Olympia and exuberant about the triumph of the San Francisco conference. Perched on the back of an open car, he smiled and waved his gray hat to the crowd. Some people were not sure whether to call him "Harry" or "Mr. President."

That evening, he was the guest of honor at a surprise stag dinner of his World War I "buddies," the veterans of Battery D of the 129th Field Artillery. Then he spoke in the crowded, flag-decorated auditorium of the Reorganized Latter-Day Saints (the branch of the church that had stayed in Independence and not gone west). Just behind him sat his old schoolteacher, Miss Caroline Stoll, now age eighty-four. He joked that he wished he had been able to fill the hall this way when he was campaigning and told them the story of how he learned he was President two months earlier. He promised that what had been accomplished at San Francisco was "the first step" toward winning the peace and asked for their support. The ceremony ended with a presentation of bouquets of roses to Bess and Margaret.

When Truman moved on to Kansas City, his former barber Frank Spina came over and gave him a haircut in the President's office in the Federal Courthouse. Driving to the University of Kansas City, Truman, without warning, stopped at Eddie Jacobson's Westport Men's Wear Store at 39th and Main streets and, trailed by Secret Service men, walked behind the counter with Eddie to find some white shirts with a 15½ collar and 33 sleeve length. The store was out of stock in those war days of short supply, but once the story hit the newspapers, Truman was inundated with white shirts.

After the stop to see his old partner, he sat under an oak tree during the university's fiftieth anniversary celebration, and that evening, at the Municipal Auditorium, the university awarded him its first honorary degree of doctor of laws. Years before, he had studied law there for two years but had never graduated; he was deeply touched. "I can't thank you enough," he said. "I don't dare to stop and think about it, because I would just stand up here and shed tears; and that is not what you want to see me do."

He spelled out to the university gathering the importance of what had been achieved in San Francisco; he looked forward to "an age of law and an age of reason." He drew a hopeful parallel: "Whenever the States have a quarrel or argument they don't call out the Army, they call the Supreme Court and abide by its decision. There isn't a reason in the world why we cannot do that internationally."

He impressed on them the changes occurring so rapidly. He had just flown from Salt Lake City to Kansas City in three and a half hours, while his grandfather Solomon Young had made that trip repeatedly between 1846 and 1870 and it had taken him exactly three months each way. "That is the age in which we live."

His mother saw him off at the Kansas City airport; her final words to him were: "Now, you be a good boy, Harry."

Four days later, in Washington, Harry brought the Charter of the United Nations to the Senate of the United States. (The Senate had begun the day by unanimously confirming James Byrnes as Secretary of State.) Legislators and their guests filled the floor of the chamber; Lord Halifax, the British ambassador, and Henri Bonnet, the French ambassador, sat in the diplomatic gallery; and the visitors' galleries were jammed to the doors. Standees pressed against the walls.

The occasion was in vivid contrast to that day only twenty-six years earlier when President Woodrow Wilson had asked the Senate to adopt the treaty that would have made the United States a member of the League of Nations. Then Wilson had not even bothered to appear before the Senate in person, leaving the field to his energetic—and triumphant—opponents.

Truman, wearing a gray suit and his dotted bow tie, grinned broadly and waved a bit self-consciously as he was escorted up the aisle by a senatorial committee. This was familiar territory. Walking behind Truman, his military aide, Brigadier General Harry H. Vaughan, carried the blue-bound Charter. The President handed it up to Senator Kenneth McKellar, president pro tempore of the Senate, setting off a standing demonstration in the hall. His talk was brief, simple, and forceful. He asked the Senate to ratify the treaty quickly. He said, "This Charter points down the only road to enduring peace. There is no other."

Harry Truman would always regard the acceptance of the United Nations Charter a highlight of his career as a public servant.

Ever since he had graduated from high school in Independence in 1901, he had carried in his wallet these prophetic lines from Tennyson's "Locksley Hall." The paper had worn out, and he had recopied the lines over and over again:

> For I dipt into the future, as far as human eye could
>   see,

Saw the Vision of the world, and all the wonder that
    could be;
Saw the heavens fill with commerce, argosies of magic
    sails,
Pilots of the purple twilight, dropping down with costly
    bales;
Heard the heavens filled with shouting, and there rain'd
    a ghastly daw
From the nations' airy navies grappling in the central
    blue;
Far along the world-wide whisper of the south-wind
    rushing warm,
With the standards of the people plunging throw' the
    thunder-storm;
Till the war-drum throbb'd no longer, and the battle-
    flags were furl'd
In the Parliament of Man, the Federation of the world
There the common sense of most shall hold a fretful
    realm in awe,
And the kindly earth shall slumber, lapt in universal
    law.

Chapter 11
The Shaping of Postwar Europe

Europe was in chaos. Much of central Europe, across which the war had been fought, lay in ruins. Millions of rootless refugees, formerly enslaved people, and defeated Germans were struggling to survive without adequate food, electricity, coal, or jobs. The situation was traumatic for the victors also; in the coming months, rations in Britain would have to be cut below even wartime levels. The U.S. Department of Agriculture estimated that Europe (not including Britain) would need twelve million tons of food in the next year to avoid widespread starvation. Assistant Secretary of War John McCloy returned from Germany in late April and urged Truman to take immediate action.

Truman felt a responsibility for the survival of millions who were displaced from their homes and without means to support themselves. He observed, "A chaotic and hungry Europe is not fertile ground in which stable, democratic and friendly governments can be reared."

Not everyone shared his compassion. De Gaulle wanted economic controls clamped on Germany and demanded that France be given charge of the east bank of the Rhine from Cologne to the Swiss border. He was to write, "Yesterday was the time for battle; the hour for settling accounts had come."

Rehabilitating a devastated Europe was an awesome job. On May 16 Stimson cautioned that the nations of Western Europe would need to be fortified against famine-induced political revolution and Communist uprisings. The large wheat surpluses of the United States and Canada should be used, he recommended, to feed Europe's hungry.

Truman thought another, longer-term effective move would be to establish a free flow of trade between the food-producing areas of Hungary, Romania, and the Ukraine and the coal-producing industrial countries in the West. He envisioned linking the Rhine and the Danube with a network of canals and creating an international web of free waterways.

The part of Germany occupied by the Soviet Union held the smallest proportion of people but produced the largest proportion of food. Churchill, anticipating that the Russians would use this food to feed themselves, urged that it be used to help feed the Germans as well. And he wanted it fairly distributed among the zones of Germany.

Truman proposed that the lending power of the Export-Import Bank be increased to $3.5 billion to make more money available to hard-pressed Italy, Poland, Yugoslavia, Czechoslovakia, and Greece. But he cautiously advised that Congress appropriate such funds a year at a time so that the United States would not be committed to long-term disbursements. He later summed up, "I believe that it must be the policy of the United States to support free peoples who are resisting attempted subjugation by armed minorities or by outside pressures."

How the neophyte President handled these immediate European problems would determine in great part how the energetic, inventive continent—now shattered by depression and dictatorship, mass murder and massive war—would mend and reinvent itself.

At the suggestion of both Stimson and Forrestal, Truman invited former President Herbert Hoover to counsel him on how to deal with the threat of starvation in Europe; Hoover had had practical experience with a similar crisis when he had been in charge of food relief after World War I.

Roosevelt had exiled Hoover from the White House ever since 1933. During the intervening years, Hoover had not been a political innocent sitting on the sidelines. He had been obsessed with Roosevelt and participated in Joseph Kennedy's plans for a book to expose Roosevelt's alleged duplicity in steering the United States into war. He told right-wing columnist Westbrook Pegler that Roosevelt had solicited advertising for his son James' radio stations. Paradoxically, he had also let it be known that he was eager to take the place of the aging Stimson as secretary of war.

Some men around Truman, such as Robert Lovett, Brehon Somervell, and House Speaker Sam Rayburn, were strongly opposed to giving the former Republican President any role in solving the administration's problems, but Truman defended Hoover as "the best man that I know of, and he'll do the job for me."

The two Presidents met on May 28 and talked for forty minutes. Immediately afterwards, Truman, following Hoover's advice, told the War Department to ship a million tons of grain a month to Europe on an emergency basis. Even though Hoover continued privately to call him "really dumb," Truman eventually would appoint Hoover as the honorary chairman of the Famine Emergency Committee and send him to visit the famine areas of the world. Hoover was pleased at being asked to contribute.

What were the facts of life that in the spring of 1945 played significant roles in shaping Europe's future? The Soviet Union occupied and was determined to dominate central and southeastern Europe. Vast American and British armies were camped deep in German territory that, all had agreed, would become part of the Soviet zone of occupation. With the end of the fighting, Lend-Lease shipments to the Allies had to be reexamined. The Polish deadlock was unresolved (in Western eyes) and remained a major frustration. The United Nations conference brought to the surface differences as well as agreements. De Gaulle insisted on moving French troops into Italy. The rule of Trieste was in violent dispute with Marshal Tito of Yugoslavia. If postwar Europe was to be given any coherent shape, all these situations had to be resolved promptly.

When time allowed for perspective, the end of World War II in Europe would be seen as the culmination of a great thirty-one-year civil war that had begun in 1914 and, with a midcourse truce, continued until 1945. In the process, the Austro-Hungarian, Ottoman, and Czarist empires had disappeared; France had been crushed and occupied; Britain bled white; and Germany defeated twice. The long war had not only killed tens of millions of human beings but destroyed the imperial centralizations of power and drained the Great Powers' ability to reach out and colonize the less industrialized parts of the globe. It ended European domination of the world.

Churchill continued to sound the tocsin against the Soviet Union. On May 4 he totaled up the Soviet presence in Europe for Truman, pointing out that when the German armies surrendered, the territory the Soviet Union controlled "would include the Baltic Provinces, all of Germany to the occupational line, all Czechoslovakia, a large part of Austria, the whole of Yugoslavia, Hungary, Romania, Bulgaria, until Greece in her present tottering condition is reached. It would include all the great capitals of middle Europe including Berlin, Vienna, Budapest, Belgrade, Bucharest and Sofia." This, Churchill warned, "constitutes an event in the history of Europe to which there has been no parallel."

At the end of the European "civil war," the Soviet Union looked back at a history of repeated threats and invasions from the West and resolved to ensure its own safety by controlling its Eastern European neighborhood. The United States, an ocean away, could be more magnanimous and more optimistic. Maybe it was, as Truman believed, the difference between the men; or maybe it was where the men sat. In any case, their conflicting views led to a divided Europe, the Warsaw Pact, NATO, and the Cold War.

Although Roosevelt and Truman both dreamed of maintaining the peace through a new international organization, others who regarded themselves as hardheaded pragmatists believed that postwar Europe had to be reconstructed with the building blocks of the prewar world.

George Kennan, for one, was convinced that the West could not influence events in the areas of Europe under Soviet control "and that it would be undignified and even misleading to keep on acting as though we expected to do so." He feared "this pipe dream of a general European collaboration."

Kennan anticipated, for example, that United Nations Relief and Reconstruction Agency (UNRRA) funds would be used by the Soviet leaders for political gain and not in keeping "with the general altruistic interest in European reconstruction by which our people were motivated." His supposition that self-interest was not a part of the reason for the great American investment in the restoration of Europe was fantasy.

Kennan recommended that the United States establish the limits of Soviet expansion into Europe and "keep ourselves out of the Russian sphere and keep the Russians out of ours." He was willing to write off eastern and southeastern Europe and accept the partition of Germany. Here was the seed of the "containment policy" he would advocate publicly two years later. For him, the Cold-War-to-be was already frozen in place.

The political shape of postwar Germany itself was, of course, a major headache. The question of what treatment should be meted out to Germany divided the Truman administration as did few other issues. Morgenthau, Hull, and Hopkins favored harsh treatment; Stimson and the War Department argued for swift rehabilitation. As George W. Ball, who was to become undersecretary of state, wrote years later, "The dark spectre overhanging Europe in the early postwar years was the threat of a resurgent Germany."

Many Germans were living under no government except the victorious occupying armies, and Truman was eager to take the responsibility for Germany's future out of the hands of the military commanders ruling the separate zones of occupation and place it with an Allied Control Council. Although the generals would remain in command of the individual zones, as a council, they would, he hoped, view Germany whole. Then, Truman felt, Germany would have a chance to avoid complete collapse. He also wanted the council to work to stamp out any reemergence of Nazism and Prussian militarism.

On April 5 John McCloy had warned Eisenhower in Reims against destroying the industrial facilities of Essen, Hannover, and Düsseldorf. Predictably, Eisenhower replied that he would destroy whatever was necessary to defeat the 150,000 German troops fighting "tenaciously" in the Ruhr pocket.

Jean Monnet, the Frenchman who would become the father of the European Community, believed that the Ruhr was the root of the trouble between France and Germany. He wanted to extract the Ruhr from the two countries and make it a separate entity. Stimson, too, favored internationalizing the Ruhr, although he opposed Treasury Secretary Morgenthau's extreme remedy of obliterating the Ruhr's great industrial capacity. Both Stimson and McCloy believed in rebuilding the German economy.

Truman first faced this issue on April 27, the day Russian and American troops met on the Elbe. He conferred with the powerful Informal Policy Committee on Germany (IPCOG), which Roosevelt had appointed the previous month to guide American treatment of Germany. Before the members of the committee gathered, Truman met with Secretary Morgenthau, who persuaded him to look at the plan that Morgenthau and his staff were preparing to eradicate Germany's industrial plant and give the country over to agriculture.

Morgenthau's plan presented the question of Germany's future in stark black and white. Should Germany be pastoral, stripped of industrial and warmaking power, or should it be made industrially strong again, able to play an important economic role in Europe?

When Truman was first asked about the so-called Morgenthau Plan at a press conference on May 2, he denied knowing anything about it. And he came to oppose Morgenthau's proposal to destroy the steelmaking capacity of the Ruhr and Saar areas and to reduce Germany's economy so "that it will be so dependent on imports and exports that Germany cannot by its own devices reconvert to war production." Even before the East-West pressures of the coming Cold War built up, Truman wanted Germany to be politically denazified and economically rebuilt. Right after the Germans surrendered, he said, "Absolute insurance against German or Japanese rearmament—ever again—comes first with us." So much for prophecy.

On May 16 Stimson wrote down Truman's views as they had been given to him orally:

> Early proposals for the treatment of Germany provided for keeping Germany near the margin of hunger as a means of punishment for past misdeeds. I [Truman] have felt that this was a grave mistake. Punish her war criminals in full measure. Deprive her permanently of her weapons, her General Staff, and perhaps her entire army. Guard her governmental action until the Nazi-educated generation has passed from the stage—admittedly a long job. But do not deprive her of the means of building up ultimately a contented Germany interested in following non-militaristic methods of civilization. This must necessarily involve some industrialization, for Germany today has approximately thirty million excess population beyond what can be supported by agriculture alone. The eighty million Germans and Austrians in Central Europe today necessarily swing the balance of the continent. A solution must be found for their future peaceful existence and it is to the interest of the whole world that they should not be driven by stress of hardship into a nondemocratic and necessarily predatory habit of life.

Truman had two broad goals in mind for Germany: He wanted to carry out all the agreements that Roosevelt had made, and he wanted a unified country with a central government in Berlin. (He sought a parallel setup in Austria and Vienna, where 1.2 million Austrians had served in the Wehrmacht.

Inside Germany itself, the intellectual disarray was as intense as the physical. The Nazis had preached effectively that the state, the collective society, came before the individual. (Ironically, their enemies, the Communists, preached precisely the same thing.) But the anti-Fascist Germans who had survived the Third Reich and most of the young postwar German intellectuals sought to restore and emphasize the value of the individual.

Some Germans envisioned their nation becoming a neutral bridge between the Allies. But the Allies themselves would make such a bridge impossible, as each side in the Cold War related to a half-Germany dedicated to its partisan cause. West Germans, at least, would find this relationship beneficial; their economic ties to the West would create an economic resurgence, the *Wirtschaftswunder*. Paradoxically, said one observer, "Prosperity swelled the ranks of the middle class, while at the same time strengthening the respect for discipline, hard work, and political conformism on which the Nazis had capitalized with such success."

After Germany's defeat, Truman transferred more men and ships from Europe to the Pacific in order to finish the war against Japan. At the same time, the American public demanded that he bring home the U.S. troops who would not be going to fight Japan. Both these pressures opposed Churchill's insistence that Truman delay removing American troops from the Soviet zone of Germany and from Europe.

On May 11 Churchill cabled Truman, urging again that the Western forces stay in their advanced positions until the problems with the Russians were settled. Truman reminded Churchill that this would be reneging on their agreement that each power confine itself to its own zone of occupation. Churchill, desperate to hold on to some leverage in the continuing disputes with Stalin, even cabled Truman to ask him to stop the redeployment of American troops from Europe to the Pacific. But Truman still had a war to fight against Japan.

Persistent, Churchill followed up on May 12 with a long, reasoned telegram to Truman spelling out his prediction of what would happen to Europe if the Allied armies disbanded and the Americans sailed to the Pacific. Using a term with which he would later at Fulton, Missouri, define an era, Churchill said, "An iron curtain is drawn down upon their [the Russians'] front. We do not know what is going on behind. There seems little doubt that the whole of the regions east of the line Lübeck-Trieste-Corfu will soon be completely in their hands." He dreaded the "enormous Muscovite advance into the centre of Europe." He warned Truman, "To sum up, this issue of a settlement with Russia before our strength has gone seems to me to dwarf all others."

Finally, Truman could only reassure Churchill that he intended to remove no more troops than were essential for the war in the Pacific.

With Germany's defeat, Truman dispatched two missions to explore the changing relationships among the Allies. On May 19 he asked Harry Hopkins, who was seriously ill, to travel to Moscow and evaluate the Soviet attitudes since the end of the war in Europe. When Byrnes objected privately to sending Hopkins, Truman disregarded him, noting that Hopkins had gone on a similar mission for Roosevelt and he was reputed to be "an advanced 'Liberal' but not a professional one (I consider the latter the lowest form of politician), that he had horse sense and knew how to use it."

Hopkins explained to Forrestal, Harriman, and Bohlen, when they visited him at his home the next day, that he was going to Moscow primarily to try to reduce the widening gap between the United States and the Soviet Union. And he thought it vital that Churchill not maneuver the United States into a bloc against Russia.

Truman sent Joseph E. Davies, the former U.S. ambassador to Moscow, on a simultaneous mission to London to see Churchill. And he instructed Harriman to travel ahead and brief Churchill on Hopkins' Moscow mission and then to continue on to Moscow himself. These assignments were to be preludes to a summit meeting of the Big Three.

They also made Truman sharply aware of another reality; he was taken aback by the fact that "our three ablest foreign relations men should now be old and physically incapacitated—Hull—Davies—Hopkins." The Roosevelt-era diplomatic leaders were wearing out, just as the war was finishing and a new era, with new problems, was beginning. Left in policy positions were less astute men like Stettinius and Byrnes, and still in the wings were the Achesons and Kennans and their generation.

Truman wanted Hopkins especially to make it clear to Stalin that the Americans would carry out their Yalta commitments and they expected the Soviet government to carry out its agreements to the letter. "I told Harry [Hopkins] he could use diplomatic language, or he could use a baseball bat if he thought that was the proper approach to Mr. Stalin," Truman said. He also asked Hopkins to tell Stalin cordially that the President would be glad to see him and thought that since Roosevelt had come to Yalta, it was Stalin's turn to come to the United States.

Truman notified Stalin that Hopkins would arrive with Ambassador

Harriman on May 26 to talk with him personally and report back to the President. And he wrote in his diary with a hint of uncertainty: "So I've sent Hopkins to Moscow and Davies to London. We shall see what we shall see."

Ambassador Davies spent the night of May 26 at Chequers, the official country home of British prime ministers. The next day, coincidentally, Churchill dissolved Britain's wartime political coalition and formed an interim government in anticipation of the forthcoming general elections.

From May 26 to May 29 Davies sat privately with the prime minister for a total of eight hours at Chequers and at 10 Downing Street, where Churchill worked at a huge, round, green-covered table that almost filled the Cabinet Room.

Churchill wanted to meet with Truman before they confronted Stalin at the coming summit conference. Truman thought this was a poor idea: "Stalin already has an opinion we're ganging up on him." At the same time, Churchill picked up the mistaken idea that at the conference Truman wanted to meet with Stalin alone before Churchill joined them. Churchill took this as an affront, "however unintentional."

When Davies returned to Washington, Truman untangled the source of Churchill's annoyance. The prime minister had misunderstood Truman's wish to meet with both Churchill and Stalin individually on the site of the summit meeting and get to know them better; he had never been face to face with either man.

In Moscow, Hopkins and Harriman found Stalin just as anxious to meet with Churchill and Truman as they were to meet with him. Hopkins reviewed the American concerns about Poland, and Stalin listened carefully to his description of the state of American public opinion. Hopkins relayed Truman's feeling that without the public's support he could not continue Roosevelt's policy of cooperation into the postwar period. And at present, he said, Americans believed that the Soviet Union wanted to dominate Poland. According to Harriman, Stalin, ever the hardheaded realist, did not understand why Americans insisted on thinking about Poland in terms of abstract principles or why the United States wanted to interfere with Soviet policy on a subject so important to Soviet security.

But Stalin appreciated that he had to deal with American perceptions. He was ready to discuss which Poles should be invited to Moscow to consult about the organization of a temporary Polish government. But he required that the Warsaw group, in whose loyalty he felt secure, supply the ruling majority of the future Polish government. Hopkins offered names from London and from within Poland. Stalin insisted on a majority from the existing provisional government.

Hopkins recommended to Truman that he approve the final list, which he did on June 1. The United States recognized the Provisional Government of National Unity, and, at Truman's request, so did Britain. But the dispute was not settled; it would be a central point of discussion at the summit conference.

On another subject of immediate importance to Truman and the United States, Stalin promised Hopkins he would deploy the Soviet army in Manchuria by August 8. Of course, there was a quid pro quo: Stalin said the Soviet people had to have a good reason for going to war, and therefore China must accept the Yalta agreements, which provided for Soviet acquisitions in East Asia.

Stalin also told Hopkins he would do everything he could to achieve the unification of China under Chiang Kai-shek. He had reservations about Chiang, he said, but felt no Communist leader was strong enough to unite China.

Stalin expected that Japan would not quit the war if the Allies held to their policy of unconditional surrender. He thought they could achieve the same domination by occupation, and he affirmed that the Russians wanted to participate in that occupation.

Truman appreciated Stalin's confirmation of the Soviet Union's entry into the Pacific war. It seemed undeniable that Soviet participation could reduce the cost in American lives.

While these talks were going on, the three heads of state agreed that the summit conference would take place on July 15 at the town of Potsdam near Berlin. Truman had proposed Alaska, but Potsdam, in the Soviet zone of occupation, was Stalin's choice. Churchill accepted Potsdam and pressed the others to advance the date. He had two reasons: He feared that the American army's withdrawal from its tactical zone in the center of Germany to its occupation zone would embolden the Soviets, and he recognized that he faced an uncertain general election at home. Truman, on the other hand, secretly preferred that the Potsdam Conference be delayed until the American atomic weapon could be tested at Alamogordo, New Mexico—an event he hoped would strengthen his position at the conference.

On June 12 Truman advised Churchill that he could no longer delay withdrawing the U.S. Army from the Soviet zone to the American occupation zone. Despite Churchill's again-repeated warning that this would bring "Soviet power into the heart of Western Europe and the descent of an iron curtain between us and everything to the eastward," Truman was ready to begin pulling back American troops in less than ten days. Only then, when the Western Allies' troops were out of the Soviet zone, could the Allied Control Council be able to function. Churchill, distressed, replied, "Obviously we are obliged to conform to your decision."

Truman also notified Stalin that American troops would begin to withdraw from the Russian zone on June 21. Truman stipulated two provisions: First, American and British garrisons would move into Greater Berlin and U.S. forces would have free access to Berlin—110 miles inside the Soviet zone—by air, road, and rail from Frankfurt and Bremen. And second, adopting a proposal of Churchill's, he required that the Russians leave the British zone in Austria at the same time as the Western Allies pulled back.

Stalin unexpectedly asked that the troops' withdrawal be delayed until July 1 because he planned a massive parade in Moscow on June 24 and his troop commanders would be absent from Germany. Truman acquiesced. The first American troops reached Berlin on July 2. But Stalin totally ignored Truman's point about access to Berlin.

Lord Halifax, with great perception, telegraphed Churchill from Washington on July 7 that "the Americans in dealing with us seem to be more responsive to arguments based upon the danger of economic chaos in European countries than to the balder pleas about the risks of extreme Left Governments or of the spread of Communism." He understood Truman.

Churchill would later write, "On July 1 the United States and British Armies began their withdrawal to their allotted zones, followed by masses of refugees. Soviet Russia was established in the heart of Europe. This was a fateful milestone for mankind."

As war was changing awkwardly but swiftly to peace, an area of Europe that was experiencing intense turmoil was the Balkan Peninsula. Over the centuries, this had been a bloody battleground of ethnic and religious hatreds between subject peoples of the Austro-Hungarian Empire (Roman Catholic) and the Ottoman Empire (Muslim). A Bosnian youth with Serbian roots had assassinated Archduke Franz Ferdinand of Austria in Sarajevo in 1914 and triggered World War I. And the destruction of those two empires by 1918 had released ethnic rebellion and violence.

During World War II, Soviet armies had overrun the Balkan countries, and at Yalta the Soviet Union had agreed to reestablish in them free governments under Allied supervision. But it had unilaterally set up Communist governments in Romania and Bulgaria.

In Romania, the Russians ran the Allied Control Commission without consulting its British and American members. The Communist Party seized control of the government machinery, and Romania was cut off from trade with every nation but the Soviet Union.

In Bulgaria, no American was allowed outside the capital, Sofia, unless accompanied by a Russian. The Russians inspected every shipment of mail brought in for the American Mission. The American member of the Allied Control Commission could not even obtain copies of directives issued in the name of the Commission.

Truman instructed the State Department to remind the Soviet government that it had obligations under the Yalta agreements that prohibited such behavior. The reminder made no difference.

Josip Broz, "Marshal Tito," a Communist and nationalist, headed the Yugoslav National Provisional Government with the support of both the Western Allies and the Soviet Union. He appealed to the Yugoslavs' strong nationalist feelings and ignited an explosive confrontation with Italy in the Trieste area.

The independent Yugoslavia that had emerged out of World War I had been overwhelmed by the Nazi armies in 1941. The Germans set up a ruthless Croatian Fascist state; the Croats, as well as the Muslim Bosnians, attacked the Serbs. After a bitter civil war, Tito was able to control most of the local clashes inside Yugoslavia, but the potential for violence was undying.

Tito claimed the seaport of Trieste and its surrounding province, Venezia Giulia, which had been Italian. The province's outer area had a mixed population, but Italians dominated Trieste itself. The city was the major seaport for the entire region as well as the Danube basin and landlocked Austria. What happened there would be crucial to many peoples.

Truman and Churchill wanted the borders of Italy to be determined by the final peace settlement. Churchill especially did not want Tito's aggressiveness to decide Trieste's future. He wanted the Western Allies to seize Trieste itself; he preferred to move now and talk later. Truman was more cautious, wishing to avoid fighting between American and Yugoslav forces. But he agreed that Field Marshal Alexander, the supreme Allied commander in the Mediterranean, should establish a military government. He required that Alexander notify Tito that any Yugoslav forces remaining in Venezia Giulia must come under Allied control. If the Yugoslavs did not cooperate, Alexander was to consult with the Combined Chiefs of Staff to avoid fighting. Truman wanted to stay out of the Balkan snake pit.

Tito's partisans entered Trieste on April 30, three days before General Bernard C. Freyberg and the 2nd New Zealand Division arrived and accepted the surrender of the German garrison. Tito's forces entrenched themselves in Trieste and the nearby cities and continued to pour into the area. Tito proclaimed a Slovene government and claimed the area as his exclusive operational theater.

Tito alarmed the Italians. The Yugoslavs, backed by the Soviet Union, were not shy about demonstrating their control. Yugoslav flags flew over the public buildings. Yugoslav town names replaced Italian ones. The Italian archbishop of Gorizia was arrested and removed. The Italian government blamed the United States and Britain.

Truman, after consulting with the Chiefs of Staff and the State Department, declared Tito's actions land-grabbing reminiscent of Nazi Germany's and Japan's. He demanded that control of the entire area, including Trieste, be brought under Field Marshal Alexander and that Tito cooperate with the Allies.

Churchill called Truman's message "most welcome and strong." He added, "I need not say how relieved I was to receive this invaluable support from my new companion." And he sent a message to Alexander, saying, "This action if pursued with firmness may well prevent a renewal of the World War."

Churchill, of course, also asked Truman not to reduce the number of American troops in Alexander's command. Truman refused to guarantee the maintenance of force levels. And he would not become involved in a war with the Yugoslavs unless they actually attacked Allied forces. He warned Churchill, "I must not have any avoidable interference with the redeployment of American forces to the Pacific."

As tension built, Alexander alerted Eisenhower that the Yugoslavs could not be controlled without force. Eisenhower, at Truman's request, ordered Patton to hold three divisions, units of the Mediterranean Fleet, and several air squadrons ready to make a show of strength if needed. He hoped that would prevent a fight.

For the first time, Truman cabled Stalin for help. With Tito refusing to renounce his right to hold the territory, Truman asked Stalin to use his influence to achieve orderly and peaceful settlement of the dispute.

Stalin did quite the opposite. If Truman wanted to resolve the conflict, Stalin advised, he should simply accept Tito's position. In Stalin's view, because the Yugoslavs had driven out the Germans, they had the right to set up a temporary military government until the peace process determined the long-term settlement. To remove the Yugoslav troops now, Stalin said, would be "an undeserved insult for the Yugoslav Army and the Yugoslav people."

Tito was the one who finally compromised. He would agree to Anglo-American control if Yugoslav troops and administrators were allowed to remain in place. At least, Truman felt, he was keeping the door open for negotiations. After more wrangling and threats, an agreement was signed on June 9 creating two temporary zones. One, including Trieste, would be under Anglo-American occupation, and the other, under Yugoslav. In effect, the Allies held the city of Trieste while Tito occupied most of the province surrounding it, Venezia Giulia, which was now divided by a line along which Anglo-American troops and Yugoslav forces tensely faced each other.

The confrontation continued, and the Yugoslavs forced down and even shot down unarmed U.S. Army transport planes. Field Marshal Alexander on one occasion angrily compared Tito to Hitler and Mussolini. Stalin, indignant, jumped to Tito's defense and cabled Churchill on June 21 that Alexander's language was "absolutely unacceptable." Churchill replied that he would not make excuses for Alexander and added, "It seems to me that a Russianised frontier running from Lübeck through Eisenach to Trieste and down to Albania is a matter which requires a very great deal of argument conducted between good friends."

In this whole conflict over Trieste, Truman and Churchill had diverging priorities. Truman's was to establish a Western presence in southeastern Europe and still bring Russia into the war against Japan; Churchill's was to maintain British influence in the eastern Mediterranean and over Greece, Egypt, and the Middle East.

Chapter 12

Colonialism and Nationalism

Harry Truman regarded colonialism as un-American. "Colonialism in any form is hateful to Americans," he said. "American fought her own war of liberation against colonialism, and we shall always regard with sympathy and understanding the desire of people everywhere to be free of colonial bondage."

World War II would, in time, mark the beginning of the end of old-style colonialism. But the first thrust sped in the opposite direction—toward trying to restore the victors' colonial empires.

Roosevelt had disapproved of reestablishing the European powers in Africa and Asia. The Allies should not shed their blood to restore Indochina to France. He wanted trusteeships to prepare the former colonies for self-government and independence.

Truman believed in the same principles. But as soon as he had to face the realities of power politics, his opposition to colonialism became muddled. Although he supported prompt independence for the Philippines and self-government for other island peoples, the American military chiefs advised him that "certain strategic areas in the Pacific" were vital to the future security of the United States. These were the Marshall, Mariana, and Caroline islands, which Japan had fortified between the world wars and which Americans had fought to conquer or isolate. The War and Navy Departments argued that a hostile power could again use these islands to block the United States from the Philippines and Guam, as well as Southeast Asia, Australia, and New Zealand.

The United States, the great outspoken guardian against the reimposition of colonialism in the world, now found that it wanted colonial exceptions in its own interest. Stimson, for one, insisted that these islands belonged to the United States, which must have the absolute right to rule and fortify them. He predicted in his diary that everybody would understand if the United States announced that it was holding these islands "for the purpose of protecting freedom and peace in the Pacific."

Of course, the United States was not alone in wanting to hold on to areas of "strategic importance." Both Britain and France were determined to reestablish their important political and economic relationships with underdeveloped areas and to keep open the routes to them. And the Soviet Union was determined to control the strategic areas on its periphery.

Truman listened to the State Department debate the War and Navy Departments about the Pacific security issues, and he tried to find a middle ground. He decided that the United States should construct and control military and naval bases on the Pacific islands; but the United States, unlike the Japanese, should permit a third party (the United Nations) to oversee the social and economic conditions of the islands' inhabitants. Truman thought this a happy compromise: "We thus assured full protection to our nation against a future Pacific aggressor and, at the same time, laid the foundation for future self-government of the island people."

Truman supported the revival of Britain and France in Europe with all his heart. But did that mean he had to help America's European allies and friends reconquer their colonies in order to assist their postwar revival? Truman faced the conflict of wanting to rebuild the economy and status of France, for example, while opposing (in the beginning at least) France's reacquisition of her colonies in North Africa, the Middle East, and East Asia. The relationship between countries that had possessed colonies and their former subjects was one of the most knotted problems Truman had to unravel.

At the start of World War I, the majority of the world's people lived under the control of Western nations geographically distant from them. The imperial rulers benefited from overseas markets, raw materials, cheap labor, and jobs at home and overseas. But rivalry for overseas possessions was also one of the causes of three decades of war.

As a consequence of World War II, Britain gave up India, and within a few years the Netherlands lost Indonesia. By 1954 the French were facing an uprising in Algeria and had been defeated by the

Vietnamese at Dien Bien Phu. And this was just the beginning. The movement toward separation was worldwide and revolutionized the politics, the economies, and the cultures of the globe.

Paradoxically, as the colonial empires melted away, Americans were reversing their traditional inward-looking isolationism and beginning to play a greater role in the world. The United States was making commitments abroad and becoming a "Great Power."

At first, nationalist movements turned to the United States for support, attracted by the much-quoted declarations of principle of Wilson, Roosevelt, and Truman. But in time, partly because of the demands of the rivalry with the Soviet Union, the United States felt it needed to influence some of the underdeveloped countries. For example, the victory of the Chinese Communists that gave birth to the People's Republic of China stimulated American interest in the French struggle in Vietnam. Washington looked to Bao Dai, the former French-controlled Emperor of Annam, as a sound opponent to nationalist Ho Chi Minh, which led Ho to seek diplomatic recognition from Beijing and Moscow. By then the United States was supporting the French in their war against the Vietnamese, while the Soviet Union drew to its bosom other former Western colonies like Syria, Iraq, and Cuba.

Americans liked to speak of their altruism and anticolonialism, but history said differently. They had almost exterminated the original occupants of the continental United States, and the forces of American empire had expanded American interests into the Caribbean, the Pacific, and Latin America backed by hard-nosed Marines and their Enfield rifles.

This expansion of self-interest continued after the war. Truman appreciated that powerful Americans would like to see U.S. domination extended overseas so the country could exercise imperial power and control resources and markets. Some Americans in high places felt a vital interest in holding on to, for instance, such conquests as the Philippines. Henry R. Luce, the publisher of *Time* and *Life* magazines, visited the Pacific theater soon after V-E Day and cabled home:

> The American frontier is no longer Malibu Beach; the American frontier is a line Okinawa–Manila—and it will never be moved back from there. . . . Americans have a very acute sense of where their "home" is; from now on their home is a continent and an ocean that covers nearly half the globe. This is the political geography for the next round of the human drama.

Luce had expressed his true desires in a signed *Life* editorial entitled "The American Century," which had predicted a postwar world dominated by the United States:

> The vision of America as a principal guarantor of the freedom of the seas, the vision of America as the dynamic leader of world trade, has within it the possibilities of such enormous human progress as to stagger the imagination. Let us not be staggered by it. Let us rise to its tremendous possibilities. . . . Clearly a revolutionary epoch signifies great changes, great adjustments.

This grandiose "vision" was not one Harry Truman shared. He planned to free the Philippines immediately after the war was won, despite those who wanted Filipino independence postponed so that they could first gain control over the islands' resources. Even Secretary of the Interior Ickes opposed independence for the Philippines.

On April 19, having been in office only a week, Truman met with Sergio Osmeña, the anti-Japanese president of the Philippines, and told him he favored the earliest possible date for independence. President Osmeña asked for U.S. financial aid when the war was over, but he found Truman preoccupied with the war in Europe and the creation of the United Nations Organization. Osmeña's request was premature, but because of Douglas MacArthur's intervention, he was destined not to be in office long enough to repeat it. On May 14, Osmeña and Truman did sign an agreement to permit the United States to maintain military and naval bases in the Philippines.

Truman also promptly received T. V. Soong, the foreign minister of China, who was a member of the Harvard College class of 1915, former head of the Bank of China, and brother of Mrs. Chiang Kai-shek. After attending the San Francisco conference, Soong planned to fly to Moscow to conclude a treaty of trade and mutual assistance with the Soviet Union. Truman encouraged him, asserting that the United States wanted China to come out of the war strong and prosperous. In both the Philippines and China, the new President could not possibly anticipate how events would work out.

The British and French still had great colonial interests in the Middle East, East Asia, and Africa. And the United States was increasingly motivated by its need for oil and attracted by the wealth to be gained from markets overseas. Edward W. Said, a Palestine-born professor at Columbia University, has written:

> The United States is the last superpower, an enormously influential, frequently interventionary power nearly everywhere in the world. Citizens and intellectuals of the United States have a particular responsibility for what goes on between the United States and the rest of the world, a responsibility that is in no way discharged or fulfilled by saying that the Soviet Union, Britain, France, or China were, or are, worse. . . . So we should first take scrupulous note of how in Central and Latin America—to mention the most obvious—as well as in the Middle East, Africa, and Asia, the United States has replaced the great earlier empires and is *the* dominant outside force. Looked at honestly, the record is not a good one. . . . [I]s there not an unquestioned assumption on our part that our destiny is to rule and lead the world, a destiny that we have assigned ourselves as part of our errand into the wilderness."

The Soviet Union built an empire of adjacent territories, and overseas it actively sought the allegiance of Egypt, Iraq, Afghanistan, and North Yemen. It encouraged Ghana, Mali, and Guinea to oppose Western imperialism and to participate in the political fragmentation that was crackling around the globe, led at first by such strong, charismatic figures as Tito of Yugoslavia, Gamal Abdel Nasser of Egypt, and Jawaharlal Nehru of India.

The "Third World," which was emerging from the former colonies, struggled to stay free of domination by either the American or Soviet bloc. The U.N. General Assembly grew from fifty predominantly European and Latin American countries to more than triple that number, most of them Asian and African. This worldwide relocation of power came out of revolutions, civil wars, and border battles, which were the ugly side of the price of gaining independence.

By Truman's time, the European colonial interlude in the Middle East—based on strategic concerns and oil—was tattered, more because of the Great Powers' squabbling than because of the local peoples' rebellions.

The Middle East sits on a human fault line where cultures and ambitions collide. In 1914 the area was ruled by the decrepit Ottoman

Empire, based in Constantinople and ruled by Turkish adherents to Islam. A decade later, Christian Britain and France controlled much of the Middle East, often with League of Nations–granted legitimacy and with opposition from indigenous peoples encouraged by Wilson's principle of self-determination.

The Middle East had been a military sideshow in World War II, but the war stirred great changes in the area. At war's end, Charles de Gaulle, aways zealous to restore France's colonies and "glory," pressed both Syria and Lebanon for some degree of French hegemony. When he landed French troops in those countries, violence broke out.

Soon the Middle East became an important focal point for Cold War maneuvering, and when the Cold War was over, the United States was free to try to impose its own military solutions on the area, as signified by the Persian Gulf "war" of 1990–91.

Iran was an early hair trigger spot between the Soviet Union and the Western powers. During the war, Soviet troops had occupied the northern half of Iran, and the British had moved into the southern part in order to block any German intervention and to control Iranian oil. Since 1941, when Winston Churchill, First Lord of the Admiralty, and Lord Fisher, then First Sea Lord, had converted the British Navy to oil, the British had regarded Iran's vast oil deposits as vital to their security.

At the end of World War II, neither power wanted to withdraw its forces from Iran. The Soviet Union fomented a revolt against the ruling Shah and helped spark the formation of separatist, ethnic "republics" of Azerbaijanis and Kurds. Truman protested strongly, and Britain and the United States sided with the Shah.

Because of the need to resettle the Jewish survivors of the Nazi Holocaust, one of the most urgent and complex colonial problems was the British Mandate of Palestine, populated in the main by native Arabs and Jewish immigrants and ruled by British soldiers.

Before Truman had sat behind his White House desk a week, the State Department warned him that Zionist leaders would seek his support for unlimited Jewish immigration into Palestine and the establishment there of a Jewish state—the two prime Zionist goals. The State Department said the American people had "every sympathy for the persecuted Jews of Europe," but the United States had vital interests in the area, and the Palestine question should be treated "with the greatest care." That is, Truman's sympathy for displaced

European Jews should not interfere with American dependence on Arab oil.

On the morning of his ninth day in office, Truman was visited in the White House by Dr. Stephen S. Wise, chairman of the American Zionist Emergency Council. Truman was eager to see him. "I knew he wanted to talk about Palestine, and that is one part of the world that has always interested me, partly because of its Biblical background, of course. . . . The stories in the Bible, though, were to me stories about real people, and I felt I knew some of them better than actual people I knew."

Truman assured Rabbi Wise that he knew the history of the Jews, had read Britain's Balfour Declaration, and was familiar with the Arabs' point of view. "I also said that I knew the things that had happened to the Jews in Germany. . . . At that time I couldn't even have imagined the kind of things they found out later. But I said as far as I was concerned, the United States would do all that it could to help the Jews set up a homeland."

They discussed resettling Jewish Holocaust survivors from Europe into Palestine. Truman was skeptical of the advice he was getting from the "striped-pants boys," as he called the State Department, and said they did not care enough about what happened to displaced people. He believed, he told Rabbi Wise, that the United States could both take care of its own vital interests and help the victims of persecution. Although some "experts" in the State Department disagreed with him, he declared, he was the one who was going to make the policy.

Zionists were soon convinced that Truman would be more understanding and helpful than Roosevelt, who, they felt, had not done enough to save millions of Jews in Europe from Hitler's work-unto-death camps and gas chambers. In their eyes, Roosevelt had failed to make specific efforts to save Jews who were being exterminated; he had said that the best thing he could do for the Jews was to win the war swiftly.

V-E Day brought dancing in the streets of Jerusalem. Both Arabs and Jews joyfully expected a resolution of their conflicting hopes. But in fact the end of the war in Europe only intensified the tension in Palestine.

The issues were difficult, but Truman's course was clear. He pressed Prime Minister Clement Attlee (who by then had replaced Churchill) to admit Jewish survivors to Palestine. Truman wanted to ease the short-term Jewish refugee problem by admitting one hundred thousand Jews to the British Mandate and to leave Palestine's long-term fate to be decided by the United Nations. Attlee and Foreign Minister Ernest Bevin accused him of promoting Jewish immigration into Palestine for domestic political reasons. Bevin even said publicly that the Americans did not want the Jewish refugees flooding into New York.

The State Department opposed a Jewish state in Palestine. Loy W. Henderson, chief of the department's Division of Near Eastern Affairs, asserted that a Jewish state there would be disastrous to U.S. interests, and Dean Acheson said later, "I did not share the President's views on the Palestine solution to the pressing and desperate plight of great numbers of displaced Jews in Eastern Europe." George Kennan thought the Palestine problem insoluble.

In July, the then Labour-dominated British Parliament supported a Jewish National Home in Palestine. U.S. Navy Secretary Forrestal and Brendan Bracken, who had been Churchill's First Lord of the Admiralty, both objected. Bracken feared it would touch off an explosion in the Middle East. Forrestal was eager that the United States, and its navy, not lose access to Saudi Arabian oil.

On the other side, Clark Clifford and David K. Niles, both of the White House staff, backed the President and championed a Jewish state. Truman told Forrestal that he would act on a principle of justice, not oil. And eventually he removed Loy Henderson from Washington by appointing him ambassador to India.

Later, Truman told the press that U.S. policy was to let as many Jews into Palestine as possible, but he had no desire to send five hundred thousand American soldiers to make peace in Palestine.

A few days before the European war ended, Colonel Oliver Stanley, the British colonial secretary, told David Ben-Gurion, the chairman of the Jewish Agency Executive, that the British were unwilling to continue their mandate over Palestine much longer. But they could not decide between the demands of the Arabs and the Jews.

On V-E Day, Ben-Gurion wrote pessimistically in his diary, quoting Hosea 9:1, "Rejoice not, O Israel, unto exultation, like the peoples." He foresaw that, even with Hitler defeated, the Jews would have to oppose the British army in Palestine; the Jewish survivors in Europe would have to fight their way into their refuge; and after the British did march out, the Jews would have to battle the Arabs' armies alone. None of the Western powers was willing to risk getting involved in an Arab-Jewish war.

When Ben-Gurion, as Eisenhower's personal guest, visited the Jewish survivors in the death camps and displaced persons camps in Germany, he told them that if they built a Jewish state in Palestine, "there will not be another Holocaust."

* * *

Inside Palestine, the Palmach, the strike force of the armed Jewish Haganah militia, attacked British police stations and radar stations guarding the coast to keep Jews out. On May 9 the dissident and militant Irgun Zvai Leumi organization stormed British police headquarters in Jaffa and near Tel Aviv, and the following week blew up the oil pipeline at Haifa.

When the British Labour Party took charge of the government in London on July 26, it seemed to promise to cancel the 1939 British White Paper policy that limited Jewish immigration into Palestine. The Zionists were full of hope.

But Attlee and Bevin unexpectedly switched Labour Party policy and kept the gates to Palestine locked. The new government would not increase the number of Jews who could immigrate to the British Mandate. The Jews in Palestine reacted with bitterness. The three disparate resistance movements—Haganah, Irgun, and Lehi—cooperated against the British. This collaboration would last a year, until the Irgun blew up part of Jerusalem's King David Hotel.

Finally, on November 29, 1947, the United Nations voted to partition Palestine and create a Jewish state there; and on May 14, 1948, the British marched out and the state of Israel was born. Truman saw to it that the United States was the first to declare de facto recognition of Israel, which was immediately attacked by the surrounding Arab nations.

The emergence of the state of Israel was only the most dramatic and complicated of the many battles for freedom from colonialism that followed World War II. That one was doubly difficult because two peoples—the Arabs of Palestine and the Jews who had gone there especially since the Holocaust—were fighting for the same small, arid speck of land. And broad issues were at stake: the industrial world was dependent on Arab oil, and the Jews who had survived the Holocaust needed a homeland and some degree of safety.

No one can claim that Harry Truman achieved his desire to satisfy the wish "of people everywhere to be free of colonial bondage." The war's aftermath roused to action nationalist forces—some based on reactionary military power, some on Soviet-backed communism. Decolonialization was rarely easy or bloodless. It was difficult to separate self-interest and self-determination.

Chapter 13

Battle for a Launching Pad

Just twelve days before Truman became President—on Easter Sunday, April 1—four divisions, two Army and two Marine Corps, of Lieutenant General Simon Bolivar Buckner's U.S. Tenth Army landed on Okinawa's west coast beaches, 350 miles south of the Japanese homeland. The Americans came to seize a base from which they could launch an invasion of the Japanese home islands.

The Pacific war was now concentrated on Okinawa. The massive, brutal battle there would go on for nearly three months and involve 548,000 Americans. The Japanese had 120,000 troops on the ground. Fighting hard to keep the invaders away from their homeland, they hurled 1,900 suicide attacks from the air. The kamikazes sank 36 American ships and damaged 368 more; in the air, the Americans lost 763 planes.

The invasion of Okinawa caused major political repercussions in Tokyo. On April 7 a new cabinet came to power. General Kuniaki Koiso was replaced as prime minister by aged, retired Admiral Kantaro Suzuki. Shigenori Togo, a critic of the war who had been foreign minister at the time of Pearl Harbor, again was given that portfolio. The Japanese army's failure to halt the relentless approach of the Americans resulted in the cabinet gaining some ambivalent voices that might be prepared to end the fighting, given favorable terms. But there were no terms; and the generals, still in control, were prepared to hold out for a decisive battle on the beaches of Honshu.

On Friday, April 13, the Americans on Okinawa learned of President Roosevelt's death; many were deeply shaken. That night, Sergeant William Manchester of the 29th Marines (the future author) was leading a five-man patrol on the Motobu Peninsula near the island's northern end. Their mission was to link up in the darkness with the 4th Marines. Years later, Manchester wrote:

> Because the Nips were so skillful at infiltration, the rule had been established that after night had fallen, no Marine could leave his foxhole for any reason. Anyone moving was slain. . . . So I moved along the path as quickly as I could, and I recall ascending a little wiggle in the trail, turning a corner, and staring into the muzzle of a Browning heavy machine gun. "Flimsy," I said shakily, giving that day's password. "Virgin," said the 4th Marines' gunner, giving the countersign. He relaxed and reached for a cigarette. He said, "You heard the news? FDR died." I thought: *my father.*

The battle turned into a slugfest. Kamikaze raids hit hard; and on April 16, the 77th Infantry Division assaulted Ie Shima, off Okinawa, where a machine-gun burst killed Ernie Pyle, the beloved war correspondent.

On the nineteenth, three divisions of the XXIV Army Corps fought down the width of Okinawa. Progress was measured in yards; the Japanese had to be killed if the Americans were to advance. Lieutenant General Buckner's costly straight-ahead tactics were severely criticized; war correspondents castigated him. The Marine Corps' highest leaders tried unsuccessfully to persuade him to land a Marine division behind the enemy.

General Douglas MacArthur also condemned the way the Central Pacific Command fought the battle. He said that after the first three or four days the Americans had all the territory they needed and they should then have let the Japanese come at them. His criticisms, made repeatedly, infuriated Admiral Chester W. Nimitz, Commander-in-Chief, Pacific.

Buckner certainly fought the battle the way the Japanese hoped he would. They welcomed a ferocious fight that would enable them to buy time and inflict casualties that they thought would discourage an assault on the homeland. The U.S. Army and Marines struck the center of the Japanese defense at Shuri Ridge but could not break the Japanese line. The final charge against Shuri and its supporting strong points, designated Sugar Loaf Hill, Half Moon, and The Horse-

shoe, did not start until May 11—three days after V-E Day in Europe—
and required two weeks of hard fighting. The 5th Marines finally
seized Shuri Castle on May 28. Over the parapet, the commander of
A Company, 1st Battalion hoisted a Confederate flag he had carried
in his helmet since he had left South Carolina. On the last day of
May, the Tenth Army occupied the capital city of Shuri.

Before the eighty-two-day battle was over, 7,613 U.S. soldiers and
Marines died on Okinawa and 4,907 sailors offshore. U.S. casualties
exceeded 74,000. More than 110,000 Japanese were killed; an entire
Japanese army was destroyed. If the price for Okinawa was that
high for both sides, what would be the price of invading Japan?

Although the new President's initial attention had to go to the fast-
approaching climax of the war in Europe, at the end of his first week
in office, he had met with President Osmeña of the Philippines and
Foreign Minister Soong of China; and to launch the Seventh War
Loan campaign, he greeted and commended three of the six men
who on February 23 had raised the American flag on Iwo Jima in
Joe Rosenthal's famous photograph. The other three had been killed
on Iwo.

Once the European war was won, Truman started to shift the giant
American war machine, now finished with its task in Europe, to Asia.
On May 16 Secretary of War Stimson briefed him on the two basic
(and apparently paradoxical) elements of U.S. Pacific strategy: to
avoid fighting the Japanese in China in order to save American lives
and to mount a massive American invasion of the Japanese home
islands.

V-E Day also freed the Soviet Union to join the East Asian struggle.
Japan's leaders knew they could not defeat both the Americans on
their home islands and the Russians on the mainland. They sought
to keep the Soviet Union out of the war and persuade Stalin to stay
friendly to Japan. They even proposed to have him mediate an end
to the Pacific war. To make it worthwhile for the Soviet Union, the
Japanese were ready to return territory they had seized in the Russo-
Japanese War, forty years earlier.

The Pacific war was being fought on a scale and over an area
larger than any other war in history. Distances were enormous and
strategies complex. From San Francisco, it was seven thousand miles
to Brisbane and six thousand miles to New Caledonia.

The seeds of this Pacific saga had been sown ninety-two years earlier, when Commodore Matthew Calbraith Perry had opened Japan to Western trade and ideas. By World War I, Japan had conquered Korea and gained Port Arthur, half of Sakhalin Island, and control over the southern half of Manchuria.

By siding with the Allies in World War I, Japan had acquired the German port of Tsingtao on the China coast and the German islands in the Central Pacific—the Marianas, Marshalls, Palau, and Carolines—astride the American route to the Philippines. Japan had made herself a world power.

The first action of what was to become World War II was Japan's aggression in China in September 1931, a full decade before Pearl Harbor. Japan invaded Shanghai and occupied Manchuria, captured Peiping and Tientsin, and ruthlessly destroyed Chiang Kai-shek's capital, Nanking. The Chinese Nationalists retreated farther and farther inland and made a swift Japanese victory impossible.

The Japanese attacked southward into Southeast Asia and grabbed vast natural resources, particularly oil. When Hitler invaded the Soviet Union in June 1941, the Japanese jumped at the opportunity and seized the southern half of Indochina. In response, Roosevelt embargoed war matériel to Japan and closed the Panama Canal to Japanese shipping. This and the buildup of American strength in the Philippines and Hawaii persuaded Japan's more militant leaders that war was inevitable, and the sooner the better.

As a result, two daring and, as it proved in the end, foolhardy Japanese attacks on December 7, 1941, awoke the United States, which had been still at peace in a warring world, and brought her to battle against Japan. The Japanese caught in Pearl Harbor, Hawaii, every battleship in the U.S. Pacific Fleet, except *Colorado*, and in the Philippines they wiped out Lieutenant General MacArthur's Far East Air Force (FEAF).

The Japanese swept down and occupied the Malay Peninsula, the Philippines, the Dutch East Indies, Wake, and Guam. But the following summer, two great naval struggles—the Battle of the Coral Sea and the Battle of Midway—killed the best of Japan's pilots, sank five Japanese aircraft carriers, and finished the Japanese offensive.

By the time Truman became President, the United States had fought back mightily. On August 7, 1942, the United States 1st Marine Division landed on Guadalcanal and nearby Tulagi in the Solomon Islands—the first step. And an Australian-American army under Lieutenant General MacArthur had fought up the northern coast of New

Guinea and into the Philippines. The Marines, island-hopping in fierce, costly leaps across the middle of the Pacific, seized Tarawa, Guam, Saipan, and Tinian.

The two-Pacific-theater strategy represented a massive application of American power, as well as an awkward answer to American interservice rivalry. In retrospect, either MacArthur's Southwest Pacific campaign or Nimitz's Central Pacific campaign could have done the job. And, once Japan's navy had been mortally wounded, the Japanese troops holding many isolated outposts could simply have been bypassed—at a lower price in American lives.

Whether the two-theater strategy shortened the war and saved American lives is dubious. One military historian called it "a monstrosity."

Two years after the Marines landed on Guadalcanal, Japan's cities were in range of American island-based B-29 Superfortress bombers. Even Prime Minister Koiso thought Japan could no longer win the war it had started. But Japan would fight on stubbornly for another year and a half, hoping for a decisive victory before agreeing to stop the killing.

On February 19, 1945, the U.S. 4th and 5th Marine Divisions assaulted Iwo Jima, halfway between the Marianas and Tokyo—about 670 miles from each. The five-mile-long island would be converted into an emergency landing field for the B-29s that were fire-bombing Japan's cities and a base for the shorter-range fighters escorting the Superfortresses. Before the end of the fighting on March 26—the Marines called Iwo "the toughest yet"—26,589 Americans were killed and wounded. It was expensive in American lives; but 2,500 Superfortresses made emergency landings there and 3,081 air strikes against targets in Japan were flown from tiny, costly Iwo.

Directly ahead on the Central Pacific front waited Okinawa and then the invasion of the Japanese home islands.

In the Southwest Pacific, MacArthur had established a mighty base at Hollandia on the northern coast of Dutch New Guinea, and waded ashore on the island of Leyte in the Philippines with four army divisions on October 20, 1944. Three days later, the Japanese lost the largest naval engagement in history, the Battle of Leyte Gulf. The U.S. Sixth Army landed at the Lingayen Gulf on the island of Luzon on January 9, 1945, and dashed south into Manila, where vicious street fighting lasted until March 4.

When Truman came to office, the U.S. Army was mopping up on

northern Luzon. Japanese General Tomoyuki Yamashita based his defense at Baguio, which the U.S. 37th Division captured on April 26. MacArthur announced on June 28 that all of Luzon had been freed. (It was Bess and Harry Truman's twenty-sixth wedding anniversary.)

But U.S. divisions and Filipino guerrillas continued to battle General Yamashita and 50,000 Japanese troops in the Asin Valley northeast of Baguio. Their resistance was savage.

The Luzon campaign was MacArthur's biggest and bloodiest. There, the Americans defeated the largest Japanese army they met in the Pacific. And the Americans' job was made all the more difficult because MacArthur withdrew major elements of his command to reconquer ten islands in the central and southern Philippines— without authorization from the Joint Chiefs of Staff. In the four months between February 28 and June 25, MacArthur's forces made fifty-two landings in the Philippines at a cost of 2,100 American lives.

Historian Samuel Eliot Morison wrote that where MacArthur derived his authority for that island campaign was a mystery. But neither the Joint Chiefs nor the War Department protested. MacArthur's biographer says this reconquest of the Philippines south of Luzon "was surely MacArthur's most audacious challenge to the Joint Chiefs during the war." And it should have made his later controversial actions in Korea less surprising.

MacArthur immediately became enmeshed in Philippine politics in opposition to President Osmeña, with whom President Truman was negotiating. The Japanese had flown José P. Laurel, their Filipino puppet president, to safety in Tokyo. In mid-April Manuel Roxas, who had been a MacArthur aide before the war, and other members of Laurel's cabinet entered the American lines. The Filipino people always detested the Japanese invaders, but some of the prewar wealthy elite, represented by Laurel, had collaborated.

On April 18 MacArthur sent a special plane from Manila to bring back his friend Roxas and promoted him to brigadier general in the U.S. Army. With that endorsement, Roxas launched his campaign for the presidency of the postwar Philippines against the incumbent Osmeña, who had long differed with MacArthur. After Osmeña met with Truman and returned to Manila, MacArthur refused to work with him. Instead, MacArthur boosted Roxas, claiming he had been a source of intelligence behind the Japanese lines. But Roxas remained a controversial figure bolstered by the general's blessing. In April 1946 he would defeat Osmeña to become president of the Republic of the Philippines. He brought to an end the prosecution of wartime collaborators and carried back into power the prewar ruling class.

General Thomas A. Blamey, the Australian military commander, saw MacArthur's aggressiveness in the Philippines as having political consequences in Asia that the Australians, he felt, must match. He began to attack Japanese forces he had previously been content to bypass. The resulting Australian casualties raised questions in Parliament about the usefulness of mopping up that could not affect the outcome of the war.

MacArthur's ambitions extended beyond the Philippines. Early in 1945, he began planning to invade North Borneo, using the Australian I Corps, and then to invade Java. At Yalta, the Combined Chiefs of Staff agreed to his plan, if the invasion of Japan was postponed into 1946. MacArthur boasted to Australian Prime Minister John J. Curtin that he intended to restore to the British and Dutch their former colonies. But the shortage of shipping delayed the Borneo operation.

In early April the U.S. Joint Chiefs approved MacArthur's complex plan, although the British did not like committing their fleet to these operations and some experts belittled MacArthur's publicly stated objective to procure oil resources for the invasion of Japan. Borneo was an oil center second only to Sumatra in all Southeast Asia. But when Borneo was finally assaulted, the oil fields were found to have been so badly damaged by both Allied bombings and Japanese demolitions that they could not be used for more than a year. Thereafter, the Australians were wary of involving themselves in MacArthur's schemes.

Australian Prime Minister Curtin, the Labour Party chief who had long pressed to give the Pacific war higher priority, died in June. After Truman succeeded Roosevelt and Joseph B. Chifley replaced Curtin, MacArthur received less enthusiastic support. One MacArthur biographer wrote, "It was most fortunate for the lives of the soldiers of the Australian I Corps, the prestige of the Joint Chiefs, and the reputation of MacArthur that the war was terminated before the SWPA chief got his way on the Java plan, for that two-division invasion could have produced the most tragic blood bath of the Pacific war."

On July 1 MacArthur accompanied the veteran Australian 7th Division when it assaulted the Balikpapan beachhead in eastern Borneo. This would be the final amphibious operation of a very amphibious war. MacArthur stepped ashore and came under fire briefly for the last time.

The popular hero-general certainly had not won the admiration of his Commander-in-Chief. In his diary, Truman called MacArthur "Mr. Prima Donna, Brass Hat, Five Star MacArthur." And he mused, "I don't see why in Hell Roosevelt didn't order Wainwright home and let MacArthur be a martyr. . . . We'd have had a real General and a fighting man if we had Wainwright and not a play actor and a bunco man such as we have now."

The convergence of the two Pacific campaigns on Okinawa demanded a reorganization of the American Pacific command structure. This would determine how the United States would fight the final campaign. Because a sensible unified command was a political impossibility, on April 3, two days after the invasion of Okinawa, the Joint Chiefs of Staff, following a nasty interservice political struggle, changed the division of command essentially from geography-based to service-based. They appointed General of the Army MacArthur Commander-in-Chief, U.S. Army Forces, Pacific (AFPAC), with authority over all Army and Army Air Forces resources in the Pacific except on Hawaii and in the southeast Pacific. In June, even before additional troops began to arrive from Europe, MacArthur commanded an army of 1.4 million troops; the War Department expected to increase them by another million by December. Admiral Nimitz was given command of all Pacific naval forces except those in the southeast Pacific.

The Twentieth Air Force reported directly to the Joint Chiefs of Staff, and in June it became part of the Strategic Air Force headquartered on Guam under General Carl A. Spaatz, who had led the bomber offensive in Europe. The Strategic Air Force also included the Eighth Air Force, which was to be redeployed to Okinawa.

These changes in the command structure led to new arguments between Nimitz's and MacArthur's headquarters over control of the Okinawa campaign. The death in action of Lieutenant General Buckner on Okinawa on the morning of June 18 gave MacArthur the opportunity to appoint a new commander for the Tenth Army. Meanwhile, Admiral Nimitz assigned the job to Major General Roy S. Geiger of the Marine Corps, who thus became the first Marine ever to command a field army.

The next day, Marshall offered MacArthur his choice of General Joseph W. Stilwell, former chief of the China-Burma-India Theater, Alexander Patch of the Seventh Army, Lucian Truscott of the Fifth Army, or George Patton of the Third Army, as well as William H.

Simpson of the Ninth Army and Jacob Devers of the Sixth Army Group. MacArthur replied to Marshall that he planned to name Lieutenant General Oscar W. Griswold, commander of the XIV Corps. And if that was not acceptable, his preferences were Stilwell, Patch, and Truscott in that order. It was claimed that MacArthur did not want Patton; he was quoted as saying Patton was brilliant but erratic.

Marshall, ignoring the Griswold proposal, directed Stilwell to take command of the Tenth Army. His presence would strengthen MacArthur's hand for the invasion of Japan; they had been at West Point together and were longtime friends.

On June 23 General Stilwell took over the command from Geiger, who on the twenty-first had already declared Okinawa secured. The following day, Lieutenant General Mitsuru Ushijima, the Japanese commander on Okinawa, committed hara-kiri on a cliff overlooking the sea.

The United States now had its launching pad for the invasion of the Japanese home islands. Japan was cut off from its overseas supply of natural resources and its overseas possessions. Its cities and people were being pounded unremittingly by huge bombing raids, flown from islands the Japanese had lost. Although victory was totally beyond their reach, Japan's leaders still refused to quit.

Truman continued to demand that the Japanese surrender unconditionally. And he prepared for the ordeal of his first face-to-face confrontations with Stalin and Churchill, during which they would grapple with a host of unresolved problems, the shape of the postwar world, and the nature of a dramatically new age.

Chapter 14

Potsdam

Transporting a President of the United States overseas in wartime, accompanied by a sizable part of the executive branch of the government, requires a massive effort. Truman elected to travel to the Big Three conference at Potsdam, Germany, in a U.S. Navy warship to allow time to prepare himself. He had documents to study, advisors to consult, and arguments to perfect.

Churchill had suggested that the conference be code-named TERMINAL, and Stalin had requested that it take place at Potsdam, in the Russian-occupied sector of Germany near Berlin. Potsdam had once been the royal city of the Hohenzollerns and was the site of the grave of Frederick the Great, the martial symbol of Germany's onetime greatness. Churchill notified Truman that King George VI would be inspecting British troops in Europe at the time of the conference. The king, he said, would like to come and host a dinner in the British sector of Berlin for Truman and Stalin. He would, of course, not take part in the conference discussions. Truman courteously accepted Churchill's plan, but the royal visit never took place. When Stalin asked why the king was not coming to Berlin, Churchill offered the excuse that it would have complicated the conference's security problems.

After an ample lunch of fried chicken, french fries, and peaches and cream, Truman spent the whole afternoon, July 3, in his White House study, trying to clear away all possible problems before he left Washington and to prepare for the challenges of his journey. He signed documents until he was exhausted and began to review the minutes of the previous wartime summit meetings as well as memos from Secretary Byrnes, Harry Hopkins, and former Ambassador to Moscow Davies. He selected clothes for all kinds of working and ceremonial occasions and wrote Bess, "I have to take my negro preacher coat and striped pants, tails, tux, winter clothes and spring ones, high hat, soft hat, and derby. It'll be a circus sure enough."

Truman was taking Secretary of State Byrnes (Truman called him "my able and conniving Secretary of State") with him to Potsdam and leaving Secretary of the Treasury Vinson in Washington as the next in the line of executive authority.

At 7 P.M. on July 6, after attending a Friday evening concert by the Army Air Force band on the White House South Lawn, Truman was driven to Union Station and boarded an armored railroad car. The train—with accommodations for fifty-three assistants, advisors, newsmen, and help—arrived at Newport News, Virginia, just before six on a sunny Saturday morning. Truman was immediately piped aboard the heavy cruiser USS *Augusta*, the ship on which Roosevelt and Churchill had drafted the Atlantic Charter back in 1941. As always, Truman felt "blue as indigo" about leaving his wife and daughter. And uneasy about what lay ahead: "Now I'm on the way to the high executioner. Maybe I'll save my head."

Within the hour, *Augusta* was under way, accompanied by the heavy cruiser USS *Philadelphia*. The two cruisers made up all of Task Force 68; no other escort, either ship or aircraft, was used.

Philadelphia, sailing ahead to smooth a path in the heavy seas, made course for Antwerp, Belgium. As soon as *Augusta* passed the minefields at the entrance of Chesapeake Bay and reached the open sea, the crew held an abandon-ship drill. Truman went to his station at the Number 2 whaleboat on the port side of the well deck. He was impressed by the efficiency with which a naval ship was managed.

Because the war in Europe was over, the ships were not darkened at night. Truman enjoyed the thirty-piece band that played during dinner, and movies were shown every evening in Secretary Byrnes' cabin. The President was up each morning at 6:15, striding out on his daily walk around the deck and chatting with members of the crew. Afternoons he spent with Byrnes and Admiral Leahy, writing out briefs on the problems they envisaged arising at Potsdam.

Truman, Churchill, and Stalin expected to discuss, debate, and— they hoped—resolve an enormous array of issues. These included the frontiers of Germany, the German economy, reparations, Italy and her colonies, the status of the former German satellites, and the government and frontiers of Poland. Before the ocean journey was over, Truman and his aides had worked out four proposals that the President would present to the conference. The men had a sense that they were embarked on a journey of great historic significance.

On Sunday he went to church services with the ship's captain and Secretary Byrnes. That afternoon, he enjoyed "a probabilities game . . . [which] ended pleasantly with my doing some satisfactory guessing on my opponents' hole cards." Monday, he watched gunnery practice from the navigating bridge. "Nice entertainment for an artilleryman," he thought. "I'd still rather fire a battery than run a country." He ate a meal in every crew mess, taking his place in the line with an aluminum tray.

He was introduced to a sailor named Lawrence Truman from Owensboro, Kentucky, who, he wrote his mother and sister, "is the great grandson of our grandfather's brother. He's a nice boy and has green eyes just like Margaret's. Looks about her age." Of the trip, Truman wrote them, "I hate it. But it has to be done."

Press Secretary Charlie Ross embargoed news of the trip until the President was safely ashore at Antwerp; but radio commentator Drew Pearson in Washington broke the story the second day out. The Associated Press immediately picked it up, and this forced the release of news stories from *Augusta* the next day.

The President was also receiving important information. Political problems back in Britain would interrupt the conference. The British had held a general election on July 5, but the results would not be known until July 26 to allow time to collect and tally the soldiers' vote. Churchill told Truman that the political members of the British delegation would have to leave the conference on July 25; they could return to Potsdam on July 27 and then stay until August 5 or 6.

The British had enjoyed a coalition government throughout the war; but now, since the German surrender, partisan politics was reviving. Labour Party leaders were already blaming Churchill and the Conservatives for the growth of suspicions that, they charged, were eroding British-Soviet relations.

As *Augusta* and *Philadelphia* entered the English Channel, HMS *Birmingham* and six British destroyers met and escorted them. On the extremely hot Sunday morning of July 15, the American cruisers moved slowly toward Antwerp harbor while hundreds of undemonstrative Belgians and Dutch lined the shore of the Schelde Estuary.

Truman, peering through field glasses, was surprised that he saw few signs of war, except for about a hundred German POWs on the shore crowded behind the barbed wire of an Allied prison camp. When the ships reached Antwerp's municipal dock, Pier 23, he viewed for the first time a devastated, bombed-out city. *Augusta* had sailed 3,387 miles from the peacefulness of Virginia.

General Eisenhower was responsible for the arrangements for the conference's American members and came aboard with other diplomatic and military dignitaries to greet the President. For Eisenhower, this was a unique chance to present his views, especially about Germany, to Truman and Byrnes in person: the State Department should take over responsibility for Germany from the military as soon as possible, and Germany should be encouraged to rejuvenate and rebuild herself. And he voiced strong feelings against the Soviet Union joining the Pacific war; that war was coming to an end, and the Russians were all too eager to get into it.

Eisenhower and Admiral Harold R. Stark, commander of American naval forces in Europe, rode with the President to the Meller Ook Airport northwest of Brussels. During the hour-long drive, Truman witnessed war's destruction up close. Along part of the automobile caravan's route were posted GIs of the 35th Division, in which Captain Truman had served during World War I. Then, on the flight to Berlin's Gatow Airport, the President's C-54, *Sacred Cow*, flew over war-flattened Kassel and Magdeburg—whole cities in ruins. "I could not see a single house that was left standing in either town. The German countryside, however, seemed to be under cultivation and presented a beautiful appearance."

At Gatow, he was again welcomed by a delegation—Secretary Stimson, Ambassador Harriman, Admiral King, and Ambassador Gromyko—and was driven ten miles south to suburban Babelsberg. Green-capped Soviet border guards lined the road. Babelsberg, a summer resort and the prewar seat of Germany's movie colony, would be home for the heads of state during the conference. The conference's plenary sessions were to be held three miles away at Potsdam in Schloss Cecilienhof, the 176-room country estate of former German Crown Prince Wilhelm. During the war, both Germans and Russians had used the palace as a hospital.

In Babelsberg, President Truman lived in a compound at 2 Kaiserstrasse, a three-story stucco mansion that became known as the "Little White House," even though it was painted yellow. On the shore of narrow Lake Griebnitz and surrounded by groves of trees, the gabled building had been the residence of a prominent publishing family until the Russians had removed them on one hour's notice. Prime Minister Churchill, who had flown in the previous afternoon, was housed in a similar compound a couple of blocks away, and Generalissimo Stalin, who was arriving by armored train, was to live down the road about a mile closer to Potsdam.

Precisely at eleven on Monday morning, Truman and Churchill met for the first time. (It was the day of the atomic Trinity test—a tremendous blast in the remote New Mexico desert near Alamogordo.) Churchill came to call at 2 Kaiserstrasse, bringing his daughter Mary, Foreign Secretary Anthony Eden, and several aides. Truman felt he already knew Churchill and took to him instantly, although one observer did think Truman seemed nervous meeting this overpowering world figure. Truman believed Churchill and he were in complete agreement on principles. If the two men had any personal differences, they were minor: Truman thought the prime minister too given to flattery. "I liked to listen to him talk. But he wasn't very fond of music—at least my kind of music." Churchill's reaction was also positive: "[I] was impressed with his gay, precise, sparkling manner and obvious power of decision." He told Mary he was sure he could work with the new President.

Stalin was scheduled to call on the President that afternoon, but he had not arrived from Moscow. He was said to be delayed by a mild heart attack, which was being kept secret from the public. Some Westerners speculated snidely that he only wanted to point up his own importance.

That hot afternoon, Truman seized the break in the schedule to take an automobile tour of Berlin with Secretary Byrnes and Admiral Leahy. Near the city, the President transferred to an open half-track reconnaissance car and passed slowly down the line of the U.S. 2nd Armored Division, the largest armored division in the world. In Berlin, the motorcade drove along Wilhelmstrasse to the remains of the Reich Chancellery. Truman was shocked by the destruction; the grand buildings of this proud city were now massive piles of stones.

The long lines of weary, forlorn old men and women and the children pushing or pulling the remnants of their belongings depressed him. He said quietly, "That's what happens when a man overreaches himself." And he wrote in his diary, "I fear that machines are ahead of morals by some centuries." He was thankful that the United States had been spared the tragedy of war at home.

After he returned to the Little White House that evening, Secretary of War Stimson brought him a secret cable from Washington. It said, with hidden meaning, "Operated on this morning. Diagnosis not yet complete but results seem satisfactory and already exceed expectations." The atomic Trinity test at Alamogordo, New Mexico, had been a success. Although for the moment only a handful of people knew what had happened, the world had changed forever.

Just before noon the next day, in a cold, driving rain, Josef Stalin, attended by Molotov and interpreter V. N. Pavlov, arrived at Truman's mansion. Secretary Byrnes and interpreter "Chip" Bohlen were waiting with Truman. Brigadier General Harry Vaughan ran down the stairs, shook Stalin's hand, and led him to the President, who was sitting at his desk. The two world leaders, destined to play paramount roles in a vast ideological conflict, were face to face for the first time.

Truman wore a double-breasted gray suit; Stalin, a fawn-colored uniform with red epaulets. Five years older than the President and only five feet five, the powerful Russian had a pockmarked face and a crippled left arm; he was smoking a cigarette, his teeth were discolored, his mustache streaked. He was plain and laconic but known for calculation and ruthlessness. He seemed tired and worn, and acknowledged to Truman that his health was not good.

Truman ventured that since he wanted to treat Stalin as a friend, he would be direct. That was his style, in strong contrast to the charm and finesse with which Roosevelt had dealt with the dictator. Sitting in large, comfortable chairs, Truman and Stalin discussed Germany's defeat; Stalin was certain that Hitler was alive and hiding in Spain or Argentina.

Stalin volunteered the promise that the Russians would enter the war against Japan in mid-August—that was what Truman wanted to hear most of all. Stalin had first proposed that the Soviet Union declare war on Japan to Roosevelt and Churchill at the Teheran Conference in November 1943. At that time, he had been trying to persuade the Western leaders to attack Germany across the English Channel. Now Germany was defeated and it was too soon for the realization to sink in that the success of the Trinity test might have made Soviet intervention superfluous.

Shortly after this meeting, Truman recorded the experience in longhand:

> Promptly a few minutes before twelve I looked up from
> the desk and there stood Stalin in the doorway. I got to

my feet and advanced to meet him. He put out his hand and smiled. I did the same. We shook. I greeted Molotov and the interpreter and we sat down. After the usual polite remarks we got down to business. I told Stalin that I am no diplomat but usually said yes or no to questions after hearing all the arguments. It pleased him. I asked him if he had the agenda for the meeting. He said he had and that he had some more questions to present. I told him to fire away. He did and it is dynamite—but I have some dynamite too which I'm not exploding now. He wants to fire Franco to which I wouldn't object and divide up the Italian colonies and other mandates, some no doubt that the British have. Then he got on the Chinese situation told us what agreements had been reached and what was in abeyance. Most of the big points are settled. He'll be in the Jap War on August 15th. Fini Japs when that comes about.

We had lunch talked socially put on a real show drinking toasts to everyone then had pictures made in the back yard. I can deal with Stalin. He is honest—but smart as hell.

Truman asked Stalin to stay for lunch; when he declined, the President insisted with midwestern directness. "You could if you wanted to," he said. Stalin stayed, and they talked through a generous lunch of liver and bacon and a California wine, which Stalin praised so ardently that Truman had a case sent over to the Soviet compound.

He found Stalin impressive, a man who looked him in the eye when he spoke. "I had heard that Stalin had a withered arm, but it was not noticeable. What I especially noticed were his eyes, his face, and his expression," Truman said later. "I talked to him straight from the shoulder." When Stalin left, Truman took a nap.

Ambassador Harriman, who had conferred with Stalin many times during the war years, had come to an assessment very different from Truman's: "Stalin remains for me the most inscrutable, enigmatic and contradictory person I have ever known." The Western Allies were frustrated by Stalin's interpretation of the political agreements reached at Yalta, but they also recognized that he had kept his word in military matters during the war. Harriman summed this up encouragingly:

It is significant that Stalin kept his military commitments during the war. He had agreed that after we landed at

Normandy in June 1944 he would attack in the east. People forget there were at the time about two hundred Nazi divisions and about fifty satellite divisions on the Eastern Front. Our plans were based on the premise that we could not land successfully in Normandy if there were more than about thirty mobile German divisions in the west of Europe. Therefore the transfer of a relatively small number of divisions from the Eastern Front to the west could have been disastrous. One of the reasons why General Marshall and General Eisenhower believed for some time after the war that we could get along with the Russians, and why they were so reluctant to finally agree that we couldn't, was because Stalin has carried out his military commitments.

The West was about to learn how Stalin handled his political commitments.

The Potsdam Conference officially opened at 5:10 P.M. that Tuesday. The center courtyard of Schloss Cecilienhof was sparkling with a brilliant twenty-four-foot red star of geraniums, pink roses, and hydrangeas planted by the Russians. Churchill, Stalin, and Truman, each with four aides, sat crowded around a large round table in the middle of a huge forty-by-sixty-foot, oak-paneled conference room. Truman sat with Byrnes and Leahy on his right and Bohlen and Davies on his left; behind them sat Harriman and a half-dozen experts.

If the heads of government could hammer out agreements on three clusters of problems affecting the world's future—the nature of the occupation of the defeated German Reich; the political and economic future of Eastern Europe, especially Poland; and the Soviet Union's help in finishing the war against Japan—they would have the chance to create a world at peace. After three decades of savagery, this conference was offering a brief but unique opportunity.

Stalin immediately proposed that Truman, the only one of the three who was also a head of state, be the presiding officer, and Churchill seconded the motion. The Westerners felt cheered that the Soviet Union did not lay claim to being the host but rather viewed the conference as a meeting of three coequals.

Then the pleasantries were over. Truman went to work. First, the Big Three had to agree on an agenda, and Truman put before the conference the four proposals that he had worked out on the voyage over.

There needed to be, Truman said, a council made up of the foreign ministers of Great Britain, Russia, China, France, and the United States—the permanent members of the United Nations Security Council. He said the Great Powers must avoid repeating the mistakes made after World War I, and a Council of Foreign Ministers could be the machinery to develop peace negotiations and territorial settlements. The council should meet as soon as possible after the conference and, as one of its first objectives, begin work on peace treaties.

Stalin questioned the inclusion of China in the Council of Foreign Ministers intended to deal with the European peace. Truman had included China because it was one of the permanent members of the Security Council. Churchill agreed with Stalin; until the Japanese were defeated, he said, China could contribute little to the solution of European problems. Truman did not insist, and the three leaders finally not only dropped China but at the same time limited the French role in the proposed council. In the end, they referred the idea of a council of foreign ministers to Byrnes, Eden, and Molotov to study and recommend a course of action.

Truman's next proposal was that the Allied Control Council begin at once to manage Germany. He even spelled out the principles by which Germany should be governed: the end of German militarism, the destruction of Nazism, and the bringing to trial of German war criminals. On the economic side, he wanted Germany treated as a single unit and industry that could be used for military production eliminated. This proposal, too, was referred to the foreign ministers, who were asked to report back the next day.

Truman's third proposal was that the Big Three prepare a statement in which they would reaffirm their governments' obligations, undertaken at Yalta, to the liberated peoples of Europe and to those of the former Axis satellite states. For example, the governments of Romania and Bulgaria were to be reorganized on a democratic basis. Here he was clearly presenting a viewpoint not acceptable to everyone at the table. Churchill politely said he needed time to study the document. Stalin was more direct: he was, of course, not prepared to accept a Western-style democratic government for either Romania or Bulgaria.

Last, Truman proposed a revised policy toward Italy. Because Italy had entered the war against Japan, he said, she should be admitted into the United Nations. Churchill interrupted to remind them all that Italy had attacked Britain in the dire days of 1940, an act that Roosevelt had described as "a stab in the back." And the British had fought the Italians in Africa and in the Mediterranean for two years before the United States had entered the war.

Then it was the others' turn. Churchill wanted the Polish problem added to the agenda. Stalin put forth a list of questions that the Soviet Union wished to discuss: the division of the German merchant fleet and navy, German reparations, trusteeships for the Soviet Union, and relations with the Axis satellite states and the Fascist regime of General Francisco Franco in Spain. At this point Stalin interrupted his agenda to declare that the Franco government had been imposed on Spain by Germany and Italy and was a threat to the United Nations; the Great Powers should help free the Spanish people.

Stalin returned to his list. He added three more items to the agenda: the question of Tangier, the problem of Syria and Lebanon, and the Polish question, by which he meant the determination of Poland's western border and the liquidation of the London Polish government-in-exile. Churchill, who had brought up the Polish problem himself, retorted that every aspect of the Polish issue should be discussed.

In the end, the three foreign ministers were directed to draw up a "menu" for the next day, starting, as Churchill said, with "the least disagreeable points." And Stalin quipped: "As all the questions are to be discussed by the foreign ministers, we shall have nothing to do." His remark drew the conference's first laughter.

Edgily, Truman told his peers they should decide some issues each day. "I don't want just to discuss. I want to decide." If they could not accomplish something, he said, he meant to go home. And he asked them to meet at four o'clock instead of five in order to get more done. This was accepted as a constructive idea, and then Truman suggested they adjourn.

But before they could, Stalin turned on Churchill and wanted to know why he refused to give the Soviet Union its share of the German fleet. Churchill replied evenly that the fleet should be either destroyed or shared. Stalin retorted, "Let us divide it. If Mr. Churchill wishes, he can sink his share."

Truman came away from the first session with a swarm of impressions. Churchill's command of the spoken language was masterful; Stalin "just grunts" and was impatient with anything except questions of power. But Truman hoped that the Soviet Union's enormous sacrifices during the war would stimulate Stalin's desire for peace and that he would keep his agreements. "We had much to learn on this subject."

As Truman was driven back to Babelsberg with Leahy and Byrnes, a Soviet lieutenant held up their car at a crossing. After a few minutes more senior Soviet officers appeared and "proceeded to scare the life out of the lieutenant for making such a blunder." Leahy turned to Truman and said, "I'll bet that lieutenant is shot in the morning."

Byrnes and Leahy applauded Truman's performance at the conference. He wrote Bess that they "seemed to be walking on air." But he, the novice at summit conferences, added, "I was so scared I didn't know whether things were going according to Hoyle or not." He had been President for three months now and had gained a lot of confidence in the White House, but this was quite a different setting. How would he do bargaining with Churchill and Stalin face to face?

He was particularly pleased that Stalin had earlier agreed to go to war against Japan "with no strings to it." Because of that, he wrote home, "I'll say that we'll end the war a year sooner now, and think of the kids who won't be killed! That is the important thing."

That evening, he worked late on his share of a planeload of mail that had arrived from Washington. At 11 P.M., Sergeant Harry Truman, his brother Vivian's son, arrived. "He is a good soldier and a nice boy."

Back in Antwerp, the President had said he would like to see his nephew, who was in the European Theater. The President's wish was his aides' command. Young Harry had been located aboard the *Queen Elizabeth* in Glasgow ready to sail for home; he had promptly been flown to Babelsberg. His uncle proudly introduced him to all the VIPs, and after three days he was flown to Washington and rejoined his unit as it debarked from the *Queen Elizabeth* at Norfolk.

On Wednesday morning Truman walked over to 23 Ringstrasse, two blocks away, for a return visit with Churchill. They lunched alone. Truman told the prime minister about the Alamogordo atomic test, and they debated how to tell Stalin. Truman wanted to tell him informally after a conference meeting. They tried to evaluate the Japanese inquiry about peace terms and the Soviet Union's joining the war against Japan. Truman noted afterwards, "Believe Japs will fold up before Russia comes in. I am sure they will when Manhattan [the atomic bombs from the Manhattan Project] appears over their homeland."

Churchill steered Truman's attention to the enormous debt the war had piled on Britain. Truman appreciated how much Americans owed the British: "If you had gone down like France, we might be fighting the Germans on the American coast at the present time."

They discussed tariffs and the disposition of wartime airfields and communications. Truman accepted Churchill's offer to fit American warships with proper torpedoes and shells at Gibraltar. Churchill also suggested that they continue the American-British Combined Chiefs of Staff after the war. But before they could talk through this subject, Truman was pulled away to repay his visit from Stalin.

After the luncheon, Churchill noted admiringly, "I felt that here was a man of exceptional character and ability, with an outlook exactly along the lines of Anglo-American relations as they had developed, simple and direct methods of speech, and a great deal of self-confidence and resolution."

Truman discovered that Stalin also had an elaborate meal waiting for him. At this second private meeting, Stalin shared the peace feeler he had received from Emperor Hirohito and Foreign Minister Togo. The Emperor wrote that it was his "heart's desire" to see the war ended, and he proposed sending Prince Fumimaro Konoye, a respected senior diplomat who had been prime minister before Pearl Harbor, to Moscow to negotiate peace terms. But for "the honor of the homeland" he could not accept unconditional surrender.

Stalin asked how Truman felt the Emperor's approach should be handled. He replied that he had no respect for the good faith of the Japanese. Stalin suggested that they stall; he would ask the Japanese to clarify the nature of the visit by Prince Konoye. With Truman's concurrence, that is what was done.

Truman invited Stalin to the United States and even offered to send USS *Missouri* for him.

> [Stalin] said he wanted to cooperate with the U.S. in peace as we had cooperated in war but [it] would be harder. Said he was grossly misunderstood in U.S. and I was misunderstood in Russia. I told him that we each could help to remedy that situation in our home countries and that I intended to try with all I had to do my part at home. He gave me a most cordial smile and said he would do as much in Russia.

Since it might have been in the Soviet Union's interest to conceal the Japanese peace feeler, Stalin's apparent candor made Truman feel that the Soviet leader wanted to deal openly with him. Still, they remained wary of each other. Truman did not let on that he had already known about the peace feeler from coded intercepts, and

Stalin did not hint that he knew of the atomic tests at Alamogordo from his espionage network.

The conference convened again at Schloss Cecilienhof at 4 P.M. But before they could begin, Churchill raised a question about the limits that had been placed on press coverage of the conference. He offered to explain to the nearly two hundred reporters waiting outside the compound why the press was being excluded. Truman objected—the problem should be left to each delegation's press representative; the Allies were still at war with Japan and had many delicate problems to solve in Europe. Churchill replied lightly, "I only offered myself as the lamb and, in any event, I would only go if the generalissimo [Stalin] agreed to rescue me."

As chairman, Truman presented the three agenda items that the foreign ministers had reviewed overnight: the makeup of the proposed Council of Foreign Ministers, the governance of Germany, and the Polish questions.

The foreign ministers recommended that the membership of the Council of Foreign Ministers be limited to representatives of countries that had signed terms of surrender with the enemy. This left the door open for China to join the council after Japan's defeat—a happy compromise that was accepted.

Going on to discuss how the foreign ministers' council should approach peace treaties, Truman soon recognized that he and Stalin had a fundamental disagreement. Stalin wanted the Big Three to settle all world problems, while Truman believed that every nation, large or small, should participate, thus giving substance to the United Nations. Churchill feared that Truman's desire to submit peace terms to the United Nations would create a laborious process. So they finally approved referring treaties to the United Nations only after the Great Powers had first agreed among themselves.

Next, they had to settle on what they meant when they spoke of "Germany." Such a seemingly simple definition was, in fact, a minefield threatening millions of lives. To Churchill "Germany" meant prewar Germany, not necessarily the Germany occupied by the Soviet army. Stalin disagreed; Hitler had annexed Austria in 1938, but it was not part of Germany. Stalin wanted their discussion based on Germany as it existed at the moment—in 1945—which would leave the Soviet-created borders in place. Truman suggested that "Germany" meant the Germany of 1937, before Hitler had started expanding. And Stalin replied immediately and emphatically: minus what Germany had lost in 1945. ("Germany lost all in 1945," Truman retorted.) Stalin had already detached part of eastern Germany and added it to Poland in exchange for territory the Soviet Union had taken from the eastern side of Poland. He wanted the border between Germany and Poland fixed immediately. When Truman proposed using 1937 Germany "as a starting point," Stalin accepted the compromise, saying, "We cannot get away from the results of the war."

Once Stalin and Churchill went along, Truman as chairman declared that the starting point of the discussion would be the Germany of 1937—the Germany of the Versailles Treaty. What goes around, comes around. Germany was back to square one—where it had been before Hitler had begun to rip the world apart.

Stalin tried to seize the initiative on the foreign ministers' third agenda item—Poland—by introducing a draft proposal. This issue was coming to represent the chasm between East and West.

Stalin asked that all members of the United Nations withdraw recognition from the London-based Polish government-in-exile and that its assets be transferred to the provisional government in Warsaw. The Polish Communists would thus acquire all the property of the 150,000-man Polish Army, equipment that had been supplied by Britain and the United States.

Churchill accepted this proposal, provided he was given assurances that any Poles who had fought on the side of the Allies would not be forced to return to Poland against their will. Britain, he said, would offer them citizenship. Stalin said he did not want to complicate things; he only wanted to end the government-in-exile.

Truman, although eager for an agreement on Poland, still pressed for free elections there. Stalin denied that the Polish government had ever refused to hold elections. They finally referred this bundle of sticky questions back to their foreign ministers to sort out.

Truman was already growing impatient "for more action and fewer words." He wrote in his diary, "I'm not going to stay around this terrible place all summer just to listen to speeches. I'll go home to the Senate for that."

That evening, Truman telephoned Bess in Independence, the first transatlantic radiotelephone call placed from Berlin to America since 1942.

Churchill and Stalin, on the other hand, spent the evening together, eating, drinking, and talking until after 1:30. They managed to stay away from serious issues—well, not entirely. Stalin complained that he was hurt by the American demand for the democratization of the governments of Romania and Bulgaria; he had not meddled in Greek affairs. And Churchill mellowly told Stalin that he thought Russian ships should have access to all the oceans of the world. "Russia had been like a giant with his nostrils pinched by the narrow exits from the Baltic and the Black Sea," Churchill said. He was willing for the Soviet Union to have clear passage through the Dardanelles, a longtime Russian goal, and also through the Kiel Canal, as well as into the warm waters of the Pacific. Stalin, pleased, put in still another bid for a share of the German fleet.

Thursday, the summit's third session began on a positive note. After easily accepting the foreign ministers' draft on Germany, as presented by Anthony Eden, they took up the thornier question of whether the German merchant fleet and Navy should be regarded as reparations or war booty. Truman insisted the merchant fleet be classified as reparations, but first he wanted to make use of it against Japan. The United States would need every vessel available for that war—as well as for carrying food and supplies to Europe.

But as far as Stalin was concerned, surrendered war matériel was booty. Therefore, the German Navy was booty. He conceded that whether or not the merchant fleet was booty was open to negotiation. If it was acknowledged that the Russians were entitled to one third of the German merchant and naval fleets, he did not object to their use in the war against Japan.

Churchill wanted the U-boats destroyed and all other German naval vessels divided equally; the Soviet Union could have its share. He ended the tedious, rambling discussion—at least temporarily—by getting everyone to postpone resolving the question until the end of the conference.

Secrecy plagued this discussion of the fleets. Stalin complained that Soviet representatives had not been allowed to inventory or inspect the German ships, which were primarily in British custody. Churchill retorted that the Western Allies had not been allowed to inspect the forty-five submarines the Russians had captured at Danzig. "All we want is reciprocity," he said.

The Russians could look at anything they wished in the American zone of Germany, Truman said, but he, too, expected reciprocity. He was trying to lay the ground for the Allied Reparations Commission to inspect everything the Russians had seized. He had already witnessed how the Russians were gutting the industrial plants in Berlin's Soviet sector and shipping the machinery and equipment back to the Soviet Union.

These seizures of "war booty" were all mixed up with the heated question of reparations, the traditional arrangement by which the victors require that the losers pay for some of the damage the war had wrought.

While the reparations negotiations were going on, Truman received reports of the wholesale removal of industrial plants and equipment from the Soviet zone of Germany under the guise of "war booty." The Soviet Union was stripping Germany of economic assets. Comparatively, the United States did little; but it did send a unit to Nordhausen to remove four hundred tons of German rocket equipment. The equipment was shipped out before the Russians entered Nordhausen and delivered to White Sands, New Mexico.

It was obvious to Truman that Germany could not pay heavy reparations, and he did not wish to create an impoverished Germany that would become prey to communism. He knew that after World War I the United States had ended up paying the reparations Britain and France had demanded from a bankrupt Germany. He did not want to repeat this.

At Yalta, the Russians had proposed a flat $20 billion in reparations, with 50 percent going to the Soviet Union. Britain and the United States would not accept a bill that size. The Allied Reparations Commission had been set up to examine the subject and make further proposals before the next summit meeting. The commission's job was to moderate the huge demands that the Soviet Union, devastated by the war, was making.

When the commission met on June 21, the Soviets stuck to the $20 billion figure proposed at Yalta. They called for large withdrawals from Germany's national wealth for two years, followed by annual payments from current production over ten years.

The American delegation asked for data to explain the $20 billion figure; it received none. And the Russians, with delaying tactics, prevented the full commission from meeting again. Finally, the steering committee of the commission agreed on a formula of 56 percent of the total reparations to go to the Soviet Union and 22 percent each to Britain and the United States. When other nations presented their claims, payment would be pro-rated on the same basis.

The use of forced labor as reparations was among the controversial questions needing Truman's resolution. The Russians had no qualms about using enemy slave labor. But Truman ordered the U.S. delegates to refuse any reparations in the form of forced labor. The United States' position was that none of the victors should use compulsory labor except in the cases of convicted war criminals. There had already been too much of such ugly demeaning of human dignity. By the time the three leaders gathered at Potsdam, reparations had become an onerous and expensive problem that everyone knew would be extremely difficult to solve.

Next, the Great Powers tried to find common ground on a future relationship with Franco's Spain; this also was difficult. In view of General Franco's hostility to the Soviet Union, Stalin demanded that the United Nations break off relations with Spain. Franco had sent Churchill a secret proposal that the Western nations collaborate against the Soviet Union; Churchill had replied coldly, with a copy to Stalin to demonstrate his friendship. Despite this, Churchill added, Spain had not endangered the Allies, and the United Nations Charter provided against interfering in a nation's domestic affairs. To break off relations based on conditions inside Spain would create a dangerous precedent. Truman, while candidly expressing his dislike of Franco, conceded that only Spain could determine the nature of her own government.

Stalin argued that Franco's regime was not an internal matter because Hitler and Mussolini had imposed the dictatorship on the Spanish people. If severing relations was too severe, he asked, how else could the Big Three show that they were in sympathy with the Spanish people but not with Franco? Franco should not be ignored; silence might be interpreted as approval. Stalin demanded that the foreign ministers find a way to display what they all agreed on— that these heads of government disapproved of Franco.

For once, Churchill did not want the problem referred to the foreign ministers; it should be settled by the heads of government themselves. But after more prolonged and fruitless discussion, Truman, foreseeing a stalemate, had the subject tabled until later.

Stalin also had strong opinions about the next agenda item, Yugoslavia. To begin with, he objected to discussing it because the Yugoslavs were not present. After all, they were allies. Anthony Eden reminded him that the Big Three had agreed on Yugoslavia at Yalta, and the Yugoslavs had not been present there either. Stalin said that had been different: then, there had been two Yugoslav governments; now there was one, and it should be respected. There were, in fact, still two possible Yugoslav governments, Churchill replied. He and

Stalin began to argue over whether to invite Yugoslav representatives to Potsdam.

Truman's temper flared. Putting aside diplomacy, he said he had come to the conference to discuss world affairs, not "to hold a police court hearing." If they started doing that, they would have to bring in many representatives—including de Gaulle, Franco, and others—and deal with everyone's political grievances. If they were not going to stick to the main issues, he would pack up and go home.

Stalin laughed and said he wanted to go home too. Churchill calmly but pointedly commented that he had thought Truman was interested in carrying out the Yalta agreements. Truman shot back that as far as the United States was concerned he intended to see that they were carried out, and he suggested that the matter of Yugoslavia be postponed and they move on to more urgent matters.

Truman was gaining confidence. Presiding over the Senate as vice president had helped prepare him to chair this conference, and he was increasingly sure of himself. But this had been "a tough meeting," he wrote Bess:

> I reared up on my hind legs and told 'em where to get off and they got off. I have to make it perfectly plain to them at least once a day that so far as this President is concerned Santa Claus is dead and that my first interest is U.S.A., then I want the Jap War won and I want 'em both in it. Then I want peace—world peace and will do what can be done by us to get it. . . . They are beginning to awake to the fact that I mean business.

The day's final agenda item was Churchill's accusation that a stockpile of oil pipe which the British had owned in Romania, had been stolen by the Germans when they had overrun the country. And now the Soviet Union had seized the oil pipe as reparations. The British wanted their pipe back. Both Britain and the United States disapproved of the Russians picking up whatever they found lying around and shipping it home. Truman sided with Churchill on the oil pipe issue (American pipe was also involved), but again they left the question for their foreign ministers to try to resolve.

Stalin dismissed this as a trifling matter that should be settled through diplomatic channels. Truman was amused by Stalin downplaying an issue whenever "the Russians had stolen the coffin and disposed of the body." After three days of the conference, the Big Three had decided very little.

That evening, Truman hosted a state dinner in the Little White House. Churchill sat on his right, Stalin on his left. For the gala occasion, they put aside the arguments of the afternoon. They toasted everyone from the British king to the pianist, young U.S. Army Sergeant Eugene List, who, with violinist Private Stuart Canin, played several Chopin nocturnes and Chopin's Waltz in A-flat Major, Opus 42 (Truman always said that waltz, not the "Missouri Waltz," was his favorite). Truman, who unexpectedly stood by the piano and turned the pages of the score, had chosen the program to please Stalin, who was also fond of Chopin. (Churchill was not.) Stalin was so delighted he shook Sergeant List's hand and drank a toast to him. Proudly, Truman wrote Bess, "Our boy was good." Later, in the bonhomous spirit of the evening, Truman himself went to the piano and played Paderewski's Minuet in G, to the fascination of the stellar array of guests.

On Friday, Truman made full use of the daytime hours before the conference assembled again. He lunched with Generals Eisenhower and Bradley, and they reassessed the Pacific war. The down-to-earth Bradley quickly formed a judgment of the President: "He was direct, unpretentious, clear-thinking and forceful. His knowledge of American history, particularly U.S. military history, was astonishing."

They talked about the potential of the atomic bomb, which had just been tested so successfully. Truman seemed prepared to use the bomb; Eisenhower believed it should not be employed because Japan was, in his view, already defeated. Eisenhower also continued to oppose bringing the Soviet Union into the Japanese war, but he was convinced that in the end nothing would keep it out. Truman did not agree with either position; he was worried about Americans landing on the beaches of Japan's home islands in the face of massed gunfire.

Then Truman and the generals were driven to U.S. headquarters in Berlin to lend their presence to the official raising of the American flag over the U.S. sector of the city—the same flag that had flown over the Capitol in Washington when war was declared against Germany and that had been raised in Rome after its capture by the Allies. Truman called it "the flag of victory." Also in the ceremonial party were Stimson, McCloy, General Patton, and Lieutenant General Clay, the American high commissioner for Germany.

At the flag-raising ceremonies, Truman said, "We want to see the time come when we can do the things in peace that we have been able to do in war. If we can put this tremendous machine of ours, which has made victory possible, to work for peace, we can look forward to the greatest age in the history of mankind. That is what we propose to do." But so far the world's three most powerful leaders had not been able to.

He emphasized, "There is not a piece of territory or one thing of a monetary nature we want out of this war." But the American people do want "a world in which all the people will have an opportunity to enjoy the good things of life not just a few at the top."

Like any tourist, Truman took time to perform some family chores. Bess had asked for Chanel No. 5 perfume, but he could not find any, "not even on the black market." He did his best, he explained to his wife. "I managed to get some other kind for six dollars an ounce at the American P.X. They said it is equal to No. 5 and sells for thirty-five dollars an ounce at home. So if you don't like it, a profit can be made on it." And with money he had won playing poker on the ship coming over, he bought her an expensive Belgian lace luncheon set. He did not tell her what that cost.

The devastated German capital disgusted Truman. He wrote Bess, "This is a hell of a place—ruined, dirty, smelly, forlorn people, bedraggled, hangdog look about them. You never saw as completely ruined a city. But they did it . . ."—a mixture of sympathy and "we told you so."

Riding back to Babelsberg, Truman and Eisenhower talked about the future. Eisenhower said he wished to retire quietly. Truman praised the Supreme Commander, and, although they did not really know each other well, Truman volunteered: "General, there is nothing that you may want that I won't try to help you get. That definitely and specifically includes the Presidency in 1948." Eisenhower (and Bradley) found this statement astounding, and Ike tried to treat it lightly. He laughed and said, "Mr. President, I don't know who will be your opponent for the Presidency, but it will not be I."

(Many years later, after Eisenhower had served as President himself, Truman recalled that in the car that day in Germany Eisenhower and he had discussed "wartime heroes" going into politics. But he denied categorically having said he would support Eisenhower if he ran for the presidency. By that later time, however, Truman had changed his view of Eisenhower. He thought the general had been a poor President and labeled him "a coward" for not defending General Marshall against slanderous attacks by Senators Joseph McCarthy and William Jenner. He contrasted Eisenhower's silence with his own immediate defense of the general in August 1945, when an Army Pearl Harbor Board report had criticized Marshall, among others, for failing to warn the commanders at Pearl Harbor adequately before the Japanese attack in 1941.)

When Truman reconvened the conference that afternoon, Molotov reported on the foreign ministers' progress. They had not been able to resolve the dispute over the supervision of elections in Bulgaria, Romania, and Greece. Both Truman and Churchill immediately interrupted and corrected the Soviet foreign minister: they did not want to supervise elections, they only wanted to make sure elections were held and that they were conducted fairly.

Truman began his own agenda by trying to direct Churchill's and Stalin's attention back to his wish to ease Italy's terms of occupation while a peace treaty was being worked out. Stalin still would agree only if the same treatment were given to the German satellites: Finland, Hungary, Romania, and Bulgaria.

Truman persisted. They should deal with Italy first. She had been out of the war for twenty months now; her Fascist rulers were gone; and the United States expected to spend as much as $1 billion feeding Italy during the coming winter. Behind the geopolitical reasons for his initiative was his awareness of the interests of the large number of Americans of Italian origin and of the Catholic Church

This time Churchill, in effect, sided with Stalin; he spoke at length in favor of maintaining the harsher terms of the Italian surrender. Truman noted to himself that when the Mediterranean was involved, Churchill always seemed to feel a need to make a long statement and then agree to what had already been done. The Mediterranean was still vital to Britain as the route to India and Australia, and Churchill had his mind fixed on "the British imperial highways to the East." He seemed to be shrewdly laying the groundwork for the peace treaty negotiations. When Churchill went on at length, Stalin would pull on his mustache and lean over and ask Churchill why he didn't agree, because he would eventually. That would stop Churchill.

The futures of Italy and the Nazi satellites were significant questions of international policy, Stalin said. These countries had to be weaned away from their association with Germany. Speaking with

218 — Mr. Truman's War

quiet certainty, he made his longest speech of the entire conference, the burden of which was that revenge and complaints of suffering were unimportant compared to the goal of separating the satellites from Germany.

Stalin could talk this way, Truman reflected, but he still kept the "iron heel" of the Soviet army on the German satellites the Soviet Union now occupied: Estonia, Latvia, Lithuania, Poland, Bulgaria, Hungary, Romania, and Czechoslovakia.

Every piece of what Churchill had called the "Russianised frontier" through the middle of Europe from Lübeck to Albania became a political battleground between East and West.

Poland was still the most difficult frontier problem. In the face of all odds, Truman and Churchill hoped to make some progress on Poland at Potsdam. The Soviet Union had only to stand fast.

In Austria, the Soviet Union had set up a provisional government and announced that it represented the whole nation. The United States protested that this government had been formed without consulting the Western Allies—and therefore the government had no authority in the American zone of occupation.

Stalin would not permit Western troops to enter Vienna, despite the agreements to the contrary. For example, the Soviet representative on the European Advisory Commission had recommended that American forces use the airport at Tulen, twenty kilometers northwest of Vienna, instead of the airport in Vienna. Truman pointed out to Stalin that no American had been allowed to examine the Tulen airport, which was in the Soviet zone of occupation, in order to make a practical decision. Stalin replied that he would agree to American and Allied representatives visiting the city, but he wanted the zones of occupation to be settled by the European Advisory Commission, not locally in Vienna. (As someone would say wryly, Vienna had become an imperial city without an empire.)

Czechoslovakia, too, was on the frontier. The Russians had invaded from the east and the Americans from the west. And a line was agreed upon that left Prague in the Soviet sector. Czechoslovakia became a Soviet satellite.

Further south, the Soviet Union had moved to dominate Greece and Turkey. When Dean Acheson, by now the U.S. undersecretary of state, recommended to the White House that "they should be resisted at all costs," Truman mobilized a show of naval force in the waters around Istanbul with the battleship *Missouri* and the supercarrier *Franklin D. Roosevelt.*

By the time of Potsdam, the partition of Europe between East and West was virtually complete; and in the East, Soviet control was backed by Soviet tanks.

Struggling to channel the conference's discussion and to focus on priorities, Truman emphasized that they had to establish conditions under which all the war-ravaged countries of Europe could take care of themselves. The United States wanted to create a feeling of peace in the world, and this could not wait for the final peace conference.

Stalin stood fast: Italy must be considered along with the Eastern European satellites. Truman was just as adamant. Until the Eastern European satellites established democratic governments, the United States would not recognize them. The line of the emerging division of Europe was plain for all to see.

The way around such impasses had become almost routine: The matter was referred to the foreign ministers to study and report back to the principals. Time and again, this device was used when the Big Three found that they held irreconcilable positions. This may have served to tamp down the level of personal animosity, but it did not solve many problems. And the Western governments surely failed to thwart the Soviet Union from dominating the smaller nations of Eastern Europe.

Only one matter was resolved with dispatch that afternoon. British troops had not been allowed into the sector assigned to them in Vienna; the Russians, Churchill complained, were turning them away. That was no longer a problem, Stalin replied; zones inside Vienna had been agreed upon only the day before, and he was willing for Western troops to move into Vienna at once. Churchill was pleased that this had been settled.

That evening, Truman relaxed with Colonel L. Curtis Tiernan, chief of army chaplains in the European theater and an old friend. In France during World War I, Monsignor Tiernan had served as the chaplain of the 129th Field Artillery and had ridden for many hours at the head of the column with Captain Truman, the commanding officer of Battery D, discussing the problems of the world. Now President Truman had invited Colonel Tiernan, who was stationed in Paris, to Babelsberg, and he spent several days at the Little White House.

At the conference's fifth session on Saturday, Truman was clearly more sure of his ability to deal with Churchill and Stalin and less patient with their endless confrontations. Churchill saw it too. "He was a changed man," he confided to Stimson. "He told the Russians just where they got on and off and generally bossed the meeting." Not only had Truman found he could participate in this summit effectively, but his self-assurance had been greatly bolstered when, earlier that afternoon, Stimson had read to him General Leslie R. Groves' detailed report on the success of the Trinity test.

At this session, Poland dominated the discussion. The foreign ministers had not been able to resolve Poland's border and had been forced to bring that problem back to the heads of government.

But first they dealt with two easier Polish questions. Stalin, despite stonewalling by Molotov, went along with Truman's and Churchill's insistence that the liabilities of the former Polish government in London should be met before Polish assets in Britain and the United States were turned over to the regime in Warsaw. And, second, Stalin did not resist allowing the press to observe the Polish elections.

The question of Poland's western border, which had been left hanging ever since Yalta, still faced them. At Yalta, Truman reminded them, it had been explicitly decided that the ultimate borders would be determined at the peace conference. In the meantime, however, the Soviet army had fought westward all the way to the Oder and Western Neisse and had turned over forty thousand square miles of Germany and the city of Stettin to the Poles to administer. The Russians could not, Truman protested, unilaterally assign a zone of occupation to the Poles and create a fifth occupier of Germany.

Stalin's justification was that the Germans had fled before the advancing Soviet army and the Poles who remained had to administer this territory. The Soviet Union, he insisted, was not committed to keeping this area Polish, and the western frontier of Poland remained an open question. But it would be difficult to reestablish a German administration there because the majority of the population was now Polish. "There is nobody left to plough the land except Poles."

Stalin had been unable to stop the Poles from moving into the vacuum, or so he said. And he questioned why Truman and Churchill were supporting the Germans against the Poles—unless they were trying to strengthen Germany to menace the Soviet Union.

Truman countered that he had been told that nine million Germans were still in the disputed area; that seemed a large population to him. Not so, Stalin said. The Germans had fled; not a single German remained in the territory given to Poland. Admiral Leahy leaned over to Truman and whispered, "Of course not, the Bolshies have killed all of them!"

Truman did not believe that the western boundary of Poland should be determined by the army on the ground. He did not want pieces of Germany given away bit by bit. Churchill complained about another aspect of the problem: The parts of Germany that the Poles were now administering had been a crucial source of food for Germany, and the Western Allies would have to feed the Germans who had been driven out. Stalin simply suggested that the Germans buy bread from Poland.

The Soviet plan would mean shifting eight million Germans, Churchill said, and he did not want to be left with a mass of starving Germans cut off from their sources of food. Stalin replied abruptly, "There will be none."

Truman would not back down; he was angry that the Russians were trying to change the map of Europe. The Poles had no right to the territory the Soviet Union had given them—and on which Germany depended for food. Stalin responded that it was better to make things difficult for the Germans than for the Poles.

Stalin was determined that the rich farmland between Germany's 1937 eastern border and the Oder-Neisse line be Polish. But Truman could not accept the Poles' seizure of Pomerania, Silesia, and half of East Prussia, as well as the German cities of Stettin, Breslau, Kolberg, Allenstein, and Rastenburg. Stalin told him not to blame only the Poles; the Russians were also to blame. Truman said that was precisely his point.

By now Truman was frustrated with the endless arguing—and certain that Stalin was lying about the facts. Were the Big Three going to "give Germany away piecemeal"? He barely contained his temper: "On a number of occasions I felt like blowing the roof off the palace," he wrote Bess. "There are some things we can't agree to. Russia and Poland have gobbled up a big hunk of Germany and want Britain and us to agree. I have flatly refused."

Stalin, too, was annoyed; he cut off the debate. "Are we through?" he interrupted brusquely. Truman declared the issue at an impasse and promptly adjourned the session.

That evening, it was Stalin's turn to host a state dinner. He orchestrated an enormous feast with musicians imported from Moscow and twenty-five toasts, one every five minutes. Churchill, bored, grumbled that he wanted to go home, but Truman enjoyed himself. Sitting next to Stalin, he was amazed at how much vodka the generalissimo appeared to drink from his tiny, thimble-sized glass. Finally,

Truman asked him and Stalin smiled. He said to his interpreter, "Tell the President it is French wine, because since my heart attack I can't drink the way I used to."

Truman thought he had never heard better musicians than Stalin provided, although he suspected "Uncle Joe" had tried to upstage him by providing two pianists and two violinists. (The Americans had had only one of each.) When he remembered the evening years later, he said, "The night Stalin was host I had some very nice conversations with him. I liked him. I didn't like what he did, of course, but I liked him."

Sunday was no day of rest. Early in the morning, Stimson arrived to discuss target cities for the atomic bomb. Hiroshima led the list. Stimson wanted Kyoto, Japan's historic capital and a center of art and culture, removed from the list, and Truman agreed.

Truman attended two church services, one Protestant and one Catholic. After lunch, Churchill came by the Little White House to visit. And then the conference resumed where it had left off.

Truman, having reread the Yalta Declaration overnight, was more convinced than ever that the Soviet Union could not unilaterally assign Poland a zone of occupation in Germany without consulting the other powers. Shifting his ground, he now emphasized that he did not so much object to Poland having a zone as resent the way it had been done. That, he said, "was my position yesterday, that was my position today, and that would be my position tomorrow." He could not move Stalin; he was beginning to live with the inevitable.

Churchill again declared that the uprooting of eight or nine million Germans to make way for the Poles on former German territory "would be entirely wrong." He wanted the number of Germans transferred from eastern Germany matched to the number of Poles transferred from east of the Curzon Line, which was to be the Russian-Polish border. That would move two or three million of each people.

Stalin continued to profess that no Germans remained in the disputed territory; and he now tried the tactic that, since the Big Three were not in agreement about the western Polish frontier, they should hear from the representatives of the new Polish government. And if the heads of government did not want to hear them, the foreign ministers should.

Stalin acknowledged that at Yalta the frontier Roosevelt and Churchill had proposed started at the estuary of the Oder and followed the Oder to where it is joined by the Eastern Neisse. This left the cities of Stettin and Breslau in German hands. Now Stalin wanted the line to be drawn instead along the Western Neisse, which would give the two cities to Poland. He walked around the table and showed Truman the lines. Truman said that what had been decided at Yalta was the way it should be. But, recognizing that he could not persuade Stalin, he once again declared that the frontier question should not be finally settled until the peace conference. He feared that Stalin's *fait accompli* would become permanent.

Truman and Churchill did acquiesce to inviting Polish representatives to Potsdam. They would be heard by the foreign ministers, who would report back to the heads of government. Truman, as the presiding officer, issued the invitation to the Polish representatives specifically to discuss borders that would exist until they were finally fixed at a peace conference.

Almost as a relief, the meeting then turned to the question of trusteeships. At stake was the future of Italy's colonies (and, after Japan's defeat, Korea's future). Molotov cited press reports that Italy had lost its colonies, and he wanted to know who had received them. Churchill answered that the British had conquered them and held them. That prompted Molotov to interject that the Soviet army had conquered Berlin. Churchill ignored him and said if anyone else wanted the Italian colonies or if they should be returned to Italy, the conference should make that clear. Truman asserted that the United States wanted neither the Italian colonies nor a trusteeship over them. And Churchill acknowledged, half tongue-in-cheek, that he had not even considered that the Soviet Union might desire a large part of the African shore of the Mediterranean. The question was referred to the foreign ministers.

Turkey was next on the agenda, and Churchill acknowledged that Soviet ships should have free movement in and out of the Black Sea. But it was important, he cautioned, not to alarm the Turks, who were already disturbed by the presence of Soviet troops in Bulgaria and by attacks in the Soviet press.

Molotov was anxious to keep the Soviet Union free to make its own bilateral arrangements with Turkey; the Turkish government, he claimed, had sought an alliance with Russia. Churchill challenged the right of the Soviet Union and Turkey to deal bilaterally with the Black Sea straits, the waterway made up of the Straits of the Bosporus and the Dardanelles and linking the Black Sea and the Aegean. Molotov reminded him of the treaties between Russia and Turkey in 1805 and 1833. The whole subject, like so many others, needed more study.

* * *

President Truman had brought with him to Germany a draft of a declaration, which he and Secretary Byrnes had been editing, calling on the Japanese to surrender. It had evolved from a conciliatory message that former Ambassador Grew had wanted to send, encouraging the enemy to surrender. Now, incorporating Byrnes' hard-line attitude and the knowledge that the Trinity test had been successful, it had become an ultimatum. Truman intended, after showing it to Churchill, to issue it as a joint declaration from the United States, Britain, and China. Stalin could not be a party because the Soviet Union was not at war with Japan.

Monday morning, July 23, Stimson came to the Little White House to try to convince Truman and Byrnes that the proposed declaration should drop the demand for unconditional surrender and contain reassurances that the Emperor would be preserved. The secretary of war was startled to find that the secretary of state disagreed. Byrnes was adamant that anything less than unconditional surrender would appear to be appeasement, and he wanted to make no commitment to keep the Emperor. Truman stuck by the policy of unconditional surrender he had announced to the Senate when he first took over the presidency. This was the final effort to soften the terms of the so-called Potsdam Declaration.

The conference that evening returned to the knotty problems surrounding Turkey and the Black Sea straits. Churchill objected to a Soviet military base in the straits. Stalin's comments grew heated. The Russians, he retorted, had fewer troops in Bulgaria than the British had in Greece. Churchill asked just how many troops Stalin thought the British had in Greece. Stalin answered, "Five divisions." Only two, Churchill said; the British had forty thousand troops there. Stalin countered that the Russians had only thirty thousand soldiers in Bulgaria; the Turks, with twenty-three divisions, had nothing to fear from the Russians. What were they afraid of?

The argument over the Black Sea straits gave Truman the chance to restate his conviction that all nations should be guaranteed the freedom of the seas. He wanted every narrow water passageway kept open to cargo and passengers—the Kiel Canal in Germany, a Rhine-Danube waterway from the North Sea to the Black Sea, the Black Sea straits, the Suez Canal, the Panama Canal. Territorial adjustments could be settled between Turkey and Russia, but the straits concerned the world.

Although Truman and Churchill favored international control of important waterways, Stalin did not want Turkey, backed by Britain, to be able to choke off the Soviet Union. The Montreux Convention of 1936, Stalin reminded them, had given Turkey control of the straits and the right to close them to all warships whenever Turkey felt threatened. The British, he argued, would not stand for such a condition on Gibraltar or the United States on the Panama Canal. Since Turkey was too weak to guarantee Soviet ships free passage to and from the Black Sea, the Soviet Union must share in the control of the straits, have the right to build bases there, and if necessary keep them open by force.

Truman insisted that the waterways remain open to the world in peace or war and be guaranteed by all the powers. Stalin, he felt, was touching only on this part of a larger problem because it affected his self-interest. Truman had come to this proposal, he said,

> after a long study of history, that all the wars of the last two hundred years had originated in the area from the Black Sea to the Baltic and from the eastern frontier of France to the western frontier of Russia. In the last two instances the peace of the whole world had been over-turned—by Austria in World War I and by Germany in this war. I thought it should be the business of this conference and of the coming peace conference to see that this did not happen again.

Both Truman and Churchill felt that at the least the Montreux Convention should be revised, and they asked Stalin to give up the idea of a Soviet naval base in the straits in return for a Great Power guarantee of free passage of all Soviet ships in peace and wartime. Stalin said he would study the suggestion.

He then turned to the city of Königsberg in East Prussia on the Baltic Sea, asserting that the Soviet Union was entitled to an ice-free northern port at Germany's expense. Truman and Churchill did not protest strongly, although they wanted a final settlement held off until the eventual peace conference. Stalin was satisfied.

Molotov next proposed that the future of Syria and Lebanon be settled by a four-power conference of the Big Three plus France. Churchill immediately opposed such a conference; he was not eager to help the Soviet Union gain a foothold in the Middle East. During the war, Britain had ousted the Germans and Vichy French from the area and now wanted its future settled by Britain and France, in consultation with Syria and Lebanon. Of course, if the United States wished to replace Britain in the area, Churchill would welcome that. Truman shot back, "No thanks!"

The British had promised de Gaulle that as soon as he signed treaties with Syria and Lebanon guaranteeing the independence of both countries, the British would withdraw their troops from them. But until then, the British claimed, their withdrawal would leave the French there in danger of an Arab revolt. And they feared that an outbreak in the Arab world could spread to Egypt and endanger the Suez Canal, now so vital for the war against Japan.

Truman appreciated that British troops should stay in Syria and Lebanon to protect the line of communication to the Pacific war. But he disapproved of France having a quasi-colonial position in the Middle East. Stalin, recognizing Britain's wartime interest in the area, withdrew the Soviet proposal for a four-power conference.

Iran, the last subject on the day's agenda, brought apparent agreement. At Stalin's suggestion, they settled on withdrawing troops from Teheran and having the foreign ministers review the status of British and U.S. troops in the rest of Iran. Stalin seemed in no hurry for the Western garrisons to leave and promised that the Soviet Union would not take any action against Iran as the United States troops departed for the Pacific. Truman thanked him for this assurance.

As the meeting came to a close that Monday evening, Churchill reminded Truman and Stalin that he—as well as Clement Attlee, his Labour Party deputy prime minister in the wartime coalition government, and Foreign Secretary Eden—would have to leave on Wednesday to be in London for the British election results. If they lost the election, they would not return to Potsdam. But whatever the results, a British delegation would be back in time for the conference's Friday evening session; and in the meanwhile Sir Alexander Cadogan, the permanent undersecretary of foreign affairs, would stand in. Churchill requested that they hold an extra meeting on Wednesday morning before he had to depart.

At 8 P.M., Truman walked over with Byrnes and Leahy to Churchill's house on the Ringstrasse for a state dinner. During the evening, Stalin proposed that once they had defeated the Japanese together, they should hold their next meeting in Tokyo.

On Tuesday morning, July 24, Truman and the American military leaders met at British headquarters with Churchill and the British military chiefs to review the strategy for defeating Japan. At this session, Truman also received Churchill's approval of the Potsdam

Declaration, the ultimatum meant to convince the Japanese that they had no alternative but to surrender.

That afternoon, representatives of the Polish Provisional Government visited Churchill at his house. He reminded them that Britain had gone to war for Poland's sake six years earlier. But he could not accept this Polish government appropriating one quarter of Germany's arable land and displacing millions of people. The Poles and Russians would end up with the food, and the British would have the mouths to feed. His appeal, he sensed, had no effect.

Tuesday evening's conference session erupted into what Truman regarded as the most bitter dispute of the conference. By this eighth session, the Big Three were cutting close to the bone of the difficulties between East and West. The evening's hostility began when Stalin again asked the others to recognize the governments he had installed in Romania, Bulgaria, and Hungary. He repeated his assertion that there was no distinction between these Eastern European countries and Italy. None of them, he said, had had democratic elections.

Truman immediately protested. There was a difference. Italy was open to all the Allies, while Britain and the United States did not have access to the former German satellites. Certainly, the United States would recognize them and support their entry into the United Nations as soon as they allowed free access of travel and information—and not before. He demanded that they be reorganized along democratic lines as agreed at Yalta.

These were not fascist governments, Stalin replied; the government of Argentina was far less democratic, and it had been admitted to the United Nations.

Now Churchill intervened. Italy, he said, was free of censorship and was planning democratic elections, but the British knew nothing of conditions in Romania and Bulgaria. He described the problems the British Mission was having in Bucharest and said that "an iron curtain" had come down around the British representatives in Romania.

"All fairy tales!" Stalin exploded.

Churchill mildly but firmly countered that statesmen could call one another's assertions fairy tales if they wished, but that did not change the facts. Truman confirmed Churchill's charges; the U.S. Missions in Romania and Bulgaria had encountered the same constraints as had the British. This tense exchange ended only when Truman, using the conference's usual escape hatch, referred the dispute to the foreign ministers.

Truman was still angry when he wrote Bess, "We have unalterably opposed the recognition of police governments in the German Axis countries. I told Stalin that until we had free access to those countries and our nationals had their property rights restored, so far as we were concerned there'd never be recognition." Then, with a bit of humor, he added, "He seems to like it when I hit him with a hammer."

The conference then tried again to resolve the question of the Black Sea straits. Truman sought to join this specific issue to the futures of the Danube and the Rhine. "I do not want to fight another war in twenty years because of a quarrel on the Danube," he flared up. Churchill supported his attempt to broaden the discussion; he endorsed Truman's effort to make the waterways of the world free.

Molotov asked derisively if the Suez Canal was under international control such as was being proposed. Churchill replied that the question had not been raised. Molotov retorted, "I'm raising it." If international control was such a good idea, he asked, why not apply it to Suez? Exasperated, Churchill reminded him that they were discussing international control of waterways in order to help the Soviet Union gain free movement in and out of the Black Sea. And the Russians should not underestimate what they had heard.

Truman was astonished by what he regarded as Molotov's repeated demonstrations of assertive and tough rigidity. Truman found him more difficult to bring to agreement than even Stalin, and he speculated that Molotov, who was one of the old Bolsheviks of the 1917 Revolution, kept facts from Stalin when he could. Truman wrote Bess that he still liked Stalin. "He is straightforward. Knows what he wants and will compromise when he can't get it. His foreign minister isn't so forthright." Truman felt he could get along with someone who spoke his mind honestly, even if they differed fundamentally.

The conference's ninth session was held on Wednesday morning, as Churchill had requested, before the British left for home. But first the three leaders posed in the palace garden for the initial formal photographs of the conference. Then the meeting plunged once again into the Polish questions.

Eden and Byrnes had met with the Polish delegation the previous evening. They had determined that about 1.5 million Germans remained in the area under dispute.

Churchill said he was prepared to barter coal from the Ruhr in exchange for food for the German people. Stalin was willing to discuss this. But when Churchill repeated that the Poles were driving

Germans into the British and American zones without considering questions of food, fuel, and reparations, Stalin said coldly that they should understand that the Poles were taking their revenge. Their revenge, Churchill insisted, should not throw eight million Germans into the American and British zones to be fed.

Truman had opposed giving the Poles a de facto zone of occupation, but now he shifted his position ever so slightly. Acknowledging the inevitable, he said that if the Poles were to occupy a part of the Soviet zone of Germany, they should be responsible to the Soviet Union. The Poles were not one of the recognized occupying powers of Germany. The implication was that the forced removal of vast numbers of Germans could not be reversed.

Now Truman tried another approach. He explained the limitations of his constitutional powers regarding peace treaties. A treaty could be concluded only with the consent of the Senate, and its consent depended on the political sentiment in the United States. He wanted to be in a position to persuade the Senate to approve what the conference agreed on. Even beyond that, world peace would require the cooperation of all three powers at the table.

Stalin asked if Truman's limitations related only to peace treaties or to all the topics under discussion at the conference. Truman said he had broad war powers, but he wanted the American public's support for his policies.

Stalin said he understood, and then he seized the opportunity to bargain for access to the industrial resources of the Ruhr basin. He said that, just as Churchill wanted Germany's food supply to be shared among all the occupied zones, so should the coal and steel produced in the Ruhr. Churchill had a problem with that. The British would be short of coal in the coming winter because they were exporting it to help the people in Holland, France, and Belgium. Stalin was not sympathetic. He responded sharply that if he described the shortages and conditions in Russia, which had lost millions of people in the war, Churchill would burst into tears.

If Britain was so short of coal, Stalin advised, "Then use German prisoners in the mines; that is what I am doing. There are forty thousand German troops still in Norway, and you can get them from there."

Shortly thereafter, Churchill, referring to his impending departure for London, announced that he was finished.

"What a pity!" Stalin quipped.

Churchill replied quickly, "I hope to be back."

* * *

Taking advantage of the fact that the conference was adjourned until the return of the British delegation, Truman turned the next day, Thursday, July 26, into his most enjoyable in Germany. He flew to Frankfurt to meet again with General Eisenhower. Despite the ninety-seven-degree heat, he inspected the 3rd Armored and the 84th Infantry divisions and then rode for an hour in Eisenhower's armored car to the 84th Division's headquarters in Weinheim. After lunch, Truman met with 286 GIs from Missouri and then was driven back to Eisenhower's headquarters in Frankfurt.

Along the way, Truman joked that he had seen many Missourians but no soldiers from South Carolina, the home of Secretary Byrnes. The driver spoke up; he was from Spartanburg, Byrnes' hometown. Delighted, Truman stopped the caravan and summoned Byrnes from the following car to meet the driver. It turned out they lived around the corner from each other.

Back in Frankfurt, Truman recognized with a jolt that, among all the endless mountains of rubble, one huge yellow building had somehow not been touched: the great central offices of the I. G. Farben industries. It was now Eisenhower's headquarters. It was so big it reminded Truman of the Pentagon. It must have been hard to miss.

Eisenhower introduced the President to Kay Summersby, his English secretary-chauffeur, with whom he was very close. She found Truman "a very appealing man." The general told Truman that Summersby wanted to become an American citizen, and as a result of that conversation she flew to Washington three months later to take out her first citizenship papers.

By 7 P.M. the President had returned to Babelsberg. On that busy day, he still found time to be introspective and wrote in his diary:

> The Communist Party in Moscow is no different in its methods and action toward the common man than were the Czar and the Russian Noblemen (so called: they were anything but noble) Nazis and Facists [*sic*] were worse. It seems that Sweden, Norway, Denmark and perhaps Switzerland are the only real peoples governments on the Continent of Europe. But the rest are a bad lot from the standpoint of the people who do not believe in tyranny.

At 9:20 that evening, he announced to the world the Potsdam Declaration, the ultimatum warning Japan to accept unconditional surrender or expect to be destroyed. It promised "the inevitable and complete destruction of the Japanese armed forces and just as inevitably the utter devastation of the Japanese homeland." The alternative to unconditional surrender is "prompt and utter destruction." But it also made clear that "we do not intend that the Japanese shall be enslaved as a race or destroyed as a nation."

The declaration did not mention the Emperor. The draft that Truman and Byrnes had brought with them to Potsdam had said that a postwar Japanese government "may include a constitutional monarchy under the present dynasty if it be shown to the complete satisfaction of the world that such a Government shall never again aspire to aggression." In the final declaration, even this assurance was watered down to establishing "with the freely expressed will of the Japanese people a peacefully inclined and responsible government."

This ambiguous and conditional statement was designed to deal with political opinions in Washington. It certainly did not assuage Japanese fears of surrendering. But this was as much as Truman would modify the demand for unconditional surrender.

Truman also received an invitation from Churchill in London, proposing that after the conference Truman fly to Plymouth, England. USS *Augusta* could pick him up there, rather than in Antwerp. King George VI would be aboard a British cruiser in Plymouth harbor and wished to invite the President to lunch. The king would then pay a return visit to *Augusta* before she sailed for home. Truman readily accepted the invitation.

In London that same day, Churchill announced to the British people that they had voted him out of office. They had thus retired the most imposing and charismatic leader of the era—excepting perhaps Franklin Roosevelt—both from the world scene and from the ponderous attempt at Potsdam to bring peace and order out of Europe's chaos. Winston Churchill would not be going back to Potsdam. Truman was not at all thrilled to have to deal with Churchill's successor, the Oxford-bred Clement Attlee; but he was reassured because Attlee had been quietly present as Churchill's deputy throughout the Potsdam deliberations so far; the President felt Attlee grasped the problems before them.

In Paris, Charles de Gaulle commented eloquently on the historic change of the British government: "Winston Churchill lost neither his glory nor his popularity thereby, but only the general adherence he had won as a guide and symbol of the nation in peril. His nature, identified with magnificent enterprise, his countenance, etched by the fires and frosts of great events, had become inadequate to the era of mediocrity." De Gaulle regarded Churchill's departure with "melancholy" because, although they had often been adversaries, Churchill "had vitally aided the cause of France."

The next day, the leaders of the reconstituted British delegation had not yet arrived, so again there was no meeting in Potsdam. Truman spent the time working on his mail and meeting with his advisors.

Late on Saturday afternoon, the British flew into Gatow Airport. With Prime Minister Attlee came Ernest Bevin, who had replaced Eden as foreign secretary. The two Labour Party stalwarts promptly called on Truman at the Little White House, primarily to introduce Bevin to the American President.

Truman thought to himself that the arrival of the new British delegation demonstrated the peaceful way in which a democracy changes its government. But he also decided that, compared to the likable Churchill, both Attlee and Bevin were "sourpusses" and that the new foreign minister promised to be "a tough person to deal with." He wrote Bess, "Bevin is an English John L. Lewis. Can you imagine John L. being my Secretary of State?" But over time, he would come to regard Bevin as reasonable and clearheaded.

Coincidentally, the plane of Navy Secretary Forrestal, who was only now arriving at the conference, had to delay its landing until Attlee's and Bevin's planes had put down. That evening, Forrestal dined with Truman, who told him he was not finding Stalin too hard to do business with. And reflecting on Churchill's defeat, Truman felt confident that it was not yet time for such a political reversal in the States.

Forrestal soon learned that others did not share Truman's optimism about dealing with the Russians. In fact, Averell Harriman said that Hitler's greatest crime had been enabling the Soviet Union to dominate Eastern Europe, which was precisely what he had supposedly come to power to prevent. And Forrestal discovered that one crucial American objective at Potsdam had changed. Truman had left Washington convinced that his main task would be to bring the Soviet Union into the war against Japan. But now Byrnes was eager to finish the Pacific war before the Soviet Union could join it. Once the Soviet Union was allowed in, he feared, it would be difficult to dislodge.

Forrestal asked Bevin whether he agreed that the Allies should insist on removing the Emperor as part of the Japanese surrender. Bevin, surprisingly at this late date, said that this would require a bit of thought. He had always believed, he said, that if the kaiser had survived World War I, perhaps Germany could have been guided to a constitutional monarchy and the psychological doors would never have been left open for an extremist like Hitler.

Even though the British had arrived so late in the day, it was decided to meet that evening; and at 10:15 the tenth session began. But first Stalin wanted to make an announcement. The Soviet government had received a response to its inquiry (which had been made with Truman's secret concurrence) asking why the Japanese government wanted to send Prince Konoye to Moscow.

The Japanese had originally asked on July 13 whether Prince Konoye would be welcome in Moscow. At that time Stalin, after consulting with Truman, had stalled and replied that he would have to know what the prince wanted to discuss.

Now Tokyo confirmed what Stalin and Truman already knew: Prince Konoye had been charged by the Emperor to tell Stalin that he desired to avoid more bloodshed. The Emperor wanted the prince to seek Stalin's help to mediate an end to the war. He would also be authorized to negotiate Soviet-Japanese relations during and after the war.

Stalin said he would again discourage the Japanese approach, and Truman thanked him. The Potsdam Declaration, which had been sent to Tokyo through Switzerland and Sweden, was on the table. What else was there to discuss? Then, as if to confirm the basis for this tough-minded stance, U.S. radio monitors, on this same date, reported that Radio Tokyo had broadcast the Japanese government's decision to reject the Potsdam Declaration and continue the war. The government in Tokyo condemned the American ultimatum as "presumptuous."

The offical conference session began by taking up once again the question of recognizing Italy and the former German satellite countries, on which the foreign ministers were stalemated. The heads of government also failed to come to an accommodation. Truman then raised the subject of reparations from Italy, which the Russians demanded and the Americans opposed. He explained that the United States had already contributed $500 million for the feeding and rehabilitation of Italy, and still more would be needed to keep the Italians from starving. The American people would not stand for diverting this money to pay for reparations to the Soviet Union. Prime Minister Attlee supported Truman, even though, he added, he was totally sympathetic to the suffering the Russian people had endured. But Stalin was unyielding; the Russian people would not understand if their leaders did not exact reparations from Italy, which had sent its army as far as the Volga River to fight the Russians and lay waste their country.

They finally permitted the Soviet Union to take Italian military equipment and war plants as reparations. Stalin was pleased; he would accept equipment as reparations. "Military equipment," Bevin interjected, pressing the distinction. "Yes, military equipment," Stalin conceded.

For Truman, the important point was that Stalin promised that the Russians would not touch the American monetary advances to Italy. "I do not wish to ignore the interests of America," Stalin said. With at least that point settled, the meeting was adjourned shortly after midnight.

Back at the Little White House in Babelsberg, Truman stopped by the Advance Map Room to look for news of the Senate debate over the ratification of the United Nations Charter. Just before he went to bed, he was handed a flash from Washington informing him that the Senate had ratified the charter by a vote of 89–2. In contrast to the Senate's rejection of the League of Nations only twenty-five years earlier, the United States was now committed to participate in the post–World War II world.

Elated, Truman immediately wrote out a statement for the press: "It is deeply gratifying that the Senate has ratified the United Nations Charter by virtually unanimous vote. The action of the Senate substantially advances the cause of world peace."

The next day was Sunday, and when Truman returned from attending Protestant church services, he found Molotov and his interpreter waiting for him at the Little White House. They reported that Stalin had a cold and his doctors had ordered him to remain in his residence; he would not be able to attend the conference session later that day. Molotov had come over to see what he could accomplish while his boss was incapacitated.

Truman sent Stalin a note expressing his regrets at his illness, and he later speculated in his diary:

If Stalin should suddenly cash in it would end the original Big Three. First Roosevelt by death, then Churchill by political failure and then Stalin. I am wondering what would happen to Russia and central Europe if Joe suddenly passed out. If some demagogue or house hack gained control of the efficient Russian military machine, he could play havoc with European peace for a while. I also wonder if there is a man with the necessary strength and following to step into Stalin's place and maintain peace and solidarity at home. It isn't customary for dictators to train leaders to follow them in power.

Molotov suggested that he and Truman discuss some of the conference's outstanding issues—without Stalin. Truman called in Byrnes, Leahy, and his interpreter "Chip" Bohlen; and they talked for an hour.

Although Molotov had created this unexpected and unprecedented meeting, Byrnes seized the initiative. He told Molotov that in his view the two most important issues they had to settle were Poland's western boundary and German reparations. He handed Molotov a proposal defining the western boundary of Poland until a peace treaty was signed. It broached a compromise by which Poland would continue to administer East Prussia and Danzig but not the area between the Eastern and Western Neisse rivers. Molotov objected instantly; Stalin would not agree. Truman asked him to present it to Stalin anyway.

As for German reparations, Molotov sought to set a fixed sum in either dollars ($2 billion) or equipment (five to six million tons). Byrnes said his staff felt it was impossible to settle on a fixed amount on either scale, but the United States would offer the Soviet Union 25 percent of the total equipment finally available from the Ruhr. Molotov dismissed the offer: 25 percent of an undetermined figure meant little. Truman spoke up. The percentage was not the point. Since he was trying to arrive at a workable reparations plan, he would be willing for the Soviet Union to receive even 50 percent of the total. Everyone acknowledged that the Soviet Union had suffered the most from the Nazis; it could expect the largest share of reparations.

They also discussed again the Soviet interest in the German merchant and naval fleets. Truman reminded Molotov that the Soviet Union was to get one third of the Navy now and one third of the merchant fleet after it had been used in the war against Japan.

When the meeting was almost over, Molotov revealed the real reason he was there. Unexpectedly, he brought up—on behalf of Premier Stalin, he claimed—the Soviet entry into the Japanese war. He now suggested that the Allies formally request the Soviet government to intervene against Japan on the basis of shortening the war and saving lives.

Truman was shocked. He calmly told Molotov he would study the idea. But the request exasperated him. Stalin had assured him of Soviet participation against Japan, and he had felt he had won the most important single victory possible at Potsdam. It would save American lives. Now the rug was being pulled out. Hadn't the Russians repeatedly committed themselves to come in? Why did they need a public invitation? This seemed like a cynical maneuver to make the world think that the Soviet Union was the key to victory.

Truman certainly had reason to feel deceived. At the Teheran Conference, Stalin had promised Churchill and Roosevelt that the Soviet Union would enter the war against Japan when Germany was defeated. At Yalta and again at Potsdam, Stalin had confirmed that the Soviets would enter the Pacific war within three months after V-E Day. The only condition was that the Soviet Union and China first conclude a treaty of mutual accommodation. To Truman and his advisors there was no question that the Soviet Union had obligated itself to enter the war.

After Molotov left, Truman promptly notified Attlee of this surprising development. And two days later, he sent Stalin a diplomatic letter saying, in effect, that the Soviet Union was pledged to enter the war under the Moscow Declaration of July 1943 and the provisions of the U.N. Charter "with a view to joint action on behalf of the community of nations to maintain peace and security."

He wrote his mother and Bess in a harsher tone than he ever had before. The foreign ministers, including "the able Mr. Byrnes," were getting some things accomplished, he said. But he was caustic about Stalin: "I rather think Mr. Stalin is stallin' because he is not happy over the English elections. He doesn't know it but I have an ace in the hole and another showing—so unless he has three or two pair (and I know he has not) we are sitting all right." He added, "You never saw such pig-headed people as are the Russians. I hope I never have to hold another conference with them—but, of course, I will."

With Stalin absent, the conference did not convene on July 29 or 30; it met next on the thirty-first. Then, after so many tedious discussions in which their self-interests frustrated agreement, the three leaders now strove to resolve some of the problems in the little time remaining.

Hoping to break the impasse, the U.S. delegation sought to link three major issues: reparations, Poland's western border, and satellite membership in the United Nations. Stalin protested that these were quite separate questions. Byrnes conceded that, but they had been studying the questions for weeks without result and the United States now wanted to speed up action on all three. Perhaps this coupling would force compromises.

On reparations, Stalin and Molotov haggled over the percentages the Soviet Union would get from the British, French, and American zones. When they arrived at a formula, Bevin argued that the percentages they were giving the Soviet Union plus the reparations from the Soviet zone would give Stalin more than 50 percent of the total. Stalin insisted it was less than 50 percent. (Truman commented privately, "The Russians are naturally looters.")

Truman moved on to the second of the three: Poland's western border. In order to conclude the matter, Truman was now prepared to allow the Poles to administer the area bounded by the Oder and the Western Neisse rivers. Taken aback, Bevin said his instructions were still to hold out for the Eastern Neisse. He warned that the U.S. proposal meant that the disputed area would be ruled by the Polish state and not be part of the Soviet zone of occupation or Soviet responsibility.

Truman disagreed: cession of territory must wait for the peace treaty, and the American proposal referred only to the area's temporary administration. Bevin asked sardonically whether the British could give away parts of their zone without the approval of the other governments. Stalin replied that Poland was a unique case, a country without a western border, and they had to determine its border with Germany. Byrnes also insisted that this was not a cession of territory; the Soviet Union was just letting the Poles administer this territory for the time being. Finally, Truman simply declared that they all agreed on the Polish question.

Stalin, as though he could not quite believe that the Americans had given in, declared, "Stettin is in the Polish territory." Yielding, Bevin said, "Yes. We should inform the French."

Then, as though in exchange, Stalin accepted without significant objection the American position on the admission of the former satellite states into the United Nations—which earlier had been the subject of such prolonged and acrimonious debate.

They next took up the economic control of Germany. Both Truman and Stalin asserted that the Ruhr should remain part of Germany. Bevin asked why the subject was being raised at all. Stalin explained that at one time the Great Powers had considered separating the Ruhr from Germany and placing it under international control, but they had changed their minds. Now Stalin merely wanted to make sure that Germany would not be dismembered. The Americans and Russians were both prepared to leave the Ruhr's great industrial potential in German hands. But Bevin felt he had to discuss this development with his government, so they turned the matter over to the Council of Foreign Ministers.

The Potsdam Conference began its twelfth session at 4 P.M. on August 1. Byrnes announced that the foreign ministers had not been able to resolve the question of reparations because the Big Three had not agreed on the Soviet Union's claim to German gold and foreign assets. Stalin proposed that the Soviet Union would not claim gold that the other allies had found in Germany; but, to apportion foreign investments, they should draw a geographical line of demarcation between the Soviet and Western zones from the Baltic to the Adriatic. The discussion dragged on, and they finally settled on the Soviet demarcation line. Stalin apparently was having second thoughts about how this division of spoils would appear to the rest of the world; he wanted the agreement put into the protocol but not published. Truman objected immediately; he saw no reason for secrecy, and Stalin conceded the point.

Truman had learned that Stalin was willing to bend on minor or procedural points; but on basic issues he would remain rigid and often resort to diversionary tactics.

Then Byrnes was ready to report on the question of Nazi war criminals, and Stalin made an issue out of the fact that he was not prepared to name names. Byrnes wanted the prosecutor to identify the war criminals. Stalin wanted them named now. He included Alfried Krupp's name because he was especially insistent that the industrialists who had cooperated with the Nazis be tried and the world know about it.

Truman warned that naming only some war criminals would let others think they could escape, and Justice Robert Jackson had told him that naming the criminals in advance might handicap the commission. Relenting a bit, Stalin still wanted them named as examples, but he said he would be satisfied with three names. When Attlee suggested that Hitler be one of them, Stalin wryly responded that Hitler was not available but he had no objection to naming him.

Surprisingly, Stalin was the one who stressed that the public was interested in the fate of war criminals. In fact, he wanted to know why Rudolf Hess, Hitler's former Nazi Party deputy, was living so comfortably in Britain. Attlee curtly dismissed the criticism: "You need not worry about that." Stiffly, Stalin said the people in the occupied countries cared. Bevin assured him that Hess would be turned over for trial and added that Britain would send along a bill for his care. Unfazed, Stalin asked that the first list of war criminals be named in one month, and they finally settled on that.

The last hurdle they faced was the protocol—the formal record of understandings reached—and the final communiqué. Truman had a special request; he asked that his proposal for the international control of waterways be included. Stalin objected emphatically, but Truman insisted: it had been considered by the conference, after all. He even made a personal appeal to Stalin. The premier wanted to know why the Black Sea straits would not be mentioned, and Truman assured him they would be. Truman intended to tell the Senate about the discussion of inland waterways, and he wanted no one to charge that secret agreements had been made at Potsdam. Stalin said there were no secrets, and Truman concurred. Later he wrote, "I had made up my mind from the beginning that I would enter into no secret agreements, and there was none."

Actually, one significant secret agreement had been made at Potsdam. Truman, Churchill, and the Combined Chiefs of Staff had decided that at the end of the war Indochina would be divided for purposes of disarming the Japanese and recovering Allied prisoners. China would be given surrender authority above the 16th Parallel and the British below. This was not made public on the excuse that it was a military arrangement and therefore classified. And since the Soviet Union could not participate in the decision, the matter was not officially a part of the conference. But eventually the arrangement was to take on a permanence of its own, open the door to dividing Vietnam, and make it easier for the French to return.

They argued over whether the exact line of the Russian-Polish border would be decided by the Russians and Poles alone (as Stalin wanted) or whether the other Allies would be involved. Attlee recommended a commission of experts appointed by the peace conference to lay out the frontier. In the end, Stalin dropped his objection and accepted the wording as it had been drafted. Truman was getting impatient with what he labeled the "prolonged and petty bickering." At times, when the discussion bogged down, he would leave the table, pace the floor, and even stroll out into the halls and gardens.

They finally agreed on the protocol. Stalin did not want minor decisions listed in the communiqué, but he had no objection to Bevin reporting them to the House of Commons.

The thirteenth and final session of the conference convened at 10:40 P.M., after the delegations had had time to draft the protocol and communiqué. When the drafts were presented, the principals still debated wording and amendments. They even argued over the order in which they would sign the communiqué. Stalin thought he should come first. Attlee jokingly suggested alphabetical order. Truman typically did not care who signed first.

When Truman announced the conference was ready to adjourn, he said he hoped the next meeting would be in Washington. Stalin said, uncharacteristically, "God willing." The Potsdam Conference adjourned at 12:30 A.M. on August 2. There was much handshaking all around and well-wishing for safe journeys. Truman and Stalin would never meet again.

The ink on the communiqué was barely dry before the hard-liners, who would soon turn into containment advocates and Cold Warriors, voiced their dismay at what they saw as Truman's naïveté. George Kennan wrote with indignation, "I viewed the labors of the Potsdam Conference with unmitigated skepticism and despair. I cannot recall any political document the reading of which filled me with a greater sense of depression than the communiqué to which President Truman set his name at the conclusion of these confused and unreal discussions."

Kennan was convinced that the Soviet Union would give no agreed-to meaning to terms like "the principles of democracy" or resolve such issues as reparations with any sense of fairness. He opposed conducting trials of war criminals jointly with the Russians, and preferred that Nazi leaders, when they fell into Allied hands, simply "be executed forthwith." In his view, the Stalinist regime had perpetrated so many atrocities and brutalities itself that it did not deserve to participate in such judgments.

As the conference adjourned, Truman had no idea that such indignation and disapproval existed in the Foreign Service. He returned to the Little White House and within hours was driven to Gatow Airport, eager to get back to Washington. He left Potsdam confident that several important agreements had been reached. He was proud that he had suggested the creation of the Council of Foreign Ministers as an international consultative body. He believed the formula for reparations meant the United States would not have to pay the reparations bill again and left Germany able to "develop into a decent nation." The Polish frontiers, of course, were a compromise and subject to a peace conference. He had received from Stalin reaffirmation of the Soviet Union's entry into the war against Japan, although this had been outside the conference agenda.

For a practical man like Harry Truman, this was not a bad record, given the contentious interests around the table. And highly important to him had been meeting personally with Stalin and the Russians: "It enabled me to see at first hand what we and the West had to face in the future." Truman had changed; he had come to recognize the Soviet leaders as tough, relentless bargainers, always pressing for advantage. They believed, he was told, that the West was headed for a major economic depression, and they intended to take full advantage of it; he was persuaded that the Russians were ready to fight not for peace but for national advantage. And he interpreted Stalin's refusal to accept his proposal to internationalize all the major waterways as meaning that the Soviet leader wanted to control the Black Sea straits and the Danube. Years later, looking back at that moment, he would even write, "The Russians were planning world conquest." Even if that statement was the expression of later hindsight, he came away from Potsdam with strong impressions that would affect the postwar world. He had lost much of the hopeful idealism with which he had sailed for Germany.

The final summit of World War II was now over, and a great, last opportunity had been lost. The men at the table in Potsdam were occupied with their nervous national self-interests and with winning the war still being fought in Asia. Having been so close to the problems (and not having the perspective that time and experience would afford), they had trouble seeing the larger canvas. They could have advanced postwar peace through international cooperation. Present at the moment of the birth of the atomic age, they could have explored the dangerous planetary future. Hard-headed and practical as they were, they instead opened the door on what was, in fact, to be the postwar world.

Truman was tired and glad to be going home. That morning, he flew in the *Sacred Cow* to an airfield near Plymouth, England, the port from which the Pilgrims had sailed for America 325 years before.

And just before noon he, Leahy, and Byrnes boarded the battleship HMS *Renown*, anchored in Plymouth Roads. King George VI met them on the quarter deck, extended his hand, and said, "Welcome to my country."

At lunch the king was particularly curious about the atomic bomb. After Truman returned to *Augusta*, the king in turn came aboard the American cruiser. He inspected the Marine guard, toured the decks, and descended to Truman's quarters and "took a snort of Haig & Haig," the President noted. These formalities over, *Augusta* got under way, sailing at twenty-six knots and making 645 miles every twenty-four hours.

On August 6 Truman and Byrnes were lunching with the enlisted men when the President was handed a message confirming that, just hours before, the first atomic bomb had been dropped on Hiroshima. A second message from Stimson said the bombing had been even more successful than had been expected. The President announced the dramatic news to the crew in the mess hall and was greeted with applause and cheers. Maybe now the Japanese would surrender—maybe now an American invasion of their homeland would not be necessary.

Chapter 15

"The Great American Illusion"

Arriving in Washington on August 7, Harry Truman had been away from the White House for a month and a day. Although the first atomic bomb had just exterminated Hiroshima, the Japanese were showing no willingness to surrender unconditionally.

Truman's attention was now concentrated on Asia. Climactic events were taking place there, but he had no clear vision of what postwar Asia would be like. Its future, as far as the Great Powers could shape it, was totally unsettled. East Asia looked like shattered glass, made up of a thousand random pieces, and he moved into that puzzle step by step, problem by problem.

World War II had actually started in China, and Asia had been ravaged by more than a dozen years of warfare; millions had died, and millions more had been uprooted. Now China teetered on the lip of a massive civil war; Japan's expansive and ruthless militarism had not yet been squashed; the Soviet Union was poised to seize territory and power, and the winds of nationalism were sweeping through the vast continent.

As late as May 1, Navy Secretary Forrestal had asked at a policy meeting whether the government should begin studying American objectives in East Asia. Surprisingly, his basic questions had not yet been addressed: Did the United States want to destroy Japan's industrial structure and "morgenthau" the islands, or was the goal for Japan to rejoin "the society of nations" after it was demilitarized? Did the United States seek in Asia a postwar counterweight to the Soviet Union and, if so, should the balancing force come from China or Japan?

Twelve days later, in a State Department meeting, Ambassador Harriman also raised questions about the whole range of American policies on Asia: Was Soviet participation in the war against Japan still essential? Should the Soviet Union share in the occupation of Japan? Should there be a trusteeship for Korea? Should the United States try to ease the British out of Hong Kong? Should the French be permitted a free hand in Indochina?

But it was not enough for politicians to sit in Washington and ask astute questions. What was desired or decided in Washington, or London or Paris or Moscow, would not necessarily determine the nature of postwar Asia. The people who lived there would have a lot to say.

Years later, Secretary of State Dean Acheson summed it up in a foreign policy speech: "In Asia, population differences in race, ideas, languages, religion, culture and development are vast. Blended, they had evoked throughout Asia the revolutionary forces of nationalism. Resignation had given way to hope and anger." Certainly, in Asia the tremendous explosion of World War II had cracked the crust of resignation. And certainly, hope had paired itself with anger.

The polities that would over time influence most strongly what was to happen in Asia were China and Japan; the weight of Western Europe and the United States was diminished by distance. But China, suffering from the long Japanese occupation, was itself torn apart by civil and ideological conflict. And Japan was still battling the combined powers of the world. Beyond them, any number of smaller Asian countries, which had been dominated by Western or Asian imperialism, now nursed the seeds of rebellion and national revolt. Great Power leaders who wished to help determine what kind of world would emerge from World War II had to take all this into account.

When Truman had first arrived in the Oval Room, American East Asian planning was predicated on a democratic China, not a resurrected Japan. United States policy favored the Nationalist government of the Kuomintang and Chiang Kai-shek but also sought the cooperation of the Communists led by Mao Tse-tung. The United States wanted China to settle its internal turmoil, integrate its great Nationalist and Communist military strength, marshal its vast manpower resource to help defeat Japan, and become a strong and unified democratic power for postwar stabilization in Asia. The American objectives for China, so deeply torn between two power centers, were unity and democracy. Afterwards, Dean Acheson said, "Only later did we understand that we were, in effect, seeking the reconciliation of irreconcilable factions."

Just five days in office, Truman was introduced to the paradoxes in U.S. China policy when Secretary of State Stettinius sent him two contradictory messages. The first came from Patrick Hurley, the U.S. ambassador to China. Hurley, a colorful Oklahoma lawyer and ex-cowboy, had been a secretary of war to President Herbert Hoover and was an ardent supporter of General MacArthur. In March Roosevelt had personally sent Hurley to discuss policy toward China with Churchill and Eden and with Stalin and Molotov. Hurley now informed Truman that Churchill would support American efforts to unify the military forces in China, but the prime minister regarded the expectation of democracy evolving in China as "the great American illusion."

Hurley also reported that Stalin and Molotov denied that they were supporting the Chinese Communist Party and promoting civil war in China. Surprisingly, the Soviet leaders said they would accept both the United States' short-term goal of the unification of China's military forces and its long-term wish for a democratic government in China.

In addition to Hurley's report, Stettinius sent Truman a radically different point of view expressed by George Kennan, who was serving as chargé d'affaires in Moscow during Ambassador Harriman's absence. This was in the form of a personal message to Harriman in which Kennan took it upon himself to reinterpret what Stalin had said to Hurley. Kennan and John Paton Davies, the Moscow embassy's China expert, felt that Hurley's report, if left standing alone and without their analysis, would give Washington "a serious misimpression" of Stalin's true attitude toward affairs in China. Kennan's more skeptical and less gullible judgment was that Stalin accepted the ideas of the unification of China's armed forces and of a politically united China only because he knew these could not take place without the Chinese Communists' agreement. Stalin, Kennan said, would accept a free and democratic China because to him that meant a China free of all foreign influences except the Soviet.

Stettinius added his own interpretation: "Kennan is convinced that Soviet policy will remain a policy aimed at the achievement of maximum power with minimum responsibility." Truman welcomed Kennan's cautions; he was already troubled by "the attitude Russia had assumed."

* * *

Truman, as he initially did on all issues, continued FDR's policy toward China—trying to unify the Chinese armed forces under the Nationalist government and support "the great American illusion" of a democratic Chinese government. On May 12 he ordered Ambassador Hurley to continue working toward Roosevelt's so far unrealized objectives.

The United States had supplied China with top-level advisors and extensive economic support. Congress had approved a $500 million credit to China in 1942. And now, on May 14, Foreign Minister T. V. Soong visited Truman to ask him to release the final $200 million in gold to help China fight inflation. Truman ended up releasing the gold but also approving a letter from Secretary of the Treasury Morgenthau sternly insisting that China carry out effective economic reforms.

Hurley, always vastly overoptimistic about what he had accomplished, reported to Truman on May 20 that he was gaining cooperation between the Chinese Nationalists and the Chinese Communists. When the Nationalists included a Communist in their delegation to San Francisco, Hurley regarded that as their recognition of the Communists. He was also convinced that he had brought about meetings between Communist and Nationalist leaders that he claimed had averted civil war and moved toward the United States' goal of uniting the two factions' armies under one commander in order to fight Japan. Of course, Hurley was grasping at straws.

China actually contributed little to the war against Japan because Chiang Kai-shek's Nationalist government was inefficient, corrupt, demoralized, and oppressive. And following a long Chinese tradition, Chiang was preserving his strength in order to overcome the Chinese Communists and the warlords when this foreigners' war was over.

For a few months in 1944–1945, the U.S. 20th Bomber Command, based in India and led by Major General Curtis E. LeMay, bombed Japan from forward airfields in China. Before each mission the 20th Bomber Command had to ferry its own fuel from India over the Himalayas ("the Hump")—seven supply flights were required for each B-29 Superfortress bombing strike. And even under LeMay's hard-driving leadership, the 20th Bomber Command managed only two sorties per bomber per month against Japan.

Major General Claire Lee Chennault, who had earlier led the Flying Tigers, American volunteers flying combat for Chiang Kai-shek, commanded the Fourteenth Air Force in eastern China. Its fuel was also flown laboriously over the Hump to bomb Japanese bases on the Chinese coast.

In the spring of 1944, two significant military events occurred. The Japanese effectively attacked the Fourteenth Air Force's bases, and the U.S. Central Pacific offensive came within B-29 range of Japan. By January 1945 LeMay was transferred to the Marianas to run his bombing campaign from there. Later, he declared that the entire strategy of bombing Japan from China had been "absurd." And Roosevelt and Churchill began to depend less on Chiang and his flagrant ineffectualness. Instead they looked to the Soviet Union to neutralize the Japanese on the Asian mainland.

American military leaders repeatedly sought an alternative to committing sizable U.S. forces to the Chinese mainland. Major General Albert Wedemeyer, the highest American officer in China after General Joseph Stilwell was removed in October 1944, tried to persuade the Chinese to mount an offensive to open a port in southeast China, shorten the supply lines into China, and tie down Japanese soldiers who might otherwise reinforce the defense of Japan. He wanted to include Chinese Communist forces in his plans but was overruled by Ambassador Hurley, who was supposed to be working out a political coalition between Nationalists and Communists. (Wedemeyer's efforts would come under attack during the McCarthy witch-hunt after the war.) The Chinese Nationalists did not launch the Wedemeyer-inspired offensive until July 1945, when it was too late to be useful. China was more a victim than a participant in World War II.

Chapter 16
Ready to Invade Japan

Harry Truman told Congress that his goal was to win the war against Japan "completely . . . to win it as quickly as possible." If Japan resisted "beyond the point of reason," it would be destroyed as Germany had been destroyed. Japan would not be blockaded and starved into submission; it would be invaded—and victory would be total. The United States, he promised, would force an unconditional surrender.

Truman's repeated call for unconditional surrender certainly did not encourage the Japanese military to quit the fight. Although Prime Minister Suzuki's new cabinet in Tokyo secretly began to explore whether the Soviet Union would mediate an end to the war—on Japan's terms—the Japanese military would fight to the end.

If they surrendered unconditionally, what would the ruthless, vengeful Americans do to the Emperor? Unconditional surrender would put the Emperor at risk. Whether the Emperor would be kept as head of the Japanese state was a life-and-death question for most Japanese.

To his people, Emperor Hirohito was descended from gods. To Westerners, he was an ordinary little man, absent-minded, shy, with a receding chin. His mustache was straggly, and he wore thick spectacles. His passion was marine biology, and he loved to spend hours in his laboratory with his microscope and slides. Ironically, he had named his reign "Showa," which meant "bright peace" or "enlightened peace." (Some in the West interpreted this to refer to the elimination of all Western influences.)

Despite his unimposing appearance, Hirohito was to most Americans evil incarnate. They had learned to hate him. Sentiment in the United States was overwhelmingly "Hirohito must go!" The Gallup Poll in June 1945 showed that 35 percent of Americans wanted the Emperor executed as a war criminal; only 7 percent were willing to have him retained, even as a puppet.

Among Truman's advisors, James Byrnes, Harry Hopkins, Dean Acheson, and Archibald MacLeish believed that if Hirohito stayed in place the war would have been worthless. They opposed easing the surrender terms and supported Truman's personal dedication to unconditional surrender. Acheson also made the pragmatic argument that Hirohito should be removed because he was weak and could not be relied upon to keep the Japanese military under control in the future.

There were other voices Truman could have listened to. Assistant Secretary of War John McCloy urged that in order to end the war the Japanese be promised that they could retain the Emperor. General Marshall and Admiral Leahy were beginning to favor keeping the Emperor. Secretary Forrestal and the U.S. Navy believed Japan could be forced to surrender by a naval blockade and opposed invading Japan; they argued for reconsidering a negotiated settlement. MacArthur declared it madness to expect the Japanese to renounce their Emperor. At Yalta in February, even Churchill suggested relaxing the unconditional-surrender requirement to shorten the war. And French philosopher Raymond Aron went so far as to call unconditional surrender "completely unreasonable."

Many serious people had opinions; but the responsibility for winning and ending this war, in which the Japanese had already killed 92,000 Americans (and wounded another 200,000), belonged to Harry Truman—with guidance from Secretary of State Byrnes, Secretary of War Stimson, and Army Chief of Staff Marshall. Together, their job, plain and simple, was to defeat Japan.

The Americans were assembling a massive army to assault Japan's home islands. Already in the Pacific theater west of Hawaii were 1.25 million American soldiers and Marines. And in the European theater, when the Germans surrendered, Eisenhower commanded three million Americans; all but one of his sixty-one U.S. divisions had seen battle action. Truman approved moving a million of these GIs—thirty divisions—from Europe to the Pacific. Troops began to be shipped around the globe.

The invasion of Japan would be one of the most dread assaults ever attempted. Hundreds of thousands of dedicated Japanese would meet the Americans on the beaches to defend their homeland, families, and Emperor. General Marshall told Truman to expect 500,000 American casualties; Secretary of War Stimson predicted a million.

These numbers were not overblown. In battle after battle, the nearer the fighting had approached Japan, the larger had grown the toll of American dead and wounded. Okinawa, the last battle before the invasion of Japan and the most expensive, had cost 49,151 American battle casualties, plus 26,211 "nonbattle" casualties, mostly neuropsychiatric cases.

The battles for the home islands would be still bloodier. Marshall and MacArthur agreed that the first assault—against Kyushu, the southernmost home island—would cost 31,000 American casualties in the first month alone. The second invasion, of the main island of Honshu, would be much more expensive. Pentagon planners used the figure of a total of 500,000 casualties in preparing for the invasion.

These troubling, almost intolerable, projections came from sober, conservative men now experienced in war. Truman listened to them. Their predictions helped him decide to bring the Soviet Union into the Pacific war and to drop the atomic bombs. The Joint Chiefs of Staff even studied the use of toxic gas to decrease the loss of American lives.

The Japanese understood the threat they faced and prepared to deal with it. They would drive the invaders back into the sea. They had some four million men under arms to defend their home islands, Korea, Manchuria, and North China; two million of them were on the home islands. On Kyushu, where the terrain was rugged and very defendable, fourteen divisions and five independent brigades waited—an army as large as the Americans' invasion force. The Japanese were holding back several thousand planes—for use as kamikazes if necessary—and soldiers were training for suicide attacks against the superior American M-4 and flamethrower tanks. The military was also building a "national volunteer army" to make a last-ditch stand. The Japanese were preparing for Armageddon.

Most U.S. Army generals were eager to defeat the Japanese Army on the ground and occupy the islands; but some top U.S. naval officers, including Admirals Ernest J. King and Raymond A. Spruance, commander of the U.S. Fifth Fleet, were convinced that the Navy could win the war without an amphibious assault. American sea- and airpower would cut off Japan from its food and fuel supplies and strangle her. Admiral Leahy, chief of staff to both Roosevelt and Truman, said "a completely blockaded Japan would then fall by its own weight."

The interservice debate was fierce, even though the Navy was clearly in the minority. Navy strategy was to seize bases on the South China coast from which to bombard Japan. Army planners argued that the cost of fighting the Japanese on the mainland of China would be prohibitive and would not eliminate the need to invade Japan. MacArthur pointed out that intensive air bombardment had failed to defeat Germany; he supported an early invasion of Kyushu. When Nimitz came around to MacArthur's position and King finally went along, the dice were cast for the invasion.

The loss of Okinawa left the Japanese home islands naked before the enemy. In Tokyo, Prime Minister Baron Kantaro Suzuki opened the Diet on June 9 with a call to arms: "The Japanese will lose the meaning of their existence if the national polity is impaired. An unconditional surrender as proposed by the enemy, therefore, is tantamount to the death of all 100 million people of Japan. We have no alternative but to fight."

On June 22, in his first outspoken act of the war, Emperor Hirohito summoned the prime minister, foreign minister, and military chiefs and urged that the war be ended by diplomatic means.

In early July, just before the Potsdam Conference, American code breakers intercepted radio messages from Japanese Foreign Minister Togo instructing Ambassador Naotake Sato in Moscow to ask the Soviet Union to mediate an end to the war on favorable terms. If such terms were not possible, Japan was determined to fight to the death to avoid unconditional surrender. Togo offered to send to Moscow as negotiator Prince Konoye, who would come bearing the Emperor's personal letter.

Togo ordered Ambassador Sato to see Molotov before the Russian leaders left for Potsdam and inform him of the Emperor's strong desire to end the war. The message from Tokyo reemphasized that the Japanese would not accept unconditional surrender. Ambassador Sato replied that these proposals were unrealistic, that the Soviet Union could not be divided from its allies, and that Japan should realize it had been defeated. He was ordered to carry out his instructions.

Sato was unable to see Molotov before he left for Potsdam but did arrange that he would receive a written request. When Stalin shared with Truman at Potsdam the information about the Japanese overture, they agreed to stall on receiving Prince Konoye. Sato was informed that a reply to his request would have to wait until after the Big Three conference.

In this same period, Allen Dulles, the OSS chief in Switzerland, approached a Japanese naval official in Berne about discussing an end to the war. The Navy General Staff in Tokyo ordered its man to make no reply to Dulles.

No one in power in Tokyo gave any sign that Japan was ready to accept unconditional surrender. And no one who made policy in Washington was prepared to soften the demand for unconditional surrender and guarantee allowing the Emperor to stay. It was not yet time to talk.

As plans to invade Japan solidified and assault forces moved into place, the U.S. Army Air Forces were systematically leveling Japan. B-29 bombers now based in the Marianas were destroying cities and their populations with incendiary bombs.

In mid-May MacArthur and Nimitz met in Manila and came to an agreement on the principles for the invasion. Then, on May 25, the Joint Chiefs of Staff set the invasion of Kyushu for November 1 and gave MacArthur the primary command.

In mid-June General Henry H. "Hap" Arnold, commander of the Army Air Forces, also went to Manila to discuss interservice relations and the organization of the Pacific war. MacArthur, Arnold noted, was prepared to use gas, "any kind of gas," against the Japanese. MacArthur also supported the entry of the Soviet Union into the Pacific war. The Russians should pin down the Japanese divisions on the Asian mainland before the Americans struck Japan proper.

Not surprisingly, MacArthur's new power and responsibility as commander of the invasion of Japan incensed many Navy officers. It also aggravated another festering interservice disagreement. Throughout the war, the unification of the armed forces had become a subject of intensifying debate and controversy. A committee appointed by the Joint Chiefs reported in April 1945 that almost all Army and Air Corps officers and about half the Navy officers interviewed—including Nimitz and Admiral William F. "Bull" Halsey, Jr., commander of the U.S. Third Fleet—favored unification. In good part, this discussion of unification stimulated by the experience of fighting the Pacific war through two separate commands, which had generated so much interservice rivalry.

When President Roosevelt died, many naval officers felt their service had lost a champion; Truman had long favored unification and was regarded as an Army partisan. And now the reorganization in the Pacific added to the distress of the Navy leaders, who shuddered at the news that the Army, through the flamboyant MacArthur, had gained control of all ground combat and service forces fighting Japan. The Navy nervously pulled away from accepting unification; the issue would have to wait until the war was over.

Truman's June 1 message to Congress revealed how the war against Japan would be pursued. The President said that no matter how hard the Japanese were hit from the air and sea, "the foot soldier will still have to advance against strongly entrenched and fanatical troops, through sheer grit and fighting skill. . . . There is no easy way to win."

By now the Joint Chiefs of Staff were working out a detailed plan. The overall operation against the Japanese home islands, called DOWNFALL, would consist of two parts: OLYMPIC and CORONET. The Sixth Army under General Walter Krueger, which had conquered Manila, would first carry out OLYMPIC, the amphibious invasion of southern Kyushu. This invasion would be executed by eleven U.S. Army divisions and three Marine divisions—650,000 men.

OLYMPIC's purpose was to establish bases for the main assault of Honshu, in the Kanto Plains area near Tokyo, four months later. That final invasion, CORONET, would be conducted by Lieutenant General Robert L. Eichelberger's Eighth Army and General Courtney H. Hodges' First Army, transferred from Europe. The initial assault would be made by fifteen divisions, with a total of twenty-two divisions committed. The battle was expected to be ferocious, and victory was predicted in not less than six months.

On Monday afternoon, June 18, the military secretaries and the Joint Chiefs of Staff came to the White House, where Truman convened the most important meeting yet on the planning of the invasion. General Marshall informed the President that in the judgment of the Joint Chiefs invasion was the only option. He read a digest of a memo from the Joint Chiefs stating that they, MacArthur, and Nimitz agreed that Kyushu should be invaded on November 1. (After that date, weather could delay the invasion by up to six months.) The memo said, "The Kyushu operation is essential to a strategy of strangulation and appears to be the least costly worthwhile operation following Okinawa."

The Joint Chiefs' memo predicted that the number of casualties during the first thirty days on Kyushu would be similar to that of the Luzon campaign, which had resulted in 31,000 American casualties, of whom 13,742 had been killed. The Joint Chiefs also offered advice: "It is a grim fact there is not an easy, bloodless way to victory in war and it is the thankless task of the leaders to maintain their firm outward front which holds the resolution of their subordinates."

They endorsed using Soviet forces "to deal with the Japs in Manchuria (and Korea if necessary) and to vitalize the Chinese to a point where, with the assistance of American air power and some supplies, they can mop out their own country." Soviet participation against "the already hopeless Japanese may well be the decisive action levering them into capitulation at that time or shortly thereafter if we land in Japan."

Marshall read a telegram from MacArthur, who espoused the plan and added a further thought regarding the Russians: "The hazard and loss will be greatly lessened if an attack is launched from Siberia sufficiently ahead of our target date to commit the enemy to major combat."

In Marshall's view, the assault on Kyushu was the only course to pursue. Airpower alone could not do the job; it had not defeated the Germans. Admiral King immediately supported what Marshall had said, and the Joint Chiefs, Secretary Stimson, and Secretary Forrestal all told the President that they concurred.

Admiral Leahy held back, and Truman turned to him specifically. On Okinawa, the admiral pointed out, total casualties had been 35 percent. Marshall interjected that the total assault troops on Kyushu would number 766,700—35 percent of that would be 268,345 casualties. Truman noted that, even if the Joint Chiefs differed about numbers, they unanimously predicted a high casualty rate.

Truman then wanted to know what Lieutenant General Ira C. Eaker, who was sitting in for General Arnold, thought as an airman. Eaker confirmed that he and Arnold were in complete agreement with Marshall's statement. The assault of Honshu would require airdromes on Kyushu; he stressed that any delays would favor the enemy.

Truman summed up by saying he understood that the Joint Chiefs unanimously favored the Kyushu operation. Then he called on Stimson, who acknowledged that there was no other choice. He was concerned, however, that an invasion would mobilize those in Japan who did not support the war. Did he mean, Truman wanted to know, that invasion by white men would unite the Japanese? Stimson replied that this was likely.

Forrestal finally joined the discussion, conceding that even if Japan were besieged for a year and a half, it would still be necessary to invade Kyushu.

Truman told them that at the coming Big Three conference at Potsdam he would seek to get all possible aid from the Soviet Union. At that point Leahy spoke up. He did not agree with the idea that without unconditional surrender the Allies would have lost the war. Indeed, he thought insistence on unconditional surrender would just increase Allied casualties and was unnecessary. Truman remained firm. He said he had left Congress room to reconsider the issue of unconditional surrender if it wished, but he did not want to reverse policy and attempt to change public opinion.

The President then approved the military plan to invade Kyushu and told the Joint Chiefs to go ahead with it. But he warned that he did not want another bloody Okinawa campaign, sloughing from one end of Japan to the other.

Admiral King interjected that he believed that the Russians were not indispensable, even if their absence did result in more American casualties. He offered this thought, he said, to strengthen Truman's hand at the forthcoming summit conference.

As the historic meeting closed, Truman realized that John McCloy had not entered the discussion and asked him to speak. What he said is not recorded in the top secret memorandum on the meeting by the Secretary of the Joint Chiefs, but McCloy later revealed that he proposed that the Japanese be informed about the atomic bomb in an effort to persuade them to surrender. Truman said he would think about it.

The invasion would proceed.

Decades later, some historians of a later generation charged that the estimates of invasion casualties had been purposefully exaggerated to rationalize using the atomic bombs. The exact number of casualties was, of course, not determinable in advance—but whether 500,000 or 100,000 Americans would be killed and maimed, the desire to save American lives by avoiding an invasion of Japan was overriding. Truman asserted later, "It occurred to me that a quarter of a million of the flower of our young manhood were worth a couple of Japanese cities, and I still think they were and are."

After the June 18 meeting, three war issues continued to be debated: unconditional surrender, use of the atomic weapon, and Soviet participation. The differences over unconditional surrender would never be resolved, and unease about the atomic bomb continued to plague those responsible for its use. Stimson presented a formal memorandum to Truman on July 2 urging that the Japanese be carefully warned of "the varied and overwhelming character of the force we are about to bring to bear on the islands." As usual, the actual name or nature of this "force" was not openly mentioned; it was masked in secrecy.

Finally, the Soviet Union's entry into the war, in addition to its obvious benefits, created a number of problems. Truman, faced with the Joint Chiefs' estimates of the invasion's cost in American lives, grew more and more determined to make sure that Stalin kept his promise to attack the Japanese in Manchuria.

But despite Truman's eagerness to benefit from the Soviet army's fighting power, he refused to give Stalin a share in the rule of postwar Japan. He did not want to experience again the Soviet intransigence that he had had to deal with in Germany and Eastern Europe. Once Japan was conquered, he had decided, MacArthur would be given complete command over the defeated nation.

To his surprise, Truman discovered that he had inherited some awkward obligations as the result of a secret agreement made at Yalta. They were spelled out in a paper that Admiral Leahy had carried home from Yalta and locked in Roosevelt's personal safe. It had been signed by Roosevelt, Churchill, and Stalin. In it, the Soviet Union was granted major concessions in East Asia at China's expense. In exchange, Stalin had promised to enter the Pacific war within three months after V-E Day and well before the invasion of Japan.

This arrangement had been made without the knowledge — much less the agreement—of Chiang Kai-shek, or even of Secretary of State Stettinius. (Harriman and Bohlen had been the only other Americans present.) Roosevelt and Stalin had negotiated the deal; Churchill had simply signed it. And Roosevelt had committed himself to obtaining Chiang's agreement when the time came. Two months later, FDR was dead and Truman was left to carry out this mission.

Under the agreement, Japan would be stripped of everything she had conquered from China since 1894, as well as territory the Japanese had taken from the Russians in the Russo-Japanese War of 1904–1905. The Soviet Union would get back the lower half of Sakhalin Island and the Kurile Islands (which had been Japanese since 1875). Dairen would become a free port under international control, and Port Arthur would contain a Soviet naval base. The Manchurian railroads would be operated jointly by the Russians and

Chinese. And they would both accept and recognize the status quo in Outer Mongolia.

The Joint Chiefs of Staff made no objections to these terms; their eyes were focused on drawing the Soviet Union into the war. And MacArthur applauded the arrangement by which the Soviet Union would engage the Japanese in Manchuria before the United States invaded the home islands.

But after Brigadier General William L. Ritchie, head of the Southwest Pacific Section of the War Department Operations Division and the Pentagon's frequent liaison with MacArthur, briefed the general on August 2 in Manila on the details of the agreement, Ritchie reported that MacArthur was "shocked."

MacArthur's "shock" was hard to accept. He had repeatedly told representatives from the War Department and from General Marshall's staff that Soviet expansion in East Asia was inevitable but that the Soviet Union must earn it by invading Manchuria. He had given Secretary of the Navy Forrestal essentially the same opinion. MacArthur had even sent a message to the Joint Chiefs for their June 18 meeting with Truman, urging that the Soviet army attack from Siberia before the American invasion of the home islands. But in his memoirs MacArthur wrote that by 1945 Russian participation was "superfluous." (Ten years after the war, MacArthur denied that he had been consulted and that he had condoned the Yalta deal. William Manchester, his biographer, wrote bluntly, "He was lying.")

Chiang Kai-shek was naturally reluctant to give the Russians rights in Manchuria and Korea. Truman cabled Ambassador Hurley in Chungking that Stalin wanted to discuss these issues with Foreign Minister Soong in Moscow before July 1 and expected assurances before the Soviet Union entered the Pacific war.

George Kennan was convinced that the Soviet Union intended to attain predominance in China, although in Moscow in early June Stalin had assured Harry Hopkins, Truman's emissary, that he would make no territorial claims on China itself and that he wanted a strong, unified China. Stalin claimed he would support Chiang Kai-shek, despite reservations about him and his government, because he saw no other leader strong enough to unify China. He said that only the United States could help rebuild China; the Soviet Union did not have the resources to help.

Truman and Soong met on June 14, and the foreign minister let the President know that he had severe problems with the Soviet expectations. The most difficult was the lease of Port Arthur, because the Chinese government was opposed to the old imperialistic system of foreign powers leasing Chinese ports. Truman reiterated that he wanted the Soviet Union to come into the war against Japan as soon as possible, but he did not want to harm China's interests. When Soong departed, Truman sent off messages to Stalin and Churchill alerting them of the pending problems that would affect the final stages of the Pacific war and the future of Asia.

Soong arrived in Moscow on June 30, and Stalin immediately insisted that China recognize the independence of Outer Mongolia. Soong said that no Chinese government could last if it ceded Outer Mongolia, even though the Nationalist government realized it could not exercise sovereignty there.

Stalin then proposed a secret agreement on the independence of Outer Mongolia that would be published only after the defeat of Japan. Soong said he would have to cable Chiang Kai-shek for instructions, and he asked Harriman to get a reading on the American attitude.

Stalin pressed for concessions on the ownership of the Manchurian railroads but promised that the Soviet Union would not station troops in Manchuria. Soong was mollified when Stalin said he would allow representatives of the Nationalist government to accompany the Soviet army into Manchuria.

Stalin and Soong differed over the internationalization of the port of Dairen. Stalin wanted it to come under Soviet and Chinese control, with the Soviet Union preeminent and managing the port. Soong countered that Dairen should be a free port under Chinese administration, with some Soviet assistance. Regarding Port Arthur, Stalin said he would drop the word "lease," which had such an ugly historic connotation to the Chinese, but he wanted both nations to have naval facilities there. Stalin accepted a four-power trusteeship over Korea, but Harriman cabled Truman that Soong was concerned because the Russians were training two Korean divisions in Siberia. Even if Korea were placed under a trusteeship, Harriman feared, Stalin was preparing to dominate Korea.

Truman informed Harriman that the United States did not want to take a role in the Sino-Soviet negotiations. He would communicate the U.S. views to Soong informally—especially the American belief that Outer Mongolia belonged de jure to China even if de facto this sovereignty would not be exercised.

When it came to U.S. interests, Harriman was instructed to inform both the Russians and the Chinese that the United States, as a party to the Yalta agreements, expected to be consulted before any final arrangements were concluded. And the United States did not want to be closed out of the port facilities of Dairen or the use of the railways.

Chiang Kai-shek's answers to Soong's queries were explicit: China would recognize the independence of the Mongolian People's Republic after the war if the Soviet Union would respect its sovereignty and integrity. The Soviet Union could have joint use of Port Arthur but not joint control; Dairen would be a free port but under Chinese administration. The railroads would be operated jointly under Chinese ownership. And the Soviet Union was not to support the Chinese Communists. Chiang said those were his "maximum concessions."

The Chinese and Soviet negotiators went over each point, but the gap between them could not be closed to both parties' satisfaction. Truman noted, "Stalin was always asking for as much as he could get."

On July 10 Stalin accepted the Chinese compromise on Outer Mongolia and promised not to support the Chinese Communists. (Soong told Harriman that Stalin had said he would support only the Nationalist government in China.) But Stalin did not bend on the ports and railroads, and he tried to twist Soong's arm by telling him these issues should be settled prior to the summit meeting at Potsdam because the key to the Soviet Union's entry into the Pacific war was now this agreement with China.

Chiang Kai-shek cabled Truman on July 20 to ask for his help in persuading Stalin that China had gone as far as it could to meet the Soviet terms. From Potsdam, Truman asked Chiang to send Soong back to Moscow to continue to try to work out a complete agreement. Then the long, drawn-out negotiations were suspended for the Potsdam conference.

Chapter 17

"An Opportunity to End This War"

In Potsdam on Tuesday, July 24, Truman interrupted his concentration on European problems to meet with Churchill and their leading military advisors and review the strategy for the final battle against Japan.

The Combined Chiefs of Staff, British and American, had been meeting daily in Potsdam and now presented Churchill and Truman with a completed plan to assault Japan's home islands with naval blockades, persistent air bombardments, and invasion. The British fleet and long-range bombers would help engage the Japanese, but operational strategy would remain in the hands of the U.S. Joint Chiefs of Staff. The entry of the Soviet Union into the war would be encouraged, and efforts would be continued to convert China into an effective ally against Japan. The climactic invasion would achieve absolute military control over Japan and the liberation of all Japanese-occupied territory. The Combined Chiefs predicted that by November 15, 1946—almost precisely a year after the planned invasion of Kyushu—organized resistance should end. Truman and Churchill approved the report.

That same afternoon, the Combined Chiefs of Staff sat down and talked for the first and only time with the Soviet Chiefs of Staff. Admiral Leahy presided. General Aleksei Antonov, the Soviet army chief of staff, announced that Soviet troops were already assembling in Asia, ready to start operations against Japan in the latter half of August. The exact date depended on the conclusion of the negotiations with the Chinese. The Soviet objectives, he said, were to destroy the Japanese army in Manchuria and to occupy the Liaotung Peninsula. After the defeat of Japan, he offered, the Soviet army would withdraw from Manchuria.

General Marshall briefed the Russians on the disposition of Japanese troops, as well as the American positions in the Pacific. He reviewed possible courses of action open to the Japanese. General Arnold and Admiral King covered the air and sea campaigns against the Japanese. The bombing of Tokyo had already been stepped up for two weeks. General Antonov was particularly interested in whether the United States intended to undertake operations against the Kuriles or Korea. King replied that it would not move against the Kuriles; Marshall also assured him that it had no plans for amphibious operations against Korea.

Two days later, American and Soviet military officers met again to work out cooperation between their two forces. They agreed to exchange liaison groups and to make Soviet airfields and ports in Siberia available for repairs and emergency use once the Soviet Union entered the war. They settled on weather stations and drew lines separating areas of operations for their respective air and naval forces. These lines ran generally from the northern tip of Japan across extreme northern Korea. No lines were established for land operations on the Korean peninsula because American military leaders did not anticipate fighting there.

In Berlin that same evening, Harry Truman issued the Potsdam Declaration, the most important Allied approach to Japan's leaders to stop the war. The declaration was not a part of the summit meeting, although it was announced during it. In fact, the declaration had a strange history.

On May 28, while Secretary of State Stettinius was in San Francisco and U.S. B-29s were firebombing Japanese cities, Acting Secretary of State Grew urged Truman to make a statement that would ease the "unconditional" demand and encourage surrender.

Grew had long sought a rapprochement with Japan. He had served ten years as the prewar U.S. ambassador in Tokyo, and his views about Japan were valued in Washington. He also was an early Cold Warrior with a vision of the United States as a global peacemaker and of the Soviet Union as the United States' most dangerous postwar rival. He anticipated that, given the chance, the Soviet Union would dominate East Asia, as it was already doing in Eastern Europe. He said, "A future war with Soviet Russia is as certain as anything in this world can be certain. It may come in a very few years."

In such a world, Grew argued, Japan could serve as an anti-Soviet bastion. Therefore, unconditional surrender would hamper working out a world that would benefit the United States most.

As originally proposed by Grew, the statement would have assured the Japanese that if they stopped fighting, the United States would permit the Emperor to remain as head of state. Specifically, Grew's draft said the United States would retain in Japan "a constitutional monarchy under the present dynasty."

Grew made two major arguments to Truman for leaving the Emperor in place. The first was that the United States would be able to rule the country more effectively if it kept intact Japan's fundamental political and societal structure, which demanded loyalty and obedience. The second reason was that Grew had learned in October 1941, while he was the U.S. ambassador in Tokyo, that the Emperor had tried, to the limited degree that he had the power to act, to rein in the military. The Emperor had made his views known to his military leaders at an imperial conference on September 6, 1941, when they had notified him that they had decided to place a time limit on negotiations with the United States. The Emperor had wanted diplomatic efforts to be exhausted first.

Faced with Grew's proposal, Truman was not ready to desert Roosevelt's policy or his own conviction about unconditional surrender. He instructed Grew to discuss his idea with senior American officials and collect the reactions of the cabinet and Joint Chiefs before he, Truman, dealt with it.

The next day, Grew reported back to Truman that he had the agreement of the key top officials to keep the Emperor. This was not quite accurate. He did not have Jimmy Byrnes aboard, and that omission, as it turned out, would be crucial when, by the end of June, Truman replaced Stettinius with Byrnes as secretary of state.

Also, Grew did not have unanimous support inside the Department of State. Assistant Secretaries Acheson and MacLeish both protested that the American public would react badly to any suggestion that the Emperor be kept in place. And Grew obtained the military leaders' agreement with two caveats: They wanted the declaration delayed until they were more nearly ready to invade if it were rejected. And they cautioned that if Truman did decide on such a statement while heavy fighting continued on Okinawa, it might be interpreted in Tokyo as a sign of weakness.

At the President's request, Stimson, Grew, Forrestal, and McCloy met on June 12 to reargue the ramifications of unconditional surrender. Stimson and Forrestal agreed that this issue was one of the most serious facing the nation about the Pacific war. Stimson reminded them that unconditional surrender meant the Allies would demilitarize Japan but not subjugate it permanently, enslave its people, or dictate its form of government.

Grew and Stimson both believed that the Japanese had to be told that if they surrendered, the United States would seek to eradicate all traces of militarism but not to change their form of government or their religious institutions. This suggested that, in some manner, the Emperor could stay—which would make surrender less than unconditional.

Grew continued to press on Truman the idea that unconditional surrender would only guarantee the invasion of Japan. And the 35 percent casualty rate on Okinawa, he warned, would undermine American public support for an invasion that would be even more expensive in American lives. Instead, he wanted to encourage a peace movement in Japan.

Truman decided to issue a proclamation urging the Japanese to surrender. He would announce it from Potsdam to dramatize the Allies' unity. The draft that Truman took with him to Potsdam was based on Grew's original proposal. But when Byrnes read it to former Secretary of State Cordell Hull, he said it sounded too much like appeasement.

Stimson, who strongly wanted the proclamation to allow explicitly for "a constitutional monarchy under the present dynasty," drew up his own version and then tried to avoid having it altered by sending it directly to the President. But Stimson lost whatever advantage he might have hoped for when Truman sailed for Europe with now-Secretary Byrnes. Stimson still managed to arrange for Truman to invite him to Potsdam, where he encouraged Churchill to urge his position on the President.

On the crucial point of keeping the Emperor, serious disagreement continued. By now, Truman fully realized the centrality of retaining the Emperor for the Japanese. But despite Stimson's efforts, Byrnes, with the backing of the Joint Chiefs, deleted all reference to keeping the Emperor. Truman went along with Byrnes because he doubted that most Americans would accept the idea of retaining the Emperor. The resulting ambiguity of the final Potsdam Declaration may have helped the American decision makers, but it neither reassured the Japanese leaders nor induced them to surrender.

Byrnes also cut from the declaration any mention of Soviet involvement in the war and any hint of the use of atomic bombs against Japanese targets. If it had revealed these two points, the declaration might conceivably have weakened the determination of Japan's leaders. Leon V. Sigal, an historian of the period, says: "By omitting the two most compelling threats that Japan would face, he [Byrnes] defused the ultimatum. . . . When Byrnes had finished with it, the Potsdam Declaration no longer contained much new of substance. Neither a gesture of conciliation nor an ultimatum, it was reduced to mere propaganda."

The declaration's failure to use either of these crucial pieces of information to pressure Japan to stop fighting was especially strange because Truman always stressed that he had put off issuing the Potsdam Declaration until the participation of the Soviet Union had been assured and the Trinity test had proven successful. Truman and Byrnes continued to demand unconditional surrender, but they did not use these rather significant straws, which might have broken the back of resistance in Tokyo to such an outcome. And the Potsdam Declaration gave no indication to the Japanese that the President of the United States would accept less than unconditional surrender or even convert the retention of the Emperor into a noncondition.

When Truman and Byrnes learned the results of the Trinity test on July 16, they began to question the importance of Soviet intervention. Byrnes now tried to make sure that Foreign Minister Soong did not give away to the Soviet Union more than he needed to. Truman agreed, and on July 23 he asked Stimson to check Marshall's current view on Soviet intervention. The general recommended that the possibility of Soviet help should be kept alive; he was not sure that the atomic bomb by itself could win an unconditional surrender.

The next day, Stimson brought Truman a cable from Washington, informing him when the atomic bombs would be ready. This was the trigger that released the Potsdam Declaration.

The United States, Britain, and China were to issue the declaration jointly. So, on the twenty-fourth, at the Combined Chiefs of Staff meeting on strategy, Truman gave Churchill a copy of the draft declaration. The prime minister immediately agreed in principle, and before he left for London the next day he approved the language.

Stalin was not consulted; the Russians could not, of course, join in the declaration because the Soviet Union was still at peace with Japan. But Truman spoke with Stalin privately about the declaration during a conference meeting.

When Truman instructed Ambassador Hurley in Chungking to

obtain Chiang Kai-shek's concurrence as swiftly as possible, there was no reply or even acknowledgment from Chungking for twenty-four hours. Truman's message had, incredibly, been stalled in the Honolulu communications center, and then communications traffic to Guam had been heavy. It was after midnight in Chungking before the message reached Hurley and was translated into Mandarin. He delivered it to now–Prime Minister Soong.

Chiang Kai-shek was staying in the mountains across the Yangtze River. At that hour, it was difficult to find a ferry to cross the river, and Soong refused to go with Hurley in the night.

The next morning, K. C. Wu, assistant minister of foreign relations, accompanied Hurley to the generalissimo's residence at Yellow Mountain. Chiang read the translation carefully and said he concurred. But he asked that the order of listing the heads of the three sponsoring governments be changed to put him ahead of the British prime minister, because it would help him at home. Then, because the telephone was not working, Hurley had to travel back to Chungking to transmit Chiang's reply to Truman. The order of listing was changed to accommodate the generalissimo.

The final version of the declaration said that the United States, Britain, and China agreed that "Japan shall be given an opportunity to end this war." It promised the destruction of the Japanese armed forces and the devastation of the Japanese homeland. It stated the Allies' demands as these: Irresponsible militarism shall be driven from the world. The government of Japan shall proclaim the unconditional surrender of its armed forces, which shall be completely disarmed. (Some later interpreted this language as a retreat from totally unconditional surrender, but that was a misinterpretation based on hindsight and wishful thinking.) Until a new order was established, the Allies would occupy points in Japanese territory. Justice would be meted out to all war criminals. Freedom of speech, religion, and thought would be established. "The alternative for Japan is prompt and utter destruction."

Truman still intended the Potsdam Declaration to persuade the Japanese to end the Pacific war. But he was using the stick, not the carrot. What Grew had initiated as an inducement to stop the fighting had become a preinvasion ultimatum. Leon Sigal says, "Yet the tough tone that the proclamation maintained throughout was better suited to selling its terms to Americans than to the Japanese."

When Truman issued the Potsdam Declaration from Berlin on the evening of July 26, he ordered the U.S. Office of War Information to send the message to the Japanese people in every possible way. It was radioed to Japan from San Francisco.

That same night, five C-54s carrying parts of the atomic bombs arrived at Tinian in the Marianas; and plans for the invasion of Japan moved forward.

Foreign Minister Togo reported the receipt of the declaration to the Emperor. In a cabinet meeting, the Japanese leaders debated their reaction. The military and naval leaders opted for immediate rejection; the prime minister and foreign minister wanted to keep the door open a crack. On the afternoon of July 28, the world was given the Japanese answer. Prime Minister Suzuki told a press conference that the declaration would be ignored—the word used was *mokusatsu*, meaning "treat with silent contempt." Japan would fight on.

Foreign Minister Togo complained to Ambassador Naotake Sato that he could not understand why the Allies insisted on the formality of unconditional surrender, which forced Japan to hold out against that one abstraction. In a coded message on July 22, which the Americans intercepted, Togo was unyielding: "With regard to unconditional surrender . . . we are unable to consent to it under any circumstances whatever. Even if the war drags on and it becomes clear that it will take much more bloodshed . . ." Sato was ordered not to ask the Russians to seek peace without conditions.

Even though Prime Minister Suzuki was known to be trying to manipulate the Russians to mediate an end to the war on Japanese terms because the Emperor sought it, President Truman correctly accepted the prime minister's statement as a rejection of the Potsdam Declaration.

Ambassador Sato queried Togo as to "whether the Imperial Government has a concrete and definite plan for terminating the war." As late as July 30, six days before the atomic bomb dropped on Hiroshima, the absence of an answer meant that the Japanese government had no plan to propose.

With the Japanese political and military leadership refusing to end the war on American terms, Truman was left with the options of granting "conditions" or using the atomic weapon and invading Japan.

As soon as Stalin returned to Moscow from the Potsdam Conference, he reopened the negotiations with China and met with Prime

Minister Soong and the new foreign minister, Wang Shih-chieh. Soong continued to keep Ambassador Harriman informed of the discussions.

The Soviet Union added a new demand: China should not fortify any islands for a hundred miles south of Port Arthur. The Chinese refused, and Stalin finally accepted the Chinese position. He also agreed to a Chinese-Soviet military commission to supervise Port Arthur, if the administration of the city and port would be in Soviet hands. And he kept insisting that Dairen be managed by a mixed commission headed by a Soviet official.

By pressing for more and more concessions, Stalin was endangering the Soviet entry into the war. He clearly did not understand that the atomic bomb would soon change the entire picture and diminish his bargaining power.

Truman was discouraged by the interminable negotiations. And Harriman feared that China might buckle under Soviet pressure and make concessions that were not in the interest of the United States. He urged Byrnes to intervene and put an end to the endless Soviet demands. But Byrnes was in no hurry to see these negotiations settled because he no longer sought the Soviet Union's entry in the Pacific war.

Truman disagreed with his secretary of state. He had no intention, in this pre-atomic era, to cancel the invasion, and he still believed that the Soviet Union could tie up Japanese troops in Manchuria and prevent them from being present in Japan when the Americans landed.

Truman did put an end to Stalin's constantly rising demands. On August 5, sailing home from Potsdam, he directed Byrnes to instruct Harriman in Moscow to tell Stalin that the President believed China had met the requirements of the Yalta agreements and need make no further concessions.

Truman particularly did not want the port of Dairen included in the Soviet military zone or used as a Soviet naval base. In this, he followed Roosevelt's insistence that Dairen become a truly internationalized free port. And he restated FDR's desire that the Soviets provide written assurances that they supported the American "Open Door" policy. The United States had arranged for China to pay the price for Soviet intervention, but it wanted guarantees that its own interests in the area would be honored.

Stalin continued to demand a Soviet presence at Dairen. And, always pressing, he brought up the new subject of "war trophies," referring to Japanese properties in areas occupied by the Soviet army. Truman recognized that Stalin wanted to strip Manchuria of industrial facilities as he had Germany. The President had the State Department object vigorously that Manchuria was an integral part of China. Stalin dropped that probe, but he pushed for every concession until the very finish.

After the explosion of the atomic bomb over Hiroshima, American enthusiasm for Soviet participation in the war against Japan evaporated. Even General Marshall advised Truman that the Soviet Union was no longer needed.

But the Russians could not be turned away. They would move against Japan as it suited their purposes. Marshall knew this and said as much to Stimson. So now the American government switched tactics and wanted Chiang Kai-shek to drag out his negotiations with the Russians; stalling—the tactic that Stalin had recommended in Potsdam be used against Japan—was now to be used against Stalin.

A final Sino-Soviet agreement was not signed until August 14, as the war against Japan ended. Stalin obtained the Kurile Archipelago, half of Sakhalin Island, and control of Korea above the 38th Parallel. And he forced Chiang Kai-shek to withdraw from Outer Mongolia in return for a promise not to intervene in China's internal affairs. China agreed to recognize Outer Mongolia's independence after a plebiscite. On Dairen, the Chinese gave the Soviet Union a thirty-year lease for half the port and accepted a Soviet harbormaster. On the American request for a written assurance of the Open Door policy, Stalin proved uncooperative. Actually, the United States did not need special concessions but wanted to stop the Russians from setting up a Soviet republic in Manchuria and keeping everyone else out.

While the United States was mobilizing its forces, assembling its atomic bombs, and involving its Soviet confederate in an invasion of Japanese territory, contingency plans were under way in case the Japanese should suddenly prove willing to end the war without an atomic bombardment and an invasion.

Although there was never any suggestion that the Japanese were prepared to meet the Allied demand for unconditional surrender, the Joint Chiefs ordered MacArthur and Nimitz to prepare contingency plans for a possible peaceful occupation. Nimitz designed the Campus Plan, under which the Navy would send the Third Fleet and Marines to occupy the Tokyo Bay area. And MacArthur came up with the Blacklist Plan, under which the Army would move massive forces, including twenty-two infantry divisions, into Japan. He believed that the occupation of a nation that still had an intact army was the job of the Army, not the Navy. Finally, the Joint Chiefs approved a modified Blacklist Plan, plus the sending of two Marine divisions to guard Chinese ports.

The first five thousand American troops from the European Theater of Operations arrived in Manila on July 22 for the invasion of Japan. Nimitz went to Manila again and met with MacArthur to plan the landing on Kyushu. Blacklist was strictly a contingency plan; invasion was still the reality.

Chapter 18

"Dimples Eight Two"
—Opening the Nuclear Era

"The final decision of where and when to use the atomic bomb was up to me," Harry Truman wrote years later. "Let there be no mistake about it, I regarded the bomb as a military weapon and never had any doubt that it should be used."

Throughout the Saturday night after Roosevelt died, soft, forgiving snow covered the isolated mesa and the hastily built town of Los Alamos, New Mexico. On Sunday morning a memorial service was held in the theater. Everyone gathered there was sharing a feeling of great loss. Dr. J. Robert Oppenheimer, the gaunt genius whose weight was now down to 110 pounds and who was perpetually smoking a cigarette or pipe, said that when they learned of Roosevelt's death,

> Many of us looked with deep trouble to the future; many of us felt less certain that our works would be to a good end; all of us were reminded of how precious a thing human greatness is. . . . All over the world men have looked to him for guidance, and have seen symbolized in him their hope that the evils of this time would not be repeated; that the terrible sacrifices which have been made, and those that are still to be made, would lead to a world more fit for human habitation.

Only in the previous few days had Oppenheimer learned of the first experiment that determined successfully the critical mass of pure uranium U-235. The atomic bomb was now a matter of time.

*   *   *

In Washington, on Tuesday, April 24—Truman had been President for twelve days—Secretary of War Stimson sent the new President a discreet note, asking for an appointment to discuss "a highly secret matter." The secret matter, Stimson wrote, has "such a bearing on our present foreign relations and has such an important effect upon all my thinking in this field that I think you ought to know about it without much further delay."

Although Truman knew virtually nothing concrete about the atomic project, he did know that a major secret project existed, and he understood Stimson was referring to that. He had Matthew J. Connelly, his appointments secretary, who earlier had been an investigator for the Truman Committee, arrange for Stimson to come in at noon the next day. Coincidentally, this was the same day the United Nations conference opened in San Francisco.

Stimson arrived with Brigadier General Leslie Groves, the director of the Manhattan Engineer District, the *nom de guerre* for the organization that was building the atomic bomb. Stimson first went alone into the Oval Room to brief Truman on the nature and anticipated power of the atomic bomb.

By now, the Manhattan Project had already produced enough U-235 at Oak Ridge, Tennessee, to make an atomic bomb, and preparations were under way for a definitive test in the New Mexico desert.

The Secretary of War told the President that within four months the United States hoped to have a weapon so powerful that one bomb could destroy an entire city. Thus far, the United States alone had the knowledge of how to do this; but, he warned, the nation could not expect to keep the secret indefinitely. The new weapon, he informed Truman, seemed on the brink of success and would, if it worked, shorten the war, revolutionize warfare, and change America's relations with the world. He expressed deep concern about the long-range consequences of the bomb's existence.

Stimson later wrote, "The possible atomic weapon was considered to be a new and tremendously powerful explosive, as legitimate as any other of the deadly explosive weapons of modern war. The entire purpose [of the Manhattan Project] was the production of a military weapon; on no other ground could the wartime expenditure of so much time and money have been justified." Not only was Stimson confident that a bomb would be made in the next few months, he assumed that it would be used as soon as possible because it would save American lives. He was also aware that it might have the potential to destroy civilization.

This candid judgment delivered, Stimson brought in Brigadier General Groves, who handed the President a twenty-four-page report on the Manhattan Project. Stimson said they would wait while the President read the report. Truman was reluctant; he would have preferred to study the report at his own careful, thorough pace. But they pressed him, and he read it through. When he had finished, he looked up and said quietly that he now understood the importance of the Manhattan Project.

From the beginning, the question for Truman was not whether the bomb was to be used, but how and when and against what targets. There was a terrible war to be won, at the lowest cost possible in American lives. And afterwards, how would this new weapon be controlled for mankind's benefit rather than its destruction? Churchill summed up the attitude at the time: "The decision whether or not to use the atomic bomb to compel the surrender of Japan was never even an issue." Truman, of course, soon became aware that debates were raging among the few informed people over whether the atomic weapon should be used at all. But he himself had no doubts.

As to the future, Stimson advised the President that no political system then in existence would be able to control this "menace." He urged the President to appoint an able and prestigious committee to study the implications of the atomic bomb and to recommend action. The idea of forming such a committee had come up earlier, but Roosevelt had never acted on it. Truman approved the establishment of an ad hoc committee, to be called the "Interim Committee," with Stimson its chairman. He admired the older statesman as "a man of great wisdom and foresight," and he wanted Stimson's guidance.

Truman would have to decide how the atomic weapon would be used and how knowledge about it should be handled both within the United States and with other nations, especially the Soviet Union. As the war raced to its conclusion, his most important decisions— decisions dangerous to the entire world—would involve this untested and still mysterious weapon.

Building the atomic bomb required 100,000 men, more than two and a half years in wartime and the expenditure of $2.5 billion— the largest sum ever spent on a scientific project. The work had been accomplished, with cooperation between Britain and the United States, under great secrecy and enormous pressure.

Both policy makers and scientists were driven by the fear that the Germans, too, were trying to harness atomic energy for use as a weapon. After all, the earliest fission, converting matter into energy, had been accomplished by Otto Hahn and Fritz Strassmann in 1938 in Nazi Germany. And the German Army had confiscated 1,200 tons of high-grade uranium ore in Belgium in 1940. As long as all that ore was unaccounted for, there was good reason to be concerned that the Germans might be using it for atomic weapons.

Curiously, the Western Allies mounted no espionage effort to determine whether the Germans were actually developing an atomic weapon until the Anglo-American armies penetrated Germany. Then, fast-moving Manhattan Project intelligence teams located documents in Strasbourg that convinced them that the Germans neither had an atom bomb nor were near perfecting one. On April 12 they found some of the confiscated Belgian uranium ore in Toulouse; subsequently, they found some in the small town of Stadtilm, near Weimar, at Germany's atomic research headquarters, and some more near Stassfurt, a salt-mining city twenty-one miles south of Magdeburg. They moved the ore out of reach of the Russians. Ironically, some of it was used at Oak Ridge in the building of the first American "Little Boy" bomb.

The intelligence teams also rounded up a number of German scientists to keep them out of the Soviet Union. In the Black Forest in southwestern Germany, they picked up Otto Hahn and Werner Heisenberg—as well as a sophisticated atomic pile. But they discovered that the fear of a German atomic bomb had been baseless.

Some scientists close to the Manhattan Project worried about the possible apocalyptic consequences of the atomic reaction. No longer were religious fundamentalists the only ones who worried about the end of the world.

One physicist knowledgeable about this fearsome frontier of science tried to reach Roosevelt and then Truman to persuade them to impose restraints on the use of atomic power. Back in 1939 Leo Szilard, a short, stocky Hungarian-born theoretical physicist and student and friend of Albert Einstein, had obtained Einstein's support to alert President Roosevelt to the discovery of the fission process and the danger that the Germans might develop a nuclear weapon. Roosevelt had acted on the warning. And that had led to the creation of the Manhattan Project, which had begun on December 6, 1941, the very day before Pearl Harbor.

In March 1945 Szilard had gone back to Einstein and asked him to write another letter to Roosevelt. Szilard wanted the President to start planning immediately for a postwar world with atomic power and atomic weapons. He opposed both testing and using the atomic bomb because he feared they would trigger a nuclear arms race.

On April 12, in Chicago, Szilard tried to reach the President through his wife, and Mrs. Roosevelt agreed to see him. Szilard walked into scientist Arthur H. Compton's nearby office and told him of his call to Mrs. Roosevelt. Szilard returned to his own office, and five minutes later Compton's assistant knocked on the door and told Szilard that the news had just come over the radio: Roosevelt was dead.

Szilard had to start again, and he began a relentless pursuit of the new President. He believed his mission was crucial to the world. He located in his own laboratory a young mathematician named Albert Cahn who had worked for Tom Pendergast in Kansas City to earn money for graduate school. Cahn and Szilard traveled to Kansas City together, impressed Pendergast's colleagues, and won their help to arrange an appointment at the White House. But before Truman would see Szilard, he told his appointments secretary, Matthew Connelly, first to send Szilard to see Byrnes in Spartansburg, South Carolina.

Szilard, with scientists Walter Bartky and Nobel Laureate Harold C. Urey, took the train to Spartansburg. There, on May 28, they showed Einstein's letter to Byrnes. But Byrnes bridled at a memorandum in which Szilard tactlessly said that only scientists could evaluate the situation. Byrnes vigorously disagreed with Szilard's opinion that the bomb should be neither tested nor used, knowing that the United States had the bomb would impress the Soviet Union and make the postwar period more manageable. Szilard, Bartky, and Urey returned to Washington thoroughly dejected about mankind's future.

Meanwhile, on May 2, Stimson presented Truman his recommendations for membership on the all-civilian Interim Committee. In addition to himself, he suggested Vannevar Bush, head of the Carnegie Institution; Harvard President James Bryant Conant; MIT President Karl I. Compton; Assistant Secretary of State William L. Clayton; Undersecretary of the Navy Ralph A. Bard; and New York Life Insurance Company President George L. Harrison; and he urged the President to add his own representative. Truman approved Stimson's selections and added Byrnes. It was an appointment that would affect many decisions about the atomic bomb.

The first, informal meeting of the Interim Committee took place in Stimson's office a week later. Stimson, in the chair, opened by saying, "Gentlemen, it is our responsibility to recommend action that may turn the course of civilization." They promptly appointed a scientific panel to assist them: Arthur Compton, Ernest O. Lawrence, J. Robert Oppenheimer, and Enrico Fermi.

The Interim Committee met again—formally—in the Pentagon for two days, starting at 10 A.M. on May 31. Stimson emphasized that they were dealing not merely with a larger piece of ordnance but with a revolutionary discovery that could prove to be either a Frankenstein or an expediter of world peace. Oppenheimer was impressed that someone was already thinking seriously about the bomb's implications for mankind.

The committee took up a series of crucial questions:

How long could the United States expect to hold on to an atomic monopoly? Arthur Compton judged that any other nation would need at least six years to catch up to the United States' achievement. When James Bryant Conant raised the subject of creating the next-stage thermonuclear weapon, Oppenheimer estimated that it would take three additional years.

How powerful would the atomic bomb be? Oppenheimer figured that the first-stage atomic bombs would create blasts equivalent to 2,000 to 20,000 tons of TNT and that thermonuclear weapons would be equal to 10 million to 100 million tons of TNT. These numbers thoroughly frightened Byrnes; he could see what it would mean to the United States if another nation possessed such power.

What should atomic scientists concentrate on in the future? Ernest Lawrence advocated that they focus on staying ahead of the world; in effect, he anticipated a nuclear arms race. Arthur Compton and his brother Karl Compton sided with Lawrence. But Oppenheimer said that the scientists should go back to their universities and stick to basic research, and Vannevar Bush felt the same way. These were two quite different roads; the future was not at all clear.

Should the United States share atomic information with other nations, especially with a nation like the Soviet Union, which was so dependent on secrecy that it could not reciprocate? Oppenheimer favored offering other nations fundamental scientific knowledge about atomic power even before the bomb was used; that, he felt, would strengthen America's moral position. But the Soviet Union should not be given information about producing the atomic bomb.

General Marshall, rather surprisingly, supported Oppenheimer's willingness to share basic information. The Soviet Union's reputation for being uncooperative, he argued, was based on its need to maintain security. In the past, Marshall said, like-minded powers could force a totalitarian state to come into line; but now one nation with the atomic bomb could stand up to the world. He suggested inviting two Soviet scientists to the Trinity test to witness the explosion of the first nuclear device.

Byrnes was uneasy. Would giving Stalin such information lead him into a nuclear race or perhaps encourage him to seek a role in a nuclear partnership? The United States, Byrnes believed, should push ahead with atomic production and research and make sure it stayed ahead. Byrnes, with his status as the President's personal representative, received general agreement from those present and carried the day.

The meeting adjourned, but their explorations continued in the Pentagon dining room. Should Japan be warned or an atomic demonstration arranged? Stimson expressed his horror at the mass "conventional" bombings of Dresden, Hamburg, and Tokyo. Someone said that the number of people killed by an atomic bomb would not be greater than those killed by firebombs. Lawrence and Oppenheimer believed a demonstration, which would do little damage, would be enough to persuade the Japanese government to stop fighting. Byrnes saw it differently. If the Japanese were told the bomb would be used in a certain locality, would they bring American POWs there? And if the Japanese were warned and then the bomb failed to explode, would the Japanese militarists be strengthened and American credibility damaged?

These men were deeply troubled. They had the responsibility to advise the President how to enter a new and unmapped world where no one had yet walked. They tried to weigh their options and the consequences. They returned to Stimson's office and continued their discussion into the afternoon.

Before Stimson had to leave the meeting at 3:30, he summed up his understandings. As he wrote later, "I felt that to extract a genuine surrender from the Emperor and his military advisers, there must be administered a tremendous shock which would carry convincing proof of our power to destroy the Empire. Such an effective shock would save many times the number of lives, both American and Japanese, that it would cost." This concept of an effective shock became the rationale for dropping the atomic bombs on Japanese cities. Stimson insisted that the target of the atomic bomb should not be a civilian residential area—that the bombs should be used to destroy military targets, not civilian lives. To achieve the greatest psychological "shock," said Conant, the target should be a vital war plant employing a large number of workers, even though workers and their families would be destroyed. No one envisioned the vast devastation this weapon would create—far beyond such distinctions between war plants and residential neighborhoods.

The next day, while Stimson was absent, Byrnes won the committee's agreement to recommend that the bomb be used as soon as possible and "on a war plant surrounded by workers' homes."

At the committee's final session, Stimson stressed again that they needed to deal with the atomic bomb not as "a new weapon merely but as a revolutionary change in the relations of man to the universe." It could prove to be either civilization's boon or its doom.

The Interim Committee's advice to President Truman was that no mere demonstration would be able to end the war. The bomb's "shock value" might. Therefore, the bomb should be used against the enemy without warning and as soon as possible. Its target should be something like a war plant that would prove the bomb's power.

When the committee adjourned, Byrnes immediately went to Truman and reported these recommendations. With reluctance and pressed by Byrnes, Truman confirmed, Byrnes said in his memoirs, that "so far as he could see, the only reasonable conclusion was to use the bomb." By this time—June 1—Truman had decided that there was no way to invade Japan without using the atomic bomb.

Five days later, Stimson brought Truman the Interim Committee's official report; the President acknowledged that he had already heard about it from Byrnes. Stimson said the bomb should be used to deliver "a tremendous shock," but where and when to use the bomb were decisions the President would have to make.

The decision-making process did not mean the committee handed Truman a systematic selection of alternatives out of which he then chose the option of dropping atomic bombs on Japanese cities without prior warning. Essentially, he was asked to approve or veto the decisions the committee brought to him.

To the managers of the atomic project, and particularly Brigadier General Groves, it was important that the bomb be used against a city not already wrecked by "conventional" air raids and large enough so the bomb's damage could be confined within it. This would enable them to measure the results in order to justify their effort and expense. The recent conventional bombing of Japan's cities had raised the level of destruction needed to create the atomic bomb's "shock value."

One man who ran the bureaucratic gauntlet and actually managed to present a contrary view to Truman was Navy Undersecretary Ralph Bard, the Navy's representative on the Interim Committee. He continued to hold the U.S. Navy view that the war could be won by a naval blockade. He believed that the Japanese should be warned of the atomic bombing and explicitly told that they could retain the Emperor. He opposed invading the Japanese home islands.

Bard resigned from the government, but, at Secretary Forrestal's suggestion, he arranged to see Truman in person and pleaded: "For God's sake, don't organize an army to go into Japan. Kill a million people? It's ridiculous." Truman assured Bard that he had carefully considered both the planned invasion and offering Japan a chance to surrender before dropping the bomb. But he stood firm; he was not about to change his mind about invasion.

After the war, Oppenheimer voiced to President Truman his tortured regrets about having made the bomb. "Mr. President, I have blood on my hands," he said. When he had gone, Truman said, "Don't you bring that fellow around again. After all, all he did was make the bomb. I'm the guy who fired it off." Nevertheless, Truman wrote, "More than any other one man, Oppenheimer is to be credited with the achievement of the completed bomb."

Decisions also had to be made about the atomic bomb and the Soviet Union. Stimson took Truman the Interim Committee's additional initial recommendation that the bomb should not be revealed to the Soviet Union before it was used; it was a trump card that the United States should keep close to its chest. The Interim Committee discussed using atomic power to gain concessions from the Soviet Union. Later, the committee modified its view and unanimously advised the President that at Potsdam he should tell Stalin that the United States was developing a bomb to use against Japan but give no details. Truman followed that advice.

An argument that carried weight was that the atomic bomb would cost fewer lives on both sides than continuing the firebomb campaign and climaxing it with an invasion. Stimson continued to be appalled by the B-29 firebomb raids that were demolishing Japan and killing civilians, and he told Truman so. He recalled that the world had regarded the Japanese bombing of Shanghai in 1937 as a horrendous atrocity, and President Roosevelt had asked both sides to refrain from bombing civilians. The world would condemn, Stimson felt, the raids on Dresden and the repeated firebomb raids on Tokyo as atrocities like Hitler's. He wanted the slaughter stopped.

*　*　*

Knowledgeable people differed vehemently with the Interim Committee's recommendations. On June 12, for example, Nobel Laureate James O. Franck delivered to Stimson's office a plea from a group of leading scientists at the Metallurgical Laboratory in Chicago who feared that a surprise use of the bomb might scare the Russians into a nuclear arms race. They advocated a system of international control. Over the weekend of July 16–17, the Scientific Panel, still troubled by plans to use the bomb against a city, met to try once more to envisage an effective atomic demonstration. Frustrated, they concluded: "We can propose no technical demonstration likely to bring an end to the war; we see no acceptable alternative to direct military use."

To the very end, one of the last of the skeptics about the value of the atomic bomb was Admiral Leahy, who even on *Augusta*, sailing for Potsdam, offered to bet Charles Bohlen that the bomb would never work. Leahy accused the "longhairs" of gypping the government out of billions and the whole Manhattan Project of being a scam. He would assert that the bombing of Hiroshima and Nagasaki "was of no material assistance in our war against Japan. The Japanese were already defeated." But later in life, he admitted that he had misjudged the atomic bomb's effectiveness. He said he had been wrong because "It is not a bomb. It is not an explosive. It is a poisonous thing that kills people by its deadly radioactive reaction, more than by the explosive force it develops."

Churchill told Truman he favored using the bomb if it could end the war. On July 4 the Combined Policy Committee met in Washington, and the British formally gave their approval for using the bomb against Japan. The final decision remained Truman's. Churchill wrote, "I never doubted what it would be, nor have I ever doubted since that he was right."

The fact is that most of those whom the atomic bombs killed would be civilians, but the retrospective moral outrage seems strange. No one conceived of them as battlefield weapons; the military targets considered were never troops in the field. To put it another way, the World War II battles of Nanking, Leningrad, Coventry, London, Dresden, Hamburg, Tokyo, Hiroshima, and Nagasaki suggest that the battlefield had expanded. The expectation that the model in World War II should be Waterloo or Gettysburg or even Verdun is archaic and unrealistic in the world of the bomber and the atomic bomb.

What would have happened if Truman had decided, as he might

have, not to drop the atomic bomb? There seems no doubt whatsoever that an invasion of Japan's home islands would have been necessary to finish the war. The bombings and the battles would have gone on for months more. This he was determined to prevent.

There is no ironclad evidence of exactly when Truman "made up his mind" to use the atomic bomb. The decision was incremental; surely, the decisions made at Babelsberg during the Potsdam Conference—culminating in his written approval on the morning of July 31—meant that dropping the bomb was inevitable.

Another fact was always in his mind: The nearer American forces approached Japan, the greater had been their casualties. The price of invading Japan itself would be enormous, and nobody thought the Japanese would surrender on American terms. Churchill had it right; the decision to drop the atomic bomb was really not an issue.

Giant B-29s of the 21st Bomber Command had started flying against Japan from the Marianas the previous November 24. When Major General LeMay arrived in January to command the 21st and step up the Pacific air attack on Japan, 345 B-29s were already based there—only 1,200 miles from Tokyo. LeMay was a hard-driving, cigar-chewing bomber pilot who had a reputation for getting a job done. He said, "I'll tell you what war is about. You've got to kill people, and when you've killed enough they stop fighting."

If he did not get results, LeMay was told, the United States would have to assault Japan from the sea at the cost of thousands of American lives. But his high-altitude incendiary raids on the Japanese city of Kobe on February 4 and on Tokyo on February 25 had only modest success. Then he learned the results of the raid on Dresden on the night of February 13, when 1,400 low-flying British bombers with high explosives and 650,000 incendiaries had wiped out the German city. The next day, 1,350 American bombers had followed up—but had found nothing left to bomb.

The Dresden raids showed LeMay that he could firebomb at low altitudes effectively—and not get his men killed. On the night of March 9–10, he sent 334 B-29 bombers on low-altitude runs against Tokyo, carrying 2,000 tons of incendiary bombs. They ignited a huge flaming "X," incinerated the densely packed wood-and-paper homes of 750,000 people, and created a tremendous conflagration, a wind-whipped wall of inescapable fire. That night the bombers burned out 15.8 square miles of Tokyo and killed 83,793 Japanese.

That March 9–10 raid completely changed the method of bombing

Japan and set the pattern for strategic bombing for the rest of the war. In the next ten days, LeMay's fliers firebombed Nagoya, Osaka, and Kobe.

The air assault on Japan was made more efficient when three divisions of U.S. Marines conquered five-mile-long Iwo Jima at the end of March. The price was 25,851 Marines killed and wounded; it was the costliest battle in Marine Corps history. But they eliminated a base from which the Japanese on the home islands gained advance warning of approaching B-29s, and they provided a landing field for B-29s in trouble. Thereafter, fewer B-29s and their crews were lost. By the end of the war, 2,500 B-29s had made emergency landings on Iwo Jima.

On April 12, B-29s bombed Tokyo again and burned to the ground the buildings that housed Japan's own atomic bomb project. On May 24, 400 bombers dropped another 3,646 tons of bombs on Tokyo. Among others, they killed sixty-two Allied airmen who were prisoners of war. It was later charged that the POWs had deliberately been locked in a wooden cell block while Japanese jailers and prisoners fled to safety.

The next day, an even greater armada of 464 B-29s attacked Tokyo. During the next three months, LeMay's men bombed Nagoya, Osaka, Kobe, Yokohama, and Kawasaki and killed a quarter of a million Japanese.

The devastating pounding of Japan from the air convinced LeMay that airpower could indeed end the war without an invasion. His 600 superbombers roamed over Japan virtually at will, causing 806,000 civilian casualties, of whom 330,000 were killed.

Following the Interim Committee's recommendation, the President instructed Stimson that the atomic bomb, which was then still untested, should be used against a major war plant. "In deciding to use this bomb I wanted to make sure that it would be used as a weapon of war in the manner prescribed by the laws of war. That meant I wanted it dropped on a military target."

Choosing the target for the bomb became the next big controversy. Aiming the bomb at a war plant in the center of a city promised to maximize death and destruction. But historian Leon Sigal later charged that the targeting policy was "deliberately aiming at noncombatants with only tangential involvement in the war effort."

By May, a "Target Committee" of Air Force officers and scientists was analyzing where the bomb should be used. Brigadier General Groves kept tight control of the Target Committee; he was wary of the Joint Chiefs because of Admiral Leahy's lack of faith in the atomic bomb's effectiveness. The Target Committee listed potential targets that had two primary characteristics: They should be military, and they should not have been destroyed by conventional air raids.

The largest city, Tokyo, was eliminated because, the committee said, it was already "practically rubble." Also, it was pointed out, if the capital were atom-bombed, no one would be left to surrender.

On May 30, a confrontation erupted between Stimson and Groves over whether to target Kyoto, the ancient capital of Japan and a treasured cultural and religious shrine. Stimson himself deleted Kyoto from the atomic target list because destroying this revered city would only strengthen the Japanese will to resist. General Arnold sided with Groves because Kyoto was also a center of military activity.

Stimson brought the issue to Truman, who agreed that destroying Kyoto could stigmatize the United States as competing with Hitler in atrocities. But Kyoto was still endangered. As late as July 21, military leaders were still urging Stimson to agree to make Kyoto the prime atomic target. He refused to change his mind, but the Joint Chiefs kept Kyoto free from conventional bombing. The next day in Potsdam, Stimson again brought the question to Truman, who continued to oppose including Kyoto on the atomic list. General Arnold substituted Nagasaki, although he still tried to convince Stimson to restore Kyoto to the list.

Stimson had to go to Truman still again, and the President reiterated his position that bombing the ancient capital would create postwar bitterness. Truman wrote in his diary, "Even if the Japs are savages, ruthless, merciless and fanatic, we as the leader of the world for the common welfare cannot drop this terrible bomb on the old Capital or the new." Neither Truman nor Stimson ever did manage to remove Kyoto from the Air Forces list, but it was placed after Nagasaki. Although the generals were certainly disobedient, Kyoto was out of harm's way for the moment. This decision on Kyoto was the only targeting issue that seemed to have been decided with an eye toward postwar reconciliation.

In the end, the Target Committee chose four cities: Hiroshima, Kokura, Niigata, and Nagasaki—in that order.

Hiroshima, the largest city that had not yet been ravaged by the 21st Bomber Command, was the most likely target. The delta city on the Ota River was an important army assembly point and port of embarkation in the middle of an urban industrial area. It contained some 280,000 civilians and 43,000 soldiers. From there, the Japanese Army General Staff planned to direct the defense of Kyushu. And although the Americans did not know it at the time, it was only thirty miles from the poison gas factory at Okunoshima, which had been manufacturing the poison gas that had been used hundreds of times in the war against China.

When, on July 30, General Carl Spaatz, the new commander of the Strategic Air Forces, telexed Washington that of the four target cities only Hiroshima did not have an Allied prisoner-of-war camp, he was given permission to make that city his number one target. But he was given latitude to make the final choice of target based on weather and other operational considerations.

The Trinity test was the first step. It proved whether or not the theoretical premise really worked. Oppenheimer used a prototype of the large spherical bomb known as the Fat Man.

The thunderous explosion of the first atomic bomb took place just before dawn at 5:30 A.M. on Monday, July 16, thirty miles west of the Sacramento Mountains at a remote desert site known as the Jornada del Muerto ("Journey of Death") on the enormous Alamogordo Air Force Base in New Mexico. A blinding flash of light—"the light of many suns in one"—and a giant green fireball 2,500 feet across, followed by a wind of hurricane force, inaugurated the nuclear age. Scientists had converted matter into energy, an achievement more spectacular, and more significant to mankind, than the alchemy that had professed to turn lead into gold.

The force of the explosion equaled that of 18,600 tons of TNT, ten times what even the experts at Los Alamos had expected. All animal and plant life within a mile of Ground Zero was destroyed. Windows two hundred miles away were blown out. In reply to startled inquiries from the public, both the Alamogordo Army Air Base and the Pentagon issued press releases claiming a "remotely located ammunition magazine" had exploded.

J. Robert Oppenheimer watched this momentous event, and through his mind went the line from the Hindu scripture the *Bhagavad-Gita:* "Now I am become Death, the destroyer of worlds." It has been quoted many times since.

Four hours after the Trinity explosion, the heavy cruiser USS *Indianapolis* left Hunter's Point in San Francisco Bay, slipped under the Golden Gate bridge, and set out on the ten-day voyage to Tinian.

To its deck was lashed the first combat-ready atomic bomb, informally called "Little Boy."

Secretary Stimson brought Truman the historic news of Trinity while they were in Potsdam. And the next day, Stimson received a follow-up message from his special assistant, George Harrison, in Washington, which reportedly confused the Women's Army Corps (WAC) radio operators in Babelsberg:

> Doctor has just returned most enthusiastic and confident that the little boy is as husky as his big brother. The light in his eyes discernible from here to Highhold and I could have heard his screams from here to my farm.

(Highhold was Stimson's home on Long Island, New York; the farm referred to was fifty miles outside of Washington. The little boy was, of course, not a baby son of the seventy-seven-year-old secretary of war.)

The scientists swelled with pride at their mastery over nature. But then came the overwhelming realization of the massive scale of death let loose on the earth. Truman wrote in his diary: "We have discovered the most terrible bomb in the history of the world. It may be the fire destruction prophesized in the Euphrates Valley Era, after Noah and his fabulous Ark. Anyway we think we have found the way to cause the disintegration of the atom."

He recognized the discovery's good and bad potentials and added, "It is certainly a good thing for the world that Hitler's crowd or Stalin's did not discover this atomic bomb. It seems to be the most terrible thing ever discovered, but it can be made the most useful."

How would the Trinity test change the United States' strategy against Japan? Truman met on July 21 in his quarters at Babelsberg with Byrnes, Stimson, Leahy, Marshall, Arnold, and King to review their military planning. Now there was less reason than ever to compromise on unconditional surrender, and they might not need the Soviet Union's intervention. Truman confirmed that the decision to use the atomic bomb would hold unless the Japanese accepted the Potsdam ultimatum. But because the effect of an atomic weapon on an enemy was still uncertain, they stood by their decision to invade the Japanese home islands.

Years later, Truman wrote his sister, "It was a terrible decision. But I made it. And I'd made it to save 250,000 boys from the United

States and I'd make it again under similar circumstances. It stopped the Jap war."

Despite Truman's determination to use this most destructive but American-life-saving weapon, the admirals, Leahy and King, held to their position that the Navy had already won the war de facto and the atomic bomb was unnecessary. And General Arnold remained certain that conventional bombing would win the war. How much of their certainty was the product of interservice partisanship and how much was moral horror at the prospect of the atomic bomb's destructiveness cannot be determined.

What can be said is that Truman had been listening to all these varied opinions, pro and con, repeatedly and had decided both to use the atomic bomb and to invade Japan. It was difficult to untangle all the threads of information and interests hurled at him in the multitude of recommendations. But he was a man who would make a decision and who had the buck stop at his desk. Although still a novice with little more than three months in the White House, as he said, he "never had any doubt" about the decision to use the atomic bomb. He was not a man to stay up nursing second thoughts after he had made a decision.

He may have been a novice in the Oval Room, but he was no novice in judging men and their desires—he was an experienced politician. And he understood that his purpose was to end the war swiftly and at the lowest cost possible. As Stimson said in retrospect, it was almost impossible to see how Harry Truman could ever have explained to the American people why he had made the decision to invade Japan at an enormous cost in American lives if he did not first use this new weapon.

The debate would also go on, long after the event, about what kind of a target Truman thought his airmen were aiming to destroy. Did he believe a target like the city of Hiroshima was "a purely military one"? After the firebombing of Tokyo and most every other major city in Japan, did it make any difference which target was chosen?

Between May and August, LeMay and his B-29s bombed fifty-eight of the sixty Japanese cities that the Air Forces figured were necessary to complete the war by conventional weapons from the air. The Japanese did not quit. General Marshall, of course, disagreed with the airmen's assessment; he, in true army tradition, still believed you had to seize and hold the ground.

Carefully, key people were told about the Trinity test. On July 18, two days after Trinity, Churchill—who, of course, had long known about the atomic bomb—tried to convince Truman that the test of this weapon eliminated the need for an invasion. "Now all this nightmare picture had vanished. In its place was the vision—fair and bright indeed it seemed—of the end of the whole war in one or two violent shocks." He also believed the Russians would no longer be needed in the Pacific war. "We had no need to ask favours of them."

There was one decision they both agreed on. Churchill said:

> At any rate, there never was a moment's discussion as to whether the atomic bomb should be used or not. To avert a vast, indefinite butchery, to bring the war to an end, to give peace to the world, to lay healing hands upon its tortured peoples by a manifestation of overwhelming power at the cost of a few explosions, seemed, after all our toils and perils, a miracle of deliverance.

Churchill informed Truman of the message that Stalin had received from the Japanese Emperor exploring the possibility of a compromised end to the war. The prime minister explained that Stalin had not wanted to seem to be swaying Truman toward compromise but suggested that perhaps unconditional surrender could be achieved without use of those words in order to preserve the Japanese military honor. Truman reacted coldly: the Japanese had had no military honor at Pearl Harbor. Churchill cautioned that perhaps the Japanese had more reason to die defending Japan than the Allies had attacking it.

Truman and Churchill agreed that Stalin should be told about the bomb but not given any particulars. They both felt that the Soviet Union was no longer needed to conquer Japan. But Soviet troops had been moving east on the Trans-Siberian Railway since early May.

When de Gaulle learned about the bomb, he was deeply stirred by the arrival of a means to annihilate mankind, but, always the parochial patriot, he forecast a benefit for France. He theorized that Japan's post-atomic surrender would eliminate the United States veto, which, in his view, was keeping France out of the Pacific and Asia. He wrote later, "Indochina from one day to the next became accessible to us once again."

Stimson had dinner with Eisenhower on July 21 and told him of the Trinity results. When Stimson asked for his reaction, the general said the Japanese were ready to surrender, and he hoped that the United States would never use the atomic bomb and that other nations could somehow remain ignorant of the fact that the puzzle of nuclear fission had been solved. As Eisenhower recalled later, his naive reply made Stimson furious.

Over lunch on Tuesday, July 24, Truman reviewed with Byrnes the question of how to tell Stalin about the atomic bomb. Byrnes opposed telling Stalin anything. But at the end of that afternoon's conference session, when everyone had gotten up from the large round table and was standing about chatting informally, Truman left his interpreter, Charles Bohlen, behind, walked around the table and "casually mentioned to Stalin" that the United States had a new weapon.

This is one of the dramatic and prescient moments in modern history, and no one knows precisely what the President said to Stalin. Harry Vaughan claimed to have overheard him say to the Russian interpreter, Pavlov, "Will you tell the Generalissimo that we have perfected a very powerful explosive which we are going to use against the Japanese and we think it will end the war." According to all accounts, Truman never mentioned the term "atomic bomb." Truman himself reported that Stalin replied almost offhandedly that he was glad to hear it and hoped it would be put to good use against the Japanese.

From a distance, Bohlen observed the encounter intensely. He says in his memoirs:

> Across the room, I watched Stalin's face carefully as the President broke the news. So offhand was Stalin's response that there was some question in my mind whether the President's message had got through. I should have known better than to underrate the dictator. Years later, Marshal Georgi K. Zhukov, in his memoirs, disclosed that that night Stalin ordered a telegram sent to those working on the atomic bomb in Russia to hurry with the job."

Churchill had been standing five yards away, searching Stalin's face, and he thought that Stalin appeared delighted. A few moments later, while they waited for their cars, Churchill asked Truman, "How did it go?" Truman said simply, "He never asked a question."

In fact, Stalin already knew about the Manhattan Project and the

Trinity test from his spies in the United States. Klaus Fuchs, a German-born physicist who had left Germany in 1933 and worked for the British and Americans, had long been passing important atomic secrets to the Soviet Union. Fuchs was present at Alamogordo for the Trinity test. And on July 9, a British physicist, Dr. Alan Nunn May, in Canada had handed a Soviet official a sample of uranium.

The same day that Truman spoke of the bomb to Stalin, Brigadier General Groves in Washington drafted an operational order that was approved by Marshall and Stimson at Potsdam and the next morning sent it to General Spaatz. (This was one day before Truman issued the Potsdam Declaration.)

General Spaatz was instructed to have the 509th Composite Group, Twentieth Air Force, deliver "its first special bomb" as soon after August 3 as weather would permit visual bombing. He was to prepare to strike one of four cities—Hiroshima, Kokura, Niigata, and Nagasaki—that the Target Committee had selected. Additional bombs, he was told, would be supplied for the remaining designated targets as soon as available. The mission was to be totally secret, but copies of the order to Spaatz went to General MacArthur and Admiral Nimitz.

By authorizing the atomic bomb's use "after about 3 August," when the Potsdam Conference would be over, Truman would, incidentally, avoid a lot of explaining. The formal military orders gave the air generals liberal choices, because Groves wanted the bomb used as quickly as possible, to prove its worth in case the Japanese quit.

The 509th Composite Group, commanded by thirty-year-old Colonel Paul W. Tibbets, was already waiting with seven modified B-29 Superfortress bombers on Tinian. Many regarded Tibbets as the best American bomber pilot; he had led the first B-17 bombing mission from England over Europe.

Tibbets' new silver planes had fuel injection systems, pneumatic bomb doors, and reversible electric propellers. Their group insignia were painted over. They sat on the world's largest airport; it had six runways, each the width of a ten-lane highway and two miles long. The materials for the bomb and specialists to assemble them were being rushed to Tinian.

On July 26, two days after Truman spoke to Stalin about the bomb, USS *Indianapolis* arrived at Tinian with the Little Boy bomb, and three C-54 cargo planes took off from Kirtland Air Force Base at

Albuquerque with additional parts of Little Boy and two more C-54s with elements of the Fat Man bomb.

Little Boy, to be used on the first mission, was a uranium 235–fueled bomb ten and a half feet long. It was an armored cylinder twenty-nine inches in diameter and weighing 9,700 pounds. Made of blackened steel, it had a rounded nose and a tapered tail. One crew member said it looked like "an elongated trash can with fins."

Fat Man (named for Winston Churchill), which was intended for the second mission, was a larger, more sophisticated, egg-shaped plutonium bomb of the type tested at Alamogordo. Altogether, nine bombs would be available by November 1, the date of the invasion of Kyushu, and another five the following month.

Indianapolis unloaded its atomic cargo and sailed on to Guam and then to Leyte to train for the Kyushu invasion. The cruiser was sunk on Sunday night, July 29, by the Japanese submarine I-58, whose commander, Lieutenant Commander Mochitsura Hashimoto, was a veteran of the attack on Pearl Harbor. *Indianapolis* was the last major warship to be lost at sea in the war. Of its crew of 1,196 men, 850 survived the sinking, only to endure a horrible fate in the ocean. They were without drinking water and drowned or were eaten alive by sharks before the survivors were spotted by a Navy plane on Thursday, August 2. *Indianapolis* had not even been reported missing, and more than 500 men died needlessly during the eighty-four-hour ordeal. The 883 men killed made this the greatest loss at sea in the history of the U.S. Navy.

The Little Boy bomb was ready on Tinian on July 31, and on that day Tibbets' B-29s flew a final test run with a dummy Little Boy. On Wednesday, August 1, a typhoon approached Japan and delayed the mission. The next day, the three B-29s bringing the parts of three Fat Man bombs were able to land on Tinian; one Fat Man shell was to be used for a drop test and a second for combat. The third would be held in reserve, waiting for a second plutonium core expected in mid-August.

Beginning at 3 P.M. on Saturday, August 4, Tibbets briefed the crews of the seven B-29s that would fly the mission. The bomb would be aboard Tibbets' plane. Three weather planes would fly ahead to assess the cloud cover over the designated targets. Two planes would accompany Tibbets' plane to observe and photograph. The seventh would be held as a spare on Iwo Jima with facilities to unload and reload the bomb in case needed. The mission was scheduled for early Monday morning.

Sunday afternoon, Little Boy was transported into its pit for loading into the belly of the plane designated as B-29 "82." Tibbets dragged a sign painter away from a softball game to paint on its nose in foot-high letters the given names of his mother, the former Enola Gay Haggard of Glidden, Iowa.

The usual pilot of the *Enola Gay*, who would fly this mission as copilot, was Captain Robert Lewis of Brooklyn, New York, stocky, blond, and twenty-six years old. He came over to inspect his plane, was incensed by the unexpected name, and went to confront Tibbets. But rank had its privileges.

The final briefing came at midnight. Tibbets asked a chaplain to say a prayer. The men breakfasted on ham and eggs and Tibbets' favorite, pineapple fritters. Most of the twelve crew members of the *Enola Gay* posed for endless pictures. Navy Captain William S. Parsons, a 1922 Annapolis graduate and the man who would arm Little Boy in flight, refused to be photographed. At 2:45 A.M., *Enola Gay*, referred to over the radio ludicrously as "Dimples Eight Two," started down the runway.

The crew of the *Enola Gay* flew at just under five thousand feet on automatic pilot; when they passed over Iwo Jima at 5:52 A.M., Tibbets climbed to nine thousand feet. The men drank coffee and ate ham sandwiches; they were two hours away from the target. At 7:30, Parsons armed the bomb. A weather plane reported in, and Tibbets told the crew the target would definitely be Hiroshima. They climbed again and leveled off at thirty-one thousand feet. The men put on heavy flak suits. Twelve miles from the city, the bombardier, twenty-four-year-old Major Thomas Ferebee, took charge and flew the B-29 through his Norden bombsight at 328 miles per hour. The aiming point was the T-shaped Aioi Bridge near Second Army Headquarters.

The single bomb fell away from the plane. Nearly five tons lighter, the B-29 leaped upward. Tibbets banked into a violent turn. At 8:16, 1,900 feet above Hiroshima, the bomb exploded. Already more than eleven miles from the target, *Enola Gay* was slammed by two massive shock waves. Looking back, Tibbets saw over Hiroshima the mushroom cloud.

No one knows precisely how many people died in Hiroshima that Monday morning. The Strategic Bombing Survey estimated that 71,000 people died that day. And within five years the deaths related to the bombing may have reached 200,000.

One of the brightest of the theoretical physicists involved with the bomb, Richard Feynman, figured that the atomic bomb dropped on Hiroshima could be mass-produced at the cost of one B-29 bomber, but that the power it delivered equaled that of one thousand airplanes each carrying ten tons of conventional bombs.

On August 6, four days into his voyage home from Potsdam, President Truman was eating lunch with members of USS *Augusta*'s crew when Captain Frank Graham, the White House Map Room officer, handed him a message from Stimson: "Big bomb dropped on Hiroshima August 5 at 7:15 P.M. Washington time. First reports indicate complete success which was even more conspicuous than earlier test."

Truman was overwhelmed. He telephoned Byrnes aboard the ship and told the sailors sitting around him, "This is the greatest thing in history. It's time for us to get home."

A few minutes later, he was handed a second message with details about the bombing, and he announced to the sailors that a new bomb twenty thousand times as powerful as a ton of TNT had been used. He went to the wardroom, told the officers there the news, and called a press conference of the correspondents aboard ship. He was sure the war would now be over quickly.

A statement from Truman was released by Stimson in Washington. He promised to destroy completely Japan's power to make war. He had issued the Declaration of July 26 to spare the Japanese people, but their leaders had rejected it. If they did not accept it now, they would receive "a rain of ruin from the air, the like of which has never been seen on this earth." And it would be followed by invasion.

Truman's statement said: "It is an atomic bomb." *The Washington Post* ran a front-page story headlined: WHAT'S AN ATOM? HERE'S DESCRIPTION FROM DICTIONARY.

Truman spoke of the significance of atomic power for the future and said he would set up a commission to control the production and use of atomic power in the United States. He declared, "What has been done is the greatest achievement of organized science in history."

At 11 P.M. on August 7, Truman was back in the White House. Since he had left, the U.N. Charter had been ratified and the atomic bomb had been used. In *The New York Times* that day, Hanson Baldwin wrote, "Yesterday we clinched victory in the Pacific, but we sowed the whirlwind."

The Japanese did not surrender. General Marshall, among many others, was surprised that they did not sue for peace. General Spaatz was ordered to continue bombing as planned. That day, the Twentieth Air Force sent out 130 B-29s, and on the next it flew 420 "conventional" day and night sorties against Japan.

On August 8, two days after the atomic bomb was dropped on Hiroshima, Molotov in Moscow suddenly summoned Japanese Ambassador Naotake Sato and announced that the Soviet Union regarded itself at war with Japan, at the request of its allies, as of August 9. Stalin had decided not to wait until China met his terms.

Molotov called in Harriman and the British ambassador and told them the same thing. The British ambassador asked Molotov how Ambassador Sato had taken the news that the Soviet Union was declaring war on Japan. Molotov replied that he had explained that the Soviet Union wanted to shorten the war and decrease the sacrifices. Ambassador Sato resignedly predicted that the war would not last much longer.

The atomic bomb had accelerated the Soviet timetable; Stalin had to get into the game before it was over. Truman met with the White House correspondents and told them simply that the Soviet Union had declared war on Japan.

Soviet armies rolled into Manchuria, Sakhalin Island, and Korea. A three-column attack in Manchuria actually hit the Japanese Army in strength on the eighth, and the fighting there continued until the twenty-first, six days after the supposed end of the war. In the estimate of some, this attack and the closing off of any possibility of Soviet mediation shocked the Japanese leaders as much as the atomic bomb did.

Stalin told Harriman he thought the Japanese were looking for an excuse to set up a government that would surrender, and the atomic bomb might provide that excuse. He now showed great interest in the bomb and said its secret would have to be closely guarded.

From the White House, Truman shared with the American people his rationale for dropping the bomb: "We have used it in order to shorten the agony of war, in order to save the lives of thousands and thousands of young Americans. We shall continue to use it until we completely destroy Japan's power to make war. Only a Japanese surrender will stop us."

The atomic bomb was a monstrous step in the constant evolution of the weapons of war. New weapons can have a major impact on the conduct of war. For example, John Ellis wrote of the machine gun in 1914:

The generals never came to terms with this power. Time and time again they threw their men forward. . . . They never realized that they were not fighting [the enemy's] "will," but his machine guns. And they were implacable and unshakeable. Morale was an irrelevancy to them; all they needed was enough water and bullets. Man counted for nothing. The machine had taken over. . . . This dehumanization of war has continued unabated. . . . Men are merely helpless bystanders. With the advent of nuclear weapons this process has been carried to its logical conclusion. Now the destruction of the whole world is contingent upon the mere pressing of a button.

There was little—but enough—time for Japan to react before the next bomb was dropped. Originally, a second bomb had been scheduled for two weeks after the first, but the date was moved up partly because Groves wanted it and partly because the weather was expected to turn bad.

The decision to drop a second atomic bomb had been recommended by the Interim Committee back on May 31, and the July 24 directive to General Spaatz allowed the military to act on it. This was regarded by some as a surrender of civilian control. At Potsdam, however, Truman had told Stimson that, while he hoped one bomb would be enough, he would not limit the military even if the first bomb was successful. But most significantly, after the destruction of Hiroshima, no peace offers came from Tokyo.

On Tinian, Fat Man bomb F31, a five-foot sphere weighing two tons, was assembled with a feeling of urgency. The men there felt that the sooner the second bomb was dropped, the better the chances that the Japanese would be terrified and surrender.

Late on August 8, Fat Man was loaded into a B-29 named *Bock's Car* after its usual pilot, Captain Frederick C. Bock. This time the plane was to be piloted by Major Charles W. Sweeney, who had flown one of the two observation planes on the Hiroshima mission. His primary target was Kokura's arsenal; his secondary, the old Portuguese and Dutch port city of Nagasaki, the home of many Christians.

At 3:47 A.M. on August 9, *Bock's Car* lifted off Tinian in a storm of tropical rain and lightning. Sweeney arrived over Kokura at 10:44 A.M.; ground haze and smoke prevented the bombardier from seeing the aiming point. Japanese fighters and flak began to come up. The B-29s made three runs over the city; then, with the weather still socked in, Sweeney went for their secondary target—Nagasaki, the site of the factory that had perfected the Mitsubishi torpedoes used in the attack on Pearl Harbor. They had enough fuel left for only one run over that target. The weather had closed in there also, but a twenty-second opening in the clouds allowed the bombardier to release his bomb.

Fat Man exploded at 11:02 A.M. 1,650 feet above Nagasaki. Thirty-eight thousand people were killed immediately, and in the next five years another 100,000 would die.

Some analysts speculate that the bomb was finally dispatched by radar, against orders. It was unlikely that the men aboard *Bock's Car* were eager to land back on Tinian carrying a fully armed atomic bomb. Fat Man exploded a mile and a half north of its aim point, a distance that greatly reduced the damage it caused. The Mitsubishi dockyards, containing the torpedo factories and the city's main war industry, escaped unscathed.

The human devastation from the two bombs was literally incredible. "The dead are too numerous to be counted," announced the Tokyo radio. "The destructive power of these bombs is indescribable."

One eyewitness, however, tried to describe it. An Australian soldier named Kenneth Harrison had been captured by the Japanese at Singapore at the beginning of the war and in 1945 was a prisoner of war at Camp Nakamura in Japan. When on August 22 his jailers finally admitted that the war was over, the ex-prisoners were escorted around much of Japan. Harrison, with others, visited Hiroshima and wrote a vivid account of what he saw:

> The reality was the girl with scarred features who passed with averted face. And the listless people who went by so dully; the scarred people; the burnt people; the apathetic people. And the people who even now showed not the slightest sign of hostility or resentment. Saddened and depressed beyond words at the magnitude of the tragedy, and feeling like ghouls, we decided to leave Hiroshima that same day. . . . Fortunately for our peace of mind we knew nothing of such atomic age refinements as radiation sickness, and although we occasionally picked up a statue or kicked over a strangely fused piece of metal for a closer look, we were never tempted to take a souvenir. One does not rob a tomb.

The genie was out of the bottle, and the world was dramatically and dangerously different. Atomic power would be both a blessing and a curse. The immediate postwar geopolitical question was its impact on the emerging tension between the Soviet Union and the West, and the answer depended on one's view of that tension.

Churchill saw American nuclear power, and later NATO, as the main guarantors of peace; but immediately after the two bombings he spoke of atomic power as "this terrible means of maintaining the rule of law in the world." Dean Acheson did not think the Soviet Union threatened Western Europe directly but would try to exhaust the democracies by drawing their strength and treasure to the periphery, places like Korea and Indochina. Beyond these concerns hung the mushroom cloud of the potential of planetary doom.

I. F. Stone, the radical journalist, wrote on August 12:

> I wish it were possible to throw on some gigantic screen for all to see some fraction of the suffering, the treachery, the sacrifice, and the courage of the past decade. For how are we in America to fulfill our responsibility to the dead and to the future, to our less fortunate allies and to our children's children, if we do not feel a little of this so deeply in our bones that we will be unswervingly determined that it shall never happen again?

Secretary Stimson, who had as great an influence as any man on the use of the atomic bomb, later reflected:

> The face of war is the face of death; death is an inevitable part of every order that a wartime leader gives. The decision to use the atomic bomb was a decision that brought death to over a hundred thousand Japanese. No explanation can change that fact and I do not wish to gloss it over. But this deliberate, premeditated destruction was our least abhorrent choice. The destruction of Hiroshima and Nagasaki put an end to the Japanese war. It stopped the fire raids, and the strangling blockade; it ended the ghastly specter of a clash of great land armies. . . . The bombs dropped on Hiroshima and Nagasaki ended a war. They also made it wholly clear that we must never have another war.

"The atomic bomb is too dangerous to be loose in a lawless world," Truman told the nation in a broadcast from the White House. On August 15, he ordered all information about the development, design, and production of the atomic bomb stamped SECRET.

Robert Oppenheimer drafted a report for the Scientific Panel of the Interim Committee, which unanimously favored an international control agreement. Secretary Byrnes immediately opposed this idea as impractical.

On the other hand, Secretary Stimson, who at Potsdam had expressed to Truman his opposition to any atomic disclosures to the Russians, now turned 180 degrees and recommended seeking an agreement with them and mutually controlling the atomic bomb. To do otherwise while "having this weapon rather ostentatiously on our hip" would only increase Soviet distrust of the United States and Britain. The United States, he proposed, should openly offer to stop development of the bomb as a military weapon if the British and Russians agreed to do the same.

Now, at seventy-seven and ten days from retirement, he memoed Truman with a personal observation: "The chief lesson I have learned in a long life is that the only way you can make a man trustworthy is to trust him; and the surest way to make him untrustworthy is to distrust him and show your distrust." (Two years later, Stimson would no longer believe that his lifelong lesson applied to Josef Stalin.)

Whether or not to share information about atomic energy was hotly debated. Among those who felt secure in the American atomic monopoly, there was widespread opposition to sharing atomic information even with Britain and Canada. Both Lewis Strauss and Brigadier General Groves rejected such sharing. (Historian John Morton Blum calls Groves "a xenophobic superpatriot.") But Dean Acheson led a group favoring full international cooperation on all atomic energy matters, including weapons.

Physicist Richard Feynman wrote in his notebook soon after Hiroshima:

> Other peoples are not being hindered in the development of the bomb by any secrets we are keeping. . . . [S]oon they will be able to do to Columbus, Ohio, and *hundreds* of cities like it what we did to Hiroshima.
>
> And we scientists are clever—too clever—are you not

satisfied? Is four square miles in one bomb not enough? Men are still thinking. Just tell us how big you want it!

At the cabinet meeting on Friday, September 19, Stimson pressed his conviction. The United States must take the initiative and belay Soviet suspicions by sharing with them the basic scientific data about atomic power. Word was spread that Truman wanted to share the bomb with the Soviet Union, and there was a national uproar. But what Truman was really advocating was an interchange of information on the conditions that weapons development be renounced and adequate opportunity be provided for inspection.

The entire cabinet meeting of September 21, Stimson's last, focused on this subject. The discussion was candid and vigorous. Stimson again spelled out his proposal; Undersecretary of State Dean Acheson, sitting in for Byrnes, agreed, as did Schwellenbach, Wallace, Hannegan, and Paul McNutt. Treasury Secretary Vinson was adamant that there be no exchange of information; he was certain it would be one-sided. Attorney General Tom Clark agreed with him. Henry Wallace, concerned about American-Soviet tensions, asked whether the United States would follow a line of bitterness or a line of peace. To Forrestal the bomb was the property of the American people and should not be given away. Vannevar Bush favored the exchange of scientific information but not the details of the construction of the bombs. He framed the basic question: Can we trust the Russians?

Everyone had an opinion, but there was no consensus. The decision was up to Harry Truman. The President had already decided to keep atomic energy severely controlled under a government agency, and now he saw he had to resolve these varied views of an atomic world. After the "stormy Cabinet meeting," as he called it, he wrote Bess, "I'll have to make a decision and the 'Ayes' will have it even if I'm the only Aye. It is probably the most momentous one I'll make." He was right.

Truman was determined to turn atomic energy into a weapon of peace, not war. He sent Congress a message on October 3 recognizing both atomic power's danger and its revolutionary potential for good. Action had to be taken against the hazards of misuse. He anticipated that the knowledge that the United States now possessed would in time become known to scientists and engineers abroad and the only solution lay in international agreements renouncing the use of the atomic bomb and encouraging the use of atomic energy for peaceful ends. He wanted Congress to create an Atomic Energy Commission appointed by the President with the consent of the Senate.

Although his proposal was sensible, it created a commotion. But Harry Truman told the Congress what he had come to understand: the world had entered "a new era in the history of civilization."

Chapter 19

"The Day We Have Been Waiting For"

At the moment the second atomic bomb exploded over Nagasaki, the Japanese Supreme Council for the Direction of the War was meeting in Tokyo. The council members debated, once again, the Potsdam Declaration and its demand for unconditional surrender. By then they knew that the Soviet Union had declared war. Prime Minister Kantaro Suzuki and Foreign Minister Shigenori Togo still recommended surrender. The minister of war, General Korechika Anami, earnestly insisted he would still pull victory from defeat: "There is really no alternative for us but to continue the war." The Americans should be forced to invade—and then Japan would defeat them. The vote was deadlocked: 3–3. Incredibly, the two atomic bombs had changed not a single senior Japanese leader's mind.

But the bombs did reinforce Emperor Hirohito's judgment that Japan must sue for peace. Suzuki and Togo met secretly with the Emperor, reported the deadlock in the Supreme Council, and asked him to call another meeting of the Supreme Council and to preside over it. Thus, shortly after midnight, the Emperor, in an extraordinary step, met with his ministers in his underground shelter in the palace and appealed to them to break their stalemate and accept the Allied offer. They talked for two hours. Then Hirohito told the council that the time had come "to bear the unbearable." The Emperor had decided.

At 7:33 A.M. the next day, August 10, in Washington, U.S. monitors picked up a shortwave message from Radio Tokyo addressed to the

Swiss and Swedish governments for transmission to the United States, Great Britain, China, and the Soviet Union. The message said that at the command of His Majesty the Emperor and in the cause of peace, the Japanese government was ready to accept the terms of the joint declaration of July 26 "with the understanding that said declaration does not comprise any demand which prejudices the prerogatives of His Majesty as a sovereign ruler."

This was not quite the unconditional surrender that Truman had been demanding. And the Radio Tokyo broadcast was not an official communication of surrender. Truman told Admiral Leahy to summon a meeting at 9 A.M. of Secretaries Byrnes, Stimson, and Forrestal. Should he regard this reply, he asked them, when officially received, as acceptance of the Potsdam Declaration? Should the Emperor be allowed to stay in office, or did this "condition" contravene unconditional surrender?

The President faced pressures to accept the Japanese "understanding." The U.S. Army wanted to use the Emperor's authority to control the occupation, and the Navy wanted to end the war before the Army could invade Japan. Some highly placed Americans, including Stimson and Grew, wished to keep the Emperor in place in any case. Political leaders were eager for an end before the Soviet army could stake out too large a claim in Manchuria. And everyone wanted to minimize American casualties.

But strong voices also spoke against acceptance. Not only many leaders but the vast majority of the American people wanted retribution and vengeance after the long, bloody, brutal war; and these voters had the power, if they wished, to make politicians who permitted the Emperor to stay pay a high political price at home.

Even before the official version of the Japanese petition was received, Stimson reminded Truman of the old adage that when you punish your dog, you do not stay sour on him all day after the punishment is over if you want "to keep his affection." It was, he said, the same with the Japanese if you wanted their cooperation in the long run. Win the war, the elderly Secretary of War advised the President, and then be generous.

Just before noon, Byrnes brought Truman the official communication from the Japanese government; it followed the substance of the radio broadcast. Byrnes also carried a draft reply to the Japanese message.

Truman discussed the Japanese offer with Byrnes while they

grabbed a bite of lunch at his desk. Again, he wanted to know: Did the Japanese proviso about the Emperor meet the American requirement for unconditional surrender? He called a cabinet meeting at 2 P.M. to review the Japanese message and the State Department's proposed reply.

To Stimson it made "good plain horse sense" to accept the Japanese offer. It was to America's advantage to retain the Emperor. Only the Emperor could insist on the surrender of the Japanese forces in Manchuria, China, and Southeast Asia; and the longer the war lasted, the larger part the Russians would play. Leahy also wanted the offer to be accepted, and promptly.

Byrnes strongly opposed this course. He held out for strict unconditional surrender. Why, he asked, accept less than we had demanded at Potsdam before we had the atomic bomb and before the Soviet Union was in the war? "I do not see why we should retreat from our demand for unconditional surrender," he said. "If any conditions are to be accepted, I want the United States and not Japan to state the conditions."

Navy Secretary Forrestal came up with a shrewd and simple solution: Accept the offer and declare that it accomplishes what the Potsdam Declaration demanded. Say that the Emperor and the Japanese government will rule subject to the orders of the Supreme Commander for the Allied Powers. This would imply recognition of the Emperor while tending to neutralize American public passions against the Emperor. Truman liked this. It would be close enough to "unconditional."

From Washington, Admiral King sent a message to Admiral Nimitz beginning "This is a peace warning . . ." It echoed memories of November 27, 1941, ten days before the attack on Pearl Harbor, when the U.S. Navy had sent out its first alert, starting: "This dispatch is to be considered a war warning."

In keeping with Forrestal's proposed strategy, the U.S. draft reply presumed that the Japanese had accepted the Potsdam Declaration. From the moment of surrender, the Emperor and the Japanese government would be subject to the Supreme Commander for the Allied Powers (SCAP). The Emperor and the government would be required to sign the surrender and to order Japan's armed forces to give up their arms. Allied prisoners of war and civilian internees would be transported to places of safety. The ultimate form of the Japanese government would be established in accordance with the Potsdam Declaration and by the freely expressed will of the Japanese people.

Allied armed forces would remain in Japan until the goals set forth in the Potsdam Declaration were achieved.

This draft was dispatched to London, Moscow, and Chungking. In London, Attlee and Bevin approved, but they thought it a mistake to require the Emperor to sign the surrender personally. They suggested the Emperor authorize and ensure the acceptance of the surrender by the government. Even though Chiang Kai-shek specifically wanted the Emperor to sign, the British change was accepted.

The Australians, who had done a lot of fighting against Japan, went along with the draft reluctantly. They predicted that if the Emperor stayed, the Japanese system would also remain and so would the Japanese people's militaristic ways.

In Moscow, Harriman and the British ambassador were with Molotov when Harriman received the American draft reply from Washington. Molotov had just informed them that he did not regard the Japanese message as unconditional. Harriman understood that the Soviet foreign minister was in no hurry to end the war while the Soviet army was advancing in Manchuria.

When the message was translated for Molotov, he informed Harriman that he would have to wait until morning for the Soviet reply. Harriman insisted he needed it that night; and at 2 A.M. August 11, Moscow time, it was handed to Harriman. The Russians accepted the draft but wanted representation on an Allied High Command to which the Japanese Emperor and government would be subordinated. This demand would inject the Soviet Union into the Supreme Command for the Allied Powers—a job Truman had already reserved for MacArthur.

In the dark of the night, Molotov and Harriman dueled over this proposal, which would give the Soviet Union a veto over the selection of the Supreme Commander. Because the Russians had briefly been at war against Japan, Molotov was insisting that the High Command should consist of an American and a Soviet general, Marshal Aleksandr Vasilevsky, the Soviet commander in the Far East. Harriman rejected this outright. He told Molotov heatedly that it was unthinkable that the Supreme Commander would be anyone but an American.

Harriman, of course, was simply articulating American policy—that Japan would be controlled by an American commander, acting on behalf of the Allies, whose wishes would be coordinated by a Far Eastern Advisory Commission. Moreover, as Harriman pointed out to Molotov, the United States had been fighting Japan for four years, and Russia had been in this war for two days.

Molotov was incensed; he made comparisons with the European war, where the Soviet Union had carried the tremendous burden since 1939 and the United States had not come in until after Pearl Harbor and had not invaded Europe until the middle of 1944. He demanded that Harriman forward his requests to Washington.

Harriman returned to his communications center and was dictating the message to Washington when Molotov's interpreter telephoned to say that the foreign minister had just consulted Stalin. There had been a misunderstanding. He had only wanted to be consulted on the governing of Japan. Harriman had no objection to that as long as the Russians were given no voice in the appointment of the Supreme Allied Commander.

Truman was unyielding on this point. MacArthur would have complete command of Japan. There would be no divided control or separate zones in Japan.

From Washington, a statement went out advising the Allies of General MacArthur's selection as the Supreme Commander in Japan. MacArthur was directed to have various Japanese forces surrender to Admiral Lord Louis Mountbatten, to the Soviet high commander in the Far East, and to Generalissimo Chiang Kai-shek.

At about the same time, a confidential message came in from Ambassador Edwin W. Pauley, who was in Moscow trying to negotiate agreement on reparations questions. He urged that U.S. forces occupy as much of the industrial areas of Korea and Manchuria as they could, as quickly as possible. He suspected that the Soviet Union would try to seize these resources. Harriman also urged landings in Korea and at Dairen if the Japanese surrendered before Soviet troops occupied those areas.

After all these consultations, Truman had Byrnes hand the United States' final reply to Max Grassli, the chargé d'affaires of Switzerland, to be transmitted through Berne to Tokyo. The United States accepted the Japanese offer; the Emperor and the Japanese government would be subject to the Supreme Commander for the Allied Powers. Clearly, the Japanese had won their most significant concession; they were assured that the Emperor would not be eliminated.

Even then, the U.S. reply did not break the political deadlock in Tokyo. As before, Foreign Minister Togo favored acceptance; the military continued to reject it. Prime Minister Suzuki vacillated. The Emperor stalled for time. The argument dragged on for three more days.

Meanwhile, the war did not stop. Truman kept the pressure on the Japanese. At the morning meeting on August 10, Stimson recommended halting the bombing of Japan, and Forrestal agreed. They felt there was no purpose in adding to Japanese hatred. Truman refused. But in the afternoon cabinet meeting, he shifted his position. He ordered that no more atomic bombs be dropped; but conventional bombing would continue, as the Joint Chiefs wanted, until Japan had actually surrendered.

At the same time, Brigadier General Groves accelerated production of the more sophisticated Fat Man bombs. Another would be ready by August 17 or 18. But based on Truman's decision, Marshall made certain Groves understood that no third atomic bomb would be dropped on Japan without the President's explicit permission.

As the Japanese leaders debated the U.S. reply, everyone in Washington grew impatient. Sunday, August 12, was a long day of waiting. Harry Truman had been President for precisely four months.

General Spaatz continued to advocate dropping a third atomic bomb on Tokyo; but instead of Spaatz's bomb, the Japanese capital was blanketed with a less lethal barrage of leaflets carrying the Japanese surrender proposal and the American reply. At Byrnes' request, General Arnold ordered the Strategic Air Force to drop millions of leaflets over all major Japanese cities informing the people of the peace negotiations—about which they knew nothing. It is dubious, however, that this information barrage was helpful to the Emperor's delicate effort to bring adamantly opposed leaders to accept the unbearable. Admiral Nimitz dispatched an order to the Pacific Fleet saying that neither the Japanese nor the Allies had stopped fighting and that vigilance against attack must be maintained.

On Monday, there was still no reply from Japan, and Truman re-escalated the war. He ordered the resumption of areawide incendiary bombing. U.S. Navy planes attacked Tokyo in one of the biggest carrier-based raids of the war. General Arnold staged a "finale" with 1,014 aircraft dropping twelve million pounds of high-explosive and incendiary bombs on Japanese cities. The bombs carried the message that the only way out was to surrender. The bombardment lasted without letup for fourteen hours until past 2 A.M. August 15, Tokyo time. By then Radio Tokyo was already broadcasting Japan's decision to surrender.

At 11 A.M. on August 14, Emperor Hirohito assembled his ministers in the imperial air raid shelter. He said he found the Allied reply acceptable; further resistance would reduce the nation to ashes. He requested that the prime minister accept the Allied reply. He was prepared to surrender and stop the bloodshed without further reassurances about the preservation of the throne. All fifteen members of the cabinet respected the Emperor's decision to agree to the Allied terms.

The Emperor also expressed a wish to broadcast to the nation— an unprecedented proposal. The Japanese people had never heard his voice. An Imperial Edict was prepared for him to broadcast personally to the nation, and the Emperor recorded it for broadcast the next day. Hirohito meant his broadcast to forestall any coup d'état and to refute in advance any future claim that surrender was not his wish.

The army generals issued an order to all field commanders:

> The Emperor has made his decision. The Army expects you to obey the decision and make no unauthorized moves that would put to shame the glorious traditions of the Imperial Army. . . . The Minister of War and the Chief of Staff dispatch this order with grief in their hearts, and they expect you to appreciate the emotions of the Emperor when he himself broadcasts the Imperial Rescript terminating the war at twelve noon tomorrow.

That afternoon, after the Emperor sought the obedience of the armed forces, the official Japanese news agency announced that an Imperial Proclamation would be made soon. Radio Tokyo informed the world.

Hours later, a thousand soldiers attacked the Imperial Palace to prevent the transmission of the Emperor's proclamation. They assassinated the commander of the Imperial Guards Division before they were repulsed. General Anami and other senior officers committed suicide.

On both sides, political leaders were trying to terminate the war, but without an actual invasion it was hard to stop. To the very end, American military commanders believed that an invasion would be required; and Japanese military leaders remained certain that an invasion would be so costly that it would lead to American concessions.

Thus, generals and admirals, who had won and lost the war, did not finally end it. And Japan's political leaders were paralyzed by the threat to destroy the Emperor's godlike status. Only Hirohito's intervention could halt the killing; his announcement that he was willing to risk his revered position and his future finally ended the war.

Of course, it is only logical to realize that if Emperor Hirohito had the power to stop the war after the atomic bombing of Hiroshima and Nagasaki, he had the power to stop it before those disasters. Daikichi Irokara, professor of modern Japanese history at Tokyo University of Economics, estimates that the war was no longer winnable after Japan's defeats at Saipan and Burma in 1944, and if the Emperor had acted then, 1.5 million Japanese lives would have been saved. Contrary to what Westerners have been taught to believe, Professor Irokara calls Hirohito "the person most responsible for the war" and says "the Emperor's responsibility is irrefutable."

At midday August 15, Tokyo time (which is fourteen hours ahead of Washington time), the Emperor's voice was heard over the radio for the first time ever, reading the proclamation he had recorded the day before. Because of "a new and most cruel bomb," he accepted the Potsdam Declaration and asked "our loyal subjects" to carry out his will.

It was 1:49 A.M. on Tuesday, August 14, Washington time, when the Japanese news agencies flashed a bulletin to expect an imperial message. Later that morning, a coded telegram from Tokyo arrived in Berne and raised hopes in Washington; but it turned out not to be the answer to the Allies' message. The wait continued.

Crowds started gathering in American cities, anticipating the official announcement of the end of the long war. At 3 P.M. the true message was received in Berne, and at 4:05 Secretary Byrnes impatiently telephoned the U.S. minister in Berne and had him read it. At 6 P.M. the Swiss chargé d'affaires brought Byrnes the formal Japanese notes.

Truman gathered the cabinet and invited former Secretary of State Cordell Hull, now seriously ill, and Mrs. Truman to his office. At 7 P.M. Truman, fresh from a swim, called in the reporters, who swarmed around his desk. Standing, he announced to all the world the unconditional surrender of Japan.

He read his statement rapidly. The Emperor had issued an Imperial Rescript accepting the Potsdam Declaration and authorizing and ensuring the signature of representatives of his government and the Imperial General Headquarters on the terms necessary to carry out the Potsdam Declaration. He was also ordering Japanese forces everywhere to cease active operations and to surrender their arms.

Truman said, "I deem this reply a full acceptance of the Potsdam declaration which specifies the unconditional surrender of Japan. In the reply there is no qualification."

The press conference was over in less than two minutes. Shouting congratulations, the correspondents rushed out to flash the word.

The war was over.

Thousands jammed Lafayette Park in front of the White House in the lingering daylight of Washington's summer time. Bells were rung, car horns blared. Some of the crowd formed a conga line. They chanted for the President: "We want Harry!" He and Bess came out onto the north lawn of the White House. People surged across Pennsylvania Avenue, pressing the police and MPs against the White House's iron fence. Truman walked along the fence, throwing the crowd the V-for-victory sign in Churchill's manner, and a great cheer went up. He waved to the crowd until his arm ached. Then he went back inside.

The chanting continued, and the crowd kept growing. Truman stepped onto the north portico and spoke over a microphone. "This is a great day—the day we have been waiting for." The crowd roared. He knew that Americans in cities and towns across the country were celebrating the victory, and he was deeply moved.

The President ordered all American field commanders to cease fighting. He telephoned Mrs. Roosevelt and told her he wished it had been her husband and not he who had announced the news to the nation. He cut the monthly draft from eighty thousand to fifty thousand and gave all federal employees a two-day holiday.

General MacArthur was notified that his assignment as Supreme Commander for the Allied Powers was effective immediately. He was ordered to obtain an imperial proclamation authorizing the Emperor's representatives to sign the Instrument of Surrender. He was to receive the signed instrument for the four governments concerned and in the interests of the other nations at war with Japan. Each of the four powers was to designate a representative to be present at the surrender. The U.S. representative would be Fleet Admiral Chester W. Nimitz. And MacArthur was instructed that from the moment of surrender the Emperor and Japanese government were to rule subject to his orders.

On Okinawa and in the Philippines, thousands of young American soldiers, sailors, and Marines celebrated the victory and the news that Japan would not have to be invaded and they would live. The night sky above Manila lit up with the firing of tracers and flares.

Chapter 20

The Shaping of Postwar Asia

Two atomic bombs had finally closed the gap between what Harry Truman and Hirohito were willing to settle for. And the prospect of dropping more atomic bombs made further Japanese resistance insane.

The atomic bombs had also eliminated the need for Americans to die invading Japan. As Churchill wrote later, on the Japanese home islands

> stood an army of more than a million men, well trained, well equipped, and fanatically determined to fight to the last. What remained of the Japanese Navy and Air Force was just as resolute. These two great operations [the invasions of Kyushu and Honshu] would have entailed bitter fighting and great loss of life, but they were never required. We may well be thankful.

Ever after, some historians and strategists have speculated that the Japanese surrender could have been won without using the atomic bomb. Truman had made his decision based on two convictions: that the American people wanted a definitive victory and that the Japanese required a clear-cut, unmistakable reason to quit. Stimson wrote in his memoirs, "It was not the American responsibility to throw in the sponge for the Japanese; that was one thing they must do for themselves. . . . As it turned out, the use of the bomb, in accelerating the surrender, saved many more lives than it cost."

The invasion had become an occupation. The U.S. Sixth and Eighth armies were readied to occupy Honshu, and other army elements were earmarked for Kyushu, the southern half of Korea, and Hokkaido. Special units were assigned to occupy the Yokosuka naval base on Tokyo Bay and other military installations and to rescue Allied prisoners of war.

Plans for the surrender had already been worked out. General Order No. 1 designated to whom the Japanese commanders in the field would surrender. Despite its limited intent, this order would have enormous consequences on the shape of postwar Asia.

The plans were complicated. The Japanese forces in Manchuria, in Korea north of the 38th Parallel, and on Karafuto would surrender to the Soviet commander. In Southeast Asia, from the 16th Parallel south, and from Burma to the Solomons, they would surrender to either Vice Admiral Lord Louis Mountbatten, Supreme Allied Commander, Southeast Asia, or the Australian commander. In Japan, in the Philippines, and in Korea south of the 38th Parallel, MacArthur would receive the surrender. In China, Formosa, and Indochina north of the 16th Parallel, the Japanese were to surrender to Chiang Kai-shek. Elsewhere in the Pacific area, they would surrender to Admiral Nimitz.

These complexities reflected the difficulties in the practical aspects of the Japanese surrender. Trouble started immediately.

On August 16, Stalin reacted critically to General Order No. 1. He demanded assurance that the Liaotung Peninsula was accepted as part of Manchuria. He wanted Soviet commanders to receive the surrender of the Japanese in the Kurile Islands, which were, he pointed out, in the possession of the Soviet Union. And he wanted the northern part of the island of Hokkaido, part of the Japanese homeland, to surrender to Soviet troops.

These demands set off two weeks of stiff negotiations that reminded Truman of the arguments over Poland and Yugoslavia. He accepted the inclusion of the Kuriles in the Soviet surrender area on condition that the United States have air base rights on one of the Kurile Islands for both military and commercial use.

With regard to Hokkaido, however, Truman insisted that forces on all the islands of Japan itself surrender to MacArthur. On August 22, Stalin replied slyly that the American reaction about Hokkaido was unexpected and the request for a Kurile air base was incomprehensible.

Through Ambassador Harriman, Truman explained that an air base was needed in the Kuriles for military purposes during the occupation of Japan and for commercial purposes until a peace settlement determined the final status of those islands. Stalin seemed to accept the idea of military landing rights during the occupation. But in exchange for commercial landing rights at a Soviet air base in the Kuriles, he asked for the right to land Soviet commercial planes at an American base on one of the Aleutian Islands. His purpose, he said, was to connect Siberia more closely with the American Northwest. Stalin also bid again for a role in the occupation of Japan; Truman rejected that flatly.

There was more. General Andrei Antonov, the Soviet military leader, sent MacArthur requests for changes in the Instrument of Surrender. These would give the separate Allied High Commands (including the Russian) equal power with the Supreme Commander regarding all military and civilian property and control over the surrendered forces. They would also make the authority of the Emperor and the Japanese government subject not only to the Supreme Commander but also to such organizations as the Allies might create.

As Truman saw these proposals, they would approve in advance anything the Russians might do in Manchuria and open the door for an Allied Control Council for Japan. But when MacArthur referred General Antonov to Washington, he backed down, saying that if these suggestions made any difficulties, the General Staff would not insist on them. Stalin had again been testing the waters.

On the Korean peninsula, the United States had sought to select a dividing line to separate the areas in which the Russians and Americans would receive the Japanese surrender. Secretary Byrnes urged that the United States accept the surrender as far north as possible. U.S. Army leaders did not want to advance too far in case the Russians chose to challenge the point.

During an August night meeting of the State-War-Navy Coordinating Committee (SWNCC) in Washington, John McCloy asked Colonel Dean Rusk of the Operations Division of the War Department General Staff and Colonel Charles H. Bonesteel III, both former Rhodes Scholars, to draft a proposal within American logistical capabilities. After hours of work, Rusk, who had served as deputy chief of staff in the China-Burma-India theater under Stilwell, and Bonesteel recommended that the line be drawn at the 38th Parallel.

They did not know the history of the line they had chosen. In 1902 Russia had suggested a division there. Korea had then been a political football kicked around by China and Russia; but that had changed when Japan annexed Korea in 1910 and treated it as a colony of inferior people.

The determining reason for the Rusk-Bonesteel solution was that it would keep Korea's capital, Seoul, in the American zone. It would also give the United States control of the ports of Inchon and Pusan for the repatriation of Japanese troops. The SWNCC accepted the recommendation—as later did the Soviet Union. Chiang Kai-shek, busy with troubles at home, made no objection to the 38th Parallel, even though China had controlled all of Korea before the Sino-Japanese war of 1894 and had claimed it ever since.

This line was intended only to define the areas in which the Japanese would surrender. But both the Soviet Union and the United States pressed their national interests. The division of Korea gave the Soviet Union a buffer it could make sure would be friendly and allowed the U.S. State Department to nurture its enterprises in southern Korea. Soviet forces moved into northern Korea, and the United States accepted the Japanese surrender in the south. This division of the peninsula would lead directly to the Korean War in 1950 and would become a long-term obstacle to peace in the area.

China, in this same period, jumped from the horror of the war that Japan had waged on its soil ever since the summer of 1937 straight into a Nationalist-Communist civil war. On V-J Day, the Nationalists had three million men under arms; the Communists, a million. They immediately confronted each other.

The Chinese Communists moved swiftly to take advantage of the Japanese collapse. General Chu Teh, commander of their armed forces, ordered his troops to seize any areas occupied by the Japanese. Truman condemned this as bald defiance of Chiang Kai-shek and a violation of the Potsdam Declaration.

Emperor Hirohito ordered the million Japanese troops in China to surrender to Chiang. This presented the Nationalists with a grave problem: the Communists' stronghold was in northern China, and thus they were in a better position to receive the Japanese surrender. The Communists empowered their 170,000 regular troops in the north to accept Japan's surrender there. Chiang demanded that the Communists remain at their posts. But no one was listening.

General Chu Teh petitioned Washington through Major General Wedemeyer that the Communists, not Chiang, had carried the war against the Japanese, and therefore, they should both accept local surrenders and represent China at the surrender ceremonies. Wedemeyer urged MacArthur and Nimitz to help the Nationalist government so that the Communists could not seize Japanese arms and Japanese-held territory.

Meanwhile, the Russians, who were to receive the Japanese surrender in Manchuria, stretched their interpretation of what was Manchuria to include the northern Chinese province of Jehol. Chiang protested, but the United States could only point out that Soviet troops were already in Jehol and were entitled to accept the surrender in their areas of operations.

The Americans lifted more than 400,000 of Chiang's troops to northern China by air and sea to accept the surrender of Japanese troops. And the U.S. 1st and 6th Marine Divisions landed 53,000 men in northern China to disarm and ensure the surrender of the Japanese, occupy ports and cities, and guard mines and railroads. They were also assigned to prevent huge caches of Japanese arms from falling into Communist hands. They engaged the Communists in firefights, and Marines were killed and wounded. Before the year's end, the Marines were ordered to supply the Nationalists with arms, ammunition, and replacement parts. The civil war escalated.

On November 27, Truman asked Ambassador Hurley to go back to China and try to work out some compromise between the Nationalists and Communists. Hurley accepted the President's assignment and then promptly went over to the National Press Club and publicly criticized Truman's policy. Tony Vaccaro of the Associated Press called Truman and told him Hurley had announced that he would not go to China. That finished Hurley.

Truman telephoned General of the Army Marshall, who had been retired less than a week, and told him he wanted him to go to China. As the story goes, Marshall said simply, "Yes, Mr. President." And hung up.

The Americans continued to hope for a broad political compromise in China and even a coalition government. It proved to be a fantasy. Within months China erupted into full-fledged civil war.

Even the presence of the U.S. Marines and their "abandoning" 65,000 tons of ammunition to the Nationalists did not help; Chiang's forces kept falling apart. Neither Harry Truman nor anyone else could foresee that the convulsions in Asia would lead the United States, only five years later, into war with the new People's Republic of China.

One incident—the dispute over who would receive the Japanese surrender of the former British colony of Hong Kong—illustrated how the problems with which President Truman had to deal in Asia were complicated by resurgent colonialism.

Chiang insisted the Japanese at Hong Kong should surrender to him. The British countered that the Chinese could send a representative but the British would take the Japanese surrender. Even Prime Minister Attlee interceded, persuading Truman to instruct MacArthur to order the Japanese to surrender to the British naval force already on its way. Secretary Byrnes tried to assure T. V. Soong that this did not represent the American attitude toward the future status of Hong Kong.

Chiang Kai-shek complained personally to Truman that if the British took the surrender, it would be a unilateral alteration of the Potsdam Declaration. Under no circumstances, Chiang asserted, should British troops land on the mainland of China. Truman replied that the surrender was strictly a military matter and did not raise questions of sovereignty. He asked for Chiang's cooperation.

Chiang came up with a face-saving compromise: He would empower a British commander to receive the surrender of Hong Kong as his delegate. Truman sent him a message of appreciation, but it proved premature. The British, not too surprisingly, refused to accept the surrender as the generalissimo's subordinate. Chiang denounced the British attitude as "imperialistic, domineering and unbecoming a member of the United Nations."

In the end, British Rear Admiral C.H.J. Harcourt received the Japanese surrender. No mention was made of the generalissimo. But Chiang's headquarters continued to list Hong Kong as one of the surrenders to be effected by him.

Indochina's future had supposedly been decided at Potsdam, where it had been agreed that British forces would accept the Japanese surrender south of the 16th Parallel and the Chinese Nationalists, north of the parallel. The U.S. Department of State fully understood that the British would bring back the French.

When Japan surrendered, nationalist-communist Vietminh forces led by Ho Chi Minh seized Hanoi without resistance and proclaimed the independence of Vietnam in the north. Ho quoted the American Declaration of Independence: "All men are created equal." But his hopes of gaining Americans' support were fruitless; they were concentrating on rebuilding Europe—including France.

Chiang Kai-shek sent more than 180,000 Chinese soldiers into the north of Vietnam, recognized de facto Ho Chi Minh's government in Hanoi, and proceeded to loot the country. In time, the Vietminh gladly made concessions and induced the Chinese to leave. With no support in sight from either the United States or the Soviet Union, Ho Chi Minh prepared to face the returning French alone.

At the same time, the Vietminh in Saigon in the south staged massive public demonstrations that degenerated into riots; a number of Vietnamese and five Europeans were killed.

The commander of the British occupation forces, Major General Douglas D. Gracey, the tough, respected leader of the veteran 20th Indian Division, flew into Saigon on September 13. Lord Mountbatten had ordered him to disarm the Japanese and recover prisoners of war south of the 16th Parallel but to stay out of the country's internal politics.

Shocked by the chaos, fearing an armed uprising, and having only 1,800 soldiers at hand, Gracey unfortunately proceeded to arm 1,400 French residents, who with other rearmed French troops fought the Vietnamese. Aided by the British, the French gained control of the Saigon government; Gracey even used British-Indian and Japanese troops to help keep Saigon out of Vietminh hands. He finally confined the French to barracks, but incidents continued and the Vietminh underground abducted and assassinated Europeans.

Gracey's use of Japanese soldiers roused General MacArthur's anger: "If there is anything that makes my blood boil it is to see our Allies in Indochina and Java deploying Japanese troops to reconquer the little people we promised to liberate." And Indian leader Jawaharlal Nehru protested the use of Gracey's Indian troops to fight "our friends who are fighting the same battle as we."

General Philippe Leclerc, the liberator of Paris, arrived to command the French military forces in Indochina. On October 5, at Saigon's Tan Son Nhut Airport, he announced: "We have come to reclaim our inheritance." Initially, Leclerc was simply to take over from the British. But his mission became to reconquer Indochina for France— with British cooperation. Before the end of 1945, the French were back in South Vietnam with 50,000 troops. Gracey concentrated on securing Saigon, while Leclerc pacified the countryside.

Leclerc restored French sovereignty to Cambodia and Laos. In Vietnam, an uneasy compromise was worked out between Paris and Ho: in the north, the Vietminh government would be recognized, within the French Union; in the south, where most French capital was invested, the French would be in charge. It did not work. By mid-1946 the French and Vietminh were at war. It was a war too costly to make any economic sense for France; it really was driven by the French fear of further loss of national pride.

Truman was not directly involved in the machinations that brought the French back to power in Indochina and ignited the long war between them and the Vietnamese. But by 1949, as a consequence of the Cold War and the Communist triumph in China, the U.S. government was backing the French puppet regime of Emperor Bao Dai in Vietnam against Ho Chi Minh. At the outbreak of the Korean War, Truman was persuaded to send arms to the French in Indochina as an additional means of containing the People's Republic of China. The struggle in Indochina changed in his eyes from a question of self-determination to an integral part of the all-absorbing Cold War. Said one commentator, "Anticommunism preempted anticolonialism or pronationalism in importance." Ho Chi Minh asked Peking and Moscow for diplomatic recognition, and the Cold War became firmly established in Indochina.

By 1954 the United States was contributing $1 billion to the French colonial cause in Indochina, thus underwriting 80 percent of the French war against the Vietnamese. The myth that the French ever had a chance to regain their colony finally died that May 7, when they surrendered at Dien Bien Phu.

The most enormous by-product of World War II in East Asia was that Mao Tse-tung and the Communists conquered all of mainland China and pushed the Nationalists to the offshore island of Taiwan (Formosa). When Chiang fled with his government, army, and people, the British promptly recognized Mao. The United States continued to recognize the Nationalists on Taiwan; but Truman, Acheson, and Marshall accepted reality enough to oppose U.S. intervention even if the Communists pursued the Nationalists onto Taiwan. Churchill had been right: Truman's hope of achieving democracy in China proved to be an illusion.

The war's outcome also meant that the United States occupied and ruled Japan for years until the Japanese regained their strength and became a major world economic force. A divided Korea was liberated from Japan but then engaged in a civil war that drew the United States into battle against the People's Republic of China. And in time the United States fought a full-scale war in Indochina. The Asia born out of World War II repeatedly involved the United States.

Local peoples and governments squeezed colonialism out of Asia from New Delhi to Seoul and Hanoi, often with violence and great pain. British rule came to an end in India, Pakistan, and Palestine; the United States gave up the Philippines. The Dutch left Indonesia, while the French fought to the end before getting out of Indochina and North Africa. Hong Kong would eventually be turned over to the Chinese.

The next generations of Americans would pay a high price to learn that the western frontier of the United States had moved from the coast of California across the Pacific to the shores of the People's Republic of China. The Americans had become the masters of the Pacific, but they could not easily project their vast power ashore on the continent of Asia.

Chapter 21

"A Victory of More than Arms Alone"
Sunday, September 2, 1945

As soon as the first word of the Japanese surrender was received, Admiral Leahy and General Marshall asked the President where he wanted the formal surrender to take place. Truman had already thought about it and had decided. The surrender should take place in Tokyo Bay aboard USS *Missouri*. It should be in view of the Japanese homeland but offshore to be certain no Japanese would attempt some last-minute act of fanaticism. Truman had obvious ties to USS *Missouri*, one of the nation's newest and most powerful battleships. She was named after his home state; his daughter, Margaret, had christened her at the Brooklyn Navy Yard; and he had spoken at the launching.

Because of the American people's interest in the surrender, Truman decreed that it would be an open news event with full and competitive coverage. And because of the Allies' share in the war or their insistence on participation, he notified MacArthur that representatives of Australia, Canada, France, New Zealand, and the Netherlands would be invited to be present at the ceremonies.

The Japanese were ordered to send emissaries to MacArthur in Manila to arrange for the ceremonies. On August 19, a sixteen-man delegation of Japanese officials from Tokyo headed by Lieutenant General Toroshiro Kawabe, vice chief of the Imperial General Staff, arrived at MacArthur's headquarters after changing planes on Ie Shima on MacArthur's instructions. Despite their reluctance, they were required to use the password "Bataan."

The Japanese brought with them information on the location of prison camps, airfields, and military and naval installations. The meetings went on until the late morning of August 21. The Japanese were given the Instrument of Surrender and other documents. They were upset to see the Emperor referred to as *watakushi* when the proper term of respect was *chin*. The American representatives thought the point trivial until MacArthur was consulted and ordered the change. The Emperor's dignity should be preserved, he said, so he could help maintain orderly governance in Japan.

Meanwhile, the Russians continued fighting in north China and advanced through northern Korea toward the 38th Parallel. The Japanese complained and asked MacArthur to intervene. And on August 21 the Japanese accepted the good offices of the International Red Cross to assist Allied prisoners of war still in Japan and Manchuria.

MacArthur ordered that no formal surrenders be accepted until the main ceremony was held in Tokyo Bay. Lord Mountbatten; General Thomas Blamey, commander of the Australian land forces; and the Chinese commanders all opposed this rule, fearing it would allow local seizures of power.

On August 29 MacArthur received a document of guidance on post-surrender policy that had been prepared by a coordinating committee of the State, War, and Navy departments. (It was not approved by Truman until September 6.) It laid the ground for political, economic, and social reforms in Japan and gave MacArthur wide powers.

On August 27 the U.S. Third Fleet began moving into Sagami Bay, southwest of Yokohama, and two days later entered Tokyo Bay. The slate gray USS *Missouri* anchored off the huge Yokosuka Naval Base. The first advance party of engineers and communications experts flew into Atsugi Airdrome, fourteen miles southwest of Tokyo, at 9 A.M. on August 28. (Greeting them was a large sign, WELCOME TO THE U.S. ARMY FROM THIRD FLEET, the prank of a young pilot from USS *Yorktown* who had dashed in the previous day without authorization and ordered Japanese ground crews to paint and put up the sign.) The Japanese greeted the American paratroopers with pitchers of fresh orange juice and a lavish lunch accompanied by wine. That afternoon, units of the 11th Airborne Division landed at the airfield. And all the next day, transport planes touched down at the rate of one every three minutes, bringing in paratroopers. The reborn 4th Marines, the regiment that had served at Shanghai and been forced to surrender on Corregidor on May 6, 1942, landed at the Yokosuka Naval Base and airfield on the west side of the mouth of Tokyo Bay.

MacArthur flew into Atsugi at two in the afternoon of August 30 in his C-54 named *Bataan*. He insisted that neither he nor the officers accompanying him wear sidearms. He wanted to make a show of total fearlessness, which he thought would demonstrate to the Japanese that they had been defeated. When he appeared at the plane's door in his open-necked shirt and smoking his signature corncob pipe, he took two steps down and a couple of puffs on his pipe, pausing dramatically for the cameras. He was saluted by the 11th Airborne's band. Then he was driven in an ancient American Lincoln twenty miles to the battered city of Yokohama. The highway was lined on both sides by Japanese infantrymen, bayonets fixed, their backs to the motorcade.

That afternoon, Admirals Nimitz and Halsey also came ashore. Everyone present dreaded some violent act by a Japanese fanatic. A guard of five hundred veterans of the 11th Airborne formed a ring to guard MacArthur in the New Grand Hotel. The Japanese, on the other hand, feared that the American troops might act as bestially as Japanese soldiers had in Chinese cities, and were impressed by the Americans' discipline.

Fortunately, the Japanese gave every sign of cooperating. But Stalin warned Harriman that the Japanese were treacherous, and to prevent any incidents he advised taking hostages.

The senior POWs—Lieutenant General Jonathan M. Wainwright, who had commanded U.S. forces in the Philippines; Lieutenant General Arthur E. Percival, who had commanded at Singapore; and the others—were finally located in a prisoner-of-war camp near Mukden, Manchuria, and arrangements were made to bring them to the surrender ceremony. They arrived in Chungking on August 28 and in Yokohama on the thirty-first. MacArthur was called out from dinner to meet in the lobby of the New Grand Hotel with Wainwright, who was gaunt, aged, and leaning on a cane. Wainwright was so moved he could not speak; for the past three years he had believed he was in disgrace for surrendering Corregidor. MacArthur embraced him and reassured him, and the haggard veteran broke into tears.

The first 739 rescued POWs were taken aboard the hospital ship *Benevolence*. But it would require weeks before the hundred thousand surviving prisoners could be collected from thirty-three camps throughout East Asia. More than thirty thousand Anglo-American POWs had died or been killed in captivity.

In time, the major Japanese war criminals would be tried in Tokyo by the International Military Tribunal for the Far East, the parallel of the tribunal meeting in Nuremberg to try the German war criminals. Truman appointed Joseph B. Keenan, a former assistant to the attorney general, as chief prosecutor in Tokyo. After two and a half years, the Tribunal for the Far East judged guilty twenty-five Japanese war criminals, including Hideki Tojo, prime minister and war minister at the time of the attack on Pearl Harbor. Seven of them were executed.

Other Japanese, including two leading generals who had fought the Americans, Masaharu Homma and Tomoyuki Yamashita, were found guilty by "kangaroo courts," separate from the International Military Tribunal, and executed with MacArthur's approval. President Truman refused to intervene. Throughout Asia, Allied Military Commissions held some 2,200 trials with 5,700 defendants; they ordered the execution of 920 Japanese and sentenced another 3,000 to prison.

The Japanese government sent through the Swiss its version of how events should be planned. It asked that the entry of troops or fleets into Japan proper be announced in advance to avoid misunderstandings, that the number of places occupied be kept to a minimum, and that Tokyo itself not be occupied. The government also asked that the three million Japanese under arms overseas be allowed to disarm themselves, that they not be used for compulsory labor, and that they be shipped home promptly. Secretary Byrnes' reply was cold—all arrangements were to be made with the Supreme Commander. And Truman sent MacArthur a message from the Joint Chiefs. It stated: "Our relations with Japan do not rest on a contractual basis, but on an unconditional surrender."

At dawn on Sunday morning, September 2, after a rainy night, an awesome array of 258 Allied warships lay off Tokyo. *Missouri* was anchored six miles from Yokohama and four and a half miles from the spot where Commodore Matthew Calbraith Perry had anchored his four American warships in 1853 and opened the island nation to trade with the United States and opened Japanese minds to Western thought and technology.

Missouri raised the flag that had flown over the Capitol on December 7, 1941. It had already been flown in Casablanca, Rome, and Berlin. And on the deck where the surrender ceremonies would take place was hung the flag with thirty-one stars that Commodore Perry had carried into Tokyo Bay.

At 8:05 A.M. Fleet Admiral Nimitz arrived by destroyer at *Missouri*'s starboard side, and forty minutes later General of the Army MacArthur came up the gangway. At nine an American destroyer brought the eleven-man Japanese delegation to *Missouri*. Led by the new foreign minister, Mamoru Shigemitsu, who had lost his left leg to an assassin's bomb years before, they climbed the gangway in silence. The diplomats wore cutaways and tall silk hats. The military officers were led by General Yoshijiro Umezu, chief of the Imperial General Staff, who had opposed capitulation and was furious because he had been ordered to attend the surrender.

The generals and admirals of the nine Allied nations were assembled in a "U" behind a green-felt-covered old mess table. Stands had been built for correspondents and cameramen, and the gun turrets and decks were crowded with sailors in white.

The Japanese were shown where to stand in ranks on the starboard side of the veranda deck in front of the green-covered table. After the chaplain's invocation and the recorded playing of "The Star-Spangled Banner," MacArthur came out of the admiral's cabin between Nimitz and Halsey. MacArthur wore no medals. He walked to the microphone and said he hoped "a better world shall emerge out of the blood and carnage of the past—a world dedicated to the dignity of man and the fulfillment of his most cherished wish for freedom, tolerance and justice."

He summoned the Japanese representatives to sign the Instrument of Surrender. There were two copies, one bound in leather for the Allies, the other in canvas for the Japanese.

After the Japanese signed, MacArthur sat down and signed, using five fountain pens. He was followed by Nimitz and the other Allied representatives.

The Instrument of Surrender said at its heart: "We hereby proclaim the unconditional surrender to the Allied Powers of the Japanese Imperial General Headquarters and of all Japanese armed forces under Japanese control wherever situated."

At 9:25 MacArthur announced, "These proceedings are now closed."

As the brief, unsmiling ceremonies were over, the sun came out and an armada of aircraft swept over the warships—400 B-29s and 1,500 carrier planes. The Japanese bowed stiffly and climbed down the gangway.

MacArthur walked back to the microphone and broadcast to the world. He said, "Today the guns are silent. A great tragedy has ended. A great victory has been won. . . . The entire world is quietly at peace. The holy mission has been completed."

* * *

In Washington, it was a quiet, sunny Saturday, the beginning of the first peaceful Labor Day weekend in four years. Offices were empty; traffic was already snarled. Harry Truman sat with members of the cabinet in the broadcast room of the White House and listened to the description of the proceedings aboard *Missouri*.

Truman had decided that immediately after the Instrument of Surrender was signed, the radio networks would switch to the White House for an address by the President to the nation. Harry Truman knew in his bones, as a historian of the war has written: "Peace-making, like war-making, begins at home." At 10 P.M. September 1, Washington time, the President spoke to the American people.

Calling the Japanese surrender "unconditional" and declaring that Sunday, September 2, would be V-J Day, which he named "a day of retribution," he said, "We shall not forget Pearl Harbor. The Japanese militarists will not forget the USS *Missouri.* . . . This is a victory of more than arms alone. This is a victory of liberty over tyranny."

That evening, the flags of all the Allies were lowered in unison aboard *Duke of York* as the massed bands of the British ships in Tokyo Bay played the sunset hymn:

> The day thou gavest, Lord, is ended,
>   The darkness falls at thy behest;
> To thee our morning hymns ascended,
>   Thy praise shall sanctify our rest.
>
> So be it, Lord; thy throne shall never,
>   Like earth's proud empires, pass away:
> Thy kingdom stands, and grows for ever,
>   Till all thy creatures own thy sway.

Chapter 22

"We Stand on the Threshold"

Thus, on the deck of USS *Missouri* in Tokyo Bay, humankind's most massive and dreadful war came to an end. In this climactic "moment" between April 12 and September 2, 1945, the curtain came down on the enormous upheaval that had tormented the world since 1914. Then a battered humanity rose, phoenixlike, at center stage and walked forward into a new era.

"We won two great victories," said Harry Truman a month after V-J Day, while looping the Congressional Medal of Honor around the necks of eleven Marines and three Navy men. "We're facing another fight, and we must win the victory in that. That is a fight for a peaceful world, a fight so we won't have to do this again, so we won't have to maim the flower of our young men, and bury them."

What we call World War II, the second half of the twentieth century's worldwide military trauma, had lasted 2,174 days and killed an estimated forty-six million people between September 1, 1939, and August 14, 1945. (And counting from September 19, 1931, when the Japanese invaded Manchuria and tried to dominate China, the toll included millions more, perhaps reaching sixty million deaths.)

The cost was not evenly divided. The Soviet Union suffered twenty million military and civilian deaths and China probably fifteen million. Nazi Germany, which was responsible for so much of the gore, lost 4.5 million dead, and Japan about two million. The United States, Britain, and the countries of the British Empire together suffered about a million deaths. Around the globe, millions of civilians, men, women, and children, died unrecorded and unremembered. The numbers were numbing.

On the night after the Japanese signed their surrender, President Truman said, "The evil done by the Japanese war lords can never be repaired or forgotten. But their power to destroy and kill has been taken from them."

World War II taught once again that man's worst enemy is man.

This war was in large part a battle of pluralism against absolutism. It has been rightly said that perhaps the most important human achievement of the twentieth century was the squashing of Nazi Germany.

The Allies who destroyed the fascistic Axis included, ironically, the tyrannical monolith of the Soviet Union, as well as the Western Allies, who tried so imperfectly to be democratic. The hot war contained the embryo of the Cold War, during which the vivid contrasts among the victors would be played out. The immediate postwar challenge was whether the democracies could coexist with Communist authoritarianism. But to believe that communism with a small "c" would disappear was as foolish as to believe that nazism with a small "n" had been exterminated in the bunkers of Berlin. The challenge went on.

Virulent, aggressive nationalisms and ideologies, willing to use force and destroy human life to achieve their self-centered goals, had finally been conquered by the world's assembled legions, mainly young men mobilized to combat in their country's name. To restore freedom and peace had required the sacrifice of millions of lives. None of them would "come back from the dead."

Václav Havel, the playwright and political activist who later became president of the Czech Republic, was optimistic: "I believe we are entering an era of an end of ideologies. It is becoming clear that life cannot be crammed into these dogmas. If anyone tries to do it, it results in a violation of life and an expansion of dangers to humankind."

Although the men who won the war could guarantee neither peace nor freedom, they reshaped the world. Where were the new centers of power? At first the United States and the Soviet Union were supreme in the postwar world. In time Japan would rise literally from the ashes, while the Soviet Union slowly succumbed to its own inflexible ideology and its perceived need to prepare for war above all else. Then, with the disintegration of the Soviet Union, the freeing of Eastern Europe, and the slow lifting of the boot of the major powers, local loyalties and rivalries were freed to run rampant. All over the globe, ethnic, national, religious, and tribal interests erupted—sometimes seeking autonomy, sometimes subjecting others. These centrifugal forces had always been there, whirling people apart, except when suppressed by a Napoleon, a Hitler, or a Stalin.

But at the war's end, President Truman was able to look ahead and say, "We face the future and all its dangers with great confidence and great hope. America can build for itself a future of employment and security. Together with the United Nations, it can build a world of peace founded on justice, fair dealing, and tolerance."

At home, Truman had to lead the nation through a changeover from war to peace that was often agonizing. In the euphoric, impetuous atmosphere created by the end of the war, the United States and the other Western nations began disarming and demobilizing. While most of the nearly twelve million Americans in uniform impatiently demanded to be released to take up their civilian lives again, demobilization plans were not ready for the sudden end to the Pacific war. The veterans needed housing and jobs. The country had to deal with the largest housing shortage in its history. Labor demanded catch-up wage increases. Strikes hit many industries.

General MacArthur did not help when, in mid-September, he promised that he would send home occupation troops in Japan. Truman, angry and ever competitive, reacted to MacArthur's unauthorized pledge by upping the ante and promising that more than two million soldiers would be home by Christmas. The stampede to the exits by young men in uniform was on.

The end of the war left the United States with enormous dislocations. If war production were not reconverted to peacetime swiftly and skillfully, many feared, millions would be unemployed and the Depression would return. On August 12, 1945, a *New York Times* headline read: 5,000,000 EXPECTED TO LOSE ARMS JOBS. In the first ten days of peace, 1.8 million men and women did lose their jobs. Truman replaced a model gun on his desk with a model plow.

Prices rose rapidly and indicators of inflation appeared, and government leaders debated the perpetual modern industrial question: Does the greater danger came from unemployment or from inflation? While many demanded decontrol to restore a peacetime economy, Chester Bowles, the administrator of the Office of Price Administration, warned against relaxing controls too quickly. Should Truman continue the New Deal policies or shift to a more conservative position with a smaller government role in the economy?

Truman asked the unions, which had gained several million members during the war, to hold off on wage raises and strikes. Even before the Japanese surrendered, he was unsuccessful. Just as he had dealt severely with the United Mine Workers strike before V-E Day, in July he ordered the Navy to take over five plants of the Goodyear Tire & Rubber Company in Akron, Ohio, to prevent production from being halted by 16,500 striking Congress of Industrial Organizations (CIO) workers. The unions at the Ford Motor Company and the Westinghouse Electric Corporation also struck. Philip Murray, president of the CIO, who had felt very close to Roosevelt, accused Truman of not consulting with him on reconversion policy.

Truman tried to steer a middle course: some economic controls would be ended promptly; others would be retained. The work week was dropped from the wartime forty-eight hours to forty. On August 18 Truman issued an executive order authorizing government agencies to move toward the removal of price, wage, production, and other controls. Two days later, the War Production Board eliminated restrictions on the production of household appliances in the hope of generating jobs. Reconversion policy roused intense arguments in Washington. The rumble of quarreling rose in the land.

On September 6 Truman sent Congress a long message proposing a host of postwar adjustments: increased unemployment compensation, a raise in the minimum wage, a permanent Fair Employment Practices Committee, tax reform, crop insurance for farmers, a year's extension of the War Powers and Stabilization Act over business, federal aid for housing, and a national insurance program funded by payroll deductions.

As wartime jobs were eliminated, discrimination hit black Americans especially hard. Shipbuilding, for example, had employed nearly 200,000 blacks during the height of the war; by 1946 only 10,000 remained.

Truman always spoke up forcefully against lynching, inequality in education and employment, the poll tax, and a caste system based on race or color. He wanted federal law to eliminate all these expressions of hatred and discrimination. And he ordered the secretary of defense to abolish discrimination in the armed forces. Truman said, "I am not asking for social equality, because no such thing exists, but I am asking for equality of opportunity for all human beings." The ground was being plowed for the civil rights movement that would change American society.

* * *

Women also found themselves discriminated against in the workplace. Women came to see Truman about an equal rights amendment (he noted "a lot of hooey about equal rights").

"In the first week after the surrender of Japan, half of the workers in plants under contract to the UAW [United Auto Workers] were laid off," wrote Professor Nancy F. Gabin of Purdue University, a historian of women in the labor movement. "Women represented a disproportionate number of those laid off in the [automotive] industry." Her analysis showed that women, who had made up 26 percent of all production workers in the auto and aviation industry in 1943, represented by 1946 only 8 percent of the force, merely one percentage point more than they had way back in 1939.

A director of the Ford Motor Company's Labor Relations Department was quoted in *The New York Times* as saying, "From foreman all over the place to the highest—from the lowest to the highest level, so to speak—there was a sigh of relief when they could let women go. The general expression was, 'Thank God, that's over! And we'll pray that it never has to happen again.'"

Although many men in the union leadership disagreed, the UAW finally adopted a policy that a woman with wartime seniority had rights over a young man returning from the war with no seniority. The policy meant that the woman worker (who might have children to support) should not be responsible for providing the veteran with a job. The union defended the principle of seniority rights for all; it feared that bending on that point would harm all union members in the long run—despite the realization that women were competing with veterans for a limited number of jobs.

The experience of women in the wartime labor force contributed to societal changes in terms of economic, personal, and even sexual autonomy, competitive careers, and "family values." But for the time being, to a great degree, their war-driven employment in basic industries proved to be only "for the duration."

Swarms of changes not only transformed the American people; they circled the globe. The empires that had ruled so much of the world before 1914 had battled to their deaths like scorpions and had been replaced by two superpowers—the United States and the Soviet Union—that had played small roles in the world before the thirty-one-year-long world war. Power had shifted from Europe to the two great nations on the periphery.

The polarization of the superpowers' purposes, which had already been visible at Yalta and Potsdam, dominated the world. Their atomic buildup terrified millions. As historian Paul Kennedy wrote: "[T]o many of the public at large, the sheer extent and destructive capacity of the nuclear weaponry held in these two arsenals is an indication of political incapacity or mental sickness. . . ."

The next half century was to be "an era of threat-based strategies." Europe remained divided along the line inked on the map in 1945. Elsewhere, the superpowers tried to apportion the globe between themselves and to dominate others who threatened them or could serve them. They stretched further and further year by year until their reach exceeded their grasp—the United States in Vietnam and the Soviet Union in Afghanistan. For nearly fifty years, all-consuming tension and confrontation were the hallmarks of a risk-filled interlude during which the victors of the global war sorted out their priorities and pumped up their strengths.

The world that emerged from the war that Harry Truman finished had at its core a worldwide political revolution that offered human beings a chance to live their lives with some fundamental securities. This revolution freed millions from rule by outsiders; it brought to other millions such basics as housing, health care, and the opportunity to perform useful labor. It experimented with cooperative solutions that reached beyond national borders. It set a goal—perhaps unreachable—of human rights for everyone.

Dean Acheson saw the postwar challenge to the United States and its friends as "the main constructive work of rebuilding, out of the ruins of the nineteenth-century European imperial system, a free world to deal with local troubles real enough in their indigenous origins but magnified by efforts of our Communist opponents to increase our difficulties."

The underlying thrust in Western Europe was an attempt to broaden common interests, strengthen common democratic institutions, and slowly delegate aspects of national sovereignty. Jean Monnet led those who sought to replace nationalism, which had repeatedly proved brittle and destructive, with a United States of Europe or a European community. And, in fact, the European Economic Community would become the world's largest trading unit.

When the four Allied foreign ministers met in London soon after V-J Day to discuss the future of Europe, the growing antagonism between the Soviet Union and the West became more and more evident. The Soviet Union's attitude was that as the lone occupying power of Hungary, Romania, and Bulgaria, it alone would determine their fate.

The foreign ministers debated the future of Germany. France advocated a German federation of states with the Ruhr placed under international control—until the Soviet Union insisted on participating and putting troops into Düsseldorf. After twenty-three days of talk, each power settled for keeping control of its own zone of occupation. De Gaulle called the discussions "as futile for the present as they were unpromising for the future."

Attitudes hardened in the West. George Kennan sent a message from Moscow to Washington, asserting that the Kremlin's leaders were "cruel and wasteful" and determined to divide the West and disrupt the United States. Truman's able biographer David McCullough compared Kennan's "long telegram" to Harriman's earlier warning of the Soviet "barbarian invasion of Europe."

Fear now poisoned policy in both the East and West. Six months after Japan surrendered, Stalin declared that the capitalist-imperialist monopoly had caused the war, that communism and capitalism were incompatible, and that the Soviet Union needed to increase its production for war and delay production of consumer goods. No peaceful international order was possible, he said. Acheson identified this speech as the start of the Cold War.

President Truman was less fearful of the Soviet Union than some of the people around him were. But the United States' course was set—confirmed by Clark Clifford's report declaring that the Soviet Union was "on a course of aggrandizement designed to lead to eventual world domination by the U.S.S.R." All the hopeful statements of peaceful cooperation could not withstand the ideological, political, and nuclear rivalries.

The ultimate failure of the Soviet Union became not "the end of history" but one more difficult stage in the birth pangs of the new world. When the Soviet Union finally collapsed in December 1991, the world discovered that the "local troubles" that Acheson had warned of were terrible enough in their own right. Critic Robert Hughes called them "archaic religious and racial lunacies." No longer fearing a common enemy, people turned against their neighbors; tribe warred against tribe; fanatics murdered those who believed differently. The optimistic could only hope that these passions would be defeated by man's tolerance and good sense.

A central change in the postwar world was the new willingness of the United States to involve itself in world affairs. As a practical politician, Harry Truman believed in this involvement. The nation that had rejected the League of Nations now gave a home to the United Nations; created the Marshall Plan; participated in the Organization for European Economic Cooperation, the North Atlantic Treaty, and NATO; kept hundreds of thousands of its young men abroad in uniform; and took a responsibility for the defense of Europe and, for better or worse, for a miscellany of small, troubled lands.

Truman began his presidency hoping that the superpowers could work together. But Stalin's roughshod pursuit of the Soviet Union's self-interest combined with the exaggerated fears of Truman's own advisors turned his hopefulness into a hardheaded Missourian's determination not to be beaten at the poker table where the Great Powers played out their politics.

The result was that the United States led the "free world" into the Cold War and through it—and into hot wars in Korea, Vietnam, and Kuwait—into what Truman's successors wished could be a new world for a new millennium.

In the process, Euro-centered supremacy was deflated. As critic John Russell wrote, "What was lost to Europe between 1900 and 1950, and above all between 1939 and 1945, was the sense of predestined leadership which had been taken for granted since the days of Plato and Virgil, Charlemagne and the builders of Chartres Cathedral."

Contemporary European historians recognized that the United States had shifted the world's center from Europe across the Atlantic. British historian A. L. Rowse said, "The great cycle of English history that began with the Elizabethan Age has reached its terminus. Now Europe is rather secondary to America. America is, after all, the greatest achievement of the English people." Arnold Toynbee compared America's rise to a "son growing up and taking over the family business."

Looking at the consequences of this shift in leadership, Dean Acheson said, "[T]he period of Mr. Truman's Presidency and of the immediate postwar years, saw the entry of our nation, already one of the superpowers, into the near chaos of a war-torn and disintegrating world society. To the responsibilities and needs of that time the nation summoned an imaginative effort unique in history and even greater than that made in the preceding period of fighting."

And he added, "Only slowly did it dawn upon us that the whole world structure and order that we had inherited from the nineteenth century was gone and that the struggle to replace it would be directed from two bitterly opposed and ideologically irreconcilable power centers."

The effect of the war on the Soviet Union was also graphic. Previously, it had been bordered by a Germany and a Japan each powerful and dangerous. Now, Germany was divided and Japan disarmed. The Soviet Union faced no threatening army, and it dominated much of Eastern Europe and the Balkans. Raymond Aron wrote at the height of the Cold War, "The direct and sufficient cause of Russia's rise to world power is not Communism but the Second World War." But the Cold War, to which World War II gave birth, also contained the seed of the Soviet Union's destruction.

When that superpower struggle was finally over, the revolution had still not been won. People still suffered, starved, and died because they had not learned how to live at peace.

Simultaneously, Harry Truman led a world in which other, nonpolitical revolutions were let loose. A revolution of science and technology ranged all the way from penicillin to health care to communications and exploration of the planets. These changes enabled many people to live longer and better, but they also brought with them new problems—from overpopulation to cancer to AIDS.

The most frightening scientific invention to come out of the war was, of course, the newfound ability to convert matter into energy and to exploit nuclear power. The awesome addition within the decade of the thermonuclear bomb, a thousand times more powerful than Little Boy, provided the muscle for the fearsome superpower standoff that lasted most of the rest of the century.

The World War was won in good part on technological superiority and the ability to make steel, build ships and vehicles, and develop radar, sonar, proximity fuses, jet aircraft, penicillin, and the atomic bomb. To cite one dramatic example, the United States produced more than 296,000 aircraft during the war. The war had a large and permanent effect on the industrial nations' use of energy. The demand for electricity doubled, and Western dependence on Middle East oil increased, leading to ventures in Alaska and the North Sea.

In the physical sciences, codes were broken by bulky, awkward mechanical and electronic devices that would in time be refined into the calculating machine and the computer. During the war, punchcard-based computers were on the cutting edge and heavily in demand at Los Alamos, where atomic bomb research was centered. The next leap forward would have to wait for the development of the solid-state transistor, which would make calculations vastly faster and data storage vastly larger. Then, swiftly, a variety of uses would develop from weather forecasting to designing engines and simulating ecosystems.

Jet propulsion transformed the airplane and world travel. And strong radio waves—used as radar in the Battle of Britain to locate enemy aircraft—would evolve into a technology of higher and higher frequencies that could be used to aim guns, hunt submarines, and guide ships.

Still further in the distance, but already within the imagination of some who had worked on the atomic bomb, was emerging the idea that the science fiction dream of space travel could become a reality and in the lifetimes of some then living could carry men and women to the moon and perhaps beyond.

Medicine also experienced an explosion of knowledge. The great medical advances that were accelerated by World War II would directly affect the lives of millions. Physicians were handed an arsenal of new weapons with which to fight disease and prevent illness. Chemists produced new classes of pharmaceuticals; the electron microscope opened up the knowledge of viruses; and atomic power led to the use of radioactive isotopes. Work centered at The Rockefeller Institute in New York was climaxed in 1944 by the identification of DNA as the carrier of genetic information and led to the development of the new, powerful sciences of molecular biology, genetics, and genetic engineering.

Unlike World War I, the second World War was extremely mobile; and medical supplies and equipment from blood to X-ray machines had to be transportable and often disposable. Lifesaving air evacuation became available for the wounded on a mass basis. Some of these were not scientific advances as much as large clinical trials—of penicillin, blood transfusions, and plasma and air evacuation on large populations in uniform—and they had great impact on the postwar delivery of health care.

In past wars, the biggest killer had been not bullets but infectious disease. Preventive medicine changed this with the wide use of DDT and the widespread availability, for the first time, of defenses such as sulfa drugs against bacterial onslaughts. With a spectacular effort, penicillin, discovered back in 1928, was mass-produced and shipped to the combat theaters in time to treat the battlefield wounded against bacterial infection during the Normandy invasion and the fighting in the Philippines and on Okinawa. Late in the war, other antibiotics began to appear after the first small clinical trials at the Mayo Clinic in Minnesota using streptomycin against tuberculosis. And after the Japanese cut off the supply of natural quinine, man-made Atabrine was widely used against the serious threat from malaria in the Pacific war.

Previously, the surgeon's primitive knife, aided by early X-rays, had been the only means of entry to the human body. Now the wonders of the sonogram—which evolved out of wartime sonar—and the CT-scan were available. The first attempts at cardiac surgery were risked to save the wounded.

Every gain could have its consequences. Wartime advances benefited postwar medicine, but as historian of technology Trevor I. Williams has pointed out, "Medical progress was a major reason for the population explosion in developing countries which today is the source of so many of the world's political, social, and economic problems." This would become a worldwide puzzle.

Intellectuals reacted to all that had happened. The mass killing in the global war, the brutal occupations by Germany and Japan, the Holocaust and other attempted racial obliterations, and the specter of nuclear destruction soured optimism into despair and dread.

Václav Havel saw a dichotomy between the human soul and human intellect: "The human intellect has developed fantastic things from the computer to splitting the atom, but the human soul is not on the same level as the things it has invented. Instead of serving man, in many instances the inventions enslave him or threaten him."

One intellectual response was "existentialism," which turned its back on authority, ritual, and oppression and instead celebrated freedom, individual responsibility, and choice. Jean-Paul Sartre, existentialism's most popular and articulate proponent, believed that human beings are defined by moral choice. Certainly, in wartime France Sartre witnessed the making of fundamental choices. This philosophy of choice both challenged the exclusive power of the philosophical and theological establishments and sought to turn despair into hope.

All these revolutions were reflected in the dreams and works of the artists who sought to understand, to express and to communicate the vast changes that had come out of the war and transformed their world. The result was, as critic John Russell wrote, that "in art, as in the sciences, ours is one of the big centuries."

Artists in all media expressed their reactions to the changes—some, of course, with anger and ferocity. But almost none tried to shore up the old values; they chose to explore the new. Unlike the politicians and the soldiers, they sought not to confirm but to question.

Pablo Picasso captured in brutal line and paint the terror of the bombing and destruction of the people of the Spanish city of Guernica—a terror that was to be replicated around the globe in the next eight years. Alberto Giacometti, producing the "art of survival," carved gaunt figures that spoke silently of the experience of individuals tossed about and damaged by the horrors of war and hatred. They could have come out of a Nazi concentration camp. Paul Klee, Wassily Kandinsky, Jean Dubuffet, Hans Hofmann, and others sought to express the "irrational" madness that human beings had just lived through. The abstract expressionists groped to give voice to emotions that had no name. They tried, as Vincent van Gogh had said, to "paint things not as they are . . . but as *they* feel them."

The center of artistic creativity moved from occupied Paris to New York City, resulting in the displacement of such artists as Willem de Kooning, Fernand Léger, Piet Mondrian, and Max Ernst and the emergence of American-born artists such as Jackson Pollock, Stuart Davis, Barnett Newman, and David Smith.

To John Russell "the artist is the person who puts the world together after everyone else has let it go to pieces." Or maybe the artist is the person who reminds the rest of us that it needs to be put together. This was, in Russell's words, "the beginning of a new era for all humanity. . . . In art, as in so many other departments of life, humanity was being given a fresh start."

On returning home from Potsdam in August, President Truman had spoken to the American people over the radio and again hammered home his central worry: "Any man who sees Europe now must realize that victory in a great war is not something you win once and for all, like victory in a ball game. Victory in a great war is something that must be won and kept won. It can be lost after you have won it—if you are careless or negligent or indifferent."

Henry Stimson, on his eightieth birthday, made a similar point: "The essential question is one which we should have to answer if there were not a Communist alive. Can we make freedom and prosperity real in the present world? If we can, communism is no threat. If not, with or without communism, our own civilization would ultimately fail."

On the eve of what Truman called "the Christmas that a war-weary world has prayed for through long and awful years," he lit the National Community Christmas Tree on the White House lawn and reminded the nation, "With our enemies vanquished we must gird ourselves for the work that lies ahead. Peace has its victories no less hard won than success at arms. We must not fail or falter."

Truman was not going to be negligent or indifferent. In the twenty-one weeks between Franklin Roosevelt's death and the signing of the surrender on the *Missouri*, this man from Missouri had proven his unexpected ability to take charge and settle the great questions thrown up to him.

He wrote to Bess, "This head of mine should have been bigger and better proportioned. There ought to have been more brain and a larger bump of ego or something to give me an idea that there can be a No. 1 man in the world. I didn't want to be. But, in spite of opinions to the contrary, *Life* and *Time* say I am."

David McCullough wrote:

> In just three months in office Harry Truman had been faced with a greater surge of history, with larger, more difficult, more far-reaching decisions than any President before him. Neither Lincoln after first taking office, nor Franklin Roosevelt in his tumultuous first hundred days, had had to contend with issues of such magnitude and coming all at once . . . clearly unparalleled power and responsibility had been thrust upon him at one of history's greatest turning points.

One important thing Harry Truman did know about himself, as he said much later: "I don't give up on what I start. I'm a stubborn cuss. They all found that out when I was President. I was stubborn." This was true whether he was sowing oats, running Jackson Country honestly, investigating war production, or dealing with Churchill and Stalin. And it made a difference. It enabled a very extraordinary ordinary man to get many things settled his way.

After the war was over, Jean Monnet, the great Frenchman who led the way to the rebirth of Europe and dreamed of a United States of Europe, summed up Truman's strength:

> Harry Truman was certainly no ordinary man . . . against almost everyone's expectations, he showed himself capable of dominating the world scene. The essential reason was a quality with which he was exceptionally well

endowed: the ability to decide. Whether by nature or because the role of President had transformed him, he never hesitated in the face of great decisions. . . . In the nature of things he could not always be well-informed, and he was capable of making mistakes; but he knew how to make his mind up, which is the sign of a genuine statesman.

Dean Acheson, who worked with Harry Truman closely for years, saw the same ability:

To me his greatest quality as President, as a leader was his ability to decide. General Marshall, who also had that quality, has said that the ability to make a decision is a great gift, perhaps the greatest gift a man can have. And Mr. Truman had that gift in abundance. When I would come to him with a problem, the only question he ever asked was, "How long have I got?" And he never asked later what would have happened if he had decided differently. I doubt that that ever concerned him. He was not a man who was tortured by second thoughts. Those were luxuries. . . .

Monnet and Acheson were astute. In five months, during which so many tremendously important decisions had to be made, Harry Truman was not afraid to act. He knew his shortcomings. "Pray for me," he asked Bess, "and keep your fingers cross [*sic*] too." The sign on his desk said: "The buck stops here." He said he would have his aides and advisors "doing spade work . . . and I made the decisions."

John Hersey, a superb reporter, spent a series of weeks observing him closely during his presidency and came to admire his courage, cheerfulness, and "a mighty stubbornness," and also faulted him for snap judgments and hasty, over-positive replies. He was decisive— and human.

Once, late in life, Truman commented with his usual diffidence, "I don't think knowing what's the right thing to do ever gives anybody too much trouble. It's *doing* the right thing that seems to give a lot of people trouble." He might not always have done "the right thing," but he took the risk.

Harry Truman might have chosen to challenge Stalin in the heart of Europe before the lines were converted into walls. He might have seized Berlin and Prague and tried to alter the map of Europe. Or he might have accepted Stalin's blind need to subjugate his neighbors. He might have compromised with the Japanese warlords who refused to bend in the face of obvious defeat. He might have kept de Gaulle out of Indochina and the other former French colonies. He might have refused to use two atomic bombs against a Japan already on its knees. But he decided otherwise, and the world he shaped was the one in which we now live.

This man made decisions that made victory a certainty in both Europe and Asia and that began to guide the American people on their passage into a world totally changed from the one they had known before.

At the moment of victory, Truman issued a Labor Day statement that also looked at the future: "Today we stand on the threshold of a new world. We must do our part in making this world what it should be, a world in which the bigotries of race and class and creed shall not be permitted to warp the souls of men. We enter upon an era of great problems, but to live is to face problems."

Led by Harry Truman, the men and women who brought World War II to a close, who ended that round of genocide, and who began these revolutions of the postwar world were optimists—and realists. They understood the threats posed by carelessness, negligence, and indifference. They hoped for sanity and peace. But they knew that some self-interested people would continue to insist on dominating others, that some would gain security and material comfort while depriving others. They knew that the real war is not over. It continues into the new millennium. Harry Truman had an inexhaustible faith that this war could be won and that humankind could be free.

Bibliography

Acheson, Dean. *Present at the Creation*. New York: W. W. Norton and Company, 1969.

Alperovitz, Gar. *The Decision to Use the Atomic Bomb*. New York: Alfred A. Knopf, 1995.

Ambrose, Stephen R. *Eisenhower and Berlin, 1945: The Decision to Halt at the Elbe*. New York: W. W. Norton and Company, 1967.

American Military History. Army Historical Series, Maurice Matloff, general editor. Washington, D.C.: Office of the Chief of Military History, United States Army, 1969, revised 1973.

American Military History 1607–1953. Washington, D.C.: Department of the Army, 1956.

Appleman, Roy E., James M. Burns, Russell A. Gugeler, and John Stevens. *Okinawa: The Last Battle. United States Army in World War II, The War in the Pacific*. Washington, D.C.: Historical Division, Department of the Army, 1948.

Aron, Raymond. *The Century of Total War*. Garden City, N.Y.: Doubleday and Company, 1954.

Asimov, Isaac. *Asimov's Guide to Science*. New York: Basic Books, 1972.

Barnett, A. Doak. *China and the Major Powers in East Asia*. Washington, D.C.: The Brookings Institution, 1977.

Ben-Gurion, David. *Israel: A Personal History*. New York: Funk and Wagnalls, 1971.

Ben-Sasson, H. H., ed. *A History of the Jewish People*. Cambridge, Mass.: Harvard University Press, 1976.

Bernstein, Barton J. "Roosevelt, Truman and the Atomic Bomb: A Reinterpretation." *Political Science Quarterly*, vol. 90, no. 1 (Spring 1975).

Bird, Kai. "A Humiliating Smithsonian Retreat from the Facts of Hiroshima." *International Herald Tribune*, Paris, October 12, 1994, p.4.

Bishop, Jim. *FDR's Last Year, April 1944–April 1945*. New York: William Morrow and Co., 1974.

Blum, John Morton. *From the Morgenthau Diaries: Years of War: 1941–1945*. Boston: Houghton Mifflin, 1967.

————. *V Was for Victory: Politics and American Culture During World War II*. San Diego: Harcourt Brace Jovanovich, 1976.

Bohlen, Charles E. *Witness to History. 1929–1969*. New York: W. W. Norton and Company, 1973.

Bradley, Omar N. *A Soldier's Story*. New York: Henry Holt and Company, 1951.

————, and Clay Blair. *A General's Life: An Autobiography*. New York: Simon and Schuster, 1983.

Bullock, Alan. *Hitler: A Study in Tyranny*. London: Penguin Books, 1962, reissued 1990.

Burns, James MacGregor. *Roosevelt: The Soldier of Freedom*. New York: Harcourt Brace Jovanovich, 1970.

Buttinger, Joseph. *The Small Dragon: A Political History of Vietnam*. New York: Praeger, 1958.

Byrnes, James F. *Speaking Frankly*. New York: Harper and Brothers, 1947.

Cameron, Allan W., ed. *Viet-Nam Crisis: A Documentary History*, vol. 1, *1940–1956*. Ithaca, N.Y.: Cornell University Press, 1971.

Caro, Robert A. *The Years of Lyndon Johnson*, vol. 2, *Means of Ascent*. New York: Alfred A. Knopf, 1990.

Catton, Bruce. *Terrible Swift Sword*. Garden City, N.Y.: Doubleday and Company, 1963.

Churchill, Winston S. *The Second World War*, vol. 6, *Triumph and Tragedy*. Boston: Houghton Mifflin, 1953.

Clifford, Clark, with Richard Holbrooke. *Counsel to the President*. New York: Random House, 1991.

Cohen, Warren I. *Dean Rusk* (vol. 19 of *The American Secretaries of State and Their Diplomacy*). Totowa, N.J.: Cooper Square Publishers, 1980.

Cosmas, Graham A., and Albert E. Cowdrey. *The Medical Department: Medical Service in the European Theater of Operations*. United States Army in World War II, The Technical Services. Washington, D.C.: Center of Military History, United States Army, 1992.

Craven, Wesley Frank, and James Lea Cate, eds. *The Army Air Forces in World War II*, vol. 5, *The Pacific: Matterhorn to Nagasaki, June 1944 to August 1945*. Chicago: University of Chicago Press, 1953, Washington, D.C., new imprint by Office of Air Force History, 1983.

Daniel, Clifton, editor-in-chief. *Chronicle of the 20th Century*. Mount Kisco, N.Y.: Chronicle Publications, 1987.

Dawidowicz, Lucy S. *The War Against the Jews 1933–1945*. New York: Holt, Rinehart and Winston, 1975.

de Gaulle, Charles. *The War Memoirs of Charles de Gaulle*, vol. 3, *Salvation 1944–1946*. Translated by Richard Howard. New York: Simon and Schuster, 1960.

DeGregorio, William A. *The Complete Book of U.S. Presidents*, 3d ed. New York: Barricade Books, 1991.

Donovan, Robert J. *Conflict and Crisis, The Presidency of Harry S Truman, 1945–1948*. New York: W. W. Norton and Company, 1977.

Duchêne, François. *Jean Monnet: The First Statesman of Interdependence*. New York: W. W. Norton and Company, 1994.

Eban, Abba. *Abba Eban, An Autobiography*. New York: Random House, 1977.

Eisenhower, David. *Eisenhower: At War, 1943–1945*. New York: Random House, 1986.

Eisenhower, Dwight D. *Crusade in Europe*. Garden City, N.Y.: Doubleday and Company, 1948.

Elliott, Mark R. *Pawns of Yalta: Soviet Refugees and America's Role in Their Repatriation*. Urbana: University of Illinois Press, 1982.

Ellis, John. *The Social History of the Machine Gun*. New York: Pantheon Books, 1975.

Erickson, John. *The Road to Berlin*. Boulder, Colo.: Westview Press, 1983.

Feifer, George. *Tennozan, The Battle of Okinawa and the Atomic Bomb*. New York: Ticknor and Fields, 1992.

Feis, Herbert. *Between War and Peace: The Potsdam Conference*. Princeton: Princeton University Press, 1960.

———. *Churchill-Roosevelt-Stalin: The War They Waged and the Peace They Sought*, 2d ed. Princeton, N.J.: Princeton University Press, 1967.

Ferrell, Robert H. *Dear Bess: The Letters from Harry to Bess Truman, 1910–1959*. New York: W. W. Norton and Company, 1983.

———. *Harry S. Truman: A Life*. Columbia: University of Missouri Press, 1994.

————, ed. *Off the Record: The Private Papers of Harry S. Truman*. New York: Harper and Row, 1980.

Foreign Relations of the United States, Diplomatic Papers. *The Conference of Berlin (The Potsdam Conference) 1945*. 2 vols. Washington, D.C.: U.S. Government Printing Office, 1960.

Gabin, Nancy F. *Feminism in the Labor Movement: Women and the United Auto Workers, 1935–1975*. Ithaca, N.Y.: Cornell University Press, 1990.

Gavin, General James M. *On to Berlin: Battles of an Airborne Commander 1943–1946*. New York: Bantam Books, 1979.

Gilbert, Martin. *Churchill: A Life*. New York: Henry Holt and Company, 1991.

————. *The Second World War, A Complete History*. New York: Henry Holt and Company, 1989.

Ginsburgh, Robert N. *U.S. Military Strategy in the Sixties*. New York: W. W. Norton and Company, 1965.

Gleick, James. *Genius: The Life and Science of Richard Feynman*. New York: Pantheon Books, 1992.

Goodwin, Doris Kearns. *No Ordinary Time: Franklin and Eleanor Roosevelt: The Home Front in World War II*. New York: Simon and Schuster, 1994.

Grew, Joseph C. *A Contemporary Record Drawn from the Diaries and Official Papers of Joseph C. Grew, United States Ambassador to Japan 1932–1942*. New York: Simon and Schuster, 1944.

Groves, Leslie R. *Now It Can Be Told*. New York: Harper and Row, 1962.

Harriman, W. Averell. *America and Russia in a Changing World*. Garden City, N.Y.: Doubleday and Company, 1971.

————, and Elie Abel. *Harriman: Special Envoy to Churchill and Stalin 1941–46*. New York: Random House, 1975.

Hartman, Susan M. *The Home Front and Beyond: American Women in the 1940's*. Boston: Twayne, 1982.

Hersey, John. *Aspects of the Presidency: Truman and Ford in Office*. New Haven and New York: Ticknor and Fields, 1980.

Holton, Gerald, and Yehuda Ekana, eds. *Albert Einstein: Historical and Cultural Perspectives: The Centennial Symposium in Jerusalem*. Princeton, N.J.: Princeton University Press, 1982.

Hughes, Robert. *The Culture of Complaint: The Fraying of America*. New York: Oxford University Press, 1993.

Irokara, Daikichi. *The Age of Hirohito: In Search of Modern Japan*. Translated by Mikiso Hane and John K. Urda. New York: The Free Press, 1995.

James, D. Clayton. *The Years of MacArthur*, vol. 2, *1941–1945*. Boston: Houghton Mifflin Company, 1975.

Kagan, Donald. *On the Origins of War and the Preservation of Peace*. New York: Doubleday, 1995.

Kahin, George McTurnan, and John Wilson Lewis. *The United States in Vietnam*, rev. ed. New York: Dial Press, 1967.

Karnow, Stanley. *Vietnam: A History*. New York: Viking Press, 1983.

Keiser, Gordon W. *The US Marine Corps and Defense Unification 1944–47: The Politics of Survival*. Washington: National Defense University Press, 1982.

Kennan, George F. *Memoirs 1925–1950*. Boston: Little, Brown and Company, 1967.

Kennedy, Paul. *The Rise and Fall of the Great Powers: Economic Change and Military Conflict from 1500 to 2000*. New York: New York: Vintage Books, 1989.

Kennedy, Susan Estabrook. "Herbert Hoover and the Two Great Food Crusades of the 1940s," in *Understanding Herbert Hoover: Ten Perspectives*, edited by Lee Nash. Stanford, Calif.: Hoover Institution Press, Stanford University Press, 1987.

Lancaster, Donald. *The Emancipation of French Indochina*. Oxford: Oxford University Press, 1961.

Larrabee, Eric. *Commander in Chief: Franklin Delano Roosevelt, His Lieutenants, and Their War*. New York: Harper and Row, 1987.

Leahy, William D. *I Was There: The Personal Story of the Chief of Staff to Presidents Roosevelt and Truman Based on His Notes and Diaries Made at the Time*. New York: McGraw-Hill, 1950

Lee, Bruce. *Marching Orders: The Untold Story of World War II*. New York: Crown Publishers, 1995.

Lingeman, Richard R. *Don't You Know There's a War On? The American Home Front 1941–1945*. New York: G. P. Putnam's Sons, 1970.

Manchester, William. *American Caesar: Douglas MacArthur 1880–1964*. Boston: Little, Brown and Company, 1978.

———. *Goodbye, Darkness: A Memoir of the Pacific War*. Boston: Little, Brown and Company, 1979.

Marcus, Allan I, and Howard P. Segal. *Technology in America: A Brief History*. New York: Harcourt Brace Jovanovich, 1988.

Massie, Robert K. *Dreadnought: Britain, Germany, and the Coming of the Great War*. New York: Random House, 1991.

McCarty, Maclyn. *The Transforming Principle.* New York: W. W. Norton and Company, 1985.

McCullough, David. *Truman.* New York: Simon and Schuster, 1992.

McLellan, David S. *Dean Acheson: The State Department Years.* New York: Dodd, Mead and Company, 1976.

Messer, Robert L. *The End of the Alliance.* Chapel Hill, N.C.: University of North Carolina Press, 1982.

Miller, Merle. *Ike the Soldier: As They Knew Him.* New York: G. P. Putnam's Sons, 1987.

————. *Plain Speaking: An Oral Biography of Harry S. Truman.* New York: Berkley Publishing Corporation, 1974.

Millis, Walter, ed. *The Forrestal Diaries.* New York: Viking Press, 1951.

Minear, Richard H. *Victors' Justice: The Tokyo War Crimes Trial.* Princeton, N.J.: Princeton University Press, 1971.

Monnet, Jean. *Memoirs.* Translated by Richard Mayne. Garden City, N.Y.: Doubleday and Company, 1978.

Morgan, Kay Summersby. *Past Forgetting: My Love Affair with Dwight D. Eisenhower.* New York: Simon and Schuster, 1976.

Morgan, Ted. *FDR: A Biography.* New York: Simon and Schuster, 1985.

Morison, Samuel Eliot. *The Rising Sun in the Pacific 1931–April 1942,* vol. 3 of *History of United States Naval Operations in World War II.* Boston: Little, Brown and Company, 1948.

————. *Victory in the Pacific 1945,* vol. 14 of *History of United States Naval Operations in World War II.* Boston: Little, Brown and Company, 1960.

Morse, Arthur D. *While Six Million Died: A Chronicle of American Apathy.* New York: Random House, 1968.

Moskin, J. Robert. *Morality in America.* New York: Random House, 1966.

————. *The U.S. Marine Corps Story.* New York: McGraw-Hill Book Company, 1977, revised 1987; Boston: Little, Brown and Company, revised 1992.

Mosley, Leonard. *Marshall: Hero for Our Times.* New York: Hearst Books, 1982.

Murray, James N., Jr. *The United Nations Trusteeship System.* Urbana: University of Illinois Press, 1952.

O'Connor, Raymond G. *Diplomacy for Victory: FDR and Unconditional Surrender.* New York: W. W. Norton and Company, 1971.

Padfield, Peter. *Himmler: Reichsführer SS.* New York: Henry Holt and Company, 1990.

Parascandola, John. "The Introduction of Antibiotics into Therapeutics," in

History of Therapy, Proceedings of the 10th International Symposium on the Comparative History of Medicine—East and West, Shizuoka, Japan, September 8–15, 1985. Ishiyaku EuropAmerica, Inc., 1990.

Perlmutter, Amos. *The Life and Times of Menachem Begin*. Garden City, N.Y.: Doubleday and Company, 1987.

Piccigallo, Philip R. *The Japanese on Trial: Allied War Crimes Operations in the East 1945–51*. Austin: University of Texas Press, 1979.

Pike, Douglas. *Viet Cong*. Cambridge, Mass.: MIT Press, 1966.

Pogue, Forrest C. *United States Army in World War II: The European Theater of Operations, The Supreme Command*. Washington, D.C.: Office of the Chief of Military History, Department of the Army, 1954.

Public Papers of the Presidents of the United States, Harry S. Truman, Containing the Public Messages, Speeches, and Statements of the President, April 12 to December 31, 1945. Washington, D.C.: U.S. Government Printing Office, 1961.

Rhodes, Richard. *The Making of the Atomic Bomb*. New York: Simon and Schuster, 1986.

Rosie, George. *The British in Vietnam: How the Twenty-Five-Year War Began*. London: Panther, 1970.

Russell, John. *The Meanings of Modern Art*, rev. ed. New York: Museum of Modern Art, HarperCollins, 1991.

Ryan, Cornelius. *The Last Battle*. New York: Pocket Books, 1966.

Said, Edward W. *Culture and Imperialism*. New York: Alfred A. Knopf, 1993.

Schweitzer, Dr. Albert. "The Problem of Peace in the World Today." Nobel Peace Prize address given in Oslo, November 4, 1954, reprinted in *Reverence*, no. 16 (January 1993), p. 15.

Sigal, Leon V. *Fighting to a Finish: The Politics of War Termination in the United States and Japan, 1945*. Ithaca, N.Y.: Cornell University Press, 1988.

———. "Bureaucratic Politics and Tactical Use of Committees: The Interim Committee and the Decision to Drop the Atomic Bomb," *Polity*, vol. 3 (Spring 1978), 326–364.

Smith, Bradley F. *Reaching Judgment at Nuremberg*. New York: Basic Books, 1977.

Smith, Jean Edward. *Lucius D. Clay, An American Life*. New York: Henry Holt and Company, 1990.

Smith, Richard Norton. *An Uncommon Man: The Triumph of Herbert Hoover*. New York: Simon and Schuster, 1984.

Spector, Ronald H. *Eagle Against the Sun: The American War with Japan.* New York: Vintage Books, 1985.

Steel, Ronald. *Walter Lippmann and the American Century.* Boston: Little, Brown and Company, 1980.

Stimson, Henry L., and McGeorge Bundy. *On Active Service in Peace and War.* New York: Harper and Brothers, 1948.

Stone, I. F. *The Truman Era 1945–1952: A Nonconformist History of Our Times.* Boston: Little, Brown and Company, 1953.

Swanberg, W. A. *Luce and His Empire.* New York: Charles Scribner's Sons, 1972.

Taylor, Telford. *The Anatomy of the Nuremberg Trials: A Personal Memoir.* New York: Alfred A. Knopf, 1992.

Teveth, Shabtai. *Ben-Gurion: The Burning Ground 1886–1948.* Boston: Houghton Mifflin Company, 1987.

Toland, John. *The Last 100 Days.* New York: Random House, 1966.

Thomas, Gordon, and Max Morgan Watts. *Ruin from the Air: The Enola Gay's Atomic Mission to Hiroshima.* Chelsea, Mich.: Scarborough House, 1977.

Truman, Harry S. *Memoirs Vol. 1: Year of Decisions.* Garden City, N.Y.: Doubleday and Company, 1955.

———. *Memoirs Vol. 2: Years of Trial and Hope, 1946–1952.* Garden City, N.Y.: Doubleday and Company, 1955.

Truman, Margaret. *Harry S. Truman.* New York: William Morrow and Company, 1972.

Urquhart, Brian. *Ralph Bunche: An American Life.* New York: W. W. Norton and Company, 1993.

Von Laue, Theodore. "A Declaration of Interdependence: World History for the Twenty-First Century." *Perspectives,* American Historical Association, vol. 31, no. 4 (April 1993), p. 8.

Weinberg, Gerhard L. *A World at Arms.* Cambridge: Cambridge University Press, 1994.

Wilkinson, James D. *The Intellectual Resistance in Europe.* Cambridge, Mass.: Harvard University Press, 1981.

Williams, Trevor I. *A Short History of Twentieth-Century Technology 1900–1950.* Oxford: Oxford University Press, 1982.

Yarmolinsky, Adam. *The Military Establishment: Its Impacts on American Society.* New York: Harper and Row, 1971.

Ziemke, Earl F. *Stalingrad to Berlin: The German Defeat in the East.* Washington, D.C.: Center of Military History, United States Army, 1987.

Acknowledgments

The men and women who proposed the policies and made and carried out the decisions that changed the world so dramatically between April 12 and September 2, 1945, have left behind records that are at times illuminating and at others self-serving. Meanwhile, we have gained a half century of perspective that distances us from the fire and the tensions that accompanied this explosion of changes.

The challenge of this book was to pull together the varied, conflicting strands that made these five months one of the crucial and exciting moments in the world's history—and to enable the reader to see our world being born. Most of what happened is known. The sources so far available have been ransacked. The challenge was not to uncover but to reveal, put into perspective, and communicate what happened.

In addition to more than four years of research, this book encompasses my own lifetime. The experiences of my youthful participation overseas in World War II, followed by forty years of reporting the world's affairs, have gone into this book. Over these years of journalistic and historical work, my path has crossed those of many of the people who participated in these events and their consequences. To name just some of the best known: John F. Kennedy, Lyndon Johnson, Dean Rusk, Cyrus Vance, Willy Brandt, Teddy Kollek, Walter Reuther, Václav Havel, Chiang Kai-shek, David Ben-Gurion, Averell Harriman, George Kennan, Robert Oppenheimer, and Leo Szilard. Interviewing them (and knowing some of them) influenced, to varying degrees, the book's ultimate shape.

Writing a book is largely a solitary act, but it is never accomplished in a vacuum. Those who have contributed insights and information, encouragement and guidance to this project over the years are numerous. But at the end of the process some individuals stand in my memory and stimulate my wish to acknowledge the help they gave in many assorted ways.

My appreciation goes especially to my editor, Robert D. Loomis, whose caring and skillful interest were unique in my experience and who improved the manuscript immeasurably, and to my longtime and astute literary agent, Don Congdon, who supported and advanced the book from the beginning. I thank Harry Evans for originally listening to my desire to write this book and recognizing that it was something he wished to publish. I thank Harvey Klein, M.D., for making it possible for me to finish the book. And I thank most warmly Lynn Goldberg for being, in addition to a most loving and understanding wife, a wonderfully wise counselor.

I would also like to thank Frederick E. Allen; Robert V. Aquilina; William B. Arthur; Ambassador A. Leroy Atherton; Robert L. Bernstein; William S. Catherwood; Matt Clark; Benjamin J. Cohen; Danny J. Crawford; Jane S. DeHart; Dan H. Fenn; Helena Fierlinger; W. Gregory Gallagher; Gail Winslow Ginsburgh and the late Major General Robert N. Ginsburgh; James Hansen; the late John Hersey; Gail Russell Job; Reverend William A. Johnson; Colonel Robert Joy, M.D.; Margaret E. Mahoney; Janet and John Marqusee; Mary Martin; John Mendelsohn, M.D.; Gail Potter Neale; David M. Oshinsky; John Parascandola, M.D.; Gary Sick; Leon V. Sigal; Brigadier General Edwin H. Simmons; Walter and Mary Simons; Joseph E. Slater; Robert M. Solow; Julia and Thomas Vitullo-Martin; Kenneth W. Wheeler; and Professor Yang Biao. Carl Wohlleben has been a special help as an able and thorough archival researcher. Jane Colihan has discovered and produced the pictures with great perception and taste.

As I traveled abroad during the years that I worked on the book, a number of people were particularly helpful. That I sought out those in central Europe was no accident; that part of the world was so affected by World War II and its aftermath.

In Paris, General Juan Delmas, Colonel Paul Gaujac, and Colonel Jacques Vernet at the French Army Department of History, Chateau de Vincennes, Vincennes, Paris, deserve special mention. In Paris, I also want to thank Kristofer and the late Simonne Finnbogason and Ulane Bonnel.

In London, Professor D. Cameron Watt and Dr. John W. Young of the Department of International History of the London School of Economics were most generous with their time and thoughts, as were Miss Alex Ward, Head, Army Historical Branch; Group Captain Ian Madelin, RAF (Ret.), Head, RAF Historical Branch; and Mr. J. David Brown, Head, Naval Historical Branch, at the Ministry of Defense, London. In addition, my personal thanks to Donald Trelford, Dorothy Berwin Stein, and Nicholas Berwin.

In Vienna, my understanding was strengthened by talks with Dr.

Fritz P. Molden of Auslandsösterreicherwerk; Dr. Hugo Portisch; Dr. Oliver Rathkolb of Stiftung Bruno Kreisky Archiv; Dr. Manfried Rauchensteiner, Director, Army Historical Museum and head of Military Historical Service of the Armed Forces; and Professor Erika Weinzierl, Chair, Institut für Zeitgeschichte. I was also aided in Vienna by James W. Swihart, Jr., Deputy Chief of Mission, Embassy of the United States, and Ellen Swihart; by Wolfgang Petritsch in Washington; and by Carl W. Schmidt, Director, Salzburg Seminar, Salzburg, and his wife, Rika.

In Prague, I benefited greatly from talks with President Václav Havel; Dr. Vilém Prečan, Director, Institute for Contemporary History, Czechoslovak Academy of Science; and Prince Karl von Schwarzenberg. In addition, I want to express my appreciation in Prague to Jan Bednar; Anna Freimanova; Dagmar Obereigner; John M. Evans, Deputy Chief of Mission, Embassy of the United States; and Zdenek Prouza; and in Washington, to Jiří Setlik.

And in Israel, I was helped generously by Mayor Teddy Kollek, General Ephraim Poran, Jay Bushinsky, Shula Eisner Navon, Leora Nir, and Tirza Yuval.

Source Notes

Introduction

xvi "a turbulent age": quoted in Harriman, *America and Russia*, v.
xvi "Humanity has now entered": Von Laue, 8.
xvii "limited war for": quoted in Miller, *Plain Speaking*, 285.

1: "Jesus Christ and General Jackson!"

6 "hastened his death": Stimson, 605.
6 a social secretary: T. Morgan, 762.
6 with his thumbs: Bishop, 590.
6 "it is my sad duty": Burns, 600–1.
7 "Board of Education": Caro, 17; Acheson, 97; Miller, *Plain Speaking*, 197.
7 "It's my job": Ferrell, *Off the Record*, 13.
7 "Jesus Christ and General Jackson!": Donovan, 4.
8 "I had hurried": Truman, Harry, *Memoirs*, vol. 1, 44.
8 "Now the lightning": Ibid., 6.
8 "snow-capped and episcopal": Acheson, 90.
8 "In a voice of steel": M. Truman, 210.
9 "None of us": *The Washington Post*, April 13, 1945, 1, 6; Hersey, 68.
9 "the first decision": quoted in Miller, *Plain Speaking*, 199.
9 "They were all so broken up": Ibid.
10 On Stimson's word: Donovan, xiv.
10 "Stimson was a man": quoted in Miller, *Plain Speaking*, 200.
10 "He is straight-forward": Acheson, 104.
10 "We in the State Department": Bohlen, 212.
11 "the damnedest scramble": quoted in Caro, 122.
11 "honest and patriotic": quoted in Donovan, 13.
11 As the bells: Rhodes, 620.
11 "The war isn't lost": Donovan, 7.
11 "When I saw Stalin": Harriman, *America and Russia*, 39; Erickson, 552.
11 a physical blow: Churchill, 471.
12 "a resolute and fearless man": Ibid., 480.
12 had been infuriated: Donovan, 12.
12 "The destruction of": Churchill, 456.
12 "to win an organized peace": H. Truman, *Memoirs*, vol. 1, 12.
12 "the best thing to do": Truman diary, quoted in Ferrell, *Off the Record*, 16.
13 from his own bedroom: *The Washington Post*, April 13, 1945, 3.
13 "I was very much shocked": Truman diary, quoted in Ferrell, *Off the Record*, 16.
13 "I guess the party's off": Donovan, 14.

2: The Man

18 "Those were wonderful days": H. Truman, *Memoirs*, vol. 1, 115.
18 "I only had one sweetheart": Ferrell, *Off the Record*, 43.
18 a bit of a sissy: Miller, *Plain Speaking*, 35.

18 "a leader is a man": H. Truman, *Memoirs*, vol. 1, 119.

18 was to Mark Twain: Miller, *Plain Speaking*, 32.

19 "I managed to save dimes": Ferrell, *Dear Bess*, 20.

19 "That is moving some": Ibid., 26.

19 Eddie and his wife: Miller, *Plain Speaking*, 104.

19 "I bet there'll": Ferrell, *Dear Bess*, 52–3.

20 "The Jews claim": Truman diary, June 1, 1945, quoted in Ferrell, *Off the Record*, 41.

20 "I had never heard": M. Truman. 136.

20 "the brotherhood of man": Ibid., 128.

20 "I'm not Jewish": Ibid., 187.

20 "How does it feel": Ferrell, *Dear Bess*, 143.

21 was given command: McCullough, 120.

21 "Dear Harry, May": Acheson, 150.

21 "The silence that": H. Truman, *Memoirs*, vol. 1, 131.

21 "disgusting": Ibid., 132.

22 he eventually settled: Ferrell, *Harry S. Truman*, 86.

22 When Judge Truman ran again: M. Truman, 67.

23 "You carry out the agreement": H. Truman, *Memoirs*, vol. 1, 141.

23 "No man can get rich": Miller, *Plain Speaking*, 130.

23 "It was the era of George F. Babbitt": Ferrell, *Harry S. Truman*, 91.

24 a quarter of a million votes: Ibid., 127–31.

24 the vote in Kansas City: Ibid., 130.

24 "Boss Tom's" advice: McCullough, 213.

24 "The street gangs": Bullock, 270.

24 "I am hoping to make a reputation": Ferrell, *Dear Bess*, 365.

25 One person who helped Truman: Donovan, xi.

26 "half Judaized": Bullock, 672.

26 all his dreams: Aron, 45.

26 The Navy publicly denied: McCullough, 288.

27 he thought Byrnes: Ferrell, *Harry S. Truman*, 91.

27 "a lot of hooey": Ferrell, *Dear Bess*, 509.

27 "Don't fly": Quoted in Miller, *Plain Speaking*, 183.

27 Truman was appalled: M. Truman, 186.

28 "I knew he was a sick man.": quoted in Miller, *Plain Speaking*, 185.

28 the Communists were taking over: McCullough, 332.

28 "the last time that he saw Mr. Roosevelt": M. Truman, 190; McCullough, 332.

28 As 1945 opened: H. Truman, *Memoirs*, vol. 1, 6.

29 Stalin cooperated: Gilbert, *Second World War*, 628.

29 "Now you behave yourself": H. Truman, *Memoirs*, vol. 1, 195.

29 "a study in probabilities": Hersey, 136.

30 a dirt farmer: Donovan, 20.

3: "Plowing a Field with a Mule"

33 "Come on in, Tony": *The Washington Post*, April 14, 1945, 4.

34 had already killed: Reference Department, Marine Corps Historical Center, Washington, D.C.

34 "Boys, if you ever pray": quoted in McCullough, 353.

34 "The leader of his people": H. Truman, *Memoirs*, vol. 1, 20.

35 "a great world statesman": Ibid., 20–21.

35 "assistant president": Messer, 65.

35 "I thought that my calling on him": H. Truman, *Memoirs*, vol. 1, 23.

35 "man best qualified": Ibid., 23.

35 "an explosive great enough": Ibid., 11.

36 "I have confidence in him": *The New York Times*, April 14, 1945, 8.

37 But Truman was determined: Ferrell, *Off the Record*, 44.

37 The Soviet premier refused: Harriman, *America and Russia*, 39.

38 "like a ghost": quoted in Miller, *Plain Speaking*, 207.

38 "Stalin is a forthright": H. Truman, *Memoirs*, vol. 1, 31.

38 "he knew exactly how": quoted in Miller, *Plain Speaking*, 208.

39 "It may be of interest": Churchill, 481.

39 "one of the most remarkable men": quoted in Miller, *Plain Speaking*, 84–5.

40 seventeen-car special train: *The Washington Post*, April 15, 1945, 1.

40 "honest and friendly": Churchill, 484.

41 "Just a minute, Harry": *The Washington Post*, April 17, 1945, 1, 2; H. Truman, *Memoirs*, Vol. 1, 42.

41 "In His infinite wisdom": *The Washington Post*, April 17, 1945, 9; *Public Papers of the Presidents*, 1.

41 "America will never become a party": *The Washington Post*, April 17, 1945, 9.

41 "Give therefore Thy servant": Ibid.; H. Truman, *Memoirs*, Vol. 1, 42.

42 moving out at: Hersey, 37.

43 "I like people": H. Truman, *Memoirs*, vol. 1, 64.

43 "Plowing a field with a mule": quoted in Miller, *Plain Speaking*, 259.

4: "The So Recently Arrogant Enemies of Mankind"

47 "was acting in the void": David Eisenhower, xxv.

48 foreign policy roles: Yarmolinsky, 112–13.

49 "the final battle": Gavin, 299.

50 Churchill cared who: Author's interview with Alex Ward, Army Historical Branch, London, September 10, 1990.

50 "to disrupt any German efforts": David Eisenhower, 752.

50 "I am the first to admit": quoted Ibid.

50 "Some think that General Eisenhower": Harriman, *America and Russia*, 50.

50 Even the British government: Author's interview with Professor D. Cameron Watt, London School of Economics, September 11, 1990.

51 "an unprecedented 'personal' message": David Eisenhower, 740.

51 "will be the supreme signal": quoted in Gavin, 341.

51 "the single objective": quoted in H. Truman, *Memoirs*, Vol. 1, 212.

52 At noon on the twelfth: Ryan, 313.

52 That night—Harry Truman: Erickson, 552; Ryan, 314.

52 "Had the division been able": Ryan, 325.

53 TRUMAN BRIDGE: Ibid., 320.

53 Bradley estimated one: Bradley, *Soldier's Story*, 535; Larrabee, 506; Ryan, 321.

53 "a pretty stiff price": quoted in Lee, 432.

53 It would ultimately cost the Russians: Larrabee, 506.

53 "It was always a basic condition": H. Truman, *Memoirs*, Vol. 1, 217.

54 "The Anglo American armies": quoted in Ibid., 65.

54 The moment, he wrote, signals: *The Washington Post*, April 28, 1945, 1, 3.

54 Now he made the point: Churchill, 514; Weinberg, 794.

55 On April 12 Eisenhower, Bradley: Bradley, *A Soldier's Story*, 539.

56 "Still have trouble": David Eisenhower, 763.

56 six million of them: Dawidowicz, xiv.

56 "The Nazi campaign": Bullock, 216.

57 The three men, in their bathrobes: David Eisenhower, 763.

57 "It seemed to us": Dwight D. Eisenhower, 409.

57 Zhukov and Konev: Erickson, 568.

58 "He who gives the order to retreat": Gilbert, *Second World War*, 666.

58 On the day the Russians opened: Ambrose, 96.

58 "He has left a successor": David Eisenhower, 775.

58 "which is to Berlin": Ambrose, 11.

59 one of the most loathsome decisions: Gilbert, *Second World War*, 699.

59 "it is not advisable": Elliott, 43.

59 the Big Three: Ibid., 40.

60 Truman quietly fortified: Ibid., 112.

60 "Communism is a system that has no regard": H. Truman, *Memoirs*, Vol. 2, 460–2.

60 The Japanese held about: Piccigallo, 27.

60 "Any person guilty": *Public Papers of the Presidents*, 19.

61 "Stalin had the remainder": Elliott, 202.

61 committed suicide: Acheson, 653.

62 "Our officers were thinking": Harriman, *Harriman: Special Envoy*, 416.

62 "Despite the fact that there were three GIs": Elliott, 1–2.

62 That morning, Hitler was greeted: Erickson, 577.

62 By the Führer's birthday: Ziemke, 476.

63 Hitler was bent and trembling: Ibid., 579.

63 Among the medals: Gilbert, *Second World War*, 668–9.

63 And on this same afternoon: Ibid., 673; Erickson, 590.

64 At Torgau: Associated Press report in *The Washington Post*, April 28, 1945, 3.

64 Germany was cut in half: *The Washington Post*, April 28, 1945, 3.

64 Anticipating that the Allies would slice Germany: Churchill, 533.

64 "The enemy has been cut in two": *Public Papers of the Presidents*, 25.

64 Truman left the White House secretly: *The Washington Post*, April 26, 1945, 1, 2.

66 On the transatlantic telephone: H. Truman, *Memoirs*, vol. 1, 89–92; Churchill, 536.

66 The frantic Himmler: De Gaulle, 201.

66 A British patrol arrested him: Churchill, 538.

67 partisans shot to death Benito Mussolini: *Newsweek*, May 7, 1945, 42.

67 "Let Japan as well as Germany": H. Truman, *Memoirs*, vol. 1, 201.

67 "Through the sacrifices of our soldiers": quoted in Gilbert, *Second World War*, 677.

67 the concentration camp at Dachau: Ibid., 677–8.

68 "One could smell": Gavin, 321.

68 Hitler and Eva Braun killed themselves: Bullock, 800.

68 "Europe may rise again": Ibid., 806.

69 the 1937 boundary of Czechoslovakia: Churchill, 507.

69 "Personally and aside": Statement of April 28, 1945, quoted in Pogue, 468.

69 "I shall not attempt any move": Pogue, 468; Feis, *Churchill-Roosevelt-Stalin*, 611.

70 "meets with my approval": H. Truman, *Memoirs*, vol. 1, 216.

70 "these cities were under Russian control": Ibid., 217.

5: First of All—Poland

75 at a poker game: Dovovan, 34.

77 "In the easily foreseeable future": McCullough, 372.

77 "I became convinced": Harriman, *America and Russia*, 7

77 "Just at the time of my return to Russia": Kennan, 217

77 "occupy ourselves seriously": Ibid., 219.

78 "rather hoped, I must confess": Ibid., 223.

78 no longer support the Soviet war effort: Ibid., 211.

78 Stalin countered that: Steel, 422.

79 "I felt I had to see": Harriman, *America and Russia*, 39–40.

79 "perhaps too bluntly": Ibid.

79 "barbarian invasion": quoted in McCullough, 373.

80 Truman interjected that he understood this: H. Truman, *Memoirs*, vol. 1, 71.

80 "eye to eye": Ibid., 72.

80 an affront to the new President: *The Washington Post*, April 23, 1945, 1.

81 "My appreciation is that": Churchill, 492.

81 Perhaps, he suggested calmly: McCullough, 375.

81 go slowly and avoid: Millis, 49; Stimson, 609.

82 for Soviet participation: Bohlen, 212.

82 "we had done all the dirty work": H. Truman, *Memoirs*, vol. 1, 79.

82 If one part of the agreements: Millis, 50.

82 He would tell Molotov: H. Truman, *Memoirs*, vol. 1, 78; *Millis*, 49.

82 "go to hell": M. Truman, 236; *Millis*, 50.

82 "I am very sorry for the President": Stimson diary, April 23, 1945, quoted in Stimson, 610.

83 The United States would honor all its Yalta commitments: Bohlen, 213.

83 "Carry out your agreements": H. Truman, *Memoirs*, vol. 1, 82; M. Truman, 237.

84 "That will be all, Mr. Molotov": Bohlen, 213.

84 "unadorned by the polite verbiage": Leahy, 351.

84 "Unless you were a man": quoted in Miller, *Plain Speaking*, 47–8.

84 "How I enjoyed translating": Bohlen, 213.

84 "It is also necessary": H. Truman, *Memoirs*, vol. 1, 85.

85 "It showed plainly": Ibid.

85 "their quarrel would tear the world": Churchill, 496–7.

85 "felt as if I had lived": H. Truman, *Memoirs*, vol. 1, 111.

85 "you and I should consult together": Churchill, 499.

86 "Q. Mr. President": *Public Papers of the Presidents*, 123.

86 "Don't get this thing tangled up now": Ibid., 60–1; *The Washington Post*, June 14, 1945, 1, 2.

87 Truman told the reporters: *The Washington Post*, June 14, 1945, 2.

87 "provocative and discouraging": H. Truman, *Memoirs*, vol. 1, 320.

87 The trial opened in Moscow: *The Washington Post*, June 19, 1945, 1.

87 After three days, twelve of the Poles: *The Washington Post*, June 21, 1945, 1; Churchill, 497–8.

87 "free elections": *Public Papers of the Presidents*, 166.

6: "The Flags of Freedom"

91 Newsmen rushed in: *The Washington Post*, April 29, 1945, 1.

91 But the following day: Gilbert, *Second World War*, 684.

93 "You will, officially and personally": Dwight D. Eisenhower, 426; David Eisenhower, 802.

93 Eisenhower's face broke into a huge smile: Miller, *Ike the Soldier*, 778.

94 "Isn't that some birthday present?": H. Truman, *Memoirs*, vol. 1, 206.

94 "This is a solemn but a glorious hour": *The Washington Post*, May 9, 1945, 2; H. Truman, ibid., 206–7.

94 "Let no man abandon his post": quoted in H. Truman, ibid., 208.

94 By midmorning of May 9 in Moscow: Kennan, 240–2.

94 The fighting across Europe: Weinberg, 894; Ziemke, 500.

95 United States deaths: *American Military History*, 497.

95 "whatever the scale": Erickson, ix.

7: Unconditional Surrender

99 public opinion poll reported: Sigal, 95.
100 "If Britain were to run out on us": quoted in Ferrell, *Dear Bess*, 474.
100 Accounts differ as to whether Churchill: O'Connor, 52; Goodwin, 407.
100 "The elimination of German": O'Connor, 52.
101 the Confederate commander: Catton, 159–60.
102 Years later, Truman: H. Truman, *Memoirs*, vol. 1, 209.
102 In 1964 Eisenhower said: *The Washington Post*, December 21, 1964, quoted in O'Connor, 54.
102 "greatest single mistake": Bohlen, 212.

8: France Shall Rise Again

105 On his first day in office: H. Truman, *Memoirs*, vol. 1, 14–17.
106 "He [Stimson] had shared the aspirations": Stimson, 552.
106 With de Gaulle and the French: De Gaulle, 150.
107 "We were childish": Bloch-Michel, *Journal du désordre*, Gallimard, Paris, 1955, 10, quoted in Wilkinson, 77.
107 France would gain leverage: Author's interview with General Juan Delmas, French Army Department of History, Paris, April 30, 1990.
107 "The roses of glory": De Gaulle, 194.
108 He warned the French commander: Dwight D. Eisenhower, 413.
108 De Gaulle said sardonically: De Gaulle, 195.
108 "I don't like the son of a bitch": Donovan, 58.

108 Truman actually ordered supplies: Dwight D. Eisenhower, 413.
108 at last, on June 25: Author's interview with General Juan Delmas, French Army Department of History, Paris, April 30, 1990.
108 "possessed by the will to power": De Gaulle, 68.
109 "restored the entire city to France": Ibid., 156.
110 "Whatever happens": Ibid., 183–6.
110 "Alsace is sacred ground": Ibid., 169.
110 "The United States does not give us the impression": Ibid., 93.
110 "The result" he said: Ibid., 9.
111 "Our troops, too, would have to cross": Ibid., 174.
111 bungled the crossing: Author's interview at French Army Department of History, Paris, April 30, 1990; de Gaulle, 177–8.
113 "They would be under our command": Ferrell, *Off the Record*, 29.
113 "the extreme consequences": De Gaulle, 207.
113 "assume a clearly unfriendly character": Letter of May 30, quoted in Churchill, 567.
113 "by all necessary means": Letter of June 2, quoted in ibid., 567.
113 "All right, we will at once stop": Leahy, 373.
113 "contain the almost unbelievable threat": Mosley, 334.
113 "While this threat": Ibid., 335.
114 "I did not take": De Gaulle, 208.
115 The French were convinced: Author's interview with Colonel Paul Gaujac, French Army Department of History, Paris, April 30, 1990.
115 "An explosion followed": Churchill, 563.
115 Churchill even won Truman's approval: Donovan, 58–9.
115 "Those French ought to be taken out": Ibid.
115 The Syrian president sent Churchill: Churchill, 566.

116 "a pebble in their diplomatic pond": De Gaulle, 225.

116 "The end of the war": Author's interview with Colonel Jacques Vernet, French Army Department of History, Paris, April 30, 1990.

116 The U.S. State Department had also disapproved: Donovan, 60.

116 "French blood shed": De Gaulle, 187.

117 More than a half-million villagers: Lancaster, 128.

117 French underground activities: Spector, 470–1, see footnotes.

117 De Gaulle began assembling: Author's interview with General Juan Delmas, French Army Department of History, Paris; De Gaulle, 190.

117 "The United States recognizes French sovereignty": Cameron, 39–43.

118 On August 15 de Gaulle unwisely: Spector, 406–7; Kahin, 26; Pike, 29.

118 "a great ally": De Gaulle, 238.

118 Truman, meeting de Gaulle for the first time: The Washington Post, August 23, 1945, 1.

119 His goal, as de Gaulle saw it: De Gaulle, 238.

119 "Ultimately," he told: Ibid., 242.

120 "As Chief of State, Truman impressed me": Ibid., 243.

9: Like Running Jackson County

123 "As long as I have been in the White House": Donovan, 147.

123 And he would begin to see: Ferrell, Off the Record, 40.

124 That morning, Truman held: The Washington Post, April 28, 1945, 7.

124 Truman sent the Sacred Cow: The Washington Post, May 12, 1945, 9.

124 "Mama got a great kick": H. Truman, Memoirs, vol. 1, 219.

124 This Monday brought him chiefly

foreign policy: The Washington Post, May 15, 1945, 9.

125 "I didn't get to phone": Letter of June 7, 1945, quoted in Ferrell, Dear Bess, 515.

125 "I'm always so lonesome": Truman diary, quoted in Ferrell, Off the Record, 40.

125 "The only things worth learning": quoted in Miller, Plain Speaking, 147.

125 "very boresome speeches": Truman diary, quoted in Ferrell, Off the Record, 37–8.

126 "It won't be long": Letter of June 6, 1945, quoted in Ferrell, Dear Bess, 514.

126 "Dear Bess: Just two months ago": Letter of June 12, 1945, ibid., 515–16.

126 "the United States must be carrying a rabbit's foot": The Washington Post, June 20, 1945, 9.

127 "Second Bill of Rights": Burns, 425; Goodwin, 485.

128 CIO President Philip Murray: The Washington Post, May 23, 1945, 6; June 8, 1945, 15.

128 "most remarkable achievements": The Washington Post, May 2, 1945, 4.

128 "One of the most surprising aspects of this war": quoted in Monnet, 175–76.

129 This tragic racist action: Goodwin, 321.

129 "a distinctly healthier atmosphere": Stimson, 406.

129 Then-Senator Truman had disapproved: Miller, Plain Speaking, 421.

129 The action had special meaning to Truman: Ibid., 78.

129 "I would not stand for that": H. Truman, Memoirs, vol. 1, 223–4.

129 many smaller companies: The Washington Post, June 20, 1945, 10.

130 Labor leader Walter Reuther: Goodwin, 196.

130 The federal government was forced to order: Gabin, 54.

130 he vetoed a congressional reso-

lution: *The Washington Post*, May 4, 1945, 1.

130 "No group should be given special privileges": H. Truman, *Memoirs*, vol. 1, 225.

130 Calling racial discrimination: *The Washington Post*, June 6, 1945, 1, 6, 7; June 8, 1945, 1.

130 He advocated raising the pay: *The Washington Post*, June 8, 1945, 1, 10; June 13, 1945, 15.

131 he visited the House of Representatives: *The Washington Post*, May 2, 1945, 4.

131 Truman instructed Director of the Budget: *The Washington Post*, May 20, 1945, 1.

131 "If you just give people a chance to be decent": Miller, *Plain Speaking*, 259.

132 Stimson was infuriated: Stimson, 462.

132 "is a human characteristic": quoted in Moskin, *Morality in America*, 219.

132 "While the race question": quoted in Ibid., 197.

132 American women revolutionized: Gabin, 57–8.

133 automotive and aviation industry: Ibid., 4.

133 He walked a tightrope: *Public Papers of the Presidents*, 238.

133 Both industry and unions applied pressure: Gabin, 112.

134 the Federal Bureau of Investigation arrested: Miller, *Plain Speaking*, 63.

134 Navy Secretary Forrestal was told: Forrestal, 65.

135 *Amerasia* editor Jaffe and one other man: Donovan, 64.

135 the efforts of Congressman John Rankin: *The Washington Post*, May 23, 1945, 6.

135 Truman rescinded it: Donovan, 54.

136 self-styled anti–Soviet Union hard-liner George Kennan: Kennan, 267.

136 "I know of no justification" Ibid., 269.

136 "ill-considered": Acheson, 106.

136 years later Truman agreed: Ibid., 122.

137 an article in *Collier's:* "Our Armed Forces MUST Be Unified," *Collier's*, August 26, 1944, 16, 63–4.

137 He said that the war would have ended much earlier: Bradley, 146.

137 Eberstadt's 250-page report: Forrestal, 64.

137 That act was a compromise: Keiser, 18.

138 "In my opinion the Cabinet members": Appointment sheet, quoted in Ferrell, *Off the Record*, 29.

138 announcing the first changes: *The Washington Post*, May 24, 1945, 1.

139 he got rid of Milligan himself: *The Washington Post*, May 23, 1945, 1.

139 Stettinius, the President noted: Ferrell, *Off the Record*, 174.

139 that the line of succession be changed: *The Washington Post*, June 20, 1945, 1; H. Truman, *Memoirs*, vol. 1, 22–3.

139 "At this time I regarded Byrnes": H. Truman, ibid.

139 Truman appointed Byrnes: *The Washington Post*, June 28, 1945, 1; July 1, 1945, 1.

139 "After I got to be President": Miller, *Plain Speaking*, 176.

139 Fred M. Vinson. *The Washington Post*, July 7, 1945, 1.

10: "The Architects of the Better World"

144 "As hopeless as the outlook seemed": Bohlen, 176–7.

145 "if world federalism was impractical": quoted in Steel, 406.

146 "the architects of the better world": H. Truman, *Memoirs*, vol. 1, 95.

146 Harriman held three off-the-record press conferences: Harriman, *America and Russia*, 42; Steel, 420.

148 "those responsible for excesses": Stimson, 585.

148 Stimson felt more comfortable: Stimson in *Foreign Affairs*, January 1947, quoted in Stimson, 590–1; Piccigallo, 9.

150 "Yesterday was a hectic day": Letter of June 7, 1945, quoted in Ferrell, *Dear Bess*, 515.

151 "It was a gaudy affair": H. Truman, *Memoirs*, vol. 1, 295; Ferrell, ibid., 516.

151 Truman flew to Olympia: *The Washington Post*, June 19, 1945, 1; June 20, 1945, 1.

151 "a solid structure": *Public Papers of the Presidents*, 138.

152 That evening, he was the guest of honor: *The Washington Post*, June 28, 1945, 1, 2.

152 stopped at Eddie Jacobson's: *The Washington Post*, June 29, 1945, 5; M. Truman, 257.

152 "an age of law and an age of reason": *The Washington Post*, June 29, 1945, 1.

153 He impressed on them the changes: *Public Papers of the Presidents*, 150; M. Truman, 257.

153 "Now, you be a good boy, Harry": *The New York Times*, July 3, 7.

153 Truman, wearing a gray suit: Ibid., 1.

153 "This Charter points down the only road": *Public Papers of the Presidents*, 155; *The New York Times*, July 3, 1945, 1.

153 "For I dipt into the future": Hersey, 43; Ferrell, *Harry S. Truman*, 21.

11: The Shaping of Postwar Europe

157 "A chaotic and hungry Europe": *Public Papers of the Presidents*, 61.

157 "Yesterday was the time for battle": De Gaulle, 204.

158 "I believe that it must be the policy": Acheson, 222.

158 Truman invited former President Herbert Hoover: *The Washington Post*, May 29, 1945, 5.

159 "the best man that I know of": R. N. Smith, 342.

159 Even though Hoover continued: Ibid., 347–52; H. Truman, *Memoirs*, vol. 1, 472.

159 Hoover was pleased: H. Truman, ibid., 309–10, 465; Forrestal, 52; S. E. Kennedy, 96–7.

159 It ended European domination: Acheson, 4.

159 "would include the Baltic Provinces": Gilbert, *Second World War*, 686.

160 "it would be undignified": Kennan, 256.

160 "with the general altruistic interest": Ibid.

160 The question of what treatment: J. E. Smith, 217.

161 "The dark spectre overhanging Europe": François Duchêne, 10.

161 He wanted to extract the Ruhr: Ibid., 126.

161 Stimson, too, favored internationalizing: Stimson, 577.

161 When Truman was first asked: *Public Papers of the Presidents*, 56.

162 "that it will be so dependent": quoted in Stimson, 571.

162 "Absolute insurance against": *Public Papers of the Presidents*, 57.

162 "Early proposals for the treatment of Germany": quoted in Stimson, 582–3.

162 where 1.2 million Austrians: Author's interviews with Dr. Hugo Portisch and Dr. Manfred Rauchensteiner, head of Military Historical Service, Vienna, September 1992.

163 "Prosperity swelled the ranks": Wilkinson, 190.

163 "An iron curtain is drawn down": Churchill, 572–3.

164 When Byrnes objected privately: Ferrell, *Off the Record*, 30.

164 "an advanced 'Liberal' but not a professional one": Truman diary, quoted in ibid., 35.

164 Hopkins explained: Forrestal, 58.

164 These assignments were to be preludes: *The Washington Post*, May 25, 1945, 1.

164 "our three ablest foreign relations men": Truman diary, quoted in Ferrell, *Off the Record*, 35.

164 "I told Harry": H. Truman, *Memoirs*, vol. 1, 258; Truman appointment sheet, quoted in Ferrell, *Off the Record*, 31.

165 "So I've sent Hopkins": Ferrell, ibid., 35.

165 "Stalin already has an opinion": Truman diary, quoted in ibid., 35.

165 "however unintentional": Churchill, 577.

166 the three heads of state agreed: Ibid., 580.

167 "Soviet power into the heart of Western Europe": H. Truman, *Memoirs*, vol. 1, 301–2.

167 "Obviously we are obliged to conform": Ibid., 303–4.

167 Stalin totally ignored Truman's point: Donovan, 59.

167 "the Americans in dealing with us": quoted in Churchill, 611.

167 "Soviet Russia was established in the heart of Europe": Ibid., 609.

169 "most welcome and strong": Ibid., 554–6.

169 "I must not have any avoidable interference": H. Truman, *Memoirs*, vol. 1, 249; Churchill, 559.

170 "an undeserved insult": quoted in H. Truman, ibid., 251.

170 Yugoslavs forced down and even shot down: Acheson, 194.

170 "absolutely unacceptable": quoted in Churchill, 560.

170 "It seems to me that a Russianised frontier": Ibid., 561.

12: Colonialism and Nationalism

173 "Colonialism in any form": H. Truman, *Memoirs*, vol. 1, 275.

173 Roosevelt had disapproved: Bohlen, 140.

173 "certain strategic areas in the Pacific": H. Truman, *Memoirs*, vol. 1, 274.

174 Stimson, for one, insisted that these islands: Stimson, 600.

174 "for the purpose of protecting freedom": Stimson diary, March 30, 1945, quoted in Stimson, 602.

174 "We thus assured full protection": H. Truman, *Memoirs*, vol. 1, 275.

174 At the start of World War I: Said, 8.

175 "The American frontier is no longer Malibu Beach": Cable from Henry R. Luce, May 27, 1945, quoted in Swanberg, 235.

176 "The vision of America": Swanberg, ibid., 181–2.

176 President Osmeña asked for U.S. financial aid: James, 695.

177 "The United States is the last superpower": Said, 54–5.

178 "every sympathy for the persecuted Jews of Europe": H. Truman, *Memoirs*, vol. 1, 69.

179 "I knew he wanted to talk about Palestine": Miller, *Plain Speaking*, 213–14.

179 "I also said that I knew the things": Ibid., 215.

179 Zionists were soon convinced that Truman: Perlmutter, 163.

179 Roosevelt had failed to make specific efforts: Goodwin, 455.

180 Bevin even said publicly: Acheson, 173.

180 "I did not share the President's views": Ibid., 169.

180 Forrestal was eager that the United States: Forrestal, 81.

180 U.S. policy was to let as many Jews into Palestine: *The Washington Post*, August 17, 1945, 6.

180 "Rejoice not, O Israel": quoted in Ben-Gurion, 55.

180 "there will not be another Holocaust": Teveth, 873.

181 The new government would not increase: Eban, 59.

13: Battle for a Launching Pad

186 "Because the Nips were so skillful": Manchester, *Goodbye, Darkness*, 358.

186 The Marine Corps' highest leaders: Moskin, *U.S. Marine Corps Story*, 383.

186 His criticisms, made repeatedly, infuriated: James, 733.

186 Buckner certainly fought the battle: Moskin, *U.S. Marine Corps Story,* 383.

187 Before the eighty-two-day battle was over: Appleman et al., 473.

187 They sought to keep the Soviet Union out of the war: Sigal, 52.

188 This and the buildup of American strength: Ibid., 28.

189 "a monstrosity": Spector, 145.

189 Even Prime Minister Koiso thought: Sigal, 33.

190 "was surely MacArthur's most audacious challenge": James, 738.

190 But Roxas remained a controversial figure: Ibid., 693.

191 General Thomas A. Blamey: quoted in Ibid., 703.

191 MacArthur boasted to Australian Prime Minister John J. Curtin: Ibid., 713.

191 "It was most fortunate for the lives of the soldiers": Ibid., 716–17.

192 "I don't see why in Hell": Ferrell, *Off the Record*, 47.

193 It was claimed that MacArthur did not want Patton: James, 737.

14: Potsdam

198 "I have to take my negro preacher coat": quoted in Ferrell, *Dear Bess*, 516–7.

198 "my able and conniving Secretary of State": Ferrell, *Off the Record*, 49.

198 an enormous array of issues: *The Washington Post*, June 14, 1945, 1.

199 "a probabilities game": Ferrell, *Off the Record*, 49.

199 "Nice entertainment for an artilleryman": Ferrell, *Dear Bess*, 518.

199 "I'd still rather fire a battery": Ferrell, *Off the Record*, 49.

199 "the great grandson of our grandfather's brother": H. Truman, *Memoirs*, vol. 1, 338.

200 For Eisenhower, this was a unique chance: Dwight D. Eisenhower, 442.

200 Eisenhower and Admiral Harold R. Stark: *The Washington Post*, July 16, 1945, 1, 2.

200 "I could not see a single house that was left standing": H. Truman, *Memoirs*, vol. 1, 339.

201 one observer did think Truman seemed nervous: Bohlen, quoted in Donovan, 72.

201 "I liked to listen to him talk": H. Truman, *Memoirs*, vol. 1, 340.

201 "was impressed with his gay": Churchill, 630.

201 "That's what happens when a man overreaches himself": Letter, quoted in H. Truman, *Memoirs*, vol. 1, 341.

201 "I fear that machines are ahead of morals": quoted in Ferrell, *Off the Record*, 52.

202 "Operated on this morning": quoted in Donovan, 73.

202 He seemed tired and worn: Ibid., 74.

202 Stalin was certain that Hitler was alive: McCullough, 418.

202 "Promptly a few minutes before twelve I looked up": Truman diary,

July 17, 1945, Truman Library, Independence, MO.

203 "You could if you wanted to": H. Truman, *Memoirs*, vol. 1, 341.

203 "I had heard that Stalin had a withered arm": Ibid.

203 "Stalin remains for me": Harriman, *Harriman: Special Envoy*, 536

203–4 "It is significant that Stalin kept his military commitments during the war": Harriman, *America and Russia*, 31.

204 Stalin immediately proposed that Truman: *The Washington Post*, July 18, 1945, 1, 2.

206 "I don't want just to discuss": H. Truman, *Memoirs*, vol. 1, 349.

206 "Let us divide it": Ibid., 350.

206 "We had much to learn on this subject": Ibid.

207 "proceded to scare the life": Ibid., 351.

207 "I'll say that we'll end the war a year sooner now": Ferrell, *Dear Bess*, 519.

207 "He is a good soldier and a nice boy": Truman diary, July 18, 1945, Truman Library, Independence, MO.

207 "Believe Japs will fold up": Ibid.

207 "If you had gone down like France": Churchill, 632.

208 "I felt that here was a man of exceptional character": Ibid., 634.

208 At this second private meeting: Harriman, *Harriman: Special Envoy*, 492.

208 "said he wanted to cooperate with the U.S. in peace": Truman diary, July 18, 1945, Truman Library, Independence, MO.

209 "I only offered myself as the lamb": H. Truman, *Memoirs*, vol. 1, 352.

210 "We cannot get away": McCullough, 426.

210 "for more action and fewer words": H. Truman, *Memoirs*, vol. 1, 354.

210 "I'm not going to stay around this terrible place": Truman diary, July 18, 1945, Truman Library, Independence, MO.

211 "Russia had been like a giant with his nostrils pinched": Churchill, 634–5.

212 Comparatively, the United States did little: Gilbert, *Second World War*, 695.

212 It was obvious to Truman: Donovan, 77.

214 he had come to the conference to discuss world affairs: H. Truman, *Memoirs*, vol. 1, 359.

214–15 "the Russians had stolen the coffin": Ibid., 360.

215 that waltz . . . was his favorite: Miller, *Plain Speaking*, 358.

215 "He was direct, unpretentious": Bradley, 444.

215 Eisenhower also continued to oppose bringing the Soviet Union: Bradley, 444; McCullough, 428.

215 "flag of victory": *Public Papers of the Presidents*, 174.

216 "We want to see the time come": Ibid., 175.

216 "There is not a piece of territory": *The Washington Post*, July 21, 1945, 1.

216 "a world in which all the people": H. Truman, *Memoirs*, vol. 1, 362.

216 "I managed to get some other kind": Ferrell, *Dear Bess*, 520.

216 "This is a hell of a place": Ibid.

216 "General, there is nothing that you may want": Eisenhower, 444, Bradley, 444; McCullough, 430.

216 But he denied categorically: Miller, *Plain Speaking*, 338.

217 He thought the general had been a Poor President: Ibid., 130.

217 when an Army Pearl Harbor Board report had criticized Marshall: *The Washington Post*, August 30, 1845, 1, 6.

217 Behind the geopolitical reasons: Feis, *Between War and Peace*, 185.

217 "the British imperial highways to the East": Ibid., 189.

218 "they should be resisted at all costs": Acheson, 195.

219–20 "He was a changed man": Stimson diary, July 22, 1945, quoted in Groves, 304.

220 "There is nobody left to plough": Churchill, 655.

220 Stalin had been unable to stop the Poles: Ibid., 654; Feis, *Between War and Peace*, 35.

220 unless they were trying to strengthen Germany: Feis, ibid., 227.

220 "Of course not, the Bolshies have killed": H. Truman, *Memoirs*, vol. 1, 369.

221 Truman did not believe that the western boundary of Poland: Churchill, 657.

221 The Soviet plan would mean shifting: Churchill, 656.

221 "On a number of occasions I felt like blowing the roof off the palace": H. Truman, *Memoirs*, vol. 1, 369.

221 "There are some things we can't agree to": Ferrell, *Dear Bess*, 521.

222 "Tell the President it is French wine": quoted in H. Truman, *Memoirs*, vol. 1, 371.

222 "The night Stalin was host": quoted in Miller, *Plain Speaking*, 86.

222 "was my position yesterday": H. Truman, *Memoirs*, vol. 1, 373.

222 "would be entirely wrong": Churchill, 658.

223 recognizing that he could not persuade Stalin: Ibid., 659.

225 "after a long study of history": H. Truman, *Memoirs*, vol. 1, 377.

226 "No thanks!": Ibid., 379.

226 they should hold their next meeting in Tokyo: Churchill, 668.

227 "an iron curtain": Donovan, 86.

227 "All fairy tales!": H. Truman, *Memoirs*, vol. 1, 385.

228 "We have unalterably opposed the recognition": quoted in Ferrell, *Dear Bess*, 521.

228 "I do not want to fight another war": quoted in McCullough, 446.

228 "He is straightforward": Ferrell, *Dear Bess*, 522.

229 "Then use German prisoners in the mines": quoted in Churchill, 671.

229 "What a pity!": quoted in H. Truman, *Memoirs*, vol. 1, 389.

230 After lunch, Truman met with 286 GIs from Missouri: *The Washington Post*, July 27, 1945, 11.

230 Truman recognized with a jolt: H. Truman, *Memoirs*, vol. 1, 393.

230 it reminded Truman of the Pentagon: K. S. Morgan, 12.

230 "a very appealing man": Ibid.

230 "The Communist Party in Moscow is no different": Truman diary, July 26, 1945, Truman Library, Independence, MO.

231 "the inevitable and complete destruction": quoted in H. Truman, *Memoirs*, vol. 1, 391.

231 "may include a constitutional monarchy": Spector, 546.

231 "with the freely expressed will of the Japanese people": H. Truman, *Memoirs*, vol. 1, 392.

232 "a tough person to deal with": Ibid., 395.

232 "Bevin is an English John L. Lewis": Ferrell, *Dear Bess*, 522.

232 Truman felt confident that it was not yet time: Forrestal, 78.

233 Forrestal asked Bevin whether he agreed: Ibid., 80.

233 "presumptuous": quoted in H. Truman, *Memoirs*, vol. 1, 397.

234 "Yes, military equipment": Ibid., 398.

234 "I do not wish to ignore the interests of America": Ibid.

234 "It is deeply gratifying that the Senate": Ibid., 400.

235 "If Stalin should suddenly cash in": Truman diary, July 30, 1945, Truman Library, Independence, MO.

236 "with a view to joint action on behalf of the community of nations": Letter, July 31, 1945, quoted in H. Truman, *Memoirs*, vol. 1, 404.

236 "I rather think Mr. Stalin is stallin'": quoted in Ferrell, *Dear Bess*, 522.

236 "You never saw such pig-headed people": letter, quoted in H. Truman, *Memoirs*, vol. 1, 402.

237 "The Russians are naturally looters": quoted in Ferrell, *Dear Bess*, 522.

237 "Yes. We should inform the French": H. Truman, *Memoirs*, vol. 1, 406.

239 "You need not worry about that": Ibid., 407.

239 "I had made up my mind from the beginning": Ibid., 409.

239 Actually, one significant secret agreement: McCullough, 452.

240 "prolonged and petty bickering": H. Truman, *Memoirs*, vol. 1, 410.

240 At times, when the discussion bogged down: *The Washington Post*, August 3, 1945, 1, 2; Ferrell, *Off the Record*, 59.

240 "God willing": quoted in H. Truman, *Memoirs*, vol. 1, 410.

240 "I viewed the labors of the Potsdam Conference": Kennan, 258.

240 Kennan was convinced: Ibid., 260.

241 "develop into a decent nation": H. Truman, *Memoirs*, vol. 1, 411.

241 "It enabled me to see at first hand": Ibid.

241 "The Russians were planning world conquest": Ibid., 412.

242 "took a snort of Haig & Haig": *The Washington Post*, August 3, 1945, 1, 2; Ferrell, *Off the Record*, 59.

15: "The Great American Illusion"

245 Did the United States seek in Asia a postwar counterweight: Forrestal, 52.

246 Twelve days later, in a State Department meeting: Ibid., 56.

246 "In Asia, population differences": Acheson, 355.

246 American East Asian planning was predicated: Aron, 181.

247 "Only later did we understand": Acheson, 140.

247 "the great American illusion": quoted in H. Truman, *Memoirs*, vol. 1, 61.

247 This was in the form of a personal message to Harriman: Kennan, 237.

247 Kennan's more skeptical and less gullible judgment: Report from the Secretary of State, quoted in H. Truman, *Memoirs*, vol. 1, 84–5; Kennan, 238.

247 "Kennan is convinced that Soviet policy": quoted in H. Truman, ibid., 84.

247 he was already troubled: Ibid., 85.

248 China actually contributed little to the war: Spector, 326.

249 "absurd": Rhodes, 586.

16: Ready to Invade Japan

253 "completely . . . to win it as quickly as possible": Speech, June 1, 1945, quoted in Donovan, 65.

253 "Showa," which meant "bright peace": Manchester, *American Caesar*, 456.

253 Some in the West interpreted this to refer to: Morison, Samuel Eliot, *Rising Sun*, 10, note 5.

254 "Hirohito must go!": Donovan, 90–1.

254 The Gallup Poll: Spector, 545.

254 They opposed easing the surrender terms: Spector, 546; Manchester, *American Caesar*, 437.

254 There were other voices: Forrestal, 70–1.

254 MacArthur declared it madness: Manchester, *American Caesar*, 437.

254 "completely unreasonable": Aron, 53.

254 the Japanese had already killed: Reference Department, Marine Corps Historical Center, Washington, D.C.

255 General Marshall told Truman to expect: Stimson, 619.

255 The second invasion: Rhodes, 641.
255 Pentagon planners used the figure: Lee, 563.
255 The Joint Chiefs of Staff even studied the use of toxic gas: Sigal, 167.
255 They had some four million men under arms: Stimson, 618.
255 "a completely blockaded Japan would then fall": quoted in Moskin, *U.S. Marine Corps Story*, 399.
256 "The Japanese will lose the meaning of their existence": Sigal, 70.
256 He was ordered to carry out his instructions: Forrestal, 75; Lee, 500.
256 Sato was informed that a reply: Lee, 509–10.
257 The Navy General Staff in Tokyo ordered its man: Lee, 521.
257 "any kind of gas": James, 730.
257 MacArthur also supported the entry: Larrabee, 203–4.
258 "the foot soldier will have to advance": *The Washington Post*, June 2, 1945, 1, 4.
258 "The Kyushu operation is essential": Foreign Relations of the United States, 904.
259 "It is a grim fact there is not an easy, bloodless way": Ibid., 905.
259 "to deal with the Japs in Manchuria": Ibid.
259 "the already hopeless Japanese": Ibid.
259 "The hazard and loss will be greatly lessened": Ibid., 906; Sigal, 119.
260 But he warned that he did not want another bloody Okinawa campaign: Spector, 543; Donovan, 70.
260 Admiral King interjected: Foreign Relations of the United States, 910.
260 Decades later, some historians: Bird.
260 "It occurred to me that a quarter of a million": quoted in McCullough, 439.
261 "the varied and overwhelming character of the force": Stimson, 623.
261 To his surprise, Truman discovered that he had inherited: James, 763.
262 "superfluous": Ibid.
262 "He was lying": Manchester, *American Caesar*, 428.
262 He said that only the United States could help rebuild China: Forrestal, 67.
264 "maximum concessions": quoted H. Truman, *Memoirs*, vol. 1, 318.
264 "Stalin was always asking for as much as he could get": Ibid., 319.

17: "An Opportunity to End This War"

268 "A future war with Soviet Russia is as certain as anything": Grew quoted in Sigal, 97.
269 "a constitutional monarchy": Ibid., 114.
269 The Emperor had made his views known: Spector, 77–8; Morison, *Rising Sun*, 69, note 50; Lee, 245.
270 This suggested that, in some manner, the Emperor could: Forrestal, 69.
270 He would announce it from Potsdam: Stimson, 625.
270 By now, Truman fully realized the centrality: Sigal, 86.
271 "By omitting the two most compelling threats": Ibid., 130.
271 Truman always stressed that he had put off: H. Truman, *Memoirs*, vol. 1, 417.
271 no indication to the Japanese that the President of the United States would accept less: Sigal, 9.
271 But Truman spoke with Stalin privately: H. Truman, *Memoirs*, vol. 1, 387.
272 "The alternative for Japan is prompt and utter destruction": Ibid., 391–2; Harriman., *Harriman: Special Envoy*, 492–3.
272 "Yet the tough tone that the proclamation maintained": Sigal, 125.
273 "With regard to unconditional surrender": Lee, 524.

273 a rejection of the Potsdam Declaration: Harriman, *Harriman: Special Envoy*, 492–3.

273 the absence of an answer meant that the Japanese government: Lee, 533.

275 Marshall knew this and said as much to Stimson: Donovan, 94.

276 The first five thousand American troops: *The Washington Post*, July 23, 1945, 1.

276 Nimitz went to Manila again: James, 727.

18: "Dimples Eight Two"—Opening the Nuclear Era

279 "The final decision of where and when to use the atomic bomb": H. Truman, *Memoirs*, vol. 1, 419.

279 "Many of us looked with deep trouble to the future": Rhodes, 613–14.

280 Secretary of War Stimson sent the new President a discreet note: H. Truman, *Memoirs*, vol. 1, 85.

280 "The possible atomic weapon was considered to be a new": *Harper's*, February 1947, quoted in Stimson, 632.

281 "The decision whether or not to use the atomic bomb": Churchill, 639.

281 control this "menace": Rhodes, 624.

281 "a man of great wisdom and foresight": H. Truman, *Memoirs*, vol. 1, 87.

282 After all, the earliest fission: Marcus and Sigal, 302.

282 Then, fast-moving Manhattan Project intelligence teams located documents: Rhodes, 607; Gilbert, *Second World War*, 663.

282 Ironically, some of it was used at Oak Ridge: Rhodes, 610.

282 Back in 1939 Leo Szilard: Paul Doty, "Einstein and International Security," quoted in Horton and Yehuda, 354.

283 He opposed both testing and using the atomic bomb: Ibid., 375.

283 Szilard, Bartky, and Urey returned: Rhodes, 638.

283 Truman approved Stimson's selections and added Byrnes: H. Truman, *Memoirs*, vol. 2, 419.

284 "Gentlemen, it is our responsibility": McCullough, 390.

284 Oppenheimer favored offering other nations: Rhodes, 644.

285 Byrnes was uneasy: Sigal, 199.

285 "I felt that to extract a genuine surrender": *Harper's*, February 1947, quoted in Stimson, 617.

286 "on a war plant": quoted in Sigal, 201.

286 "a new weapon merely but as a revolutionary change": quoted in McCullough, 392.

286 "so far as he could see, the only reasonable conclusion was to use the bomb": S. E. Kennedy, 262; Sigal, 205.

287 "For God's sake; don't organize an army to go into Japan": quoted in Sigal, 206.

287 "Mr. President, I have blood on my hands": Jeremy Bernstein, "Profile: Physicist—I. I. Rabi," *The New Yorker*, October 20, 1975, 61.

287 "More than any other one man, Oppenheimer": H. Truman, *Memoirs*, vol. 1, 418.

287 The Interim Committee discussed using atomic power: Sigal, 204.

288 "We can propose no technical demonstration": Rhodes, 697.

288 Leahy accused the "longhairs" of gypping the government: Bohlen, 236.

288 "was of no material assistance in our war against Japan": Leahy, 441.

288 "It is not a bomb": Ibid.

288 "I never doubted what it would be": Churchill, 639.

289 culminating in his written approval: McCullough, 448.

289 Churchill had it right: Churchill, 553.

289 Giant B-29s of the 21st Bomber Command had started flying: Rhodes, 588.

289 "I'll tell you what war is about:" quoted in Rhodes, 586.

289 Then he learned the results of the raid on Dresden: Toland, 143.

290 By the end of the war: Spector, 502; Moskin, *U.S. Marine Corps Story*, 373.

290 Among others, they killed sixty-two Allied airmen: Gilbert, *Second World War*, 645, 648, 696.

290 The devastating pounding of Japan from the air convinced LeMay: Rhodes, 600.

290 His 600 superbombers roamed over Japan: Larrabee, 620.

290 "In deciding to use this bomb": H. Truman, *Memoirs*, vol. 1, 420.

290 "deliberately aiming at noncombatants": Sigal, 200.

291 "practically rubble": Rhodes, 627.

291 Stimson himself deleted Kyoto: Sigal, 194.

291 As late as July 21, military leaders were still urging Stimson: Rhodes, 686.

291 "Even if the Japs are savages": Truman diary, quoted in Rhodes, 690.

291 This decision on Kyoto was the only targeting issue: Sigal, 197.

292 it was only thirty miles from the poison gas factory: *The New York Times*, August 12, 1995, 2.

292 The thunderous explosion of the first atomic bomb: Gleick, 154; Gilbert, *Second World War*, 704; Rhodes, 677.

292 "the light of many suns in one": Thomas and Watts, 204.

292 The force of the explosion equaled: Sigal, 179; Rhodes, 677.

292 In reply to startled inquiries from the public: Groves, 301–2; Author's interview with William B. Arthur.

292 "Now I am become Death": Rhodes, 676.

293 "Doctor has just returned": Ibid., 688.

293 The scientists swelled with pride: Gleick, 156.

293 "We have discovered the most terrible bomb": Truman diary, July 25, 1945, Truman Library, Independence, MD.; Rhodes, 690; Ferrell, *Off the Record*, 55.

293 "It is certainly a good thing for the world": Truman diary, ibid.; Ferrell, ibid., 56.

293 "It was a terrible decision": M. Truman, 5.

294 it was almost impossible to see how Harry Truman: Sigal, 210.

295 "Now all this nightmare picture had vanished": Churchill, 638–9.

295 "At any rate, there never was a moment's discussion": Ibid., 639.

295 Churchill cautioned that perhaps the Japanese had more reason to die: Ibid., 642.

295 "Indochina from one day to the next became accessible": De Gaulle, 258.

295–6 Stimson had dinner with Eisenhower on July 21: Rhodes, 688.

296 "casually mentioned to Stalin": H. Truman, *Memoirs*, vol. 1, 416.

296 Harry Vaughan claimed to have overheard: Donovan, 93.

296 Truman himself reported that Stalin replied: H. Truman, *Memoirs*, vol. 1, 416; Messer, 111–12; Rhodes, 690.

296 "Across the room, I watched Stalin's face carefully": Bohlen, 237.

296 "How did it go?": Churchill, 670.

297 And on July 9, a British physicist, Dr. Alan Nunn May: Gilbert, *Second World War*, 702.

297 "its first special bomb": H. Truman, *Memoirs*, vol. 1, 420; Rhodes, 691.

298 "an elongated trash can with fins": Rhodes, 701.

298 Altogether, nine bombs would be available by November 1: Sigal, 179.

298 The 883 men killed made this the greatest loss at sea: Gilbert, *Second World War*, 709.

298 Beginning at 3 P.M. on Saturday, August 4: Craven and Cate, 718.

299 Sunday afternoon, Little Boy was transported: Rhodes, 583.

299 The Strategic Bombing Survey estimated: Ibid., 734; Sigal, 224.

300 One of the brightest of the theoretical physicists: Gleick, 203.

300 "This is the greatest thing in history": H. Truman, *Memoirs*, vol. 1, 421.

300 "a rain of ruin from the air": Ibid.; *The Washington Post*, August 7, 1945, 4.

300 "What has been done is the greatest achievement": Ibid.

300 "Yesterday we clinched victory in the Pacific": quoted in McCullough, 456.

301 Molotov called in Harriman: *The Washington Post*, August 9, 1945, 1.

301 Soviet armies rolled into Machuria: Weinberg, 889.

301 In the estimate of some, this attack: Sigal, 226.

301 "We have used it in order to shorten the agony of war": *The Washington Post*, August 10, 1945, 6.

302 "The generals never came to terms with this power": Ellis, 177–8.

302 On Tinian, Fat Man bomb F31: Rhodes, 660.

302 At 3:47 A.M. on August 9, *Bock's Car* lifted off: Rhodes, 393.

303 "The dead are too numerous to be counted": *The Washington Post*, August 9, 1945, 1.

303 "The reality was the girl with scarred features": Gilbert, *Second World War*, 719.

304 "this terible means of maintaining the rule of law": quoted in Stimson, 634.

304 Dean Acheson did not think the Soviet Union threatened Western Europe directly: Acheson, 599.

304 "I wish it were possible to throw on": Stone, 6.

304 "The face of war is the face of death": *Harper's*, February 1947, quoted in Stimson, 633.

305 "The atomic bomb is too dangerous to be loose in a lawless world": *The Washington Post*, August 10, 1945, 5.

305 "having this weapon rather ostentatiously on our hip": Stimson, 644.

305 "The chief lesson I have learned in a long life": quoted in Ibid.

305 Two years later, Stimson would no longer believe: Stimson, 646.

305 "a xenophobic superpatriot": Blum, *V Was for Victory*, 319.

305 "Other peoples are not being hindered": Gleick, 204.

306 But what Truman was really: Acheson, 124–5.

307 "a new era in the history of civilization": H. Truman, *Memoirs*, vol. 1, 530.

19: "The Day We Have Been Waiting For"

311 "There is really no alternative for us": quoted in Lee, 543.

311 The vote was deadlocked: Gilbert, *Second World War*, 716.

311 Incredibly, the two atomic bombs had not changed: Sigal, 225.

311 "to bear the unbearable": Gilbert, *Second World War*, 716; Sigal, 242.

312 "with the understanding that said declaration": H. Truman, *Memoirs*, vol. 1, 427; Sigal, 242.

312 and these voters had the power: Sigal, 246.

312 It was, he said, the same with the Japanese: Ibid., 249.

313 "good plain horse sense": Rhodes, 742.

313 "I do not see why we should retreat": Sigal, 250.

313 "This is a peace warning": Forrestal, 84.

315 Harriman returned to his communications center: Harriman, *Harriman: Special Envoy*, 501.

316 They felt there was no purpose: Forrestal, 83; Sigal, 252.

317 "The Emperor has made his decision": Sigal, 274.

318 "the Emperor's responsibility": Irokara, xv.

318 "a new and most cruel bomb": Morison, *Victory in the Pacific 1945*, 350.

318 At 6 P.M. the Swiss chargé d'affaires brought Byrnes: Acheson, 119.

319 "I deem this reply a full acceptance": *The Washington Post*, August 15, 1945, 8.

319 "We want Harry!" New York *Daily News*, August 15, 1945, 10.

319 "This is a great day": *The Washington Post*, August 15, 1945, 1B.

20: The Shaping of Postwar Asia

323 "stood an army of more than a million men": Churchill, 629.

323 "It was not the American responsibility": Stimson, 629–30.

325 Stalin also bid again for a role: Donovan, 103.

325 They did not know the history of the line they had chosen: Cohen, 4.

327 "Yes, Mr. President": McCullough, 475.

328 "imperialistic, domineering and unbecoming": quoted in H. Truman, *Memoirs*, vol. 1, 450.

328 Ho quoted the American Declaration of Independence: Kahin and Lewis, 419.

329 "If there is anything that makes my blood boil": Quoted in Edgar Snow, *The Other Side of the River*, 686, quoted in Kahin, 24.

329 "our friends who are fighting the same battle as we": *The New York Times*, January 1, 1946, cited in Buttinger, 449.

329 "We have come to reclaim our inheritance": Pike, 28.

330 "Anticommunism preempted anticolonialism": quoted in Kahin, 31.

330 The United States continued to recognize the Nationalists: Barnett, 171.

21: "A Victory of More Than Arms Alone"

336 The Emperor's dignity should be preserved: James, 779.

336 WELCOME TO THE U.S. ARMY FROM THIRD FLEET: Morison, *Victory in the Pacific 1945*, 360–1.

337 Then he was driven in an ancient American Lincoln: Ibid., 362; Manchester, *American Caesar*, 445.

337 MacArthur embraced him and reassured him: Manchester, ibid., 448.

338 After two and a half years, the Tribunal for the Far East: Piccigallo, xi, 263; Minear, 4, 6.

338 Seven of them were executed: Manchester, *American Caesar*, 484.

338 Truman refused to intervene: Ibid., 487.

338 "Our relations with Japan do not rest on a contractual basis": H. Truman, *Memoirs*, vol. 1, 457.

339 "a better world shall emerge": James, 790; Manchester, *American Caesar*, 453.

339 "We hereby proclaim the unconditional surrender": Morison, *Victory in the Pacific 1945*, 364.

339 "Today the guns are silent": James, 791; Manchester, *American Caesar*, 453.

340 "Peace-making, like war-making": Sigal, 310.

340 "We shall not forget Pearl Harbor": *Public Papers of the Presidents*, 256; *The New York Times*, September 2, 1945, 4; *The Washington Post*, September 2, 1945, 1, 3; H. Truman, *Memoirs*, vol. 1, 460–2.

340 "The day thou gavest, Lord, is ended": Hymn by John Ellerton,

quoted in Morison, *Victory in the Pacific 1945*, 369.

22: "We Stand on the Threshold"

343 "We won two great victories": *Public Papers of the Presidents*, 375.

343 What we call World War II: Gilbert, *Second World War*, 1.

343 And counting from September 19, 1931: Weinberg, 894.

344 "The evil done by the Japanese war lords": *Public Papers of the Presidents*, 255.

344 "come back from the dead": Russell, 419.

344 "I believe we are entering an era": Author's interview with Václav Havel, Prague, October 15, 1992.

345 "We face the future and all its dangers": *The New York Times*, September 2, 1945, 4; *Public Papers of the Presidents*, 257.

345 While most of the nearly twelve million Americans in uniform: Reference Department, Marine Corps Historical Center Washington, D.C.

345 5,000,000 EXPECTED TO LOSE ARMS JOBS: quoted in Donovan, 108.

346 in July he ordered the Navy to take over: *The Washington Post*, July 6, 1945, 1.

346 Shipbuilding, for example; had employed: Lingeman, 169.

346 "I am not asking for social equality": McCullough, 589.

347 "a lot of hooey about equal rights": Ibid., 471.

347 Her analysis showed that women, who had made up 26 percent: Gabin, 113.

347 "From foreman all over the place": *The New York Times*, February 19, 1945, quoted in Gabin, 114.

347 The union defended the principle of seniority rights for all: Gabin, 124–7.

348 "[T]o many of the public at large": P. Kennedy, 504.

348 "the main constructive work of rebuilding": Acheson, 499.

348 Jean Monnet led those who sought to replace nationalism: Monnet, 523.

349 "as futile for the present as": De Gaulle, 248.

349 "cruel and wasteful": Acheson, 151.

349 "long telegram": McCullough, 491.

349 Acheson identified this speech: Acheson, 194.

349 "on a course of aggrandizement": quoted in McCullough, 544.

349 "archaic religious and racial lunacies": Hughes, 13.

350 The nation that had rejected the League of Nations: Acheson, 707.

350 "What was lost to Europe": Russell, 258.

350 "The great cycle of English history": quoted in Moskin, *Morality in America*, 27.

350 "[T]he period of Mr. Truman's Presidency": Acheson, 725.

350 "Only slowly did it dawn upon us": Ibid., 736.

351 "The direct and sufficient cause of Russia's rise": Aron, 110.

351 the United States produced more than 296,000 aircraft: Marcus, 308.

352 the science fiction dream of space travel: Gleick, 218.

352 Work centered at The Rockefeller Institute: McCarty, 213.

352 Unlike World War I, the second war was extremely mobile: Author's interview with Colonel Robert Joy, M.D., Professor of History of Medicine, Armed Forces Medical School, Bethesda, MD.

352 Preventive medicine changed this with the wide use of DDT: Weinberg, 585.

352 other antibiotics began to appear: Gleick, 195; Asimov, 649.

353 The first attempts at cardiac surgery:

Harvard Medical Alumni Bulletin, Spring 1994, 70.

353 "Medical progress was a major reason for the population explosion": Williams, 356.

353 "The human intellect has developed fantastic things": Author's interview with Václav Havel, Prague, October 15, 1992.

353 "ours is one of the big centuries": Russell, 9.

354 "paint things not as they are": Ibid., 41.

354 "the artist is the person who puts the world together": Ibid., 403.

354 "the beginning of a new era for all humanity": Ibid., 330–1.

354 "Any man who sees Europe now": *Public Papers of the Presidents,* 211.

354 "The essential question is one which we should have to answer": Stimson, 653.

354–5 "the Christmas that a war-weary world": *Public Papers of the Presidents,* 585.

355 "This head of mine should have been bigger": Ferrell, *Dear Bess,* 524.

355 "In just three months in office Harry Truman had been faced with a greater surge of history": McCullough, 463.

355 "I don't give up on what I start": Miller, *Plain Speaking,* 89.

355 "Harry Truman was certainly no ordinary man": Monnet, 252.

356 "To me his greatest quality as President": Miller, *Plain Speaking,* 378.

356 "Pray for me": Ferrell, *Dear Bess,* 522.

356 "doing spade work": Ibid., 524.

356 "a mighty stubbornness": Hersey, 51.

356 also faulted him for snap judgments: Ibid., 144.

356 "I don't think knowing what's the right thing": Miller, *Plain Speaking,* 431.

357 "Today we stand on the threshold of a new world": *The New York Times,* September 2, 1945, 1.

Index

About the Author

J. ROBERT MOSKIN, an award-winning historian and journalist, has reported from and written about most of the places in this book: from Hanoi to Jerusalem, from Berlin to Beijing. He was the foreign editor of *Look* magazine, where he worked for eighteen years, and reported for several other magazines. He has been the editorial director of the Aspen Institute and of The Commonwealth Fund. He has written six books before this, including *The U.S. Marine Corps Story, Morality in America,* and *Among Lions,* the story of the battle for Jerusalem in 1967. He has degrees in American history from Harvard and Columbia universities and served with the U.S. Army in the Southwest Pacific in World War II. He lives in New York City and Tyringham, Mass.